The Economics and Management of Intellectual Property

For Karin and Oskar

The Economics and Management of Intellectual Property

Towards Intellectual Capitalism

Ove Granstrand

Professor of Industrial Management and Economics,
Chalmers University of Technology, Sweden

Edward Elgar

Cheltenham, UK • Northampton, MA, USA

Published by
Edward Elgar Publishing Limited
Glensanda House
Montpellier Parade
Cheltenham
Glos GL50 1UA
UK

Edward Elgar Publishing, Inc.
136 West Street
Suite 202
Northampton
Massachusetts 01060
USA

Paperback edition 2000

A catalogue record for this book is available from the British Library

Library of Congress Cataloguing in Publication Data

Granstrand, Ove, 1944–
    The economics and management of intellectual property : towards
intellectual capitalism / Ove Granstrand.
    Includes bibliographical references and index.
    1. Technology transfer—Economic aspects. 2. Intellectual
property. I. Title.
HC79.T4G679   1999
338.9'26—dc21   98–46605
                                                                    CIP

ISBN 1 85898 967 1 (cased)
ISBN 1 84064 463 X (paperback)
Printed and bound in Great Britain by MPG Books Ltd, Bodmin, Cornwall

Contents

Figures

Tables

Abbreviations

(except for special notations in particular figures or formulas)

AIPPI	Association Internationale pour la Protection de la Propriété Industrielle
BI	business image
BUSD	billion US dollars
CAFC	United States Court of Appeals for the Federal Circuit
CEO	Chief Executive Officer
CI	corporate image
DRAM	Dynamic Random Access Memory
EC	European Community
EPC	European Patent Convention
EPO	European Patent Office
FDI	foreign direct investment
FIB	'foreign is better'
GATT	General Agreement on Trade and Tariffs (agreement from 1947)
GSM	Global System for Mobile Communications
IC	intellectual capital
ICTs	information and communication technologies (infocom technologies)
IP	intellectual property
IPC	International Patent Classification
IPR	intellectual property rights
ISIC	International Standard Industrial Classification
JAPIO	Japan Patent Information Organization
JIT	just in time
JPO	Japanese Patent Office
LDC	less developed country
M-form	multidivisional corporate organization form
MITI	Ministry for International Trade and Industry (in Japan)
MNC	multinational corporation (company)
MUSD	million US dollars
NBER	National Bureau of Economic Research (USA)
NIC	newly industrialized country
NIH	not invented here

OECD	Organization for Economic Cooperation and Development
OEM	original equipment manufacturing
OTC	over the counter
PCT	Patent Cooperation Treaty
PERT	Program Evaluation and Review Technique
PLC	product life cycle
R&D	research and development
S&T	science and technology
SDNY	Southern District Court of New York
SII	Structural Impediments Initiative
TBF	technology-based firm
TNEC	Temporary National Economic Committee (US Senate Committee created 1938)
TQM	total quality management
TRIPs	trade-related aspects of intellectual property rights
UNCTAD	United Nations Committee on Trade and Development
USITC	US International Trade Commission (renamed so in 1974)
USPC	US Patent Classification
USPQ	US Patents Quarterly
USPTO	US Patent and Trademark Office
VLSI	very large scale integration
WIPO	World Intellectual Property Organization
WPI	World Patent Index
WTO	World Trade Organization

Preface

A book is like a tree. The roots of this one can be traced back to my experience as a PhD student, when I bought a small share in a patent right from a patent broker. I learned the hard way how difficult it was to make proper economic calculations and how easy it was to become legally swindled, even though the technology was sound and simple. In fact, 99.6 per cent of my invested financial capital was lost, but my intellectual capital increased since I gained considerable interest, that is, an intellectual interest, in patenting and licensing. During the 1980s, I pursued my concern within this area, as an academic instead of a venture capitalist. Inspired by the late Professor Edwin Mansfield, I made a study of patenting and technology intelligence in twelve large US corporations while at the Massachusetts Institute of Technology's Sloan School of Management during 1985–86.

The trunk to this book stems from a project conducted in 1992–93 together with Jon Sigurdson and Enrico Deiaco for the Royal Swedish Academy of Engineering Sciences (IVA). The project was commissioned by the Swedish Patent Office in connection with its centennial jubilee in 1992, which happened to occur in a pro-patent era and in the midst of the so-called 'patent war' between Japan and the USA. The major focus of the project was intellectual property management in large Japanese corporations, which was judged as representing the best practice, and included a comparison with large Swedish corporations. The project report, IVA (1993), summarizes this comparison along with an analysis of Sweden's patent position in the global patent landscape.

My work with this project then branched out into a deeper study of intellectual property management in Japan during 1994–95, followed by a study of the US situation while residing at the Center for Economic Policy Research at Stanford University in 1995–96. During these years, the work also expanded into a wider context. It gradually became clear to me that the observations in Japan and the USA were symptomatic of a much grander transition into what could be called intellectual capitalism, with technology as a key element according to my interpretation. For that reason, the book needed to be complemented by more comprehensive chapters on the history, theory and future of intellectual property, surrounding the main original study of Japan. As a technology-based state with many technology-based corporations, Japan could be considered a potential spearhead of this transition to a new form of capitalism. The USA, with technology-based regions such as Silicon Valley, is pushing the frontiers of capitalism in similar directions. Hence, this book has grown more comprehensive and ambitious than initially planned.

Numerous people and organizations have been very helpful, to whom I am deeply grateful. Jon Sigurdson worked with me in the original IVA project, together with Enrico Deiaco as Secretary for the Academy. The steering committee for the IVA project was chaired by the late Bert-Olof Svanholm, CEO of ABB Sweden, and comprised Lars Björklund (Swedish Patent Office), Ulf Rehme (Saab-Scania AB), Jan Uddenfeldt (Ericsson AB), Clas Wahlbin (University of Jönköping), Douglas Wahren (Stora AB), Claes Wilhelmsson (AB Astra) and Jerry Öster (Victor Hasselblad AB). Peter de Bellmond provided valuable assistance from the Swedish Patent Office.

In Japan, the Japanese Patent Office, Association Internationale pour la Protection de la Propriété Industrielle (AIPPI) Japan, and the large corporations studied provided indispensable help and willingness to assist. Among the many persons in and around these organizations, I would especially like to thank Professor Akira Mifune, formerly at Teijin Company, and Mr Kensuke Norichika, formerly at Toshiba, who have assisted on many occasions in various capacities and have commented on parts of the manuscript. Professor Mifune has also kindly provided a great deal of valuable material, based on his long and rich experience with intellectual property rights issues in Japan. My thanks also go to Mr Saba and Mr Takayanagi at Toshiba, Mr Yamaji and Mr Marushima at Canon, Mr Uenohara at NEC, and Mr Shiraishi, formerly at JVC and to many other company representatives and officials who spent time with me. International House of Japan provided, as always, a pleasant atmosphere for studies and reflections. Needless to say, many more were helpful and friendly in Japan, and I want to include them in this general acknowledgement. A heartfelt thanks to all of you who, throughout the years in this and other studies, have nurtured my interest and comfort in Japan as a *gaijin*.

In a similar way, I have many persons to thank in the USA. My gratitude goes first and foremost to Professor N. Rosenberg, who in numerous capacities has provided support and enabled my several stays at Stanford. I have had valuable help and discussions concerning intellectual property with Professors Moses Abramowitz, Kenneth Arrow, John Barton, William Baxter, Paul David, Paul Goldstein, Zvi Griliches, Edwin Mansfield, Robert Merges, Frederic Scherer, and many others. Thanks are also due to the Center for Economic Policy Research for housing me and to its former Director, John Taylor, and the nice and helpful staff, especially Deborah Carvalho, who helped a great deal with the manuscript, but also to Donna Holm and Alex Duncan.

Several people have spent much of their time and personal intellectual capital on reading and commenting upon the manuscript. Their help has been indispensable in improving the final result. Professor Frederic Scherer has been of invaluable assistance with his general support and rich comments, drawing upon a long career as one of the leading economists in the field. Professor Erik Dahmén, patent attorney Thomas Ewing, deputy patent commissioner Lars Björklund and former corporate patent manager Gerhard Miksche all made detailed and invaluable comments from various policy, legal, economic, management, engineering and language points of view. Thomas Ewing was moreover very helpful as a research assistant. The same is true for Sven Lindmark and Bo Heiden, who also commented conscientiously from an engineering and management point of view. Magnus Backstad and especially Bo Heiden assisted in data checks and the further collection of various material. Ulla Anson provided secretarial assistance in early drafts of the manuscript. Björn Areskough supplied much help with data organization and statistical analysis. Mats Magnusson has given valuable help in translations from Japanese and Jon van Leuven and Bo Heiden in checking and improving the English language. In finalizing the manuscript, prompt and highly professional service was provided by Eva Burford in word-processing, editorial assistance and many other secretarial capacities. With all this help, I can only claim exclusive rights to any remaining errors.

The main part of the work in completing the book has been financed by the Swedish Patent Office. Additional financial support has been provided by the Swedish government agency for technical development, NUTEK, the Sasakawa Foundation, the Ruben Rausing Foundation and internal funds at Chalmers University. Part of the work has been done under the auspices of the Institute for Management of Innovation and Technology (IMIT) at Chalmers.

Finally, book writing takes its toll on the people closest to you at work and at home. Thank you all for your continuous inspiration and support and your sacrifice and forbearance.

Ove Granstrand
Göteborg, Sweden, April 1998

1. From intellectual property to intellectual capitalism

CHAPTER CONTENTS

1.1 INTRODUCTION

Undoubtedly, you are now reading the beginning of this book. Hopefully, you have started to read it with curiosity to see whether you will learn something, making it worthwhile to continue reading. In other words, you are now judging whether your private intellectual capital will be increased sufficiently to justify your reading effort, given the alternative to read or do something else. You would probably not use such words, and you would probably protest if you were described as an intellectual capitalist just because you were considering investment in a book. Nevertheless, the underlying notion of personal value from knowledge and learning is presumably at hand. There is nothing new or special in that notion. What, then, is new or special about the concepts of intellectual capital, intellectual capitalists and intellectual capitalism? The following citation is sobering in the current vogueness of these concepts:

> The present state of the nations is the result of the accumulation of all discoveries, inventions, improvements, perfections and exertions of all generations which have lived before us: they form the intellectual capital of the present human race, and every separate nation is productive only in the proportion in which it has known how to appropriate

those attainments of former generations and to increase them by its own acquirements. (List 1841, p. 113; cited in Freeman and Soete 1997, pp. 296–7)

1.2   PURPOSE

The broad purpose of this book is to present thoughts and ideas about a general, global transition into what can be called 'intellectual capitalism', some elements of which have always been with us. The narrower purpose is to present a study of intellectual property and its economics and management in large, technology-based corporations. Such corporations can be seen as perhaps the most important drivers of intellectual capitalism, although not the only ones. Regarding intellectual property, much is known about the USA but less about Japan. However, Japan is in fact on the frontier with respect to its management. Being poor in natural resources, Japan also has had every reason to develop its intellectual capital base, which it has been doing with surprising speed and effect.

This book is also a serious attempt to raise and merge the various interests in intellectual property (IP) and intellectual capital (IC) among managers, economists, engineers and lawyers – practitioners as well as students and scholars. As a consequence of this ambition, interdisciplinary breadth and understanding have been preferred to disciplinary depth. A better interdisciplinary understanding of intellectual property and capital is profoundly needed as the interest in this topic grows rapidly in various directions and quarters. Hopefully, this book can contribute to building bridges between different disciplines and contribute to our joint understanding of this complex issue. Besides presenting research results in an accessible way, this book also paints on a broad canvas, giving the history and fundamentals of the field, as well as providing a textbook introduction. Basic concepts and terminology, such as technology, intellectual property and intellectual capital, are dealt with in various places, starting in Section 2.2, and a glossary is provided at the end of this book.

1.3   BACKGROUND

Undoubtedly, we are now in an ongoing transition to a more knowledge-based society, or information society, as shown by many indicators and recognized by many authors. We spend an increasing share of our lives on learning. Products and services have become increasingly information-intensive, firms have become increasingly dependent upon competencies of diverse kinds, investments have become increasingly intangible in character and so forth. This has been going on for a long time, but it seems that the decades surrounding the new millennium are a turning point in the sense that information, knowledge – whatever we want to call it – is becoming dominant by various measures.

This transition is not due to chance or some outside force or major event but instead is the historical consequence of cumulative learning by generations of individuals and the willingness of Mother Nature to reveal herself to inquirers. Of course, many factors may give twists and turns to this collective learning process, but essentially it is an irreversible process of accumulation, apart from major catastrophe, that will continue until limits of some kind – physical, economic, behavioural – are reached. So far, there is actually nothing new or surprising about this, and in fact this point should be emphasized. We have been aware of this evolutionary process for a long time. Naturally, the emphasis given to its various features and factors could differ. In this book, the role of the economic, management and technology factors will be emphasized.

Does a knowledge society have to be capitalistic in some sense? Not necessarily. There is a widespread notion in the West and the East that knowledge by and large is and should be a publicly accessible good. Knowledge has properties that make it difficult to privatize in the same way as physical goods. Nevertheless, knowledge and information have been subjected to private control or restrictions in various ways historically, with or without capitalism. A good example is military information. Indeed, it will be argued in this book that various factors strengthen the possibility of controlling knowledge and information for private gain by individuals and groups, including firms. This occurs to such an extent that in the course of the accumulation of knowledge a kind of knowledge-based capitalism emerges, or intellectual capitalism in the terminology proposed here. Firms and their management capabilities play an important role in this process, as do international competition and technology. In particular, information and communication technologies play a decisive role. Legal institutions and national interests also play a key role. Since the downfall of the Soviet Union and the politico-economic system associated with it, traditional capitalist economic institutions such as markets, firms and private property rights have become dominant in the world, in the 1990s. Moreover, the frontiers of capitalism – geographic and legal – are being advanced without any strong, competing economic ideology at present.

In summary we point to the following background trends of general relevance: (a) growth and accumulation of science and technology (S&T) that offers economic benefits but at the same time is becoming increasingly complex, diversified and expensive and controlled by private firms, especially large ones; (b) relative shifting of material (physical) to immaterial (non-physical) sources of economic growth; (c) strengthening of capitalism as an ideology and deployed economic order; (d) internationalization and globalization; (e) emergence of a multi-polar world that is becoming politically, economically and managerially more complex; and (f) emergence on a large scale of new information and communication technologies, referred to here as infocom technologies or ICTs for short.

1.4   INTRODUCTION TO INTELLECTUAL PROPERTY

One specific economic institution, even older than capitalist industrial society itself, is the system of intellectual property rights (IPR), covering not only patents but also trademarks, trade secrets, copyrights, designs and artistic works. The IPR system has historically not been considered a strong and important element of traditional capitalism. However, in the 1980s, the patent system became significantly strengthened in the USA, and a so-called 'pro-patent' era emerged for various reasons, one being the concern that US industry had difficulties in protecting and exploiting its research and development (R&D) investments in view of the competitive successes of several Asian economies, in particular Japan. This development can be seen as an important symptom of the transition towards intellectual capitalism, and it has focused wide attention upon patents, IPR and intellectual capital matters in general (see IVA 1993).

1.4.1   The 'Pro-patent Era'

In order for a capitalist economic system to operate properly, it is of decisive importance that markets for labour, capital, products, services and so on are functioning. However, markets for ideas, knowledge, information and intellectual products in general have difficulties in functioning in principle (see further Chapter 2). It is basically very difficult to sell an idea without disclosing it in such a way that others essentially can use it without paying properly. From society's point of view, an underinvestment in creative work and knowledge production may then result, since creators and innovators do not get sufficiently rewarded by profits from selling their creations on the market. To compensate for the deficient functioning of such markets, technology markets in particular, an IPR system (with patents, trademarks, trade secrets, copyrights, design rights and so on) has been created by society.

Patents are granted as a temporary monopoly right, functioning as an incentive both for the disclosure of technical information and for investments in generating and diffusing marketable technical inventions – granted therefore as an attempt to improve the efficiency of the capitalist economic system (see further Chapter 3).[1] Alternative government policy measures for similar purposes may work more one-sidedly, for example, public technology procurement that strengthens demand, or R&D tax deduction schemes that reduce the cost of supplying R&D. Such policy measures are usually nationally oriented and may have strong or weak effects. Until the 1980s, the patent system had been considered

Table 1.1   The top ten corporations in terms of number of US patents granted

Rank 1987		No.	1989	No.	1992	No.	1995	No.	1997	No.
1	Canon	847	Hitachi	1053	Toshiba	1156	IBM	1383	IBM	1742
2	Hitachi	845	Toshiba	961	Hitachi	1139	Canon	1087	Canon	1381
3	Toshiba	823	Canon	949	Mitsubishi Electric	959	Motorola	1012	NEC	1101
4	General Electric	779	Fuji Photo	884	General Electric	923	NEC	1005	Motorola	1065
5	US Philips	687	General Electric	818	Eastman Kodak	887	Mitsubishi Electric	973	Mitsubishi Electric	925
6	Westinghouse	652	Mitsubishi Electric	767	General Motors	863	Toshiba	969	Hitachi	922
7	IBM	591	US Philips	745	Canon	828	Hitachi	910	Fujitsu	909
8	Siemens	539	Siemens	656	Fuji Photo	742	Matsushita Electric	854	Toshiba	891
9	Mitsubishi Electric	518	IBM	623	IBM	680	Eastman Kodak	772	Sony	867
10	RCA	504	Eastman Kodak	589	Motorola	631	General Electric	758	Eastman Kodak	795

Source: Compiled from USPTO statistics.

Table 1.2 Largest patent infringement damages in the USA (up to 1995)

Patent right holder[1] (nationality, size)	Damages[2] (US$ million)	Infringer (nationality, size)	Year	Remarks[3]
Litton (US, large)	1200.0	Honeywell (US, large)	1995	A
Polaroid Corp. (US, large)	873.2	Eastman Kodak (US, large)	1991	B
Alpex Computer Corp. (US, small)	253.0	Nintendo (Japan, large)	1994	C
Smith International, Inc. (US, medium)	204.0	Hughes Tool Co. (US, large)	1986	D
Honeywell (US, large)	166.0	Minolta (Japan, large)	1994	E
Stac Electronics (US, small)	120.0	Microsoft (US, large)	1994	F
Hughes Aircraft (US, large)	114.0	USA	1994	G
3M (US, large)	106.0	Johnson & Johnson (US, large)	1991	H
Lubrizol I Corp. (US, large)	86.0	Exxon Corp. (US, large)	1988	I
Pfizer, Inc. (US, large)	55.8	International Rectifier (US, large)	1983	J
Shiley, Inc. (US, large)	44.8	Bentley Labs (US, large)	1985	K
Jan R. Coyle (US, individual)	43.0	Sega Corp. (Japan, large)	1992	L
B&H Manufacturing (US, medium)	36.5	Owens-Illinois Glass (US, large)	1991	M
Syntex (US, medium)	36.5	Paragon Optical (US, medium)	1987	N
Trans-World Manufacturing (US, medium)	31.3	Dura Corp & Kiddie (US, medium)	1986	O

Notes

1. Courts have increasingly ruled in favour of the patent right holder during the past 15 years. A patent right holder's probability of winning an infringement lawsuit in the USA has increased from 30 per cent prior to 1982 to 89 per cent after 1982 (see Sirilla et al. 1992).

2. Excluding legal fees. These run between US$0.5 and 5 million with some extreme cases like Texas Instruments, believed to have spent over US$10 million in its litigation over DRAMs, involving 347 lawyers and 29 law firms. Texas Instruments' Japanese opponents were believed to have spent nearly US$100 million in preparing their defence (*The American Lawyer*, March 1992, p. 56).

3. Remarks.

A. Following the jury's verdict awarding Litton US$1.2 billion in August 1993, Honeywell filed a motion to set aside the jury's verdict, which was granted by Judge Mariana Pfaelzer on 4 January 1995. Litton v. Honeywell, CV-90-4823 MRP (C.D. Calif.: 1995). Thus, Honeywell prevailed in spite of the jury's verdict.

B. Polaroid Corp. v. Eastman Kodak, 17 USPQ2d 1711 (1991). The total cost for Kodak is higher since Kodak also paid voluntary damages to customers, in addition to the damages awarded to Polaroid.

C. Alpex Computer Corp. v. Nintendo, 86 Civ. 1749, KMW (SDNY: 1994).

D. Smith International, Inc. v. Hughes Tool Co., 229 USPQ 81 (1986).

E. Honeywell v. Minolta. *The Nikkei Weekly*, 5 September 1994, p. 1.

F. Stac Electronics v. Microsoft. *Legal Times, The American Lawyer* Newspaper Group, 19 December 1994, p. 11.

G. Hughes v. US. *Corporate Legal Times*, October 1994, p. 1. The article states that this may be the largest patent infringement judgment against the US government.

H. 3M v. Johnson & Johnson, 22 USPQ2d 1401 (1991).

I. This case settled out of court. *Research & Development*, December 1988, **30** (12), p. 16.

J. Pfizer, Inc. v. International Rectifier Corp., 218 USPQ 586 (1983).

K. Shiley, Inc. v. Bentley Laboratories, Inc., 225 USPQ 1013 (1985).

L. Article states this is one of the largest patent infringement awards for a single individual. A federal jury in Los Angeles had awarded Mr Coyle US$33 million in damages, but Sega settled for the higher amount because the court found the infringement was intentional and the award could have been trebled. *National Law Journal*, 10 August 1992, p. 1.

M. B&H Manufacturing, Inc. v. Owens-Illinois Glass Container, Inc., 22 USPQ2d 1551 (1991).

N. Syntex, Inc. v. Paragon Optical, Inc. and Wilsa, Inc., 7 USPQ2d 1001 (1987).

O. Trans-World Manufacturing Co., Inc. v. Dura Corp. and Kiddie, 229 USPQ 525 (1986).

by industry to have weak economic effects on a broad average (chemicals and pharmaceuticals being one exception), resulting in weak management attention. In 1982 a new court, the US Court of Appeals for the Federal Circuit (CAFC), specializing in patents, was created. At roughly the same time, but by and large for independent reasons, US anti-trust policies changed in favour of strengthening the enforcement of patent rights. In parallel, US industry and politicians started to push forcefully for a general strengthening of the IP system. A new era thus emerged, referred to as the 'pro-patent era', for various reasons and with far-reaching consequences (see further Chapters 2 and 5).

The economics and management of intellectual property on the whole (thus including patents, trademarks, trade secrets, copyrights and so on) have changed considerably since the early 1980s. Both the use and abuse of the patent and litigation systems have increased, which prompted the eruption in the mid to late 1980s of what some people referred to as 'patent wars', notably between the USA and Japan.

The importance of patents as a means for a company to exploit new technologies has increased, as have the resources companies devote to IP protection. Patenting and licensing have become more strategically managed, including a shift to more offensive rather than defensive patenting in a 'patent arms race' (see further Chapters 6 and 7). Several US and many Japanese companies have been particularly active in building up patent portfolios and accumulating skills in using the patent system, including using patent information for technology and competitor intelligence (see further Chapters 7, 8 and 9). Table 1.1 shows how large Japanese corporations have consistently dominated the list of top ten corporations in terms of the number of US patents granted. For the years shown, the highest-ranked corporations on aggregate in descending order are Canon, Hitachi, Toshiba, IBM and Mitsubishi Electric. The European corporations Philips and Siemens have dropped out entirely. IBM has made the most remarkable comeback, and Motorola and NEC have entered the top four.

1.4.2   The Rising Value of Intellectual Property

During the emergence of the pro-patent era of the 1980s, the economic value of patents increased in various ways. The probability of winning a court case as a patent holder increased, as did the patent damage claims. From being a relatively minor business issue on average, patents started to gain significance. Table 1.2 gives an illustration of this.

Not only patents have increased in value and sometimes reached astonishingly high levels. Table 1.3 gives examples of how high monetary values are also attached to trademarks.[2] Although the valuations are very uncertain, the table still illustrates the possible magnitude of intellectual capital in the form of trademarks. As seen from the table, the total value of the eight highest valued trademarks in 1992 amounts to 132 BUSD, which is in the range of the GDP for a small country. As noted in the table trademark values typically increase (unless they are mismanaged). The value of know-how, trade secrets and knowledge in the form of human capital in general is also difficult to measure, but as we shall see in Section 1.5 and further in Chapter 10, there are indications that such values have increased as well.

Table 1.3   World's most highly valued trademarks[*]

Rank	Trademark	1992 Value (BUSD)	Rank	1995 Value (BUSD)
1	Marlboro	39.47	1	44.6
2	Coca-Cola	33.45	2	43.4
3	Intel	17.81	10	10.5
4	Kellogg	9.68	7	11.4
5	Nescafé	9.17	9	10.5
6	Budweiser	8.24	8	11.0
7	Pepsi-Cola	7.50	14	8.9
8	Gillette	7.15	11	10.3

Note: [*] Valuation of trademarks may be done in several ways, mostly subjective, all of which produce uncertain results (for an overview see Aaker, 1996; see also Chapter 7). The astounding magnitudes of trademark values do not result from valuation errors although the precise figures in the table may be in error. Trademarks may be kept valid permanently, and their value is built up over time through various means, primarily through advertising and positive exposure to consumers. They are thereby subjected to increasing returns or cumulative advantages, although volatile. Thus old, consistently well-managed trademarks for consumer mass markets could be expected to accumulate the highest values. This is also shown in the table although there are exceptions such as Intel, being a relatively young company (formed in 1968) with a component product. The volatility as well as the consistency of value rankings are also shown in the table. The dominance of US trademarks is noteworthy. The most valuable Japanese trademark is Sony, valued to 8.8 BUSD in 1995, and thereby ranking 15th.

Sources: *Financial World* (1993, 1996).

As the values associated with the market exploitation of intellectual properties increase, the need to foster and manage the development of these creations as well as protect their rights on an international market grows proportionately. In response to the realization of the importance of intellectual property in today's global market, different strategies have been deployed in order to reap the benefits. However, individuals, corporations, nations and society all have different goals regarding intellectual property. Its value is indisputable in the context of the present IPR system and capitalist market, but who should benefit from this value and what are the most effective methods to do so? Perhaps the system should be changed or abolished – but what would take its place? This book will elaborate on these very issues.

1.5   THE EMERGENCE OF INTELLECTUAL CAPITALISM

Intellectual capital has always existed. Individuals and groups have been able to differentiate themselves from their neighbours or their enemies using their superior intellect since the beginning of time. No doubt some cavemen were better at hunting, fighting or drawing on the walls, and these qualities surely imparted prestige that differentiated them from the others. No doubt the Inca tribes of South America were surprised when their Spanish visitors introduced them to the firearm, quickly defeating their 40 000-man army with a band of 180 explorers. The 'Blitzkrieg' and the atom bomb used in World War II were deadly combinations of both strategy and technology employed to substitute for sheer numbers and equipment. Size of a population matters, but within limits. Technology and intellectual capital allow one to do more with less. It is only natural that modern corporations have now found that intellectual capital can be used as leverage in the marketplace. Advances in knowledge have always made life easier; now they also make work more profitable. Today's companies trade brawn for brains and value information over infrastructure as they face down global competition.

The accumulation and use of intellectual capital has led to the creation of intellectual capitalism as a viable economic system that displaces the dependency on traditional tangible fixed assets as a means for commercial success. The days when land, factories, machines, natural resources and unskilled labour ruled the valley like giant dinosaurs have given way to the knowledge warrior, nimble and unencumbered by the dead weight of corporate equity. Now, corporations and nations, such as Japan, which also lack the sheer natural resources to overwhelm their competition, have turned to the use of intellectual capital as a means to win the marketplace. These corporate intellectual capitalists (for example, Microsoft, Coca-Cola, Intel, Astra, Merck, Canon, Sony and so on) are able to create enormous market value based primarily on their intangible assets, which include corporate know-how, customer loyalty, distribution networks, intellectual property, and so on.

One rough way to look at the level of intangible assets or intellectual capital in firms is to compare their tangible assets or equity with the market value[3] of the company. Table 1.4 indicates that each of the ten most valued companies in the world possesses more intangible or intellectual capital than tangible capital. Calculating the market-to-book ratio[4] for each company gives a rough indication of which companies are highly reliant on their intellectual capital. Those companies with very high ratios of intangible to tangible capital could

Table 1.4 Intellectual capital in the world's most valued companies[1]

Company	Market value[2]	Profit margin (%)[3]	Equity	Intellectual capital[4]	Market-to-book ratio[5]	Sales	R&D[7]	R&D intensity (%)	IC per employee	Kodama ratio[6]
General Electric	222 748	12.3	34 438	188 310	6.5	90 840	1 891	2.1	0.9	0.23
Royal Dutch/Shell	191 002	8.9	76 639	114 363	2.5	171 657	701	0.4	1.1	0.06
Microsoft Corp.	159 660	46.8	10 777	148 883	14.8	11 358	1 925	16.9	6.7	3.86
Exxon Corp.	157 970	9.3	43 660	114 310	3.6	137 242	529	0.4	1.4	0.07
Coca-Cola	151 288	32.1	7 311	143 977	20.7	18 868	[7]	[7]	4.8	[7]
Intel Corp.	150 838	42.5	19 295	131 543	7.8	25 070	2 347	9.4	2.1	0.52
Nippon T&T	146 139	5.9	43 068	103 071	3.4	71 143	2 649	3.7	0.4	0.11
Merck	120 757	27.3	12 614	108 143	9.6	23 637	1 684	7.1	2.0	1.16
Toyota Motor Co.	116 585	5.8	45 781	70 804	2.5	98 741	3 200	3.2	0.7	0.68
Novartis	104 468	26.5	22 432	82 036	4.7	26 098	3 091	11.8	0.9	2.40

Notes
1. All monetary values are in US$ million. Company information was found in their respective 1997 annual reports.
2. Source: *Financial Times* (1997).
3. Income before tax divided by total revenue.
4. For the basis of comparison, the market value of intangible assets has been set equal to the company's IC as a first approximation. For related approaches, see, for example, Sveiby (1989, 1997) and Stewart (1997).
5. The market-to-book ratio was calculated by dividing the company's market value by its book value.
6. The Kodama ratio was calculated by dividing a company's R&D expenditures by its capital investments (accounted for outside R&D).
7. R&D figures for Coca-Cola are confidential, as is the recipe.

be called pure IC (intellectual capital) companies while those with intermediate values are hybrid IC companies. There are indications that the IC component of corporate assets is increasing in absolute as well as relative terms (see also Section 10.3).

Taking the comparisons one step further, we can look at the ratio between intangible assets and the number of employees. Not only do Microsoft and Coca-Cola produce high profits and tremendous market value with very little physical capital investment, they do so also with a relatively small number of employees. This is consistent with the view that IC to varying degrees is more than just human capital. Personnel are not necessarily a company's largest asset, not even for an IC company.

The top IC companies in Table 1.4 are also R&D-intensive, except for a few. One should note moreover that intellectual capitalism also penetrates companies such as Shell, which are traditionally looked upon as based on raw materials but are becoming increasingly technology-based. Intellectual capital can be created and leveraged in many different ways. The technology-based firm (TBF) is a special type of IC firm that uses R&D as a main vehicle to reap the rewards of knowledge. Increasingly, such companies invest more in technology and other intangible assets than in physical assets. In Kodama's words (Kodama 1995), Japanese TBFs (Hitachi, NEC, Canon, Toshiba and so on) are no longer primarily in manufacturing industries but are instead primarily development companies in R&D industries. Viewing what we can call the Kodama ratios in Table 1.4, one can see which firms are oriented more towards research than manufacturing or other capital-intensive activities. Effective management of intellectual property, especially patenting and trade secrets, is very important to the survival of these technology-based firms. This type of firm will be discussed theoretically in Chapter 4 and empirically in Chapters 5–9.

The world's large TBFs today control the lion's share of the world's technology as generators and cumulators of technology.[5] Technology in turn could be considered a main – if not the main – driver of intellectual capitalism. Particularly, new information and communication technologies speed up the transition to intellectual capitalism. There are moreover no signs of vanishing technological and business opportunities. Mother Nature continues to reveal herself, but to a new breed of intellectual explorers and capitalists and at an increasing cost. The roots of knowledge may be bitter but the fruits are sweet.

I hope that will hold true for this book as well.

1.6   BOOK OUTLINE

This book is geared to a general public with an interest in intellectual property and its wider context of capitalism. Three groups of readers should be most concerned: practitioners in industry and government, scholars in academia, and students of engineering, management, law and economics. As this is a large and heterogeneous audience, the chapters will be of varying appeal to different types of readers.

Chapter 1 has described a fundamental shift of the overall economic system towards what can be called intellectual capitalism. The topic of patents and intellectual property has then been placed in that context. Various indicators of intellectual capitalism and the rising value of intellectual capital have also been presented and more along these lines will be presented in Chapter 10. The rest of the book is outlined below and the next section describes its research basis.

Chapter 2 gives as broad as possible an overview of the history and philosophy of intellectual property, which is relevant for academics and for all those interested in more fundamental issues. The chapter is also important for the general discussion in the final chapter.

Chapter 3 provides an introduction to the IP field, mainly for non-specialist practitioners and students, as well as some introductory IP theory, mainly for academics and students.

Chapter 4 establishes, mainly for academics and students, a frame of reference for intellectual property in the technology-based firm (TBF), thereby setting the stage for the subsequent empirical chapters. The TBF is also a key actor in intellectual capitalism, and thus the chapter is relevant to the concluding discussion in the final chapter.

Chapter 5 describes the history of the patent system in Japan and contains an introduction to contemporary patenting in Japanese industry. The chapter summarizes some of the recognized trends regarding patenting and presents some findings regarding the quantity and quality of Japanese patenting.

Chapters 6 and 7 examine findings at the corporate level regarding technology strategies and IP strategies. These chapters are aimed at practitioners, academics and students with a management and business economics perspective. Empirical results are presented in a detailed and transparent way.

Chapter 8 looks at IP organizational structure (in contrast to strategy) and IP management from a perspective similar to that in Chapters 6 and 7. The possible evolution of IP management towards a distributed IC management is explored as well.

Chapter 9 shows how patent information can be used in technology intelligence in general. The patent mapping methods used in Japan are specially illustrated.

In concluding, Chapter 10 returns to the broad perspective introduced in Chapter 1. The earlier findings are discussed in the context of emerging intellectual capitalism as a synthesizing theme. Such a form of capitalism may not prove to be terminal, which justifies some final speculation about its future. Finally, the appendices give a simple bench-mark illustration, as well as questionnaires, which could be used as a diagnostic instrument. A glossary is also included.

1.7   RESEARCH BASIS

Various studies over the years have contributed to the research basis of this book. An interview study of technology protection and technology scanning in a dozen large US corporations (for example, General Electric, Honeywell, ITT,

Table 1.5   Overall design of the main empirical study and purpose of sub-studies

Level of analysis	Data collection method		
	Public patent statistics	Survey questionnaire	Case interviews
1. National	Comparative analysis of rate, volume and quality of patenting in different countries and industries, using available data from World Patent Index (WPI), European Patent Office (EPO), Patolis, USPTO	1	1
2. Corporate	Comparative analysis of rate, volume, composition and quality of corporate patent portfolios in 2 × 22 major Japanese and Swedish corporations with a sub-sample of matched competitors[2]	Analysis of IP activities and role of IP inside 25 + 20 large Japanese and Swedish corporations. c. 400 question items[3] 1	Analysis of best-practice IP management through corporate cases in Japan and Sweden (primarily Canon, Hitachi, Sony, Toshiba, ABB, Astra, Ericsson and Tetra Laval)[4]
3. Technology	Analysis of major players and patenting activities in each technology case. (2 × 2 Swedish invention cases with/without domestic exploitation: beta-blockers (Astra), mobile telephony (Telia, Ericsson), inkjet printers (Canon), ferro-electric liquid crystals (Canon))		Analysis of the roles of IP and IP management in exploitation of the technologies for beta blockers, mobile telephony, inkjet printers and ferro-electric liquid crystals

Notes
1. No specific sub-study was designed with this combination of level of analysis and data collection method.
2. The sampling is described in Appendix 1.
3. The sampling is described in Appendix 2 together with the survey questionnaire.
4. The general interview questionnaire is provided in Appendix 3.

Monsanto, Motorola, 3M, Pfizer, RCA and Xerox) was conducted in 1985–86 and followed up by a similar study in Sweden. However, these studies are not particularly reported here but instead served as background information from which several inputs to later studies were provided.

The original core study for this book is a study of patenting and IP matters for the Royal Swedish Academy of Engineering Sciences (IVA), initiated by the Swedish Patent Office and conducted in 1992–93. The study was designed as a general comparison between Sweden and several other countries at the aggregate level and between Sweden and Japan in particular at the corporate level. In addition, four technological areas, which contained major new Swedish technologies with or without domestic technology exploitation, were studied. For these three levels of comparative study – national, corporate and technology – data were collected from international patent statistics, a unique in-depth questionnaire sent to about 50 large Japanese and Swedish multinationals, and case-studies of best-practice companies as well as case-studies of four technological areas, using interviews. Table 1.5 summarizes the overall design of this study. Details of the survey study and the company case interview study are found in Appendices 2 and 3. The chief results of the comparative study of Sweden and Japan are summarized in IVA (1993).

The material about Japanese IP management was most interesting and a subsequent broader, interview-based case-study of Japanese corporations was conducted in 1994–95. This book draws mainly on the survey and case-studies of the Japanese corporations. It is complemented by general material from the USA collected in 1995–96, especially regarding the developments from the early 1980s onwards as well as the special conditions in Silicon Valley, a frontier in IP-related practices.

NOTES

1. More specifically, patents constitute law-enforceable, restricted exclusive rights that are granted to inventors when their applications are approved by national patent offices. Patents are granted for any technical invention that is novel to the world, non-obvious to someone skilled in the relevant art, and prospectively useful or at least not considered harmful to society. Patents are granted in exchange for disclosure by the inventor of information sufficient to enable others to imitate the invention in principle (see further Chapter 3) plus administration fees.
2. A similar list of the most highly valued patents in the world is not readily available. Such a list would most likely include the patents behind the top-selling pharmaceuticals. The best-selling pharmaceutical worldwide in 1997 was the ulcer drug Losec, developed and patented by the pharmaceutical company Astra in 1978. Astra management has estimated the value of the basic patent (discounted to 1978) to fall in the range US$15–30 billion, which is of the same magnitude as the most highly valued brand names.
3. Market values are collective, subjective measurements based on continuously changing external valuations of a company's stock. According to our rough formulation, a short-run reduction in market value translates to a reduction in intangible assets or IC as equity is fixed in the short run. This is not an accurate depiction of reality as the amount of IC becomes too dependent on

factors such as the volatility and well-functioning of the financial markets. Thus, these calculations provide only rough estimates for comparative purposes.

4. Market-to-book ratios were calculated simply by dividing the market value by the company's equity. Such a ratio is related to Tobin's q-value, which is the ratio of the market value of a firm's assets to the replacement costs of the firm's assets, where it is customary to calculate the replacement costs only for tangible assets. Measuring intellectual capital in this way should be treated with much caution since it depends on the well-functioning of both financial markets and accounting procedures. In fact, measuring intellectual capital as the difference between market value and book value means measuring a residual that contains more than what we would like to call intellectual capital. Components of IC may enter into the book value as well. As measurement techniques develop this residual will be disentangled, just as the original measurement of technology as a residual has developed (see Griliches 1996). For an overview of studies of market values and intangible capital, especially R&D, see Hall (1998).

5. See Patel and Pavitt (1995). Their control of the world's science is also increasing.

2. Philosophy and history of intellectual property

CHAPTER CONTENTS

2.1 CHAPTER OUTLINE

When, where, how and why have notions about intellectual property evolved? These are the basic questions to be dealt with in this chapter. Before giving more detailed historical accounts of how the IP system has evolved, these questions will be put in a broader, philosophical context. After those accounts, the economic and technical consequences of IPR are explored. Thus, the nature and the causes and consequences of the IP phenomenon are presented here with a broad but brief philosophical and historical perspective. The next chapter will then go into more contemporary and operative details.

2.2 PHILOSOPHY OF INTELLECTUAL PROPERTY

2.2.1 General Philosophy

Basic concepts
Needless to say basic notions, concepts and terminology evolve in complex ways. Nevertheless central concepts have to be simply described as a point of departure.

In common language, the term 'property' usually refers to resources (or assets) of some sort, physical (tangible, material) or otherwise over which somebody can exercise some justified control. In a broad sense, intellectual property (IP) can be taken to mean the opposite of physical or material or tangible property, and thus becomes synonymous with immaterial property. The term 'property right' refers to a right (or a bundle of rights[1]) that has evolved in society as recognized enforceable claims to some benefits or use of the resource. The rights may be transferable and may be treated as property or resources in themselves. Thus, property right is a social construct to be distinguished from the underlying resource. To emphasize this distinction, the fuller expressions 'property rights' and 'intellectual property rights' (IPR) are used.[2] Intellectual property rights are typically comprised of patent rights, copyrights, design rights, trademark rights, trade secret rights and a few other special property rights as items in contemporary law.[3] Intellectual capital in turn essentially comprises all immaterial resources that could be considered as assets with some kind of assignable capitalized value. In the context of a firm, intellectual capital comprises IPR, human capital and what could be called relational capital, see further Chapter 4.

For the discussion that follows in this chapter we can think of intellectual property in broad terms as property directly related to the creativity, knowledge and identity of an individual. Intellectual property of a collectivity of individuals may in turn be broadly thought of as property directly related to the creativity, knowledge and identity of that collectivity. The collectivity may be a legal person, such as a company or a nation, or it may be a less well-defined group, such as a team or a community. The basic notion of property in general is to have the right of way to exclude others at will from using and/or deriving benefits from the underlying resource, thereby exercising some semblance of control. Thus, ownership is associated with the right to at least partially control the benefits derivable from a resource. What constitutes the basic notions of property and the fundamentals of rights, and how these notions have evolved over time in various societies could be further elaborated at length. (See, for example, Demsetz 1967; MacPherson 1978; and Bouchaert 1990. See also Winter 1987 for a good review of some basic notions like knowledge, asset and property from an economist's point of view.)[4]

IP notions in individuals

How do notions about IP arise in individuals and collectivities? How do they arise in a child? How do they arise, if at all, in a primitive society? Very little seems to be known about such questions. In fact, psychologists studying child development have hardly asked the question of whether and how IP notions arise in a child. To explore this question a bit further, we can then ask ourselves some more specific questions, falling into four areas. First, does a child in the absence of instructions (for example, from parents) have a sense of natural right to its secrets and creations? Will a child easily accept a demand that it hand over a secret in any circumstance? Second, if a child for some reason discloses a secret, say about a discovery it has made, does the child sense a right to exclude others (children in particular) from taking such advantage of the disclosed information that it puts the child at a disadvantage? Third, does a child object to others imitating a creation or design of some kind that it has developed? For example, if the child builds a sandcastle on the beach with a specific design, does it object in some way to other children imitating that design? Does the child object more strongly to imitation if it has laboured more on the castle? Do other children feel it is fair to imitate and unfair to be stopped from doing so? Fourth, does a child have a sense of exclusive rights to a name or a symbol it has chosen to attach to itself or its creations or belongings?[5] All these questions must be left open here for the reader's further observation and speculation. It is hoped that they will stimulate further research, and not only by child psychologists.[6]

IP notions in primitive societies
The next set of general philosophical questions concerns how IP notions emerge in primitive societies. How do such societies look upon ownership and control of ideas, knowledge, secrets, creations, symbols and cultural expressions in general? Again, it seems as if questions like these are not asked frequently in the relevant academic circles, for example, in anthropology or in the legal sciences.[7] On the other hand, questions regarding how notions of physical property (land, animals and so on) emerge and develop in primitive societies have been studied widely (see, for example, Bouchaert 1990 and Demsetz 1967, both of which give further references). Jean Jacques Rousseau's philosophical discourses on the origin and foundations of inequality in primitive societies describe the emergence of general property notions as a point of departure for his evolutionary view of human rights, but in fact he has little to say specifically on IP notions in primitive societies. Nevertheless, he considerably influenced the emergence of the natural rights movement in 18th century France, which claimed that IPRs were limited to an individual's natural right to his or her own intellectual works rather than being a means for society to stimulate further intellectual works.

IP notions among animal societies
To stretch our present type of inquiry even further, one can also ask if animals develop any IP notions. For example, if a monkey discovers a new technique for food collection, will it readily share this discovery with others in the group? Will there be any enforcement behaviours or any rewarding behaviours in the flock? Again, these types of questions have not been asked frequently in the relevant academic disciplines, like zoology, although some relevant observations

of animal behaviour have been made. For example, information-sharing among groups of the same species is universal in social species from insects to primates (in fact it characterizes a social species), while information-sharing between different species is almost non-existent (see Wilson 1975). Chimpanzees, being the closest relatives to humans, have developed more subtle and human-like ways of information-sharing and secret-keeping (see de Waal 1982). However, there are no signs of any communication between groups associated with negotiation and trading purposes.[8] (Thus, there is support for Adam Smith's well-known proposition that the propensity to barter and trade is specific to humans).

IP notions in ancient societies

The type of foundational questions asked above could be asked about ancient societies as well. Were there any recognized IPR in Hammurabi's Babylonia, in Pharaonic Egypt, in ancient Greece or in ancient China, and what was the philosophy behind them? There are various indications of the recognition of IP in these societies, but it is difficult to find historical material on the supporting philosophical issues, and it is also difficult to find historians who have tried to deal with the questions in any depth (see further Section 2.3 on the history of the IP system). It is also difficult to find explicit treatments of the issues by ancient philosophers like Plato, Aristotle and others. One can, of course, speculate that Plato would not have approved of any private ownership of ideas that he thought of as universal, subject to discovery by noble men and belonging in some sense to a societal collectivity. However, he belittled industrial crafts and technology and would perhaps not have been concerned if some IPR had been attached to inventive work in such a context.[9] At the same time, he would probably have been concerned if his writings had been copied and published with someone else making claim to them. That there was a concern in ancient Greece over who originated ideas and writings is illustrated by the fact that Aeschines was (apparently wrongly) accused of having appropriated material from Socrates, after Socrates' death, without acknowledging it properly.[10] Thus, IP notions existed and were probably complex then as they are today. This is also clear from the well-documented proliferation, long before Plato, of semi-religious organizations such as 'mystery cults' (for example, at Eleusis) whose initiates claimed to possess secret knowledge, often of practical value concerning metallurgy and agriculture (and trade).[11]

Although an open question, it is not far-fetched to assume that contemporary views on IPR are, after all, influenced by Greek philosophy. The distinctions between science and technology (S&T), between discovery and inventions and between idea and expression are central in contemporary decisions regarding IPR.[12] The distinctions are often difficult to make and perhaps more so in contemporary S&T, as well as in contemporary cultural arts, not the least since they increasingly become penetrated by technology as well as by science.[13] Nevertheless, there is a widespread acceptance of these distinctions, which more or less became articulated in Greek philosophy. Likewise, Western-type academic institutions concerned with the furtherance of knowledge in non-proprietary ways have intellectual and ethical roots stretching back to Plato's Academy and Aristotle's Lyceum.[14] Thus, one can recognize the emergence in ancient societies of different sets of IP notions or IP regimes pertaining to science, technology, culture, military activities and religion.

IP notions in S&T

The scientific society or community has, over the centuries, also developed IP notions quite different from those in the industrial technology community. Priority for new creations is important in both communities but is decidedly more vague in science on the basis of the 'first to publish' principle, rather than on the 'first to file' (a patent application, that is) or the 'first to invent' principle as is the case with technical inventions. A publisher's decision to 'grant' a publication is based on some criteria of newness, non-obviousness and usefulness of the publication, similar to but not exactly the same as the criteria used in granting patent rights for an invention (see further Chapter 3, and also Chapter 10). Scientists, then, use each other's works and, in so doing, are expected to cite them as a basis for recognition and further career, funding and award possibilities. Certainly, citing fulfils other functions in academic work as well, but in this respect citing is thus analogous to paying a royalty for using the results of someone else's work. However, the 'payment' is made 'liquid' in quite a different manner. Peer recognition for contributions that are scientifically innovative is perhaps the biggest 'payment' to academics, albeit a non-monetary reward. The monetary rewards in science are partly oriented around prizes, grants and salaries. These forms of rewards are in fact alternatives to patent rights as means to promote technological progress. Much can be said and debated about the differences and relations between science and technology.[15] However, technically speaking there is nothing in principle that prevents them from having more similar IP regimes. One could, for example, have a patent-like system in science as easily as one could have a prize or grant or inventor reward system in technology.[16] The information in a 'scientific patent' could be freely used, respecting citation practices, until it is commercially exploited in some specified sense, similar to patents in technology.[17]

IP notions in culture

In the heterogeneous cultural communities of artists and artisans of various sorts (authors, potters, painters, musicians, dancers, goldsmiths and so on) and among parties interested in their output (the ruling elite, publishers, audiences and so on), a variety of IP notions have developed over time. Many of these notions are different from those in S&T, although there are clear similarities as well (perhaps increasing, due to technology's penetration of cultural activities). It seems that certain rights and rewards (individual/societal, tangible/intangible) have always been associated with cultural innovations, based on their innate newness, uniqueness and goodness and more or less regardless of the labour effort involved. The distinction between a specific artistic expression and the underlying idea (for example, a theme or motive) has also been important. Variations on a theme or different works within a style have been appreciated, while outright plagiarism has always been frowned upon, even if it has been tolerated. IPRs were given to potters and chefs early in history (see Section 2.3), and IP notions in the cultural field may very well have been precursory and generic in some sense.[18]

IP notions in the military

Historically, the military community has developed quite different IP notions compared to the areas of both culture and S&T (at least compared to IP notions in civilian S&T). For military operations, it is essential that secrecy protection is the primary concern, since there must be reliance on self-enforceable measures to prevent imitation and maintain control over the dissemination of information in general. The closed, secrecy-oriented military IP regime obviously clashes with the open IP regimes in science and (civilian) technology.

Other closed IP regimes

Secrecy-oriented or closed IP regimes also prevail in other parts of society, for example, in criminal organizations or certain religious or professional organizations. Again, it has been deemed essential to resort to such an IP notion when institutionalized enforcement of rules by any third party is deemed to be ineffective. The impossibility of dispossessing the perpetrator of allegedly stolen information makes the damage from leakage irreparable, and explains the extreme sanctions often inflicted in closed IP regimes upon spies, traitors and undesirable informants in general.

IP notions in mythology and religion

IP notions can even be found in the fabric of mythology and religion. In Greek mythology, the gods punished Prometheus for stealing fire and giving it to mankind. Fire symbolized technology, which was the property of the gods. Thus, Prometheus was punished as a kind of IP thief. But once fire had been given, the gods could not take it back and thereby prevent mankind from using technology to challenge the gods. The gods, in turn, punished mankind for receiving and using fire, although it had not been stolen by mankind.[19] This myth counters the present practice of absolving punishment from a third party for receiving stolen property in good faith.[20]

In the Bible, Genesis provides a parallel story about how God punished Adam and Eve for eating the fruits of the knowledge tree that belonged to God. Both stories carry the notion that knowledge is basically divine intellectual property, and that once mortals have illegitimately obtained access to it, whether or not through an intermediary, they can never be dispossessed of it and are therefore subject to eternal damnation (compare royalties), that is, they must pay for it for ever. To the extent that Christian kings and priests historically considered their earthly powers to have been divinely sanctioned, it is reasonable to believe that they also found religious justification for controlling IP. However, it is unclear whether this justification was an important factor behind the custom developed among rulers in Renaissance Europe of granting certain privileges to intellectual workers. In this context, it may be noted that the mythological theme of divine penalty to mankind for using technology has an earthly parallel in 18th-century Japan, where the Tokugawa rulers forbade inventions on penalty of death (see Chapter 5). This further underscores the importance of power and the political aspects of IP, in addition to its economic aspects.

The Talmud in Jewish religion expresses another IP notion that is at least 2000 years old. It is said that he who cites the source of his teaching 'brings salvation to the world'.[21] Thus, anyone is free to use information as long as attribution is made to the source, just as in science where the use of information is free of charge as long as appropriate references are made. In this way, the reputation of the idea or knowledge creator is increased during the diffusion of the knowledge. This Talmudic rule could be interpreted as an economic incentive for producing and disseminating information in ways that benefit both the producers and the users of new knowledge.

IP notions in philosophy

Apart from Greek philosophers, what have other traditional philosophers had to say about various notions of IP? This wide question cannot be dealt with at any length here, but a few remarks and references to the literature will be made.[22] Property notions in general have been much discussed by traditional philosophers, but IP has mostly been treated as a side issue. Among Western philosophers who have had an influence on IP notions, either directly or indirectly, John Locke, David Hume, Immanuel Kant, Friedrich Hegel, Jean Jacques Rousseau and Jeremy Bentham deserve mention (see, for example, MacPherson 1978; Palmer 1990).

Inspired by the (differing) ideas of Locke and Rousseau, a so-called 'natural rights' school or movement emerged in the 18th century and became especially influential in 19th-century France. The individual was looked upon as having a natural claim to the results of all his or her labours, mental or physical. In particular, the results of an individual's intellectual labour were seen as an extension of that individual's identity, an extension of which the individual could not be deprived by others, and especially not by societal institutions. In opposition to the natural rights school, which eventually declined in influence, stood the notion that patent rights were creations by society for the purpose of serving the economic interests of its members at large (compare the citation of Thomas Jefferson, below).[23] This more economically or utilitarian- (Bentham-) oriented IP notion, dating back to ancient times and clearly codified in 15th-century Venice, gradually became strengthened as economic concerns grew in connection with industrialization. The IP notions of the natural rights school, which, as we have seen above, possibly have roots extending to primitive origins, eventually declined markedly in their influence over IP legislation.[24] The philosophical debate over IP then shifted more to the arenas of law and economics (see below). Nevertheless, the current debate about IPR in connection with software, the Internet, universities and culture might broaden into general philosophical issues, perhaps also reviving natural rights arguments. The distinction between natural rights and economically (utility) oriented rights should not be overplayed, however.

2.2.2 Legal and Economic Philosophy

In legal and economic circles, the general concept and justification of property has been dominated by notions of physical property. There is a certain convergence of general notions defining property as a bundle of rights, being enforceable within limits and bound to the use or benefits derivable from a resource that is scarce and possible to possess. Property, then, embodies the right to include some beneficiaries and exclude others, where the ability to exclude is paramount. Several attempts have been made to carry such notions over to IP.[25] This tendency to generalize from physical to intellectual property raises a question about the *extendibility* of legal and economic concepts and principles from the area of physical property to the area of intellectual property. We cannot go into a deep discussion of that question here, but a few points will illustrate some basic differences between physical and intellectual property and at the same time edify some relevant philosophical issues in the law and economics of IP.[26] Any extendibility from physical to intellectual property appears to be strongly limited by the obvious differences between physical objects and intellectual objects (typically ideas and knowledge), even if property is seen as a bundle of rights which should be distinguished from the underlying objects themselves. For example, the rights of an individual to a certain piece of physical property can be seen to derive in principle from the circumstance that the individual either has had the first (non-momentary) possession of that physical property or has had the property rights transferred to him or her.[27] The possibility of extending that principle to IP, then, seems to be limited by the fact that possession of a physical object fundamentally differs from possession of an intellectual object. One such difference is what we can call the *dispossession impossibility* (or the inalienability) of intellectual objects. This means that once an individual has received some knowledge it cannot simply be deliberately removed from him or her. (Admittedly, computers may have erasable memories, and selective drugs or treatments in the future for erasing parts of human memory are conceivable.) Thus, a stolen piece of information cannot be taken back from a thief in the same way as a stolen piece of physical property.[28] At the same time, the act of stealing does not dispossess the information owner of his or her information either; so from that point of view, it may not be important to have the information returned.[29] (This also implies that there is no absence of information to indicate that a theft has occurred.) But what is important is that the original information owner cannot return to a state of sole possession and control in normal circumstances.[30] Thus, any transfer in the possession of knowledge is more or less irreversible. This makes it difficult to base a property concept on the possession of knowledge in the same way as the concept of physical property can be based on the possession of physical things, where the sole possessor and also the first possessor can be identified more easily and dispossession is possible.

There are further differences between physical and intellectual things.[31] These differences are rather obvious, but their consequences need not be, as pointed out by Arrow (1962). In contrast to physical things, information can be shared at will, cheaply and almost limitlessly among individuals. In that sense, a given piece of open information is not scarce, so scarcity would not warrant defining a property right to it.[32] On the other hand, an individual can also choose to keep information secret, perfectly contained and at no direct cost, and thereby enforce scarcity. However, there is no guarantee that others thereby will remain excluded from the use of that information or idea, since someone else may come up with the same information or idea.[33] The exclusion from direct use of someone's secret proprietary information is perfect but sole possession and thereby scarcity cannot be kept permanent at will. In other words, exclusion from a secret may be temporarily perfect, but for how long is uncertain. Exploiting valuable information often necessitates some disclosure; therefore excluding others from its use also implies an indirect cost for the information holder, thereby lowering the incentives to create information in the first place. It is moreover impossible for an individual to prove *ex post* that he or she was in possession of some information, unless the information was disembodied and stored or registered in some form or unless something in the individual's behaviour revealed the truth.

In summary, inherent differences between physical objects and intellectual objects make it much more difficult, and frequently impossible, to establish and verify states of possession for intellectual objects, especially the states of first and sole possession. Thus, using circumstances pertaining to possession as a basis for deriving necessary property rights is less straightforward for IPR than for physical property rights. This in itself does not mean that a better basis exists for deriving IPR. Still, considering the obvious fundamental differences between physical and intellectual things, it would seem to follow that extendibility of the legal principles for property rights from the physical to the intellectual domain is limited. Even if property rights are to be distinguished from their underlying tangible or intangible objects, a closer specification of the nature of the rights can hardly be made fully independent of the nature of the underlying objects. At the very least there is some burden of proof to be carried by those claiming that extensions can be made.[34] Nevertheless, it appears that legislators and courts traditionally have attempted such extensions without a very unified or general theory of intellectual property.[35]

So, given the fundamental difficulties in extending traditional property notions from physical to intellectual property, what philosophical and theoretical justifications of specific IPR have been voiced? Generally, such justifications are categorized as *deontological* and *consequentialist*.[36] Very briefly, deontological justifications are based on moral rights and rules that are largely exogenous to the economic and legal system (they are 'natural rights'), while consequentialist justifications are based on the good (economic) consequences of the legal recognition of IP. Deontological justifications mostly refer to rights associated with one's labour (the 'labour theory' of property associated with Locke) or rights associated with one's personality or identity (the 'personality theory' of property associated with Hegel).

Consequentialist justifications are often classified as being utilitarian, referring to fulfilment of consumer preferences or utilities, or as being teleological, referring to fulfilment of the proper ends of human life. Consequentialist justifications focus on the nature of incentives which legal recognition of IPR can afford. Incentives can take the form of rights to a reward, such as a monopoly right, a prospect right, a contract, a prize or some other kind of right or privilege.

The monopoly right reward has been the most popular approach by far. The main idea is that the IPR should be tailored in such a way that the IPR holder through a limited monopoly can get a share of the benefits which can be derived from the intellectual creations. The rent-sharing should be designed by limiting the monopoly in such a way that creators are sufficiently stimulated to create wealth for themselves as a means to create wealth for others (for example, a ruler, a community, a society). This idea could be taken one step further, so as to create the best or optimal rent-sharing arrangement in some sense. The underlying presumption then is that a market economy does not sufficiently or optimally stimulate creative or inventive work. The contemporary economic theory behind IPR, and patents in particular, is dealt with further in Chapter 3.

Consequentialist justifications, and especially utilitarian ones, predominate in the contemporary legal and economic philosophy of IPR. This does not imply that there are no objections to such justifications or to some of their parts or features. Some authors object that IPR are not compatible with the justifications of property rights in general, while some object that IPR conflict with other more fundamental rights like liberty and justice; still others object that IPR are not instrumental in providing the desired consequences, and so on. For further discussions of the legal and economic philosophy of IPR, see for example Plant (1974), Penrose (1951), Machlup (1958a), Dreyfuss (1989a), Kuflick (1989), Davis (1989), Nance (1990), Bouchaert (1990) and Palmer (1990).

2.3   HISTORY OF THE IPR SYSTEM

2.3.1   General History

Here, the historical evolution of IPR systems on the whole will be outlined, covering the various IP parts, periods and places of relevance, with a special focus on some less well-known circumstances. A major reinterpretation of the common historical accounts will not be made, however. There are several such accounts which are excellent: for example David (1993) on patents, copyrights and trade secrets; Penrose (1951), Machlup (1958), Kaufer (1989), MacLeod (1988, 1991) and the special issue of the journal *Technology and Culture* (1991) on patents; Plant (1974), Rose (1993), Goldstein (1997) and Kretschmer (1997) on copyrights; Coleman (1992) on trade secrets; and Diamond (1983) and Wilkins (1992) on trademarks. Contemporary changes regarding IPR are surveyed in the special issue of *International Review of Industrial Property and Copyright Law (IIC)*, **26** (6), 1995. It must be kept in mind that the various IP components (patents, copyrights, trade secrets, trademarks, and so on) have separate histories, which were weakly interrelated until recent decades and hardly constituted an 'IP system' other than in a loose sense.

IP notions have evolved from the dawn of history, oriented especially around secrets, although identity-related symbols are also of early origin.[37] IP for gaining trade-related advantages was less important in prehistoric times, but secrets and symbols as means to gain and preserve power were important, especially in political, military and religious settings. Ancient cultures, as in Egypt and Greece, were not known to have had any patent-like institutions for technical inventions, nor did the Roman Empire (Kaufer 1989, p. 1). But there are clear indications of other forms of IP in these cultures (see Table 2.1). Particularly noteworthy is the use of trademarks and a patent-like system for 'food chemistry' in the Greek colony Sybaris in the southern part of the Italian peninsula.

Table 2.1   Chronological overview of major events in development of IP legislation

Year(s)	Event
3200 BC	Potter marks found on fired clay pots, including jars buried in tombs of the First Dynasty Egyptian kings, providing a precursor to trademark protection. Stone seals bearing such marks were used from about this time onward in both the Near East and Greece.
700–500 BC	Chefs in Sybaris, a Greek colony in southern Italy known for luxurious living, were granted 1-year monopolies on the preparation of an unusual or outstanding dish. This right applied to no other art or science.
100 BC	Trademarks used in Rome on an everyday basis to mark products such as cloth, lamps, glass vessels, cheese and medicine.
AD 337	Roman emperor Constantine decrees that artisans of certain critical trades are exempt from all civil duties. Chariot makers, engineers and locksmiths are especially favoured.
483	Roman emperor Zeno decrees that no monopoly can be granted to clothing or food, even if the monopoly was previously required by order of an emperor.
1297	A Venetian decree allows physicians to retain within their guild the secret for preparing new and novel medicines.
1323	Johannes Teuthonicus is granted a patent-like privilege by the Venetian government for a grain mill.
1324	Edward II (England) grants letters of protection to skilled German miners to induce them to come to England.
1331	John Kempe of Flanders receives a royal grant (patent) for the purpose of building a clothing industry in England. The policy is later extended to other skilled trades.
1332	The Venetian Grand Council establishes a special fund for a foreign constructor of windmills.
1353	An English statute enables a foreign merchant to obtain restitution for lost goods if his mark proved ownership.
1450	Johann Gutenberg develops the printing press. The newly acquired ease of copying written materials creates the necessity for copyright protection.
1452	Earliest recorded trademark litigation; a widow of a London bladesmith is awarded a particular mark that formerly belonged to her husband.

1474	Venice enacts the first codified patent ordinance. Inventors were permitted 20-year monopolies. Infringers would be fined 300 ducats.
1557	Queen Mary I establishes the Stationers' Co. of London, a trade association of printers and booksellers, holding a royal patent on the printing of books in England.
1559	G. Acontio of Italy petitions Queen Elizabeth I for the protection of his inventions out of fear that his work will be copied by others without royal protection. The Queen grants Acontio's request, instituting a tradition of granting inventors patents for their discoveries.
1594	Galileo receives a patent for a device which raises water and irrigates land.
1623	England adopts patent ordinance (Statute of Monopolies). Ordinance codifies a century-old practice of the English monarchy. The patent term is set at 14 years, twice the length of time required for an ordinary apprenticeship.
1641	The Massachusetts Colony grants the first patent in the Western hemisphere.
1709	Legal protection in England granted for authors for the first time. Legal protection extended for 14 years in a manner similar to the Statute of Monopolies.
1741	Denmark enacts first copyright law on European continent.
1786	All but one of original 13 American colonies have enacted copyright laws.
1787	US Constitution drafted, providing for the first time a constitutional instrument recognizing an individual's property right in the product of his invention, with both patents and copyrights.
1790	USA adopts patent legislation (first US patent law).
1791	France adopts patent legislation.
1791–1882	Patent laws introduced in most European countries.
1836	Fire destroys the US Patent Office, including 7000 invention models, 9000 drawings and 230 books. Congress authorizes funds to replace the most valuable and interesting models. Congress modifies patent law to provide for publication of the patent drawings with the issued patent – in case of another fire.
1837	First trademark case in USA decided by a Massachusetts state court.
1845	First trademark case decided under US federal law.
1875	English Parliament passes a comprehensive trademark registration statute.
1883	Paris Convention/Paris Union (establishes reciprocity, priority).
1885	Japan promulgates the Patent Monopoly Ordinance.

Table 2.1   continued

Year(s)	Event
1886	Berne Convention for the Protection of Literary and Artistic Works. First attempt to develop international protection for copyrights. Madrid Agreement; established reciprocity for trademarks among signatory nations.
1891–1947	Gestation period – AIPPI sponsored meetings in the USA (1911), London (1925) and The Hague (1935) to initiate amendments and fixes to the established system. The end of World War II brought about the need for a new start in IPR deliberations.
1947	Hague Agreement on the establishment of the International Patent Institute.
1949	The European Council advocates the foundation of a European patent office.
1957	The Nice Agreement lays down the international classification of goods and services used in registering trade and service marks.
1963	Strasbourg Agreement on partial harmonization of patent laws (paving the way for Patent Cooperation Treaty (PCT) and European Patent Convention (EPC)).
1968	Locarno Agreement establishes a classification system of industrial designs.
1970	PCT signed (in Washington).
1971	Universal Copyright Convention offers an alternative for countries unable to join the Berne Convention.
1971	Strasbourg Agreement on international patent classification.
1973	EPC signed. The treaty had been signed by 16 countries by 1995.
1975	Community Patent Convention establishes a unified European patent. Treaty has not yet come into force.
1977	EPO established. Original signatory nations are: Austria, Belgium, Denmark, France, Germany, Italy, Luxembourg, the Netherlands, Sweden, Switzerland and the UK.
1978	PCT in force. EPC in force.
1980s	Industrial countries begin changing their trade laws, classifying defective IP systems as a type of unfair trade practice.
1985	Patent law comes into effect in China.
1989	The Structural Impediments Initiative (SII) talks initiated between the USA and Japan remove structural impediments to trade between the two nations, and include IP protection.

| 1994 | World's industrialized nations agree to harmonize aspects of their IP protection under the auspices of General Agreement on Trade and Tariffs (GATT), known as trade-related aspects of intellectual property rights (TRIPs). |
| 1994 | Commonwealth of Independent States (CIS) adopts the Eurasian Patent Convention, patterned after the EPC. |

Source: Compiled from various sources with the assistance of T. Ewing and B. Heiden.

As trade and technology developed in the Middle Ages, IP notions developed. A need to protect technological advantages by means other than secrecy arose. For example, a ruler could feel overly dependent on the secret-based 'natural' monopolistic power of professional guilds and societies, as well as on that of an individual artisan such as a clever weaponsmith. Furthermore, skilful artisans could take their professional secrets with them to the grave. The idea of remunerating the disclosure of secrets, which is an ancient practice in itself, became increasingly important as technical know-how gained importance. It is likely that various types of compensation were considered – prizes, grants, patent privileges and so on. What probably made a patent-like privilege particularly attractive to a ruler was its financial feature. A privilege that protected the privilege holder from competition allowed him or her to charge higher prices. To the extent that competitive trade existed, the privilege holder was remunerated by the ruler but in such a way that the ruler, that is, the privilege granter, did not have to pay for it fully and directly.[38] A patent privilege also carried the advantage that the remuneration was tied to the actual working of a device and the demand for that device. This advantage could be achieved by a prize system as well, but then the ruler had to finance the prize. The disadvantage of a patent system from the patent holder's point of view was that a patent privilege implied an *ex post* remuneration, that is, in connection with commercial success based in turn on technical success, and it financed neither any necessary investments *ex ante* nor any failures *ex post*. This disadvantage could be mitigated by a grant or a loan in combination with the patent, however, but then at the discretion of the ruler. Thus, the emergence of the patent system can be seen partly as a reaction against secrecy in a context of the rising importance of technology and trade, and partly as a scheme for promoting inventions that provided an attractive mode of financing for the privilege granter.

A patent-like system also emerged in connection with ore-mining sites as described by Kaufer (1989, pp. 2–4). In that context, the priority rule 'first to invent' emerged, with the term 'invention' then having a meaning closer to 'discovery' in present-day language.[39] According to Kaufer, there had long been a common-law tradition in mining areas in the European Alps of granting property rights to those who were 'first to invent' an ore site.[40] As mining became a more technically complex operation, for example, going deeper into the ground, more technical devices were needed, for example, for removing water (*Wasserkuenste*, or 'water arts'). Patent-like privileges were then granted to originators and financiers of these devices by extending mining law principles. Often remuneration took the form of rights to a certain share of the mine's output, again an attractive mode of financing.[41]

In the 14th and 15th centuries, the Republic of Venice was engaged in mining and 'water arts' as well. Kaufer (1989, p. 304) and David (1993, p. 46) report on how several engineers were granted special patent-like privileges by the Venetian government. The first known example is Johannes Teuthonicus in 1323 for a grain mill. Another example is Jacobus de Valperga, who received a special privilege in Venice in 1460 for a water pump. The privilege prevented anyone from imitating Jacobus's pump without his permission as long as Jacobus lived. On the other hand, there was a compulsory licensing provision requiring Jacobus to grant licences to anyone who offered reasonable royalties. At this time, Venice had two types of privileges, invention privileges and trade privileges. Jacobus's privilege was an invention privilege that gave protection from unlicensed imitation, while a trade privilege gave protection from competition.

In 1474 Venice promulgated a formal patent code, the first one known in history. The code incorporated various ideas practised in preceding cases. Inventions shown to be workable and useful received ten years of protection subject to compulsory licensing provisions. The preamble of the 1474 code stated:[42]

> We have among us men of great genius, apt to invent and discover ingenious devices ... Now, if provisions were made for the works and devices discovered by such persons, so that others who may see them could not build them and take the inventor's honour away, more men would then apply their genius, would discover, and would build devices of great utility to our commonwealth.

The 1474 patent code and its preceding practices were a way for Venice to attract engineers from outside and stimulate orderly technical progress, although it was not the only way. This first patent law had a slow start, something that happened later with the first patent laws of other nations as well, for example, in Japan. However, these laws signified the emergence of a new era, what we can call the patent era, or rather the *national patent era*, since the patent system was a national or local phenomenon pertaining only to single city-states or countries. The rest of the history of the patent system is more widely known. Table 2.2 summarizes this history, divided into different eras.[43]

The granting of privileges, including patent-like ones, by governments or rulers was not confined to Venice. During the 16th century, patents became used increasingly in France and England as an implement of mercantilist policies.

Table 2.2   Eras in the history of patents and IP

Era	Characteristics
1. Non-patent era Ancient cultures (Egypt, Greece etc.)	Emergence of science separated from technology Emergence of cultural and industrial arts Secrecy and symbols emerging as recognized IP No patent-like rights or institutions for technical inventions
2. Pre-patent era Middle Ages to Renaissance	Emergence of universities Secrecy, copyright and symbols (artisan trademarks/names) as dominant IP, also collectively organized Emerging schemes to grant privileges and remunerate disclosure Extensions of mining laws to inventions
3. National patent era Late 15th to late 18th century	Breakthrough of natural sciences Local codifications of patent laws (Venice 1474, England 1623 etc.) Regulation of privileges Conscious stimulation of technical progress at national level, linked to economic policies (e.g., mercantilistic)
4. Multinational patent era Late 18th to late 19th century	Emergence of modern nation-states Industrialization Continued international diffusion of the patent system Local anti-patent movements Emerging international patent relations (e.g., disputes)
5. International patent era Late 19th to late 20th century	Emerging industrial and military R&D International coordination of IP (Paris Convention 1883, World Intellectual Property Organization (WIPO), PCT, EPO etc.) Separate IP regimes in socialist countries and less-developed countries (LDCs)
6. The pro-patent and emerging IC era Late 20th century to ?	IC surpasses physical capital for many entities Intensified international competition Global activism for IP from industrialized countries, especially from the USA Almost worldwide adoption of the patent system Increased international patenting
7. The global patent and IC era ?	Global harmonization and integration of IP Emergence of supra-national and global patents, IP offices and clearing procedures? ?
8. ?	?

An important event in the early diffusion of the patent system was a passage in 1623 of the Statute of Monopolies by the English Parliament, which gave a clear recognition of the underlying ideas and specific form of a patent system.[44] This later came to serve as a model, for example, for British colonies in North America, which started to adopt similar patent laws in the 17th century. An interesting feature of the statute was that monopoly privileges were granted for the true and first inventor of new manufacture but the invention had only to be new in England. This was intended to stimulate domestic technical progress, for example, by attracting foreign engineers and entrepreneurs to England. England at the time felt it had fallen back in some technical areas and needed to catch up. Another feature of the statute was that the lifetime of a patent was set at 14 years, which was twice the time needed for a master to train a generation of apprentices. This was an explicit consideration corresponding to contemporary considerations of R&D times and market lifetimes on average. A third interesting feature was the explicit shift in granting authority from a royal ruler or sovereign to a government or its bureaucracy. The government was then considered the source of patent rights, in contrast to the views that patent rights derived from sovereigns or were natural rights of the individual. The latter view underlined the French patent law at the time of the French Revolution in 1791 and lived on in 19th-century France (Penrose 1951, p. 21).

Another important event was the enacting by the USA of a federal patent law in 1790. The importance attached to patents and individual IPR in the newly created USA is clear from the fact that it was written into the US Constitution in 1787 that Congress had the power: 'to promote the progress of science and useful arts, by securing for limited times to authors and inventors the exclusive right to their respective writings and discoveries'.

Thomas Jefferson played a key role in the early days of the US patent system. His clear view of the system is illuminating and deserves citation at length (as cited in David 1993, p. 26):

> If nature has made any one thing less susceptible than all others of exclusive property, it is the action of the thinking power called an idea, which an individual may exclusively possess as long as he keeps it to himself; but the moment it is divulged, it forces itself into the possession of every one, and the receiver cannot dispossess himself of it. Its peculiar character, too, is that no one possesses the less, because every other possesses the whole of it . . . That ideas should freely spread from one to another over the globe, for the moral and mutual instruction of man, and improvement of his condition, seems to have been peculiarly and benevolently designed by nature, when she made them, like fire, expansible over all space, without lessening their density in any point, and like the air in which we breathe, move, and have our physical being, incapable of confinement or exclusive appropriation . . . Inventions then cannot, in nature, be a subject of property. Society may give an exclusive right to the profits arising from them, as an encouragement to men to pursue ideas which may produce utility,

but this may or may not be done, according to the will and convenience of the society, without claim or complaint from anybody.

The period from the late 18th to the late 19th century is characterized by continued but locally disrupted diffusion of the patent system internationally. An anti-patent movement emerged in Europe, first in Germany and somewhat later in Holland, where patent laws were repealed in 1869; Switzerland rejected several patent law proposals. Even England considered adopting significantly weaker patent laws, and France had earlier weakened patent protection at the time of the French Revolution. Essentially, the anti-patent movement was a consequence of free-trade and anti-monopoly movements, since patents were associated with mercantilistic policies as well as with monopoly privileges. However, interest groups in emerging industry and in some strong patent nations created pro-patent lobbying groups, which gradually gained influence. Finally, the worldwide depression in the 1870s revived protectionism and the anti-patent era by and large ended in the 1870s.

The case of Switzerland provides interesting illustrations of the nationalistic forces affecting the international diffusion of the patent system. After having rejected proposals to introduce patent laws for many decades, even by popular referenda, Switzerland finally introduced them in 1887, mainly because its watch industry was under pressure from foreign imitations. However, patent protection within Swiss borders was at this time limited to mechanical inventions, since the emerging Swiss chemical industry wanted to imitate and catch up with the more advanced German chemical industry. After Germany had threatened with retaliatory tariffs, Switzerland extended its patent coverage to include chemical process (but not product) inventions in 1907 (Kaufer 1989, p.10).

The patent system became more internationally diffused, concomitant with the growth of international trade and competition in industrial goods. The nation-states adopted various policies for promoting their industries, and a need for international cooperation in patent matters grew, especially since nations often discriminated against foreigners. The Paris Convention of 1883 was the first milestone in this respect, followed by many more treaties and agreements.

In the 20th century, industrial and military R&D emerged, entailing very different modes and settings for inventive work. The individual inventor, who was the original target for patent laws, has gradually become relatively less important. Inventions increasingly require large resources, and industrial firms and the military establishment have become the prime movers of technology in both the East and the West. Similarly, cultural arts have become big business, with more professional artists than ever. Socialist countries with planned economies have set up separate IP regimes. Economic and industrial differences between various categories of countries have increased and become alarmingly

Table 2.3   Chronological overview of major events in US IPR development

Year(s)	Event
1641	The Massachusetts Colony grants the first patent in the western hemisphere.
1786	All but one of original 13 American colonies have enacted copyright laws. No centralized or uniform administration system exists among the colonies.
1787	US Constitution drafted, providing for the first time a constitutional instrument recognizing an individual's property right in the product of his invention, with both patents and copyrights.
1790	USA adopts patent legislation (first US patent law). (Patent bill signed into law on 10 April.)
1793	USA revises its patent act to provide for more rigorous examinations.
1794	Eli Whitney receives patent on a cotton gin.
1811	Robert Fulton receives patent on the steamboat.
1834	Cyrus McCormick receives patent on the reaper.
1836	New Patent Act initiates inventiveness requirement and provides a fixed term of 14 years, with a possible seven-year renewal.
1836	Fire destroys the US Patent Office, including 7000 invention models, 9000 drawings and 230 books. Congress authorizes funds to replace the most valuable and interesting models. Congress modifies patent law to provide for publication of the patent drawings with the issued patent – in case of another fire.
1837	First trademark case in USA decided by a Massachusetts state court.
1839	Congress authorizes the employment of two assistant examiners to handle the increased workload.
1840	Samuel Morse receives patent on the telegraph.
1842	Design patents are provided with a seven-year term of protection.
1844	Charles Goodyear receives patent on the vulcanization process.
1845	First trademark case decided under US federal law.
1846	Elias Howe receives patent on the sewing machine.
1848	The Commissioner of Patents is given the sole power to extend a patent.
1849	US Patent Office is placed under the newly created Department of Interior.
1861	Congress creates a Board of Appeals consisting of three examiners-in-chief.
1868	C. Latham Sholes receives patent on the typewriter.
1869	George Westinghouse receives patent on the air brake.
1870	A new Patent Act is enacted to consolidate all changes made to the Patent Act of 1836. The patent term is increased to a maximum of 17 years.
1870	Congress passes another trademark act.
1871	US Supreme Court declares trademark act unconstitutional.
1876	Alexander Graham Bell receives patent on the telephone.
1880	Thomas Edison receives patent on the incandescent lamp.
1881	Congress passes another trademark act which survives constitutional scrutiny by the Supreme Court.
1888	Nikola Tesla receives patent on the induction motor.
1930	Plants are added to the items suitable for patenting.
1935	Patent number 2 000 000 issued.
1949	Patents so frequently declared invalid when litigated that Supreme Court Justice Jackson remarks, 'the only patent that is valid is one which this Court has not been able to get its hands on' (Jungerson v. Ostby & Barton Co.).
1952	The present US Patent Law is passed. Revisions have occurred continually as needed.

1961	Patent number 3 000 000 issued.
1976	Copyright Act enacted.
1979	Both the US Senate and President Jimmy Carter desire to strengthen enforcement of domestic patents.
1980	US Supreme Court declares man-made micro-organisms to be patentable. Bayh-Dole Act enacted, enabling universities to patent inventions from federally funded research.
1980s	Patent fees steadily begin rising, as the Patent Office becomes a self-funded government function.
1981	The US Justice Department revises its anti-trust enforcement activity to make it easier for patents not to violate anti-trust statutes.
1982	CAFC is established. In quick order, the court changes the validity of litigated patents from 30 per cent to 89 per cent, thus initiating an era in which patents are of much greater interest to industry.
1989	The SII talks initiated between the USA and Japan remove structural impediments to trade between the two nations, and include IP protection.
1980s	Jury trials become much more common in patent litigation.
1992	Patent number 5 000 000 issued.
1994	World's industrialized nations agree to harmonize aspects of their IP protection under the auspices of GATT, known as TRIPs.
1994	After years of favourable court decisions, all software is now clearly patentable.
1995	GATT-related TRIPs agreement causes USA to amend its patent laws to expand the patent term from 17 to 20 years, allow inventive activity abroad to be considered by the patent office, and permit the filing of provisional patent applications.
1995	CAFC holds that patent claims are a matter of law to be decided by the judge and not a matter of fact to be decided by the jury. The ruling expands the ability of the court to review patent holdings and makes patent trials by jury less desirable. The ruling is upheld by the US Supreme Court in 1996.
1998	The Digital Millennium Copyright Act enacted.

Source: Compiled by T. Ewing.

large, creating tension among institutions, including national IP regimes in developed and developing countries. Two global wars have transformed the world, including its various institutional frameworks. S&T have progressed and accumulated tremendously at an increasing pace. Still, the patent system and its essential ideas have survived and continued to diffuse internationally, not least after the downfall of the Soviet Union and the corresponding planned economy systems. This resilience of ideas and persistent adoption of a fairly well preserved and longstanding institution such as the patent system is indeed surprising. Its context has changed radically since 15th-century Venice and 17th-century England, while its basic feature of offering a temporary monopoly reward for certain inventions for a certain length of time, has changed comparatively little.[45] There are naturally numerous variants of patent laws in different periods and places, but as a whole the patent system has become a dominant institutional design. There has also been a convergence both of national patent systems and of IP regimes, although this has been slow and has left many substantial differences.[46]

Table 2.1 gave a broad chronology of IP-related events in the world throughout history, including details for Europe. A more detailed chronology for IP-related events in the USA is given in Table 2.3. IP history in Japan is treated in Chapter 5, with a chronology in Table 5.1.

2.3.2   US IP Developments in the 1980s and the Emergence of the Pro-patent Era

The anti-patent era of the 19th century more or less ended in the 1870s. Political and economic forces largely defeated the anti-patent movement. However, this did not produce a marked reversal into a pro-patent era. Patent legislation carried weight, but patent issues were by and large circling in the backwaters of business, economics and policy-making and continued to do so for a good century.

In the USA, a revival of certain anti-patent sentiments appeared in the interwar years, as large corporations with strong in-house R&D emerged, some of them blatantly using the patent system to build up dominant market positions (see Kahn 1940 and Folk 1942; Scherer 1980, p. 451). Several government committees and reports on patents, trademarks and so on appeared before and after World War II, but the pro-patent era of the 20th century did not begin in the USA until the 1980s.

There seem to be four streams of events in the USA, somewhat disjointed initially, leading up to the pro-patent era. The first concerned the creation in 1982 of a federal court of appeals, namely the Court of Appeals for the Federal Circuit (CAFC), specifically to hear patent appeals in lieu of the other circuit courts of appeal.[47] This type of specialized court had been contemplated for a long time in patent circles.[48] As the complexities in patent disputes grew, the pressures for a specialized court of appeals mounted and finally resulted in the creation of the CAFC. These pressures were generated by and large within pro-patent circles in law and industry. The origins of the CAFC were much less dramatic than the consequences, the magnitude and repercussions of which had not been anticipated. The CAFC started to act in a pro-patent manner, in stark contrast to what US courts had done previously, as was to some extent expected. The validity of patents was upheld far more often (as if they were 'born valid'), and patent damages were largely increased (see further Banner 1986; Cox 1986; Shapiro 1990).[49] All in all, the economic value of patents to patent right holders increased (see also Chapter 1).

The second stream of events behind the emergence of the pro-patent era was linked to a change of attitude within the Antitrust Division of the US Department of Justice in the early 1980s under its new director, William Baxter. Traditionally the Antitrust Division had been hostile to IP legislation and IP licensing (illustrated by the famous 'nine no-nos' of patent licensing), interpreting patents as monopolies that limited the static efficiency of price competition. Attitudes now changed with reference to upgrading the incentive aspects of patents to promote dynamic competition through R&D-based new products and processes and limiting the disincentive to R&D investments created by unauthorized imitation and 'free-riding'. This was presented as a shift from a narrow scope of static economic analysis towards a broader, dynamic analysis of the economics of technology, but still within the stated mission of the division to serve the interests of US consumers.[50]

This change in attitude could be traced back to ideas and perspectives emerging in the 1960s among economists, especially within the emerging field of law and economics.[51] The shift in anti-trust policy in the early 1980s in the USA is a good (but perhaps too uncommon) example of how changes in scholarly thinking have had a direct impact on policies.

The third stream of events emanated from large US corporations, with the chairman of Pfizer, Edmund Pratt, and the chairman of IBM, John Opel, as two leading representatives among several other industrialists.[52] Through a series of initiatives and reports, channelled through various committees, councils and task forces, US big industry pressed for stronger IP protection and enforcement against infringers and counterfeiters domestically and abroad. US industry also pressed for a 'trade-based approach' to improve IP protection by including IP matters in US trade negotiations and in the GATT framework of international trade negotiations, for which a number of TRIPs were formulated. In general, these initiatives and pressures were part of a larger movement to increase the competitiveness of US industry, for which it had become increasingly clear that technology was a key asset that had to be protected. Individual US corporations such as Texas Instruments and Motorola then started in the mid-1980s to become aggressive litigators against both domestic and foreign – especially Japanese – infringers. The economic value of patents rose accordingly due to the changes in court behaviour and anti-trust attitudes.[53]

A memo entitled 'Priorities for intellectual property', prepared in 1985 by the US Council Task Force on Intellectual Property within the US Council for International Business, an interest group composed of US corporations, illustrates the kind of problems US industry had identified concerning the protection of IP. The memo identified the following problems as of 1985 (briefly enumerated here):

1. Epidemic proportions of commercial counterfeiting.
2. Inadequate protection for chemicals.
3. Inadequate protection for biotechnology.
4. Inadequate patent term.
5. Expropriation of exclusive patent rights.
6. Inadequacy and ineffectiveness of copyright protection.

7. Procedural deficiencies.
8. Need for a multilateral framework.

The fourth stream of events, merging with the other streams behind the pro-patent era, emanated from the US government, especially the Reagan administration. This political stream of events, as well as the stream of events in industry, was embedded in the general movement in the 1980s to preserve US industrial competitiveness. This movement in turn was essentially triggered by the successful catch-up process in Japan and Asian newly industrialized countries (NICs), and the perception in the USA that these countries were free-riding on US technology as they made significant inroads into US markets and as US trade deficits grew to astounding heights. At the same time, there were signs in the early 1980s that US (civilian) R&D investments were growing insufficiently, with little or no increase in patenting, and that foreign corporations, especially from Japan, were increasing their patenting in the USA.[54] New forms of federal and state support to stimulate industrial R&D were installed, for example a new R&D tax deduction scheme, engineering research associations, R&D consortia and schemes for university–industry collaboration (including the so-called Bayh–Dole Act of 1980, enabling universities to patent inventions from federally funded research, see Henderson et al. 1995).

In the 1980s, the Patents, Copyrights and Trademarks Sub-committee was re-created (in 1982), and Congress became much more active on IP matters. Presidential commissions and task forces on IP were created, and US diplomats and delegates criss-crossed the globe advocating the protection of US IP (see Oman 1986; Simon 1986).

A good overview of US legal developments, describing the strengths and weaknesses of IP legislation, remedies and US government positions in the mid-1980s on IP, is given in 'Preserving America's industrial competitiveness. A special report on the protection of intellectual property rights', issued by the President's Commission on Industrial Competitiveness.

In summary, the report's proposals for reform asked for longer patent protection time, shorter handling of cases in the USPTO and in courts, more reciprocity towards foreign countries and increased enforceability against infringers and counterfeiters, especially in NICs and LDCs. The international trade aspects of IPR were proposed to take place primarily within the GATT framework, an arena in which the USA had more leeway than in the United Nations framework (with WIPO and the United Nations Committee on Trade and Development (UNCTAD), and so on) or the framework of other international institutions designed for IP protection, which moreover were perceived by the USA as too weak (see also Cordray 1994).

In conclusion, the four streams of events described above merged and resulted in the advent of the pro-patent era in the USA, signs of which were clear in the mid-1980s. The CAFC and the change in anti-trust policies were largely domestic matters, which paved the way for effective enforcement of the existing US IP legislation. Entirely new IP legislation was hardly decisive in bringing about the pro-patent era, however.[55] The industry lobbyists were of decisive importance in conjunction with the US government and the tie-in of IP issues to broader political issues of US industrial competitiveness and trade relations. In these respects, there were similarities with how the anti-patent movements were defeated in Europe in the 1860s and 1870s (see Kaufer 1989, p. 9).

The trade-based approach to IP protection was, to a considerable extent, successful (from the US point of view), especially since the US Congress created leverage for US trade negotiators through a number of changes in US trade laws.[56]

The pro-patent era, set in motion in the USA, gained ground internationally for various reasons. This was due especially to the shared interests among technology-based multinational companies (MNCs), not only in the USA but also in Europe and especially in Japan (see further Chapter 5). In the late 1990s, there were no signs of a reversal of the pro-patent era, on the contrary. This may be seen as a reflection of the growing strength of more fundamental forces in the international economy (see further Chapter 10).

2.4 ROLE OF IPR IN ECONOMIC HISTORY AND THE HISTORY OF TECHNOLOGY

Almost the only points of consensus regarding the role of the IPR system[57] in economic history are that its role is intrinsically difficult to assess and that there is no persuasive evidence that the IPR system has ever played a major role. At the same time, there is widespread consensus today that technical progress, the promotion of which is the direct purpose of the patent system, has probably been the major determinant behind economic progress.[58] It is then natural to turn to the history of technology for evidence of its role. However, while there are plenty of accounts of cases where patents have played major as well as minor roles in promoting as well as delaying or distorting technical progress, there are few if any studies showing the impact of the patent system upon streams of innovations and the opening up of new technological fields and industries on the aggregate. Inventors have consistently exploited the patent system, perhaps surprisingly often, but its impact on technical progress is a question that remains largely unanswered.

There were several periods and places in history without a patent system but with flourishing inventive activity. One example is ancient Greece, which in fact, at a closer look, shows an impressive rate of technical progress (see Farrington 1965; Finley 1965). Another example is medieval China. The economic incentives for inventive activities in these pre-industrialized times could possibly have been less important, compared with other incentives, than they are today. It must also be kept in mind that the most important factor during all periods, as persuasively emphasized by North (1981), is the military sector, which has an incentive system for technical progress quite different from that of the commercial sector, although competition has always played a decisive role in both sectors. One should also keep in mind that inventive activities on a broad scale in a country were historically not always sought by the ruling elite. An extreme example of this was the forbidding of inventions in 18th-century Japan by the Tokugawa rulers, as mentioned earlier (see also Chapter 5).

A patent system (or some kind of prize system) has not been necessary for technical progress on the whole, even in the 20th century, as evidenced by military technology as well as by planned economies (although the rate of technical progress in planned economies has been low relative to market economies).[59] Neither has a patent system *per se* been sufficient for technical progress on a large scale, historically. Patent systems, awarding temporary monopolies to inventors, were first legally codified in Venice in 1474 and in England in 1623, but technical progress did not 'take off' until much later in connection with industrialization in England.[60] Such an absence or delay of impact could in principle have been due to the initial weakness of the patent systems and a gestation period for their operation.[61] The US patent system during its first period of existence was weak (as was the Japanese one, although for a shorter period), but when strengthened in the 1830s, it created a traceable impact upon inventive activities (Sokoloff 1988). More importantly, however, the delay or absence of impact of the patent system upon technical progress could be attributable to the absence of complementary developments as well as the presence of overriding counteracting forces, such as war.[62] It has, moreover, been claimed that the state of technology in ancient Greece as well as in medieval Italy was sufficient to enable industrialization (Farrington 1965). If this is so, then the patent system cannot be claimed to be the missing institutional link in the developments of technology and industry.

Looking further at economic progress as represented by industrialization, it is interesting to note that most countries, including Japan, did industrialize in the presence of a patent system (see, for example, Dutton 1984). However, Germany, the Netherlands and Switzerland did not (see, for example, Kaufer 1989, p. 45). Schiff (1971), studying the Netherlands and Switzerland, moreover found no evidence that industrialization in those countries was hampered by the absence of a patent system. Thus, some countries could industrialize without a patent system.

The size and growth of a domestic market are likely to matter to technical progress, however, and perhaps more so in the absence of patents. In connection with industrialization, North (1981, p. 165) has argued that 'in the absence of property rights over innovation, the pace of technological change was most fundamentally influenced by the size of the markets'. This is so, North continues, because large and growing markets would increase the private return upon innovation, other things being equal. In addition, going back to Adam Smith's arguments, large markets would allow for specialization, in turn favouring creativity. Small, industrializing countries could then look for foreign markets. If these markets in turn had a patent system, the small countries would be more likely to have to adopt a patent system themselves sooner or later, which the Netherlands and Switzerland eventually did.

Sweden, being another small country, had a late but rapid industrialization with a spur of inventive activities, giving rise to a number of large MNCs (see Dahmén (1970) for a classic study with a Schumpeterian perspective.) In the formation of many of these large, invention-based MNCs, patents played a conspicuous role, perhaps even more so in protecting subsequent inventions that sustained the companies' economic development (Granstrand 1982).[63] Chandler makes a similar point about the role of patents in the sustained development of large US companies, although the role of patents in their early formative stage was found to be marginal on average (Chandler 1990). The case of large companies in the USA seems to lend some support to North's view of the importance of large markets where patent rights are absent or weak, while the case of Sweden points to the importance of strong patents in gaining access to large foreign markets when the domestic market is small.

In connection with the role of IPR for the rise of large, industrial corporations, it should also be remembered that – although it is difficult to assess comprehensively – trade secrets have always played an important role. Moreover, they have often complemented patents, typically so that product technology has been protected by patents while process technology, or at least part of it, has been protected by trade secrets. Trademarks, finally, have also played an apparently important role for companies in the longer run, although they have not been studied much (however, see Wilkins 1992 for an excellent study).

There are many accounts in business history indicating the importance of IPR for the economic progress of companies in various places and periods or stages of their development. Still, there are as many examples of companies that have succeeded without any significant IPR as there are of companies with strong patents that have failed. There are also examples of companies, mostly small, that have been forced out of business because of the IPR and litigation power of large competitors. The importance varies with country, period, industry, company and type of IPR.[64] The overall, long-run impact of the IPR system upon a stream of company formations and developments cannot be assessed across industries in our present stage of knowledge. It is likely, though, that new, small companies will become increasingly dependent upon the patent system as they face old, large competitors. At the same time, the large competitors are becoming less dependent upon single items of IP. Coca-Cola, for example, could probably lose its secret formula and still survive. Single patents with great blocking power could be an expensive nuisance to a large company, especially if held by inventors with no manufacturing capacity who are thus invulnerable to retaliation through counter-blocking.[65] However, such patents would not jeopardize the business of the whole company, unless really high damages resulted from litigated infringement.[66] Small companies on the other hand could be ruined by patent litigation.

In summary, the IPR system in general, and the patent system in particular, has been neither necessary nor sufficient for technical and/or economic progress at country and company level historically. This is hardly a surprising statement but is nevertheless important to keep in mind, especially since technical progress is increasingly seen as necessary for economic progress. Of course, it is difficult to infer very much from history by relating the absence or presence of an institution such as the patent system to a lower or higher rate of technical or economic progress in different periods and places. Qualifications must be made, correlations must be sought, complementary developments and counteracting forces as well as alternatives to patents must be taken into account, and so on, for a deeper understanding. However, not many studies have done this thoroughly (see Dutton 1984).

In the present stage of knowledge, there seems to be some consensus that says that the patent system has played a positive role for the rate, if not the direction at large, of technical progress but only a role secondary and complementary to other developments, particularly other institutional developments, including a general property rights system (see North 1981). A patent system, awarding temporary monopolies, was initially designed and implemented in countries mainly for their importation of new technologies and technological catch-up, for which it proved functional (David 1993). This was true for, among others, Italy, England, the USA, Japan and Switzerland. From this alone, one cannot infer that a patent system would be functional for the catch-up of the LDCs in the contemporary world, with an immensely more internationalized economic system having MNCs, foreign direct investments (FDIs), international trade and agreement interdependencies and so on.[67] Neither can one infer that a patent system initially designed for catch-up would be dysfunctional for sustaining a technological lead gained thereby. A patent system might even function better for the latter purpose in a world with increasingly globalizing companies and markets and a relative weakening of the nation-state.[68]

If the patent system has historically played a secondary, perhaps even marginal, role in the economic history of countries once they have industrialized and created a base of up-to-date industrial companies, why have the basic features of the patent system survived for so long? A common answer is that, although the patent system has often been found to be deficient, it has been better than nothing, and there has been no better incentive system for technical progress in the commercial sector. To this answer one may add that institutional inertia has over centuries gradually been built into the patent system worldwide, not least in current times as the formerly large, planned economies in Russia and China have started to adopt it.[69] The appearance of any new institutional innovations, yet to be conceived of, competing with the patent system as an incentive system is thereby hampered. Such a barrier to an institutional innovation is analogous to a barrier to technological innovation with one difference: technological innovations may be protected by patents, while institutional innovations may not.[70]

2.5   ROLE OF IPR IN THE HISTORY OF ECONOMICS

Judging from the share which the subject of patents has had in the literary output of economists of the last fifty years, and from the share which economists have had in the literature on the subject of patents, one may say that economists have virtually relinquished the field. Patent lawyers were probably glad to see them go; some said as much with disarming frankness. (Fritz Machlup, in Penrose 1951, p. vi)

Although the patent system has developed primarily to promote economic ends, economists have devoted very little attention to it and none at all to the international patent system. (Edith Penrose, in Penrose 1951, p. xi)

What matters from time to time in economics does not necessarily matter in the economy, and vice versa. The history of economics as an academic discipline differs from the history of the real-world economy, a type of difference that is common to any social science discipline. To some extent, this fact is natural (since far from all economic phenomena can be studied, and not all economic ideas can be implemented), and to some extent it is regrettable (since there is also ignorance and irrelevance). It is regrettable that it took such a long time in economics to recognize the predominant role of technology in economic growth and transformation. The minor attention paid to technology and innovations has characterized economics for the major part of the 20th century and for earlier centuries as well.[71] As a corollary, it is not surprising that IPR issues have played a minor role as well in the history of economics.

True, there has been a pulsating debate over the centuries about the pros and cons of the patent system, but the debate has been conducted in a kind of 'invisible college', indeed not very visible to the economics profession at large, or to the legal profession at large.[72] The leading economists have had little to say about the patent system, and even less about other IPR, their rationales, functioning and possible reforms. This is remarkable in view of the long history of the patent system as an economic institution, actually preceding industrialization as well as both the modern firm and the modern nation-state as economic institutions. It is also remarkable in view of the worldwide spread of the patent system, with its basic ideas remaining much the same, although with many national variations over time. The adoption of a patent system or an IPR system in a nation was not a trivial matter.

What did the leading economists in the past have to say about the patent system? To answer this is a research task in itself, and only a few observations can be offered here.[73] Adam Smith in *The Wealth of Nations* barely touched upon the patent system. Charles Babbage, who made a significant but little recognized pioneering contribution to the economics of industry and technology,[74] was largely pro-patent but did not have much to say about it either in his 1832 book *On The Economy of Machinery and Manufactures* except to complain about its cost and the difficulties of defending English patents in court (Babbage 1832, pp. 359–61).

There has been a tendency concerning patent issues to divide analysts into advocates and outright critics (rather than reformers), with fairly polarized pro- and anti-patent standpoints. This has much to do with the monopoly feature of patents, and the general hostility among economists as well as others (including Aristotle) against monopolies. A. Smith, J. Bentham, J.S. Mill, J.B. Say, Léon Walras and Ludwig von Mises accepted patents as exemptions from monopoly prohibitions, while Alfred Marshall, Friedrich von Hayek, Lionel Robbins and Frank Taussig were generally sceptical towards patents. A most outspoken critic in the 20th century was Sir Arnold Plant (see Machlup 1958a).

Marx, of course, was critical of the patent system as part of his general criticism of private property and technological change under capitalism, but he did not devote much attention to it. For example, he left largely unanalysed the patent system's feature of inducing a mixture of private and public IP; that is, a piece of IP can only be temporarily privatized by patents before being 'socialized' when the patents expire. Schumpeter is generally seen as the founding father of the economics of technology and innovation, with his pioneering emphasis on the decisive role of innovations and entrepreneurs in economic dynamics. In his first major work (Schumpeter 1912), the young Schumpeter saw inventions largely as exogenous, creating opportunities for entrepreneurs. Perhaps as a consequence of this view at the time, he did not pay much attention to the impact of a patent system upon the stream of inventions, and he did not draw the possible conclusion that an economic institution like the patent system would be largely ineffective in stimulating inventive activities if these were exogenous to the economy. In later works Schumpeter gave far more thought to the rise of large corporations, their industrial R&D, the endogenization of technological change and the importance of monopolistic positions (the 'old Schumpeter' view on inventions). Yet it is perhaps fair to say that, while he scrutinized the advantages of monopolies for R&D and innovations, he did not take a corresponding interest in the patent system, or the IPR system as a whole, as a way of fostering a certain breed of temporary monopolies that were advantageous to innovations.

Needless to say, many economists before World War II had emphasized the role in economic development of knowledge or information (Marshall and Hayek, among others), but the role of the IPR system in its production and distribution was largely unexamined.[75] This started to change after World War II, with increasing industrial and military R&D and a gradual recognition among economists of the role of R&D. Fritz Machlup wrote a major review in Machlup (1958b, 1962). Jacob Schmookler made careful empirical studies of patenting and started to use patents as economic indicators (see Schmookler 1966). Kenneth Arrow made an important analysis in Arrow (1962) of the tendency in a society to underinvest in R&D, for which the patent system was one possible corrective by raising the private rate of return on inventions. Edwin Mansfield later showed empirically that the economic returns on inventions were greater to society than to inventors on average across industry, although with large variations. Early theoretical works by Frederic Scherer analysed R&D rivalry and patent races, for example. William Nordhaus produced a major theoretical analysis along neoclassical lines, addressing, for example, the socially optimal patent protection time (Nordhaus 1969).

Further empirical and theoretical works have been made at an accelerating pace since the 1970s.[76] Through the works published after World War II, the theoretical and empirical foundations of the patent system have been considerably strengthened and some of its surrounding economic ideas have become more rigorously spelled out, analysed and recognized. Still, much research remains to be done. Entirely new economic ideas for designing an incentive system for innovations have also to be analysed (see, for example, Kingston 1987, 1990, 1994, 1997; Thurow 1997; and the whole issue of *Columbia Law Review*, December 1994, with Samuelson et al. 1994 and Reichman 1994). In addition, comprehensive economic evaluations of the patent system with its many actual and potential decision variables (for example, regarding patent length, strength, breadth, priority, licensing, differentiation) for a policymaker have scarcely been performed and agreed upon. Our state of knowledge about the patent system can still be characterized as it was in the 1950s (Machlup 1958a, p. 80):

> If one does not know whether a system 'as a whole' (in contrast to certain features of it) is good or bad, the safest policy conclusion is to 'muddle through' – either with it, if one has long lived with it, or without it, if one has lived without it. If we did not have a patent system, it would be irresponsible, on the basis of our present knowledge of its economic consequences, to recommend instituting one. But since we have had a patent system for a long time, it would be irresponsible, on the basis of our present knowledge, to recommend abolishing it.

Possibly it is reasonable to place the burden of proof upon the reformer, as Machlup indicates. But there is also a burden of disproof of misplaced notions. Such misplaced notions have grown around the patent system in the historical absence of sufficient attention to it. Two misplaced notions are of particular importance for the history of economics and the patent system. The first is the notion that a patent directly gives the patent rights holder a monopoly on output markets. In the history of economics, patents have always been linked to the much broader discussion of monopoly issues. The temporary nature of a patent-based monopoly has then generally been sufficiently recognized, but not the fact that it is basically a monopoly on an input factor market, not on an output product market. The patent rights holder can only exclude others from accessing the technology as a certain input, just as the owner of a certain raw material source can exclude others from accessing it. Sometimes an opinion of the patent system, or even an analysis of it, rests on the assumption that the monopoly position on the input side is readily converted to a product market monopoly. A strong output market monopoly may result from strong patent positions, of course, and there are many historic examples of this.[77] However, an output monopoly does not automatically obtain from an input monopoly for two reasons. First, substitute input factors may be available or be made available, including substitute technologies, sometimes due to activities for inventing around the patent. Only when a patent is necessary for a product in a given market (that is, the patent is effectively blocking others from entering the market) could an input monopoly be effectively converted to an output monopoly. (Such necessary or unavoidable patents are sometimes called 'strategic patents', see Chapter 7.) If, for example, the scope of the patent granted is broad, the patent may become strategic. Moreover, the monopolistic power of patents depends on patent length and patent scope (or breadth), both of which could be adjusted by policies or intervention by authorities. Second, complementary input factors are needed to launch an innovative new product, including other complementary technologies, whether or not protected by patents. Products, and production processes as well for that matter, also tend to become increasingly multitechnological in character, that is, new generations of products and processes need an increasing range of technologies over time to be implemented. This means that there tend to be more patents as well as more patent rights holders involved in each new product, increasing the difficulty for each one to achieve a sufficiently monopolistic position on the output market and thus forcing them into licensing, cross-licensing, pooling or other technology-swapping arrangements.[78]

The second misplaced notion is that a patent is entirely anti-competitive. This is not true, even if the input monopoly is perfectly converted to an output monopoly. A patent-based monopoly restricts short-run price competition for a certain product, but at the same time stimulates the generation of new products and processes that typically increase performance-based competition or Schumpeterian competition in the longer run. Thus, a patent is partly anti-competitive, partly pro-competitive. Therefore a trade-off must be made, but not a trade-off between the purposes of patent legislation and the purposes of anti-trust legislation, perceived as being incompatible before the 1980s, but instead a trade-off between different means to accomplish common purposes. Such a (belated) reinterpretation of the patent system also took place within the US Antitrust Division under its newly appointed head William Baxter in the early 1980s, based in fact on 'new' ideas and movements in economics which had emerged mainly in Chicago a few decades earlier.

In conclusion, one may claim that the relatively little attention paid historically in economics to the patent system paved the way for some possibly costly confusion about its impact on static versus dynamic efficiency, and concerning its input rather than output monopolistic nature.

2.6   SUMMARY AND CONCLUSIONS

This chapter has tried to trace the basic notions of intellectual property to its historical origins and to describe how a diversity of IP notions have evolved and which roles they have played. Basic distinctions are made between material (physical, tangible) and immaterial (intangible, intellectual) property (resource, asset, capital); between property and property right; between individual and collectivity; and between IPR of various kinds (for inventions, information, identity marks, cultural ideas and expressions, designs and so on). Although much research remains to be done on these issues, there are indications that IP notions are fundamental and prevalent in human nature and societies, with clear signs of several IP notions in ancient societies as well as in different religious belief systems. Different IP regimes have also developed since ancient times pertaining to science, technology, culture, military activities and religion.

Among philosophers, material property notions have commanded considerable interest while IP has not, with a few exceptions; the same could be said about economists. Physical property has also dominated property notions among jurists. This is somewhat paradoxical considering the importance of intellectual resources and creations and their inherent differences to physical resources and creations. The extendibility of physical property notions to IP was found to be severely limited as both scarcity and possession fail to serve as a basis for justifying and defining property rights in the intellectual field. The deontological, consequential and utilitarian justifications of IPRs were briefly described, together with the way in which the utilitarian use of IPRs essentially to encourage innovation has become dominant.

The chapter then gave a brief history of especially the patent system with its progression through various eras – the non-patent, pre-patent, national patent, multinational patent, international patent and pro-patent era – with their various elements of protectionism. A chronology for Europe and the USA was provided and one for Japan will be provided in Chapter 5. The emergence of the pro-patent era in the 1980s in the USA and the American success with the trade-based approach to IP legislation was described in some detail.

In summary, IP notions have evolved gradually as a social construct and in a fragmented way with many IP regimes, IP types and IP systems lacking unifying notions. Thus, one cannot talk about a coherent IP system. IP notions have also evolved in a marginalized manner very much in the backwaters of law, economics and politics.

The philosophical as well as practical complexities of intellectual property offer grounds for forgiveness of any sins of omission historically among philosophers, legislators, economists, policymakers and so on. Another ground for forgiveness is that a legal IPR system has apparently been neither necessary nor sufficient for technical, industrial and economic progress historically, as discussed in the chapter.

However the grounds for forgiving any sins of omission regarding IP have receded since the 1980s. We are entering a new IP era triggered by the events in the USA in the 1980s. There are many reasons to believe that this era is here to stay and that it will develop further, perhaps warranting further institutional innovations in the IP field.

NOTES

1. For example, an individual's right to exclude others from access to the resource in case of individual property or an individual's right not to be excluded in case of common property. Distinctions are commonly made between rights to specific uses and/or benefits (rents) of a resource.
2. As will be discussed in Chapter 4, intellectual property and resources are not fully corresponding to all immaterial property and resources. The latter would also include qualities of human relations that are commonly not referred to as being intellectual in character (compare the phrase 'emotional capital'). In addition, of course, there are borderline cases. As a first approximation we can, however, treat immaterial property and intellectual property as synonyms, with both 'intellectual' and 'property' taken in a broad sense.
3. Sometimes 'intellectual property' has been used in a very narrow sense primarily for copyright purposes, in which case the term 'industrial property' is used for patents, designs and trademarks (see, for example, Plant 1974, p. 88).
4. In what follows, we will focus primarily on notions of intellectual property, however. The first and sole durable possession of a naturally scarce physical resource or good (like a caught fish) has traditionally (at least in Western societies since medieval times) been considered as the general basis for defining an original property right (provided it is not too costly to enforce the right). However, as will be discussed below, such a notion has inherent shortcomings when applied to non-physical or immaterial resources and goods (see further Section 2.2.2).
5. Certainly a child is comfortable with having the same name as many other children, but personal names are given to the child, not chosen.

6. It should be noted that all four types of questions are amenable to experimental situations, although it may still be difficult to trace underlying factors to any experimental observations, separating influences from instructed behaviour and so on.
7. A prolific writer on law such as Posner only touches upon the issue; see Posner (1983, pp. 149, 279). Posner finds that primitive societies (at least some) give protection to a name, a spell, a song and the like but not to a productive idea or invention.
8. I am grateful to Professor Edward Wilson for helping me with these issues.
9. As is well known, it was typical among elite citizens in ancient Greece to belittle craftsmen, artisans and the like, although their output could be appreciated (see, for example, Austin and Vidal-Nauget 1980, p. 12). One illustrative observation is that, although there were many well-known potters and sculptors, who also attached their names and symbols to their work, their names seldom appeared in the literary writings of their times.
10. See Vlastos (1991, p. 103). I am grateful to Professor T. Amemiya for drawing my attention to this point.
11. This was pointed out to me by J. van Leuven.
12. As will be dealt with in Chapter 3, under current law scientific discoveries and mathematical formulas cannot be patented. Artistic expressions can be copyrighted but not their underlying ideas (such as the idea of a special type of plot or motive).
13. For example, some mathematicians refer to certain proofs as inventions rather than discoveries and some poets speak of discovering a new poem.
14. See further Farrington (1969), Finley (1965) and also Prior (1991) (compare Long 1991).
15. See especially the works by D. de Solla Price and N. Rosenberg, two leading scholars on this topic: for example, de Solla Price (1973) and Rosenberg (1982).
16. The latter was in place in, for example, the former Soviet Union. Note that for a patent system to be effective as an economic incentive some kind of competitive market economy is necessary. However, since patents give several types of advantages to individuals and firms (see Chapters 3 and 7), patenting also occurs in monopolistic industries. For example, patenting has been frequent in the telecommunications service sector in the USA, Europe and Japan in the 20th century, although the sector has consisted mainly of national telecommunications service monopolies, regulated by the government.
17. To illustrate further, it is quite conceivable (whether practical or not) to have an international system of 'publication offices', examining scientific publications in more standardized ways, following explicitly defined criteria.
18. Compare what was said about IP notions in primitive societies, above. Also note how IP notions regarding innovative chefs and their new and good dishes have changed over time as patents are no longer granted to them.
19. The punishment took the form of handing over in a cunning way Pandora's box, filled with misfortunes but with hope at the bottom, of neither of which mankind could be dispossessed.
20. The gods could, of course, have charged mankind with not acting in good faith, but of knowing in advance that fire belonged to the gods, so that mankind should have rejected Prometheus' offer. The gods could perhaps even have made the claim that Prometheus and mankind had conspired against them. This is in fact suggested by the oldest source, Hesiod (*c.* 700 BC), where the conspiracy was a misuse of fire in sacrifices to the gods. Unfortunately the myth 'Prometheus versus Zeus' is not as well documented as contemporary legal cases.
21. See the Talmud Tractate Megilla. Professor R. Aumann drew my attention to this passage. A similar importance attached to correct citations can be found in Islamic religious texts (Professor J. Hjärpe, personal communications). Muslim jurists considered the legality of IP as early as the 11th century (Azmi 1996).
22. Again, this seems to be a question that has not been researched much by historians of philosophy or other scholars.
23. See, for example, Penrose (1951).
24. However, when it comes specifically to copyrights and IP notions regarding literary works, philosophers with hands-on experience of publication have been far more outspoken. Thus, for example, Kant wrote an essay 'On the injustice of the pirating of books'.
25. See, for example, Posner (1983) and Palmer (1990). See also Section 2.3 about the 'first to invent' priority rule as an example of an extension of a physical property concept to the IP field.
26. For good discussions, see the set of papers from the symposium on law and philosophy, published in the *Harvard Journal of Law and Public Policy*, **13** (3) 1990, with Bouchaert (1990), Mackaay (1990), Mainers and Staaf (1990) and Palmer (1990), and with a summary by Nance (1990).

27. For a classic analysis in 19th-century Anglo-American law of how property rights should be derived from observable possession, see the writings of Oliver Wendell Holmes (1878). However, Holmes does not specifically address problems with the derivation of IP.
28. No important distinction between information and knowledge is made here. However, the distinction between information embodied in a human versus information embodied in a physical substrate is important, since in the latter case the substrate functions as physical property.
29. Note that the very concept of stealing usually refers to stealing physical property, with the implication that the thief acquires possession and at the same time the property holder is dispossessed. The latter does not necessarily occur when stealing information (or fire, for that matter).
30. Of course, sole possession can arise again if the information thief dies or forgets.
31. For a fuller account of differences, see Chapter 4.
32. Plant (1974, p. 36) stresses this point, arguing that property rights as patent rights and copyrights are different from rights to physical property since they are not a consequence of scarcity. Rather, such rights (that is, patents and copyrights) make it possible to create scarcity. However, Plant focuses only on scarcity in a static sense, not on scarcity of new ideas and information over time.
33. The phenomenon of independent and nearly simultaneous discoveries or inventions has been recognized repeatedly by scholars (even independently from each other) with classic studies reported in Ogburn and Thomas (1922) and Merton (1973); see Winter (1989, p. 44).
34. There is a similar problem of extendibility when IP notions for old types of intangible objects, such as old technologies, are tried out for new types of objects, such as computer software or genetically engineered living things. In IP legislation in the latter cases, legal pragmatism in some sense seems to have predominated, at least in the USA. For discussions of problems in extending current IPR to new technologies, see NRC (1993) and Weil and Snapper (1989).
35. An obvious (but still limited) possibility of letting IPR 'piggy-back' on physical property is to link them with the rights to some tangible matter or substrate which embodies the idea or creation. This may be argued from the point of view of legal pragmatism in contrast to legal foundationalism, that is, the philosophical inclination in jurisprudence to find unifying concepts.
36. It should immediately be noted that the general categorizations of justifications for IPR are closely related to those for physical property as well, which gives possibilities for extendibility at a higher level of abstraction, for example, defining rights in terms of control of rent streams of a piece of property rather than in terms of control of the property *per se*.
37. These symbols correspond to trademarks, but could also be seen as related to designs and copyrights since they involve visual expressions. Copyright of written material requires a written language, of course.
38. Thus, a patent privilege, in a way, functioned as a privilege to tax consumers for a period of time. Also, in modern times a strong patent system is attractive to a government in an advanced country as a policy measure since it is easy to finance. The government does not have to pay subsidies and the patent offices and court system can be largely self-financed. There need not be any losses to the government through business tax money, either. On the contrary, tax revenues might increase due to monopolistic pricing.
39. The 'first to invent' rule means that the one who first makes an invention has priority to the rights attached to it. This property concept is analogous to the physical property concept based on the first possession of a physical thing (see Section 2.2.2). However, the difficulty of establishing who is the first possessor of an intellectual thing, that is, who is the idea's creator, has led to the alternative priority rule that the one who registers an invention, that is, files a patent application, gets priority to any rights granted. The latter rule prevails in Europe and Japan, while the USA has stuck to the former rule.
40. This is an example of how property concepts were extended from the physical to the intellectual world.
41. As mining in one way or another is among mankind's earliest technological and economic endeavours in various parts of the world, similar legal practices could conceivably have occurred in other places and possibly earlier as well. For example, silver mining became important in ancient Greece (see Austin and Vidal-Nauget 1980, pp. 310–13.) However, it is unclear whether there were any incentive schemes used to generate and/or deploy new techniques, such as schemes for bringing in skilled workers and inventors.
42. As translated in Gilfillan (1964a, p.11) and cited in Kaufer (1989, p. 5), who also provide a fuller text in original Italian.
43. Discerning eras, epochs or stages in a historical stream of events may be a useful sorting device but it always involves some arbitrariness, even if good criteria are used. (Here the degrees of

codification and geographical diffusion of the patent system are used as primary criteria for distinguishing different eras.) Also, beneath the events that surface in an era is often an undercurrent of events that lead up to a later era.

44. In fact, the patent monopoly rights became an exemption in the Statute of Monopolies, which was generally prohibitive of monopoly privileges. The handing out of such privileges by royalty had degenerated, and the English Parliament wanted to put an end to it, apparently recognizing the exceptional importance of technical progress.

45. Note, for example, the small difference between 14 years of protection in 17th-century England and 17 years of protection 350 years later in the USA and parts of Europe (now changed to 20 years).

46. Ideas for radical reform of the patent system have not been missing, however. For some interesting current examples, see Kingston (1987) and Thurow (1996).

47. See also the Federal Courts Improvement Act of 1982, and Dreyfuss (1989b).

48. A proposal can be found, for example, in recommendations of the US Senate Committee, the Temporary National Economic Committee (TNEC) from the 1940s; see Folk (1942, pp. 281–95).

49. There have been several fact-finding studies of the outcome of patent court cases, including those of the CAFC; see, for example, Hofer (1986) and Scherer (1991).

50. See speeches and articles by Deputy-Director Roger Andewelt, for example, Andewelt (1986).

51. Professor William Baxter, personal communications. See also Baxter (1966).

52. For a good account of the lobbying activities of Pfizer executives and others regarding IP, see the Harvard Business School case no. 9-392-073, entitled 'Pfizer: global protection of intellectual property'.

53. A number of law suits were brought against infringers, as well as many out-of-court agreements. Royalty rates for licences were, moreover, increased. In general, these events signified the outbreak of the so-called 'patent war' between the USA and Japan. See Warshofsky (1994).

54. In fact, the share of foreigners' patenting in the USA rose from 22 per cent in 1967 to 40 per cent in 1980 (Evenson, in Griliches 1984, p. 92). See also Quigg (1986).

55. There were a number of other important legal IP developments in the USA in the 1980s, especially those broadening what was patentable matter to include mutational genetic engineering and computer programs (see the chapters by Barton, Samuelsson, Rathman and Goldberg in NRC 1993). The US Supreme Court decision in 1980 thus held that a live, human-made micro-organism is patentable subject-matter (the Diamond v. Chakrabarty case). The Supreme Court decision in 1981 led to the acceptance of the patentability of certain computer programs (the Diamond v. Diehr case), and a new subject-matter – semiconductor chip mask works – was given legal protection by the Semiconductor Chip Protection Act of 1984 (the first new federal form of IP protection in more than 100 years in the USA).

56. Important new trade legislation included the Trade and Tariff Act of 1984, with Section 301 (authorizing US government to take retaliatory action against countries judged to give inadequate IP protection) and Section 501 (authorizing the President to judge the adequacy of IP protection in granting tariff preferences to a country) combining to form 'a stick and carrot' approach. The Omnibus Trade and Competitiveness Act of 1988 moved further along these lines, for example, with a 'Special 301', requiring the US Trade Representative to watch, identify and investigate foreign states denying adequate IP protection to US firms.

57. It may be argued that the collection of IPR, as we know it, is not, and never has been, legally coherent enough to be called a 'system' and to be studied as an entity with causal relations. In addition, part of the IPR system is aimed at promoting cultural progress rather than economic progress in a narrow sense, although cultural arts in themselves have largely become big business. However, for the most part we shall talk about the patent system, which is narrower and more coherent legally.

58. Note that a patent is granted to a technical invention only on the merits of its technical advance, not on its economic merits (apart from a general requirement of industrial applicability of the invention), although the underlying assumption is that by so doing, economic progress will be stimulated.

59. As pointed out earlier, a competitive market economy is necessary for a patent system to be effective as an incentive system, since it holds out the prospect of a reward in the form of a temporary monopoly on a market. However, a patent system with special licensing schemes is feasible in a planned economy, for example a patent system in which royalties for non-exclusive compulsory licences are paid as a lump-sum down payment. Such a system comes close to a prize system.

60. The pace of technical progress had been significant in other places and periods, for example, in China and just after the Middle Ages, as argued in, for example, Mokyr (1990). However, in connection with industrialization, the pace of technical progress seems to have increased more than previously and has then become self-propelled and sustained in coevolution with industry.

61. By weakness is meant that legal protection or legal enforcement was weak enough to make the resulting incentive weak or perceived as weak. For a generally sceptical view of the role of patents in the industrialization of Europe see Landes (1969).

62. Compare Mokyr's point that war on the European continent delayed industrialization there (Mokyr 1990).

63. In addition, some Swedish companies could be formed on foreign technology that was by default unprotected in Sweden (like the Bell telephone invention). Some Swedish invention-based companies also by default did not patent abroad, which precluded their early internationalization. (For example, the original company of what in the 1980s became the Nobel chemical company. Alfred Nobel himself was, however, an industrious patentor, with 355 patents at the time of his death in 1896. In addition he was a skilful, internationally minded entrepreneur, creating one of the earliest industrial MNCs in history.)

64. For example, the importance of patents for the pharmaceutical industry in advanced countries is generally very great.

65. A case in point is the Lemelson patent (see Chapter 5).

66. This is unlikely but possible, especially since US law allows for trebled damages when infringement is found to be wilful.

67. Mansfield (1994, 1995) and Lee and Mansfield (1996) have shown that strong patent protection is functional for attracting FDIs. However, FDIs are not necessarily functional for catch-up. Scherer and Weisburst (1995) are also sceptical as to whether a switch from weak to strong patent protection alone can induce a catch-up, based on a study of the adoption of patent protection for pharmaceuticals in Italy in 1978.

68. The patent system is likened to a panda's thumb by David (1993) in describing its evolution into something quasi-functional from strange origins.

69. IP legislation was enacted in the Soviet Union in 1931, providing a copyright certificate and an inventor certificate. Inventors holding a certificate were entitled to remuneration from organizations using their inventions, but this was more like an inventor reward scheme. New patent and trademark laws of the Russian Federation were adopted in 1992. These laws protect a wider spectrum of IP and are of a Western type with a private rather than a state property concept. Still in 1997, however, Russia did not have an effective patent system (Alimpiev and Sokolov 1997).

70. One can point to a prize system, such as the Nobel prize in economics, as a possible incentive system for generating institutional innovations (or rather inventions) in the economy. Hopefully, such a prize system provides sufficient incentives for economic inventions and research about the IPR institution, for which there seems to be a need in society.

71. Pioneering works on the role of technology in economic growth were made by Abramowitz (1956) and Solow (1957). Abramowitz referred to the large statistical residual found as a measure of ignorance while Solow referred to it as technical change.

72. For a review of the debate over the patent system in the 19th century, see Machlup and Penrose (1950). Patent issues were widely and heatedly debated in connection with the anti-patent movements in the 19th century, with controversies among economists as well as between economists and lawyers. After the 1870s, when patent protection had largely been accepted by legislators, the interest in patent issues among economists dropped markedly and was not revived until after World War II.

73. The best exposé still up to date is made in Machlup (1958).

74. See Stigler (1991), Rosenberg (1994) and Granstrand (1994, Ch. 1) for accounts of Babbage's contribution to economics.

75. For a notable example, see Plant (1974).

76. See Chapter 3 for more details and references.

77. There are several large US corporations that serve as classic examples, for example, RCA and General Electric.

78. For example, as of 1993 there were more than 2000 patents relevant to the European mobile communication system Global System for Mobile Communications. Of these, more than 30 were so-called standard blocking patents (that is, they applied directly to a decisive feature of a standard in the system).

3. Patents and intellectual property: a general framework

CHAPTER CONTENTS

3.1 CHAPTER OUTLINE

Inventions, know-how, data, computer software, designs, trademarks and artistic works are all potential intellectual properties and may be protected by Intellectual

Property Rights. Such rights are by and large granted in contemporary society as a stimulus to creative work and innovations. IPRs pertain to specific legal systems embedded in the respective social system that provides legislation, law adherence, policing, prosecution, court practices and infringement sanctions or penalties. These elements comprise the institutional framework of the IPR system. This framework has evolved for centuries, as described in Chapter 2, and varies across countries in the same way that social and legal systems differ. It is thus important to realize that what is perceived as legally or morally right and wrong is contingent upon cultural and historical influences.

This chapter gives a brief textbook introduction to intellectual property in general and patents in particular. After some common concepts and distinctions are described, the context of inventions, innovations and diffusion is presented as a general framework for patents and IP. The basic technicalities of patenting are then described, as well as the basic rationales behind a patent system as an economic incentive system. After previous research and literature on IP and patents are surveyed, the chapter finally gives a brief introduction to the economic theory of IP and patents.

3.2   INVENTIONS, INNOVATIONS AND DIFFUSION

3.2.1   Innovations in General

Common distinctions
Innovations imply novel and accepted changes in society. As such, innovations are fundamental not only to technological and economic development but also to cultural development at large (see Barnett 1953). Table 3.1 gives an overview of the different types of innovations in general. Innovations are also often characterized as major (or radical) and minor (or incremental) related to the 'size' of the change the novelty implies. Technological innovations are, moreover, commonly sub-divided into product and process (production) innovations.

A number of additional distinctions are commonly used when discussing innovations and are therefore useful to review first. Such important distinctions are:

- inventions and innovations;
- inventions and discoveries;
- technical/commercial/economic uncertainty/success/failure;
- innovations and diffusion;
- innovations and imitations.

Although commonly used, these concepts and distinctions are not so clear-cut under closer scrutiny.

Table 3.1   General types of innovations[1]

Type	IP-related characteristics[2]	Examples
Technological/technical[3] innovation	Patentable Also protectable by trade secrets, copyrights, designs and trademarks	Wheel Telephone Incandescent lamp Transistor
Service innovation (e.g. in information services, financial services, telecommunications services, medical services, transportation services, educational services, etc.)	Non-patentable in general Supporting technologies may be patentable Protectable by trade secrets, trademarks and copyrights	Newspapers Messaging systems Heart transplantation New school courses
Financial innovation	Non-patentable Easy to imitate but diffusion may still be slow	Insurance Convertible debentures Certificates of deposit Put and call options
Managerial/organizational innovation	Non-patentable Often slow diffusion May be protected as trade secrets	Divisionalized organization (corporate organization form (M-form)) Programme evaluation and review technique (PERT) for project planning *Kanban*, just in time (JIT), total quality management (TQM), etc.[4]
Marketing/distribution innovation	Non-patentable Supporting technologies may be patentable	Supermarket Mail order Teleshopping
Institutional innovation	Non-patentable Slow diffusion	Patent system Limited liability joint stock company
Other types (social, legal, political, cultural, etc.)	Cultural innovations are protectable by IPR	European Community Opera

Notes
1. The types are not mutually exclusive.
2. The applicability of different IPR is just illustrative. The degree of protection may also be weak in many cases.
3. The concept of technology is usually taken to mean knowledge about techniques. Strictly speaking, technological innovation then refers to change in knowledge, while technical innovation refers to change in artefacts, embodying technological change. Technical innovations are generally sub-divided into product/process (production) innovations.
4. *Kanban* is a system for controlling the flow of materials between work stations in a JIT production system, originally at Toyota.

Innovation

The concept of innovation has numerous definitions, but is typically defined by a reference to a change in ideas, practices or objects involving some degree of (i) novelty or creation based on human ingenuity and (ii) success in application. The concept is used to refer to the new idea, practice or object as well as to the process leading to it, although the term 'innovation process' then is more correct. Novelty (or newness) may refer to what is novel on a global scale, to a nation, to an organization or to an individual. Typically, novelty to the world is implied when talking about invention and innovation. If there is an underlying patentable invention, novelty to the world is presumed.

Technical, commercial and economic success

The concept of success is often sub-divided into technical success, commercial success and economic success. In this context, technical success means that technical specifications have been met and/or an invention has been achieved, commercial success means that the invention has found a first commercial application, and economic success means that an acceptable return on the total investment has been achieved.[1] In a corresponding way, one may distinguish between three types of failure as well: technical, commercial and economic.

Inventions

In broad terms, an invention is a novelty or creation based on human ingenuity, but the concept of invention does not require success in application. An invention. becomes an innovation when it achieves commercial success. Inventions of all sorts are generated out of a mixture of human curiosity, the search for betterment and additional factors, more or less random. Table 3.1 again gives an overview of the different types of innovations with examples of some underlying inventions. In order to stimulate the flow of useful inventions and innovations, society may provide incentives, for example, in the form of intellectual property rights attached to the inventions. The table also gives some IP-related characteristics of the different types of innovation.

Discoveries

Inventions, being man-made novelties, are distinguished from mere discoveries of pre-existing features of nature, like an ore deposit or a natural law. Technical inventions are patentable but discoveries are not. However, the distinction between inventions and discoveries is not always as easy to uphold as it may appear (see Chapter 2).

Diffusion

The concept of diffusion refers to the process by which an innovation is adopted by individuals and organizations in a population (for example, potential buyers or users in a market, sellers or producers in an industry, departments in an organization and nations in the world). Typically, an innovation changes during diffusion. For a classic overview of diffusion literature, see Rogers (1995).

Imitation

Finally, the concept of imitation refers to a close reproduction or near duplication of ideas, practices or objects that were once perceived as inventions (or innovations). Typically, imitations are not exact copies of the underlying invention (or innovation).

3.2.2 Innovation Models

Two types of innovation models will be considered here. The first type shows the cash flow pattern associated with an innovation, while the second shows the activity pattern. In the first category one finds the so-called product life-cycle (PLC) model, which is a simple and useful point of departure here.

PLC model

In essence, the PLC model is based on the idea that a product has a finite lifetime on the market and therefore proceeds through various stages of development, including introduction, growth, maturity, saturation and decline.[2] It should be noted that this is an idealized model, and not all products conform to it. Further, there are several sets of stages that apply to different products, and sometimes there are not really any clear stages at all. Regardless of whether there are any clearly recognizable stages during the lifetime of a product, it is useful to picture the cash flows of a new product in a money/time diagram. Figure 3.1 gives an idealized picture of cash flow for a hypothetical product, divided into stages.

In relation to Figure 3.1, the following should be noted:

1. Cash flows are depicted with smoothed, continuous curves. In reality, monetary transactions occur at discrete points in time and curves connecting the values are typically not smooth.
2. The sales curve is supposed to be unimodal (that is, rising to one peak and then falling), while in reality there may be a slump and a revival.
3. Outflow of capital is counted as negative only for investment expenditures, not for direct costs and indirect costs (for example, organization costs). This is slightly inconsistent but in line with conventions to display the sales margin (or operating profit margin) more clearly as the difference between gross value of sales and the sum of direct and indirect costs.
4. Gross annual cash flows are shown. There are other variants when plotting cash-flow curves, for example, letting the money axis in the money/time diagram denote cumulative cash flow or net cash flow.

Although there is a phase of more or less concurrent investment in R&D, production and marketing preceding market introduction, investment expenditures typically continue after market introduction. For example, product variants are developed, design features are adapted to mass production, production is scaled up and further automated, and further investments in international marketing are made.

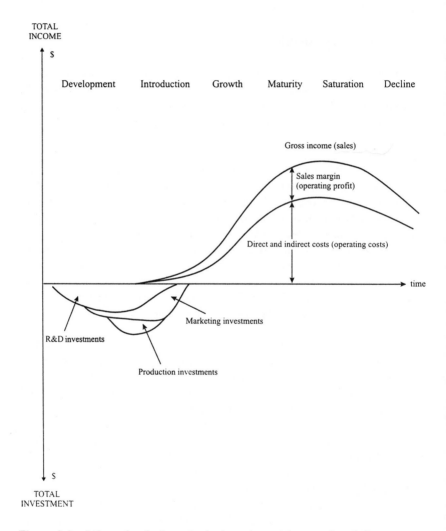

Figure 3.1   Life cycle of a hypothetical product with annual cash flows

A company usually develops new products continually. There are new variants, types, models, generations and families of new products being developed, and different products of a company are often related to each other in some way. It is thus too narrow to focus on a specific product and try to illustrate its life cycle. In fact, if the cash-flow diagrams of all of a company's products are added, the resulting picture would look something like Figure 3.2. The cash-flow curves for different products may be interdependent since they

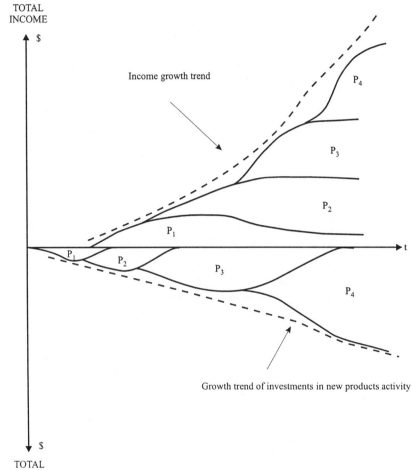

Legend: $P_1, P_2, \ldots$ denote different products with which income and investment are associated.

Figure 3.2   Corporate income growth through new products

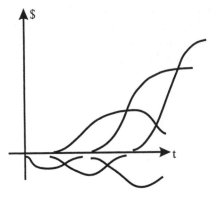

a)   Three product generations with overlapping R&D stages

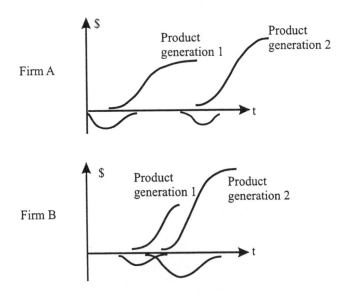

b)   Two firms with intermittent leadership over two product generations

Figure 3.3   Examples of cash-flow curves for new products

may share scarce resources. There may be synergies among the products as well, for example, they may to some extent be based on similar technologies and patents or use similar production or marketing strategies (such as the same company trademark). Two products in the same company may also compete to some extent with each other on the market, that is, they 'cannibalize' each other's sales. For example, IBM's personal computers compete to some extent with their own mainframe computer business.

If cash-flow curves refer to different models or generations of essentially the same product type in terms of functional characteristics, a type of figure similar to Figure 3.2 is obtained, see Figure 3.3a. We can then observe how, for example, R&D may be performed for different generations concurrently, just as different product generations may be marketed concurrently. In this case, it is quite natural that a new generation cannibalizes an older one, eventually outcompeting or substituting for it.

Thus far, cash-flow curves have been shown for one company with one or more products and product generations. We can also show cash-flow curves for several competing companies with one or more competing product generations. Typically, this is done for an innovator or leading company and a competitor (a follower or imitator), as illustrated in Figure 3.3b. In the case of several product generations, the roles as leader and follower may switch back and forth between the companies, with one company taking the lead in one generation and another company taking the lead in the next product generation. This pattern of intermittent leadership (in the sense of being first to market) is quite common in R&D-intensive oligopolies with a small number of competing companies.

In summary, the PLC model has many simplifying assumptions and limitations, and its division into stages is not clear. On the other hand, it is useful as a conceptual model, and cash-flow diagrams in general are highly useful as illustrations, for example, for illustrating the timing of different product generations as in Figure 3.3.

Activity models

Up to now, we have described cash-flow curves for the whole life of an innovation, typically a new product. We shall now narrow the focus and describe some activity models of the innovation process. There are several models for this, each representing different descriptive and/or normative views held by different people on how the innovation process normally looks or should look. Figures 3.4a and 3.4b give two extreme views of the innovation process as linear and one view of the innovation process as a highly interactive and iterative one.[3]

A common but far from clear-cut way to structure the innovation process or the process of product development in general is to divide it into three sets of activities and events which could be seen as constituting more or less overlapping phases (or stages).[4]

(A) Science and technology push

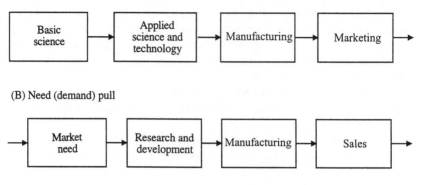

(B) Need (demand) pull

Source: Granstrand and Sigurdson (1981, p. 14).

*Figure 3.4a   Two extreme models of the innovation process – the traditional
views*

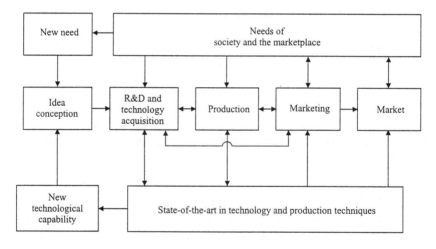

Source: Granstrand and Sigurdson (1981, p. 14).

Figure 3.4b   Interactive model of the innovation process

1. Idea phase.
2. R&D and technology acquisition phase (predominantly product and process
   technology development, but also some commercial development).

3. Commercialization phase (typically consisting of the introduction phase in the PLC model, including manufacturing start-up).

Table 3.2 gives an overview of activities and events in these phases. Activities and sub-activities in innovation and product development typically do not proceed in neat, linear sequences but rather in 'iterative spirals'. The sequencing of activities also varies between products and companies due to the influence of, for example, company management and organizational behaviour, as well as other, factors, more or less random.

Key decision problems in the R&D and technology acquisition phase are, for example: what to include in the technical specification; what to 'make or buy'; whether, when and how to patent; how to make prototypes; and on which customers or users to perform product tests (so as to prevent information leakage, for example).

Key events, often unexpected, in this phase include becoming aware of the fact that a similar patent has been granted to a competitor, discovering that unwanted side-effects exist, or finding that some item cannot meet technical specifications. There are positive surprises as well. One might accidentally discover a new phenomenon, mechanism, compound or the like.[5]

3.2.3 Diffusion Processes for Innovations

In contemporary technology-based businesses it is more or less necessary to be innovative in order to stay competitive. From an economic point of view, it is not sufficient only to be innovative, however. What is important is to create economically successful new products, that is, new products which are not just introduced to and sold on a market, but are sold in sufficient quantities with sufficient profit margins for the total investment to pay off. The standard way of expressing this criterion is that the net present value of the total investment should be positive in order to be undertaken, that is,

$$\text{NPV} = \sum_{i=1}^{L} (p_i q_i - c_i) / (1 + r_i)^i \text{ should be } > 0$$

where (the values are expected or observed, depending upon the period in which the calculation is made):

NPV = net present value of the investment;
p_i = product price in period (year) i;
q_i = number or quantity of products sold in period i;

Table 3.2   Illustration of key phases, decisions and events in the innovation process

Idea phase	R&D and technology acquisition phase	Commercialization phase
Idea search, generation and evaluation	Technical specification	Manufacturing start-up (zero batch and so on)
Idea conception and invention	Involvement of lead users, lead suppliers and other partners	Test marketing
Preliminary business analysis	Market/user analysis	Recruitment and training of sales personnel
Technology scanning and planning	Preliminary design and invention	Marketing start-up
	External technology acquisition	Market introduction
	In-house R&D	Build-up of an international market organization
	Experimentation	Introduction to foreign markets
	Design and redesign	Broadening of application areas
	Analysis of manufacturability	Start-up of mass production and mass marketing
	Testing	Shift in management
	Patent applications	
	Tooling and pilot plant design	
	Prototyping	
	Involvement of general suppliers	
	Market planning	

Note: An innovation process is often complex and irregular; general types of separate activities, events and phases are not easily discerned. The general timing of activities may differ substantially from case to case and unexpected events occur. This table is therefore aimed at illustrating a generic case. The order of activities in the table does not represent a strict order in time. Usually iterations take place among the activities, many of which may also proceed in parallel (sometimes referred to as concurrent engineering).

c_i = total cost incurred in period i for the new product (including investment expenditures);

L = lifetime (number of periods) of the product (alternatively, length of planning horizon);

r = discount rate for investments of this sort for the company, reflecting the company's cost of capital and rate of interest in period i.

Economic calculations of this kind for judging a company's investment in the development, production and marketing of a new product will be further dealt with in Section 3.6. Here we shall review qualitatively how price (p_i), sales volume (q_i), cost (c_i) and product lifetime (L) might be affected during diffusion.

The main objective of the commercialization of a new product is to build up the initial sales of the product in order to get a foothold on the market. However, the main objective in the overall process is to produce sufficient total sales at prices ensuring that the new product breaks even at some point in time, considering all investment expenditures and the relevant cost of capital. For the latter purpose, the market penetration or diffusion of the innovation is critical. It is then important to try to influence not only the diffusion or adoption of the new product among a number of buyers, but also to try to influence the diffusion or imitation of the new product and process technology among a number of sellers and producers who appear as competitors. These two different diffusion processes on the market will be called buyer diffusion and seller diffusion, respectively.

Buyer and seller diffusion

The process of *buyer diffusion* comprises a series of individual adoption processes, one for each buyer/user. Similarly, the process of *seller diffusion* comprises a series of individual imitation processes, one for each seller/producer. Depending upon when, in the buyer diffusion process, buyers adopt the innovation, the population of buyers (which in itself may be ill defined or changing over time) may be broken down into adopter categories. For example, a standard grouping has adopters broken down into early adopters, early majority, late majority and laggards. The first buyer to adopt a new product is simply called the *first adopter*. (A minority of authors prefer to call the first adopter the innovator.) Similarly, the population of sellers/producers may be broken down into innovators, early imitators, early majority and so on. The *innovator* is the main actor behind the introduction of an innovation. Sometimes there will be several innovators appearing around the same time with similar innovations. In some cases the innovator may also be the first adopter, that is, the innovator is also the first one to use the innovation. Figure 3.5 gives an overview of the buyer and seller diffusion processes.

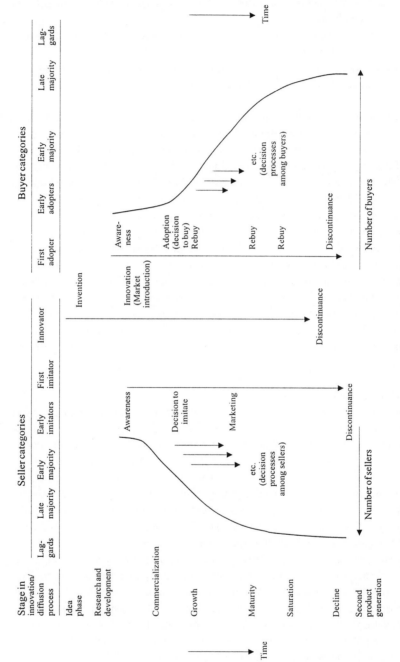

Figure 3.5   Overview of buyer and seller diffusion processes on the market for a new product

68

What happens to the new product and technology during the innovation and diffusion processes, and how are price (p), quantity (q), cost (c) and product lifetime (L) affected? The product and its technology continue to change and develop during its diffusion. These changes and developments take place partly as a result of both buyer diffusion and seller diffusion. On the buyer side, adaptations to different users are made; new applications are found and new ideas come up, often from the users themselves (see von Hippel 1976, 1988a). On the seller side, imitations are seldom true copies. Both modifications and significant changes occur as a result of adaptations to different production equipment, inventing around patents, product differentiation and new ideas. Often these changes and developments during diffusion take the form of accumulated minor improvements, but radical changes also occur. Thus, an innovation is never a one-shot affair, but is instead the first shot that triggers a swarm of mostly minor changes.

In combination, the subsequent changes and innovations lead to a series of minor improvements with a few major jumps in the technical performance parameters of the product (weight, efficiency, durability and so on). But entirely new functionalities may also be developed in addition (for example, portability and heat resistance). Improved product performance is often correlated with cumulative production as well as with the cumulative stock of products in use, and thus can be interpreted as a result of learning. This learning effect is different from the reduction in direct unit variable cost as a result of cumulative production, which stems from improvements in the performance of the production process. An important question is which factors account for this learning effect, and whether learning takes place predominantly on the buyer or the seller side. However, it may also be argued that the really important point is not whether technological change based on learning is mainly user-driven or maker-(producer-) driven, but what enables the whole system of actors to function as a learning system. Technological change may take place among makers of materials, production machinery, components and other supplies, as well as among users in different market segments and in different applications and, moreover, among other makers and users, who are connected to different value chains.

IPR influences on diffusion

From the point of view of an innovating company, it is important to try to create rapid buyer diffusion with good profit margins while preventing a seller diffusion that reduces profit margins. Marketing efforts, in which trademarks and design play important roles, may boost buyer diffusion. Patents can also be used as a marketing tool, signalling technical superiority to prospective customers. Seller diffusion may be limited and/or delayed, for example, by keeping the new product or process technology secret, creating a strong patent situation that blocks other sellers or by erecting other forms of entry barriers, such as creating costs for buyers to switch to another supplier for their rebuys (so-called switching costs). In the case of strong patent or secret protection, the diffusion pattern may look as in Figure 3.6.

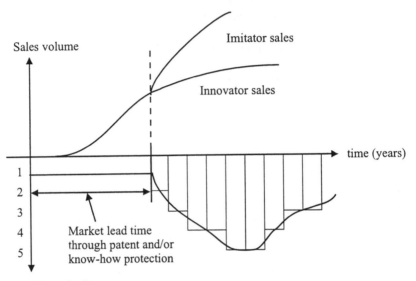

Figure 3.6   Buyer and seller diffusion with temporary monopoly

A strong patent or patent portfolio enables the patent holder to create a temporary monopoly on the market. The new product or process may also be licensed profitably to other producers in order to boost the new product. In general, studies have shown that a high market share in growing markets for new products is often associated with high profitability (at least when cost reduction due to proprietary learning is significant). But if market size can be increased by the joint efforts of many producers, it may pay off to give up a bit of the market share to other licensees.

The point to stress here is that the buyer and seller diffusion processes and their interaction jointly determine economic success and therefore must be taken into consideration in the planning and commercialization of new products. IPR may be used to effect both types of diffusion. Trademarks, designs and also patents typically speed up buyer diffusion, while patents, trade secrets and copyrights can be used to influence seller diffusion, typically by delaying it and thereby weakening competition for some time.

3.3 PATENTS

3.3.1 Introduction

The aim of this section is to give a general introduction to patents. For the interested reader, there are several good manuals and textbooks providing more detailed information. One has to bear in mind, though, that IP laws, and thus patent laws, differ between countries and vary over time. For accurate information, publications from the patent offices in various countries and from the WIPO should be consulted. There are also numerous pamphlets from law firms, patent bureaux, consultants and so on. A few suggested readings are given in Section 3.5.

3.3.2 What is a Patent?

Official definitions of a patent vary somewhat. The following one is from the EPO:[6] 'A patent is a legal title granting its holder the exclusive right to make use of an invention for a limited area and time by stopping others from, among other things, making, using or selling it without authorization' (EPO *Annual Report*).

Thus, a patent is not, strictly speaking, a technical invention or a technical document but a legal right with a possible economic value. A patent does not directly entitle the holder to exclusively sell or even manufacture the invention. In essence, it is a negative right, a right to exclude others. A patent for a drug does not entitle the holder to sell it as a medicine. For this, authorization by the national health authorities is required.

By its nature, a patent can be seen as a socio-economic contract between an inventor (or IPR holder) and society. Upon voluntary request by an inventor who fulfils certain requirements, society grants patent rights to the inventor, who in turn 'pays' for the rights by disclosing the invention to the public. Since patent offices need to be financed, an applicant is required to pay administrative fees. This is illustrated in Figure 3.7. One can say that there are two sides to the patent 'coin':

1. Patent rights are important as competitive means for the protection and commercial exploitation of new technologies.
2. Patent information is important as a means for technology and competitor intelligence.

The legal and institutional framework providing and processing patent rights (rather than inventions themselves) forms a patent system. A patent system is further characterized by the following.

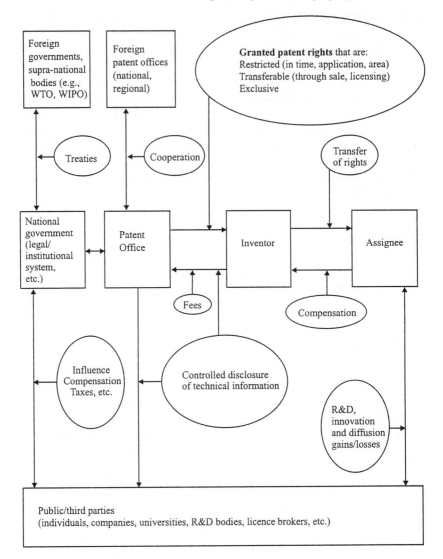

Figure 3.7   The socio-economic contract nature of a patent

1. Conditions for what is patentable.
2. Term of protection and territorial extension.
3. Protection against activities violating a patent, including sanctions and their enforcement.

A patent right is granted to an inventor or his or her assignee contingent upon the following conditions: (i) technical nature (industrial applicability); (ii) novelty; and (iii) non-obviousness (see below). Novelty and non-obviousness are determined as of the first filing date (priority date). In order to have priority to an invention, the inventor must be the first one to file a patent application with a patent office. The USA is a major exception to this rule, since priority is given there to the person who is (or is considered to be) the first to make the invention, that is, to conceive it and to reduce it to practice.

Across most major industrialized nations (such as Europe, Japan and the USA), the maximum lifetime or period of protection by a patent is now (1998) 20 years, counted from the date the application was filed.[7] The patent right is valid in each country where it has been applied for and granted.

Patent rights are national in the sense that they refer only to the country that granted them, and they must be applied for in each country of interest. Thus, there is no such thing as an international patent. However, a patent right can be extended across nations according to various procedures. Under the Paris Convention, the inventor has a 12-month period, starting from the first filing date, to file applications in other countries. The PCT facilitates the further processing of the original patent application (the so-called priority application) in the form of an international application. Ultimately, an invention matures into a family of patents in countries where applications claiming priority from the priority application have been filed and approved. An exception is European patent applications, which are filed with, processed at and granted by the EPO, a regional patent office for Western Europe (except for Norway). To be valid in a member state, a European patent has to be filed with the national office of that state within three months of the publication of the grant in the national language of that state (as of 1998).

A patent right is violated or infringed if someone exploits the invention commercially, in contrast to using it for experimentation. The patent rights holder may go to court to enforce his or her rights. That is, a patent gives to the patent holder the right to sue an infringer. This may result in the court stopping the infringer temporarily through an injunction or by the sentencing of a fraud conviction. The court may decide that the infringer should pay damages to the rights holder for economic losses incurred. Thus, ultimately, the value of a patent right as a competitive tool derives from its use as a means for litigation.

3.3.3 How to Value a Patent

The economic value of a patent derives from several sources. These sources are related to the various advantages and disadvantages of a patent, as described below. The major source of value, as traditionally conceived, is through deterred or deferred imitation and competition. This is illustrated in Figure 3.8. Another source of value arises through the licensing of a patent, as shown in Figure 3.9.

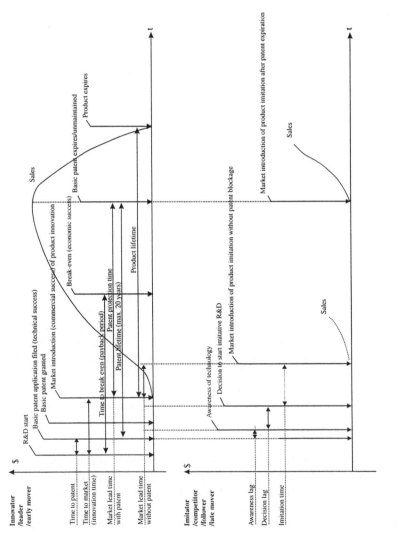

74

Figure 3.8   Time concepts in innovation and imitation

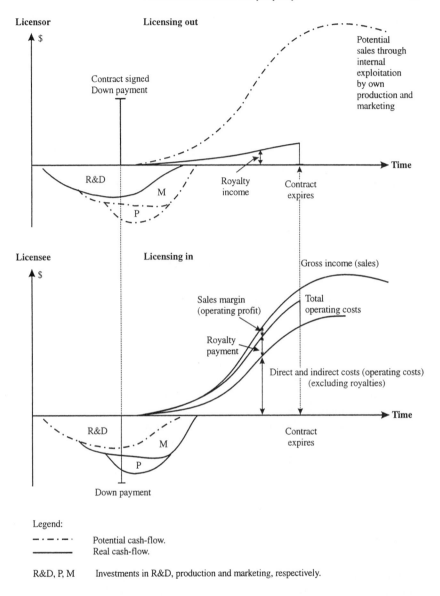

Figure 3.9 Economic value arising from licensing a patent

The licensee (licence buyer) is thereby entitled to use the patent rights and may, in turn, deter or defer imitation and competition. In return, the licensee pays a fee to the licensor (licence seller), usually in the form of a down payment and royalties that are usually calculated as a fixed or variable percentage of licence-based sales.

3.3.4   What is Patentable?

A technical invention fulfilling minimal requirements in respect of the following criteria is considered patentable:

1. It is industrially applicable or useful (exploitable within certain moral limits, not excluding weapons, however). Usually, in this context it is more specifically required that the invention has technical character and can be carried out or enabled.
2. It is novel to the world.
3. It is non-obvious to the average 'person skilled in the art' (professional practitioner), that is, the invention must exceed a certain minimum inventive step (level of invention) or level of combinatorial skill.[8]

The minimum level of patentability requirements may vary across nations (and across patent examiners as well) and over time. There is a trend towards some convergence through international cooperation and harmonization. There is also a trend towards enlarging the patentable area, for example, in biotechnology and computer software, which is a broadening of the first requirement.[9] There is also variation across technologies, for example, due to new technologies presenting difficulties to patent examiners when assessing novelty and non-obviousness. It is clear that there are never many professional practitioners skilled in a new technology. The obviousness criterion may be less stringent in such a technology, since a patent examiner may lack experience on where to draw the line between what is obvious and what is not. As a result, the minimum level of invention required by patent examiners for patentability may be lower in the early stages of an emerging technology. This translates into patents with scopes that may become too large in a new field.[10]

3.3.5   Who Can Patent?

Any individual or group of individuals can apply for a patent, and in most countries a legal person, such as a company, can do so. In the USA only individuals can apply, but this is a formality since an individual can transfer his or her rights to a company. Normally an employee in industry (but not in a university) would have to assign the right for an invention to the employer. It is then the burden of the assignee to apply for a patent and to turn the invention into an innovation in the form of a marketable product or process.

3.3.6   Why Apply for a Patent?

Firms may benefit in several ways from applying for patent protection, since a patent may do the following:

1. Deter a competitor from introducing technologically similar inventions.
2. Put pressure on a competitor who has introduced a technologically similar invention to withdraw from the market, if it has been detected that the introduction was made after the patent was applied for or granted (depending on the country under consideration).
3. Block a competitor from patenting. (This could also be achieved through prophylactic publishing, that is, publishing of information that prevents others from applying for a patent for what has been disclosed to the public and thus cannot be considered novel any more.)
4. Create an identifiable asset with certain rights attached to it, which in turn may create strength in negotiations regarding financing, licensing, cooperation, acquisition, divestment or standard-setting.
5. Create an economic asset that could be activated on the balance sheet and used for public relations, marketing, financing and tax-planning purposes.
6. Create the possibility of cross-country transfer of profits within an MNC through intra-firm licensing.
7. Create an incentive to invent among personnel within the firm.
8. Create the possibility of stimulating and measuring R&D productivity (even if this is a questionable measure).

On the other hand, a firm reaps benefits when other firms file patent applications, since they may do the following:

9. Gain easy access to the information pertaining to a patent application since it is made publicly available.
10. Conduct business negotiations with the patent holder more easily with a well-defined patented asset as a basis for financing, licensing, cooperation, purchasing and standard-setting. For example, it is easier for a firm to buy an invention from an inventor if it is patented, although the price may be higher for the same reason. Thus, in this respect, patents make it easier to trade technology for both the buyer and the seller, thereby reducing their transaction costs.

Benefits under the first three points above are usually referred to as the monopoly element of patents, since the patent system is designed in such a way that 'the winner takes all', that is, there is only one winner in the race for a patent.

A patent offers not only advantages but a mix of advantages and disadvantages. There are several ways to list these and make the necessary trade-offs. The following is a listing used in the present study (see Table 3.3 and also Table 7.1).

Thus, with respect to the advantages to a company or an individual inventor, a patent in general offers a means for the following:

1. Protecting proprietary product technology.
2. Protecting proprietary process technology.
3. Creating retaliatory power against competitors.
4. Creating better possibilities of selling licences.
5. Giving better possibilities of accessing technology through cross-licensing.
6. Facilitating R&D cooperation with others.
7. Giving a better bargaining position in standard-setting.
8. Providing motivation for employees to invent.
9. Providing a measure of R&D productivity.
10. Improving the corporate image.

This is at the expense of the following disadvantages:

1. Disclosure of technical information.
2. Direct costs of patenting.

The advantages of patenting can be summarized as follows:

1. To block competitors.
2. To improve one's bargaining position.
3. To stimulate and monitor R&D.

Blocking competitors actually means two things: first, to block their R&D and business activities, and second, to block the possibilities of their blocking the company's own R&D and business activities. The first blocking motive has traditionally been considered less gentleman-like, while the second one is considered to be fair because it involves more protective (defensive) measures. However, as competition becomes fiercer and patenting becomes more aggressive and offensive, blocking competitors outside the company's own area is becoming increasingly accepted.

It is also important to judge the pros and cons of a single patent in relation to a network or a portfolio of patents, that is, the building of a patent portfolio for a product area or for the company as a whole. For data on how companies put weight on the advantages above, see Chapter 7.

3.3.7   When to Apply for a Patent

The timing of a patent application in the innovation process is also a matter of importance. To apply early in the process provides the following advantages:

1. It reduces the risk of being blocked by others.
2. It provides for earlier revenues stemming from the patent.
3. It increases the likelihood of getting a patent granted.
4. It increases the likelihood of obtaining a broader scope of protection in case of an emerging technology.
5. It increases the likelihood of setting the inventive approach as a standard.
6. It possibly deters others from pursuing that particular approach or line of R&D.

At the same time applying early provides the following disadvantages:

7. It provides a shorter protection time for the product/process on the market.
8. It provides an early indication to competitors of the company's R&D activities.
9. It increases the risk of not securing a patent or of securing a weak patent only, due to insufficient experimental support for the invention.

Again, a patent application must be judged not in isolation but as part of the company's effort to build and maintain an IPR portfolio. For example, if a product already has patent protection one could wait a while before applying for an additional patent in order to prolong the total protection period.

3.3.8   Where to Apply for a Patent

The basic rule is to apply in those countries where the company has a business or expects to have a business within the lifetime of the patent, and where the value of the patent for protecting the company's own business exceeds the costs of obtaining and maintaining it. The latter may be high for many countries in relation to the size of the market and the competition.[11] The costs of international patenting may also be too high for small companies to absorb. However, consideration of the offensive motives for patenting, rather than the traditionally defensive ones mentioned above, may justify applications in a wider range of countries. The same is true if prospective licensing is considered.

It has also been customary to file the first patent application for a particular invention (the 'basic' or 'priority' application) in the home country of the company where most of its R&D is usually located. However, this habit is being challenged as R&D along with the patenting operation becomes more internationalized in MNCs. For example, if an Italian company acquires a German company with a good patent department, the company may move some of its patent application work to Germany, which will then become the country in which basic applications are filed.[12] There may also be advantages for an MNC to file first in a country with a large market and a strong IP regime, like the USA. Swift and cost-effective patent processing by the patent office and favourable tax conditions are other factors that may attract first filings to a country.

3.3.9   How to Apply for a Patent

There are many textbooks and manuals on how to apply for a patent, to which the reader is referred for detailed information. See, for example, Foster and Shook (1993) or Anawalt and Enayati (1996) for the USA, Hodkinson (1987) for the UK, guides from the Japanese Patent Office for Japan (for example, JPO 1994) and WIPO's *PCT Applicants' Guide*. Patent offices also provide instructional material together with application forms.

3.3.10   Pricing of Licences

As mentioned in Section 3.3.3, the value of a patent or a patent portfolio to the patenting company is derived from many sources. The market value of a patent or a patent portfolio (package) is a special matter. It is determined by the considerations of prospective buyers. In principle, the market value of a patent can be determined as the value of a corresponding exclusive, non-geographically restricted licence. Since licences can be of various types as well (exclusive, sole, non-exclusive and so on), the valuation of a patent or a group of patents is a special case of licence valuation. To make such a valuation is no easy matter. Rather, it is extremely difficult to be precise. The difficulties arise from the unique nature of a patent, the long time horizons (up to 20 years), and the technical, commercial and economic uncertainties involved. Nevertheless, numerous licence agreements are being signed every day on the basis of some kind of valuation.

Figure 3.10 gives an overview of various factors that the buyer and the seller might consider. These could be translated into ceiling price levels and floor price levels, respectively, when aggregated, and this assessment could be done in various ways. Often it is useful to distinguish between two floor price levels. The higher floor price is related to total cost, including a portion of fixed R&D costs, while the lower floor price is related only to operating costs. Similarly, different ceiling price levels could be related to different ranges of factors influencing value, for example, pertaining only to a narrow commercial value in a particular area or to a higher strategic value, incorporating spill-overs to other areas in the buying company or consequences for future licence deals.

Such economic calculations as well as contractual designs, negotiation tactics and so on can be further elaborated. The difficulties in valuation and the considerable uncertainties involved leave great freedom for exercising negotiation skills in licensing. A few useful hints are as follows:

1. Consider option agreements and letters of intent.
2. Distinguish between technical, commercial and economic risks.
3. Go for the proper jurisdiction.
4. Be critical of industry conventions regarding pricing and so on. Try to be legally and commercially creative as well, but stay within the legal framework.
5. Prepare negotiations carefully. Be aware of cultural differences.
6. Make investment calculations but do not use them rigidly.
7. Utilize legal, economic and technical expertise.
8. Have a profit-sharing attitude (try to play a win–win game with empathy regarding the partner).

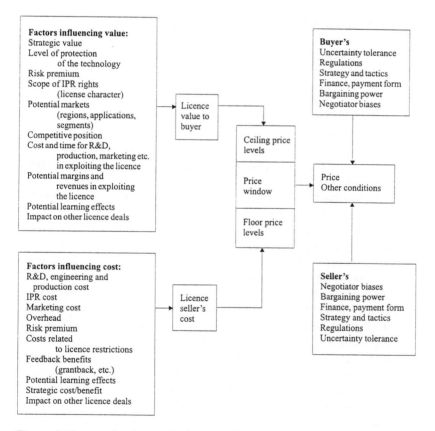

Figure 3.10   A valuation and pricing model for patents and licences

9. Consider contingencies and the need for renegotiation clauses.
10. Be prepared not to reach an agreement.

The model in Figure 3.10 could be further elaborated when determining damage claims in case of patent infringement, and it could also be used in cross-licensing situations. It should be repeated that accurate valuations are difficult to attain and that time-horizons are usually long with uncertain prospects. This has a tendency to raise negotiation costs, which makes it attractive to negotiate the cross-licensing of broad patent packages in certain industries. In many situations, patent mappings are also useful as a bargaining tool (see Chapter 9).

3.4   THE PATENT SYSTEM AS AN ECONOMIC INCENTIVE SYSTEM

3.4.1   What is a Patent System?

The patent system in itself can be viewed as a legal or institutional innovation. Its basic legal framework has diffused among the countries of the world as described in Chapter 2. The patent system will probably continue to diffuse globally. Despite longstanding public debate and concern about the positive and negative effects of the patent system, only minor modifications have taken place in recent years, which on the whole can be seen as improvements. There have been no major changes or radical legal innovations regarding the patent system in this century.[13] The basic economic and legal ideas behind the patent system have remained much the same.

In principle, the grant of a patent is a transaction between the rights holder and the state. As described earlier, this transaction means that the rights holder is rewarded for disclosing the information to the public by receiving the transferable, temporary and exclusive legal right to prevent others from commercially exploiting the invention. Furthermore, the rights holder can use legal means, which can enjoin the infringer and disgorge his or her profits, as a means to stop any further exploitation by an infringer who has been found guilty by a court. The traditional interpretation of this among economists is that the inventor/rights holder enters voluntarily into a binding contract with society, which grants a temporary monopoly right in return for information about the invention. There is, of course, a cost in setting up and running a system with legislation, patent offices and courts (with any patent policing costs deferred to the rights holder). The fixed system costs are mostly tax-financed while operating costs are mostly fee-financed. The cost for third parties to access patent information is rather low, although it may be costly to absorb it. See Figure 3.7 for an overview of the socio-economic contract nature of a patent.

3.4.2 Why Have a Patent System at all?

For a society that wants to stimulate the generation and diffusion of technical information and technical innovations, a patent system is one way.[14] More specifically, the major rationale for the patent system from a traditional economist's point of view is as follows:

1. To stimulate invention and investments in R&D.
2. To stimulate commercial exploitation of inventions through direct investments in production and marketing and/or through technology trade (licensing in and out).
3. To stimulate public disclosure of technical information.

Thus, the patent system is intended to be a stimulus not only to investments in R&D but also to production and marketing. In this respect, the patent system differs from an inventor prize system such as the one practised in the former USSR (with 'inventors' certificates'). Public disclosure of an invention is also thought of as stimulating technological progress and competition after the patent protection has ceased. The economic benefits to society have to be weighed against economic losses due to any monopolistic behaviour of the inventor/rights holder, plus the net administrative cost of setting up and running the patent system.[15] This trade-off has been at the centre of the debate about the patent system. In a country like the USA, the monopoly considerations have traditionally carried great weight. However, this has changed, as described in Chapter 2. For a more thorough discussion of the rationale behind the patent system, see Scherer (1980) and Kaufer (1989).

In addition, three things must be kept in mind when discussing the patent system as a system of incentives. First, there are different pros and cons concerning the patent system for different levels or actors in the economy; see Table 3.3. Second, there are a number of alternative policy measures for a government wanting to stimulate R&D and innovation. In this context, it may be argued that the patent system is a demand-side rather than a supply-side measure, since it affects the output markets of a firm through its supposed benefits rather than its input markets through reduced factor costs. Third, there are numerous possibilities for modifying existing patent laws and practices, and the strengths and weaknesses of their effects as incentives depend very much on the detailed design of the patent system.

Monopolistic conditions may moreover arise in a number of ways other than through patents. If markets are regionalized with local or state monopolies – regulated or 'natural' monopolies – patents do not significantly affect competition (cases in point are traditional public utility companies and old-style telephone service companies). Monopolistic conditions also arise from lead times

Table 3.3   Principal advantages and disadvantages of the patent system

Level	Advantages	Disadvantages
Nation (society, consumers)	Stimulates rate of invention by providing an incentive for investment in R&D (also for reinvestment and for inventing around work) Stimulates rate of commercialization (rate of innovation) through investment in general Stimulates rate of diffusion and technology transfer through disclosure, marketing and licensing Provides an artificial metric (yardstick) of invention	Risk of monopolistic inefficiencies (including risk of hampered commercialization of new technologies)[3] Administrative costs for setting up and running the system Risk of R&D and investment distortion Risk of overinvestment in duplicative R&D and/or substitute inventions
Company[1]	Offers restricted, transferable monopoly rights Provides bargaining power and a basis for buying or selling an identified piece of technology Provides information about technology and industry competitors Provides motivation for employees and yardsticks for technology management	Requires controlled disclosure[4] Monopolistic overpricing (including cost of acquiring technology) and/or barriers to entry induced by competitors Patenting costs, direct and indirect (including, for example, litigation costs)
Individual[2]	Provides a basis for award, negotiation of a contract or start-up of a company Provides a means for recognition Provides information on technology	Requires controlled disclosure[4] Monopolistic behaviour of holders of possibly interfering or complementary patents Patenting costs

Notes
1. These advantages and disadvantages are of course related to a company's advantages and disadvantages in taking out patents, as described above and in Chapter 7, but they do not match exactly because the pros and cons here concern the patent system as a whole, compared to a hypothetical situation with no such system at all. Moreover, seeking to take out a patent is voluntary (as is keeping it in force, once it is granted) and a company perceives the advantages of so doing in comparison with the alternative of not doing so while still having a patent system in place.
2. Typically an inventor (engineer or scientist), either autonomous or employed.
3. The commercialization of new technologies can be hampered by the dispersion of several necessary patents (and IPRs in general) among actors who cannot agree.
4. No pre-publication is allowed (that is, before a patent application is filed) and full post-publication is enforced.

on the market, for example if imitation lags and/or imitation costs are high. A third case in which additional monopolizing effects of patents are limited is when product differentiation is so high that the competing products are essentially dissimilar.

Clearly, in certain markets and with respect to certain products the patent system induces temporary monopolistic conditions. However, the monopolistic effects are then often reduced by limiting factors such as deficient infringement sanction systems.

The secrecy alternative

This said, a large number of cases remain where patents do have monopolistic effects. An obvious question, then, is what would happen if patenting possibilities ceased to exist? The main alternative open to firms is to reduce inventive activities, that is, reduce R&D in a broad sense, and/or attempt to appropriate indigenous technology through some other means, for example, through secrecy operations. Secrecy protection is substantially more effective for production technology than for product technology, since products may more easily be 'reverse engineered'. Thus, secrecy protection may to some extent substitute for patent protection regarding process inventions but less so for product inventions.

To operate within secrecy agreements would also make technology trade more cumbersome. It is well recognized in economics that any market for information works imperfectly. The moment one has to disclose a piece of information in order to sell it, one is running the risk of being cheated.[16] It would be quite possible, at least in principle, to replace a patent with secrecy agreements in business negotiations over a piece of technological information. However, the enforcement of such agreements might become very difficult since the licensor would have to show that the secret information was divulged by the licensee. Thus, the seller has to prove *ex post* that his or her invention or know-how was uniquely new and unknown to others at the time the secrecy agreement was signed. This is a formidable burden of proof.[17] Alternatively, the seller might try to establish *ex ante* that the invention is new. However, this would also be a formidable task to perform without disclosing too much. Hence, the enforcement of a secrecy agreement leads to the necessity of establishing novelty and unique proprietorship of the information passed under the agreement. The difficulty of doing so without disclosure leads one to conceive of some kind of system where novelty and unique proprietorship are established *ex ante* through public disclosure. In effect, some kind of patent system would likely result as a consequence of difficulties in enforcing secrecy agreements, as well as difficulties in disseminating information in a secrecy regime.[18] In summary, the transaction costs for conducting technology trade purely under secrecy agreements would be too high, and technology trade would shrink.[19]

Prestige system

In the absence of a patent system, one alternative open to society and firms is to stimulate invention through some kind of inventor prize system. Solely from the point of view of stimulating employee inventiveness, it is likely that such a system could be designed to substitute quite effectively for a patent system. In fact, nothing prevents companies, academies or nations from running their own such systems in parallel with the patent system, and some do so also in areas not covered by patent laws (for example, general suggestion systems in companies, or the Nobel Prize system in some sciences). However, such systems mostly provide no economic incentives for commercializing and diffusing new technologies.

Finally, it is important to keep in mind that forces other than those based on purely economic incentives play a role in advancing science and technology. Psychological motives such as curiosity, vanity and the need for achievement are important to scientists and inventors. Such non-monetary, socio-psychological incentives also often stimulate invention. Patents, too, are sometimes applied for by inventors not only for purely economic reasons, but also because a patent provides a certain amount of recognition and prestige. It should finally be noted that the prospect of a patent could be seen as a prize or a reward that could be overvalued by inventors investing in R&D. From society's point of view, it would, at least in the short run, be beneficial if firms persistently expected the patent system to function to their advantage even if it did not. To some extent this kind of false expectation can be found among young firms and inventors. (See Dutton 1984, pp. 204–5 about this 'socially wholesome illusion'.) This is analogous to what is said about entrepreneurial hubris in Chapter 4.

3.5   PREVIOUS RESEARCH AND LITERATURE

Despite the practical importance of trade secrets to the business community, the law of trade secrets is a neglected orphan in economic analysis. (Friedman et al., 1991, p. 61)

Trade marks are . . . significant business assets . . . [y]et, they have not . . . been systematically studied by economic or business historians, even though much has been written by other scholars on these intangible assets. (Wilkins 1992, p. 66)

3.5.1   General Structure of the Literature

The literature on IP has a number of interesting structural features. As a subject, IP, and patents in particular, does indeed have a long tradition in scholarly literature in economics, law, engineering, history, philosophy and so on, as well as in miscellaneous other writings (such as government investigations, biographies and debating articles). It has been a tiny tradition, however, although there is recent growth in writings on patents. In general, the IP-related literature is also highly fragmented, corresponding to the different IPR types (such as patents, copyrights and trademarks). Quite naturally, the literature is also sub-divided into disciplines, primarily economics, management, law and engineering. Also quite naturally, there is academic literature and literature for practitioners, with a substantial separation of these two general strands. (Perhaps this separation is less in some disciplines, for example, law.) Finally, there is a fragmentation of the literature by nation.

In summary, the IP literature has a long and thin, but growing, tradition, highly fragmented by IPR type, discipline, occupation and country. This makes surveying difficult. Below, the patent-related literature in English since World War II will be surveyed briefly in order to provide some different entries into the literature in general. More specific references are given in the rest of the book.

3.5.2 Surveys of the Literature

For a long time, the patent institution and its pros and cons have stirred much controversy and given rise to innumerable publications about its economic, legal and technical aspects. In this debate and literature the USA has held a central place. It is difficult to give more than a biased sample of literature surveys. For good surveys, see Machlup (1958, 1962, 1980, 1984), Taylor and Silberston (1973), Scherer (1977, 1980, 1992), Griliches (1984), Kaufer (1989), MacLeod (1988), von Hippel (1988a), Tirole (1988), Weil and Snapper (1989), NRC (1993) and Lanjouw and Lerner (1997). Good surveys on the history of the patent system are given in Kaufer (1989), MacLeod (1988) and David (1993). (See also Chapter 2.) Literature on international aspects can be found in Rushing and Brown (1990) and Albach and Rosenkranz (1995).

Surveys of patent literature related to management and business economics (rather than political economics) are rarer. A bibliography is provided in Clarke and Reavley (1993). These sorts of writings are mostly embedded in the literature that has emerged since the 1950s on the management of R&D, engineering, technology and innovation. See also Granstrand (1988).

Surveys of patent literature related to law also seem rare. Some US-oriented ones for IP more generally can be found in NRC (1993). Others are Eisenberg (1989) and Besen and Raskind (1991). See also Goldstein (1997) and Merges (1992) for textbook related surveys and Gire (1992) for a bibliography.

An increasing number of patent-related articles deal with patent information and statistics as technological and economic indicators. Surveys of this type of literature, mainly on technological indicators, are provided in Basberg (1987), van Raan (1988), Chakrabarti (1989), Archibugi (1992), Pavitt (1985, 1991), Grupp (1994) and OECD (1996). Outstanding surveys on patent information as economic indicators are given in Griliches (1984, 1989, 1990). A pioneering study using patent information for economic analysis is Schmookler (1966), which also gives an overview of a few studies from before World War II. (See also Chapter 9.)

Tables 3.4–3.6 give an overview of the academic writers on patents who are most cited in articles in the *Social Science Citation Index* for the period 1990–95. Almost all the authors in the table are economists from the USA, although law and natural sciences are represented, and almost all are alive and active in the field, although only a few work primarily in this field. Japanese authors, and authors with mainly an engineering background, are absent even in a list extended to 40 authors. Such an extended list includes only one Nobel Prize Laureate (K.J. Arrow).

Table 3.4   Academic writers of patent articles in the Social Science Citation Index, *1990–1995*

Author	Number of citations	Author	Number of citations
Scherer, F.M.	48	Gilbert, R.	18
Mansfield, E.	33	Katz, M.L.	17
Eisenberg, R.S.	28	Narin, F.	17
Griliches, Z.	28	Dasgupta, P.	16
Merges, R.P.	25	Nelson, R.R.	16
Chisum, D.S.	24	Pavitt, K.	16
MacLeod, C.	24	Scotchmer, S.	16
Nordhaus, W.D.	24	Kitch, E.W.	15
Schmookler, J.	21	Klemperer, P.	15
Levin, R.C.	19	Carpenter, M.P.	12

Note: The table is based on citations of first-listed author in all articles in the *Social Science Citation Index* for the period having 'patent' in their title. There were 442 articles published in 1990–95. I thank Dr Olle Persson, University of Umeå, Sweden for providing material for this table.

As for literature catering more to practitioners than to academics (still English-language literature), there are numerous handbooks, manuals and the like (some of them also containing good material of academic interest). The various patent offices and agencies like the WIPO also put out a substantial number of publications, apart from their legal publications. Practical guides are JPO (1994) for Japan, Foster and Shook (1993) for the USA and Hodkinson (1987) for the UK. OECD (1997) describes patents in the international context. There are also several journals, such as *Management of Intellectual Property*, *LES Nouvelles* (published by the Licensing Executive Society), *World Patent Information* and the *Journal of the Patent Office Society*. Several societies also publish IP-related material, such as AIPPI.

For licensing, there are a number of information services and intermediaries. As expected, these are neither rare nor difficult to find. Occasionally, these sources of information contain material of more general interest, not least since the field is wide open for legal and commercial creativity at the same time as it focuses on technical and artistic creativity. For some business-oriented works on licensing see, for example, Bidault et al. (1989), Parr and Sullivan (1996) and Schlicher (1996).

Table 3.5   Academic works most cited in patent articles in the Social Science Citation Index, *1990–1995*

Work		Number of citations	Work		Number of citations
Eisenberg	(1989)	21	Dasgupta and Stiglitz	(1980)	8
MacLeod	(1988)	16	Merges	(1988)	8
Nordhaus	(1969)	15	Narin et al.	(1987)	8
Schmookler	(1966)	15	Basberg	(1987)	7
Merges and Nelson	(1990)	14	Carpenter et al.	(1981)	7
Griliches	(1990)	13	Chisum	(1986)	7
Kitch	(1977)	13	Dreyfuss	(1989b)	7
Klemperer	(1990)	12	Katz and Shapiro	(1985)	7
Eisenberg	(1987)	11	Mansfield	(1986)	7
Levin et al.	(1987)	11	Tandon	(1982)	7
Scherer	(1980)	11	Taylor and Silberston	(1973)	7
Gilbert and Shapiro	(1990)	10			

Note: Based on same set of articles as in Table 3.4. The full references are given in the list of literature references.

Table 3.6   Journals with most cited patent articles in the Social Science Citation Index, *1990–1995*

Research Policy
American Economic Review
Rand Journal of Economics
Quarterly Journal of Economics
Scientometrics
World Patent Information
Yale Law Journal

Note: Based on same set of articles as in Table 3.4. The journals are ranked according to the number of articles they contain from a table of the 50 most cited works, similar to Table 3.5.

### 3.5.3	Theoretical Literature

A relatively small but recently growing number of studies of the economic theory
of the patent system have emerged since the 1960s. A seminal, even monumental,
work in this category is Arrow (1962), who presents a basic model of invention,
R&D, innovation and imitation.[20] Arrow argues essentially that there is a
tendency in industry to underinvest in R&D from society's point of view, due
to problems for a firm to appropriate the economic benefits of its R&D.[21]
Patent protection would be one way of coping with this, at least to some
extent.[22] The principal way a patent affects invention and innovation is through
its effects on the rate of imitation. In the Arrow type of patent modelling, the
innovator's profits dwindle completely by competition when imitation occurs.
Thus, a delay in imitation through patent protection would be a stimulus for firms
to invest in R&D, at the expense to society of the possible overpricing of
products by the monopolistic patent holder.

Nordhaus (1969), which is also a truly seminal work on the economic theory
of patents, makes a thorough theoretical analysis of the cost and benefits to the
firm and to society of the patent system in the Arrow type of framework.
Nordhaus distinguishes between different types of inventions, minor and major
(or 'run of the mill' and 'drastic', using his terms), and, in particular, postulates
the optimal length of patent protection time from society's point of view.
(Section 3.6 describes the Nordhaus modelling further.) By increasing the
length of patent protection, incentives for generating innovations are increased
(that is, dynamic efficiency is increased), while a longer period of monopolistic
inefficiencies is produced (that is, static efficiency is decreased). Nordhaus
triggered several works in the 1980s on the optimal length of a patent under
different conditions.

More recent work in the 1990s has shifted from focusing on the optimal length
of a patent towards the optimal breadth or scope of a patent as well as optimal
combinations of length and breadth. For works in this vein, see especially
Klemperer (1990) and Gilbert and Shapiro (1990). The scope of a patent is far
more difficult to define, however. There have been various approaches: for
example, the scope of a patent could be represented by the patentor's ability to
raise price (Gilbert and Shapiro 1990), the probability of infringement, the impact
on close product substitutes (Klemperer 1990), the number of side classifications
of a patent (Lerner 1994) and the invent around costs. The last two approaches
have the advantage that they do not rely as much on observations or estimates
of post-innovation conditions.

Another shift in focus in the theoretical literature is from considering a one-
stage innovation process towards a multistage innovation. Building partly on
Barzel (1968), Kitch (1977) introduced a new perspective on the role of patent
rights, viewing them (in analogy with prospect rights in mineral extraction) not

as rewards but as prospect rights, which were handed out at an early stage in the innovation process.[23] Kitch's work has been widely cited but also criticized (see, for example, Beck 1983). Other works using multistage models of R&D and innovation include Fudenberg et al. (1983).

Yet a further shift in thought is from considering only a single innovation towards considering multiple innovations that build upon or interact with each other. As is often the case empirically, and as studied by Mansfield, a patent loses value because new and better subsequent inventions appear before the patent expires. At the same time a strong patent influences the patentability and profitability of subsequent inventions (see, for example, Scotchmer 1991 and Aghion and Howitt 1998, Ch. 14).

Game-theoretical modelling of patent races among competitors has become popular. In many respects, stylized patent races offer a theoretically appealing application for game theory. More importantly this literature throws light on how competitive races impact incentives for R&D and innovation. For further study see, for example, Reinganum (1982), Fudenberg et al. (1983), Dasgupta (1988) and Dasgupta and David (1987).

There are many policy variables for a patent system other than patent length and breadth (for example, regarding the disclosure of patent information). More and more of these other features have become subjected to theoretical economic analysis. See, for example, Ordover (1991) on how different features affect the diffusion of technical information.

For a classic qualitative review of theories of the pros and cons of patents, see Machlup (1958) and for a current review (with a similar classification of theories) see Mazzoleni and Nelson (1998).

Finally there are some (but much fewer) economic analyses of IPRs other than patents. For trade secrets, see Cheung (1982) and Friedman et al. (1991), for designs, see BIE (1995), and for copyrights, see for example Palmer (1986) and Towse (1997). The issue of patentability versus copyrightability of algorithms, databases and computer software in general has generated a great deal of literature in recent decades, theoretical and empirical, and perhaps more legal than economic. See for example Chisum (1986), OTA (1992), NRC (1993), Reichman and Samuelson (1997), Scheinfeld and Butler (1991) and the issue of *Columbia Law Review*, December 1994.

3.5.4 Empirical Literature

When turning to empirical work, very important studies have been made by Mansfield and others on the considerable gap between the very high social returns to innovation and the private returns to innovation, as well as the importance of the rate of imitation behind these gaps. These studies indicate empirically that underinvestment in private R&D is likely because of imitation. This in turn indicates the need for something resembling a patent system. However, the studies also show that imitation is a costly and time-consuming process, affected by many more factors than just patents (see Scherer 1980; Mansfield et al. 1981). The question then is how effective the patent system actually is in practice and what would happen if it was changed or even abolished.

A classical and wide-reaching study of patenting practices in UK industry is presented by Taylor and Silberston (1973). This study also provides some data on the impact of patent lifetimes on R&D budgeting. Their main findings, based on interviews with 27 UK firms, indicate that without effective patent protection, R&D budgets would be cut marginally (by 5 per cent or less), except in certain speciality chemicals, where R&D would be cut by 25 per cent, and in pharmaceuticals, where R&D would be cut by 64 per cent. These findings can be contrasted with the empirical results of the study presented in Chapter 5 and the theoretical calculations in Section 3.6.

Mansfield (1986) sheds further light on the impact of the abolition of the patent system on the rate of invention and innovation, as estimated by firms. In essence, the study shows that the effect would be a very small decline in most industries. As almost always in these types of studies, the exceptions are pharmaceuticals and chemicals, for which the patent system is essential. However, Mansfield shows that despite this outcome the firms make frequent use of the patent system. This 'patenting paradox' requires further explanation. Since the propensity to patent was found not to have declined in the USA from 1960 to 1980, the observed decline in patenting must be due to a decline in the number of patentable inventions. Because this number is related to the amount of R&D investment, a decline in patenting without a corresponding decline in R&D investment could be due to the (temporary) presence of diminishing returns to R&D. These issues have been studied extensively by Griliches, Hall and others (see Griliches 1984, 1989, 1990; Hall 1994). The main conclusion from these studies is that there are important but complex links between the benefits of patents, R&D and innovation over time. These links are possible to study and much remains to be done.

The propensity to utilize the patent system, that is to prefer to patent an invention in face of alternatives, has attracted a number of empirical studies, see for example Scherer (1983) and Arundel and Kabla (1998).

The well-known Yale study by Levin, Nelson and others (see Levin 1986; Levin et al. 1987; Klevorick et al. 1995) investigated, through a survey of hundreds of R&D managers in more than 100 industries, the strong sector-specific variations in appropriability conditions and the role of patents in different industrial sectors. Briefly expressed, markets are imperfect and so are patents and patent systems. Thus, innovations will continue to appear even without patents, and patents will not be sufficient to recap the benefits from innovation in general. Regarding the economic value of patents, much important work has been done by Scherer; see for example Scherer (1998) and Harhoff et al.

(1997). The distribution of patent values is generally found to be very skew, sometimes possessing no finite mean and variance.

As mentioned, the empirical studies of patents have grown rapidly since the 1980s. Several factors have spurred this growth. The increased availability of large, electronic data bases concerning patents and R&D and the availability of computers have enabled and lowered the cost of many types of analyses. As is well known to investigators (for example, Schmookler), a manual analysis of the rich and varied mass of patent documents is a Herculean task. Moreover, increased international technology-based competition and the emergence of a pro-patent era in the 1980s have generally spurred the interest in patents among both practitioners and scholars.

3.6 ECONOMIC THEORY OF IP AND PATENTS

One cannot argue the relative merits or demerits of various features of the patent system without analyzing the social costs and benefits involved. This is economic analysis and no amount of legal training or engineering experience or technological research will equip the 'expert' for it. Yet, most of the economic theories enunciated in discussions about patent reform have come from lawyers, engineers and technical experts with occasional contributions from business executives. (Fritz Machlup, in Foreword to Penrose 1951, pp. vii–viii)

The patent system is much older than any formalized theories and models specifically related to patents. Theory has certainly lagged behind practice in so far as patents are concerned. It is interesting to observe how many of the significant ideas and problems with patents were experienced in Renaissance Venice, while it took the development of neoclassical microeconomic theory after World War II for significant theoretical achievements to be made regarding patents.

Seminal theoretical works include Arrow (1962) and Nordhaus (1969), with a geometric interpretation by Scherer (1972). These works all use neoclassical theory and tools. Some modelling in this spirit will be illustrated below in this section.

To put the subsequent illustrations in context, it must be recalled that the major problem to be addressed by a society that wants technical and industrial progress is the tendency to underinvest in R&D and its exploitation.[24] To correct for this tendency, incentives must be created for additional investment and its exploitation. This was as relevant a problem in Venice as it is in the various economies of today, and derives from the nature of valuable information being expensive to produce but, once generated, being cheap to reproduce (and imitate) by others. The problem can be attacked in many ways, of which setting up a patent system is one. Other ways are to use, for example, prizes, grants, contracts or R&D tax deductions, as mentioned. All these methods have their advantages and disadvantages. The first task for economic analysis, then, is to compare a patent system with its alternatives.[25] A patent system may also come in many varieties with many decision variables for inventor firms and policy-makers. Therefore a second task for analysis is how to design a specific system. Third, there are other types of IPRs besides patents and these types also come in many varieties. Below we shall focus mainly on patents but will also make comparisons to other types of IPRs.

Let us first look at the situation of a new invention from the point of view of an inventor or, rather, the firm developing the invention (the innovator). Figure 3.1, above, shows the standard cash-flow picture of a new product or a product with a new cost-saving process. In fact the picture applies to any product or service, including cultural items such as books, films, records and concerts, as long as it generates cash flows on a market and comprises some element of investment. Thus we shall refer in the sequel to any of these items as a product.

The new product is being developed during a certain period of time, which we can call time to market or innovation time and has a corresponding market lifetime. During the market lifetime it is subjected to price competition, which typically is weak at an early stage and stronger at a later stage (thereafter it can possibly be weakened again). Competition is weaker at an early stage due to delays in effective imitation.

These imitation delays or lags have various sources. They may be due to information and decision lags, entry barriers, imitation difficulties, and competitive disadvantages in general. In particular the innovator's property rights, physical as well as intellectual, may be used by the innovator to hinder imitation, since private property by its very nature confers rights on the property holder to exclude others from using the property. Thus, any resource subjected to private property (for example, a mine, a plant site or a store location) has an intrinsic monopolistic element deriving from the excludability associated with the property in question. When private property is used as an input to a production process or in a business context at large, it provides a certain type of input monopoly. Albeit narrow, this input monopoly position can be used to build up a monopoly position on the output product market or at least weaken imitation-based price competition on that market. In this sense, any private property serves as a source of potential competitive advantage. In particular, intellectual property, including secrets as well as patents, designs or copyrights, can be used by the innovator during a limited time to weaken competition (or strengthen the innovators' own competitive advantage). For patents, designs and copyrights, the time limit is fixed by law and known to the players; for secrets, time runs out when the secret is revealed or independently discovered, and thus the time limit is highly uncertain. In addition, information about the spread of certain secret information may be kept secret in turn. This is what we can call 'second-order secrets'. Thus, a secret-holder sometimes may not know if his or her secret is out or not, which poses an additional uncertainty about its duration.

Trademarks are also used to weaken competition, since a well-known trademark induces a customer preference in a purchasing situation, and the exact way this is done cannot be imitated. However, a trademark does not have a definite lifetime.

Thus we can view the innovator's IP as giving rise to a temporary competitive advantage, limited to an early stage of the product's market lifetime. This competitive advantage is used to generate a stream of operating profits (that is, profits before depreciation, financial costs and taxes). The operating profits may derive from product inventions, cost-reducing process inventions or through other advantages in production and marketing, for example, acquired through learning-by-doing rather than through organized R&D. Learning advantages in turn may be viewed as deriving from minor, cumulative improvements corresponding to minor inventions, guarded as secrets, and thus constituting IP as well.

Now let us turn to some formalized illustrations. The following variables and notation will be used below:

c = cost (total variable cost $c = c(q)$)
p = price
q = quantity sold at price p, that is, the demand function is $q(p)$ with an inverse demand function $p(q)$
r = discount rate
S = sales = $p \cdot q$
π = innovator's operating profit = $p \cdot q - c(q)$
R = R&D investment
P = production investment expenditures
M = marketing investment expenditures
I = total investment expenditures = $R + P + M$
t = time (considered continuous)
V = total value discounted to time $t = 0$, that is, present value
D = discounting operator (continuous), discounting to time $t = 0$
E = expectation operator
T = technical performance variable
L = length of period of patent or IP protection
$\hat{L}$ = maximum L as offered by law
k, α are constants
I, II, III are time intervals $[0, t_1)$, $[t_1, t_2)$, and $[t_2, \infty)$ corresponding to stages of competition, where t_1 is the market introduction time point and t_2 is the time point when IP protection ceases. (Note that since there is a time delay for an invention to reach the market, L is normally larger than $t_2 - t_1$, which in turn is normally larger than zero.)

All variables (except V, L) are functions of time in the general case, in which cash-flow variables correspond to instantaneous cash-flow intensities, that is, cash flows per unit of time.

The innovator's total discounted value V derived from a new product or process invention is then:

$$V = \int_0^\infty \pi(t)e^{-rt}dt - \int_0^\infty I(t)e^{-rt}dt \qquad (3.1)$$

If $\pi(t)$ is totally dependent upon IP protection effective in the time interval $[t_1, t_2]$ then:

$$V = \int_{t_1}^{t_2} \pi(t)e^{-rt}dt - DI \qquad (3.2)$$

Now, the profit function over time $\pi(t)$ can assume different shapes. In the simplest case π is a positive constant during a period $[0, L]$ and zero otherwise, in which case:

$$V = \pi \cdot \frac{1}{r}\left(1 - e^{-rL}\right) - DI \qquad (3.3)$$

Simple rules of thumb for valuing a patent could then be derived under these very restrictive assumptions. For example, if a patent allows an innovator to keep a sales margin of 15 per cent on roughly stable sales due to enhanced product performance and/or cost savings from the invention during ten years with a discount rate of 7 per cent, then the gross value of the patent (apart from discounted investments DI) is:

$$0.15 \cdot (1/0.07) \cdot (1 - e^{-0.7}) = 10.8\% \text{ of the total ten-year sales.}$$

Numerous extensions and variations are now possible. To be able to aid R&D investment decisions in principle, the dependence of π upon R must be specified. This could be done by introducing a function $T = T(R)$, a customer utility function $U = U(T)$ and a T-specific cost function $c = c(q,T)$. (The function $T(R)$ is sometimes called an effort curve.) Considerations of T could also be bypassed by linking c directly to R through specifying $c = c(q,R)$ instead.[26] This is the approach of Nordhaus (1969), who introduces an 'invention possibility function' for constant unit costs c (that is, $c(q) = c \cdot q$), being reduced from c_0 to c_1 by a cost-reducing patented invention derived from spending in total R on cost-reducing R&D, according to

$$c_1 = c_0(1 - kR^\alpha); \; k > 0, \; \alpha \in (0,1), \; R \geq 0, \; c_1 > 0 \tag{3.4}$$

Assuming, for example, that the patent (or patent portfolio) offers a perfect monopoly on the product market during a period of length L (stage II) and perfect competition before (stage I) and after (stage III) this period, Nordhaus derived conditions for the innovator's optimal spending on R, regardless of whether the innovator chooses to license out the invention fully or chooses to go alone.[27]

Assume moreover that the invention is sufficiently minor so that the pre-invention price $p = c_0$ and output q_0 remain the same during stages I and II. In stage III competition forces the price to fall to post-invention cost c_1 with a corresponding expansion of output from $q(c_0) = q_0$ to $q(c_1) = q_1$. Then in the Nordhaus type of modelling:

$\pi(\mathrm{I}) = \pi(\mathrm{III}) = 0$ (that is, $\pi(t) = 0$ for $t \in$ I, III)
$\pi(\mathrm{II}) = q_0(c_0 - c_1)$ for $t \in$ II $= [t_1, t_2)$
$V = \pi \cdot (1/r)(e^{-rt_1} - e^{-rt_2}) - DI$

Putting $DI = R$ and inserting c_1 according to (3.4) gives:

$$V = q_0 c_0 kR^\alpha (e^{-rt_1} - e^{-rt_2})/r - R \tag{3.5}$$

Putting $\partial V/\partial R = 0$ gives the necessary condition for any optimal R&D investment $\hat{R} > 0$:

$$\hat{R} = (\alpha q_0 c_0 k \, (e^{-rt_1} - e^{-rt_2})/r)^{1/(1-\alpha)} \tag{3.6}$$

Since $\alpha \in (0, 1)$ implies $\partial^2 V/\partial R^2 < 0$ for $R > 0$, $\hat{R}$ is in fact optimal and maximizes V if $V(\hat{R}) > 0$. This means that, for example, the length of IP protection cannot be too short in order to generate positive optimal investments in R&D.[28]

As an illustration, we can calculate the sensitivity of the theoretically optimal R&D investments to changes in the maximal patent lifetime. Assume therefore that the maximal patent lifetime is changed from 20 to 23 years. Assume moreover that $r = 0.1$ and $\alpha = \frac{1}{2}$. Then

$$\hat{R} \, (t_2 = t_1 + 23) / \hat{R} \, (t_2 = t_1 + 20) = [(1 - e^{-2.3}) / (1 - e^{-2.0})]^2 = 1.083$$

Thus lengthening the maximal possible patent protection time from 20 to 23 years induces companies in this model to spend 8.3 per cent more on R&D. If the change is instead from 17 to 20 years, the corresponding R&D increase is 11.9 per cent. A decrease from 20 to 10 years would decrease R&D by 46.6 per cent.[29]

So far the Nordhaus type of modelling has given the optimal response to patent or IP protection of the inventor or the inventing firm in terms of its investments in R&D. Now comes the question: what is the optimal patent system from society's point of view? The social planner or policy-maker has a wide variety of policy variables, such as:

1. Maximal length of patent (design, copyright) protection. (However, length of secrecy protection has not been considered as being at the policy-maker's disposal, although this is possible.)
2. Starting point in time for the protection period.
3. Minimal level of inventive step or non-obviousness of an invention or state-of-art advance.
4. Maximal scope of patent protection in terms of coverage.
5. Compulsory licensing arrangements.
6. Patenting fees.
7. To whom to grant IP protection.
8. For what to grant patent protection.

Nordhaus (1969) focuses on society's optimal, maximal length of a patent protection period. In order to illustrate how the optimal $\hat{L}$ can be calculated in a simple case, assume first a general (but declining) demand function $p(q)$ and that the invention (or innovation) reduces a constant marginal cost from c_0 to c_1 as above and as shown in Figure 3.11. The invention is minor in the sense that pre-invention marginal cost is lower than the monopolistic price for the invention. Further, assume that R occurs instantaneously at $t = 0$ and put $t_1 = 0$ and $t_2 = L$.

The benefit to society of the invention then equals the producer net surplus, which is realized as the innovator's discounted value $V(\hat{R})$ of the profit stream in stage II (assuming R&D pays off at all) plus the additional consumer surplus V^c generated in stage III by the cost savings from the invention. Then (assuming the same discount rate for consumers and producers):

$$V^c = \int_L^\infty q_0(c_0 - c_1)e^{-rt}dt + \int_L^\infty \left(\int_{q_0}^{q_1} (p(q) - c_1)dq \right) e^{-rt}dt \qquad (3.7)$$

The second term then corresponds to the dead-weight loss in stage II being turned into consumer surplus in stage III when competition forces price down to c_1.

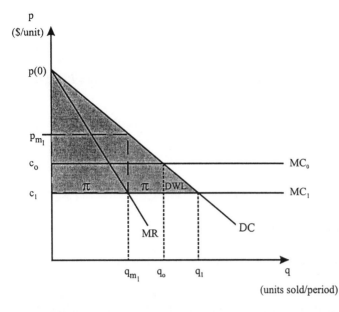

Legend:

MC	Marginal cost, being reduced from c_0 to c_1 by the innovation
MR	Marginal revenue
DC	Demand curve corresponding to $p = p(q) = -aq+b; a,b>0$
p	Price per unit
p_m	Monopolistic price for the innovation (impossible to charge in this case since it exceeds c_0)
p_c	Competitive price $=$ MC
q	Quantity sold per period. $q=q(p)$
q_c	Quantity sold under competitive pricing $=$ q_0 and q_1, corresponding to c_0 and c_1
q_m	Quantity sold under monopolistic pricing
π	Producer (gross) surplus per period under patent protection$= q_0(c_0 - c_1)$
DWL	Dead-weight loss $= \frac{1}{2}(q_1 - q_0)(c_0 - c_1)$, being lost to consumers under patent protection, allowing price to remain at c_0
π+DWL	Consumer surplus per period after patent expiration and price drop to c_1

Figure 3.11   Value of patent protection of an innovation (simple case of a minor cost-reducing innovation with linear demand curve and constant marginal cost)

Now for $q(p)$ linear in p:

$$V^c = (c_0 - c_1)(q_0 + q_1) e^{-rL} / 2r \qquad (3.8)$$

The producer's (innovator's) net surplus V^p, when $t_1 = 0$ and $t_2 = L$ and $R = \hat{R}$ (from (3.5)), is:

$$V^p = q_0 c_0 k \hat{R}^\alpha (1 - e^{-rL}) / r - \hat{R} \qquad (3.9)$$

where (from (3.6)):

$$\hat{R} = (\alpha q_0 c_0 k (1 - e^{-rL})/r)^{1/(1-\alpha)} \qquad (3.10)$$

Thus (after some simplification):

$$V^p = [\alpha q_0 c_0 k (1 - e^{-rL})/r]^{1/(1-\alpha)} (\alpha^{-1} - 1) = \hat{R}(1/\alpha - 1) \qquad (3.11)$$

Thus total net surplus or welfare to society $V^s = V^c + V^p$ is a function in L explicitly. The first-order necessary condition for any $L = \hat{L} > 0$ to maximize V^s is then given by $\partial V^s/\partial L = 0$, so that a marginal change of $\hat{L}$ gives equal but opposing changes in discounted consumer and producer net surplus, that is, at $\hat{L}$ a balancing trade-off is made between the innovator and the rest of society.

The calculation of $\hat{L}$ is in the general case not a straightforward sequence of algebraic operations. It turns out that with $p = -aq + b$ (see Nordhaus 1969, p. 78):

$$\hat{L} = -\frac{1}{r} \cdot \ln\left(1 - \left[\frac{c_0 k \hat{R}(\hat{L})^\alpha + aq_0}{c_0 k \hat{R}(\hat{L})^\alpha \cdot (\alpha+1)/2\alpha + aq_0}\right]\right) \qquad (3.12)$$

Using this expression one can analyse how $\hat{L}$ varies with the different relevant parameters.

However, a patent system does not come free of charge to society, so the costs to society for installing and operating a patent system should also be considered in addition to consumer and producer surplus. These costs include, first, the direct costs for setting up and operating patent offices and a system for enforcement of patent laws (such as courts). Second, there are the direct costs of the patenting operations for the inventors and inventor firms. These costs are neglected in the equations above but may amount to several per cent of R&D costs. Third, there are various indirect costs as well as benefits, as shown in Table 3.3 above.

Among the latter are the costs for the patent holder and the corresponding benefits to other inventors from the stipulated disclosure of information in return for patent rights. For a single patent these costs and benefits might be neglected (as in the Nordhaus model), but in total they are considerable. Just as a firm might decide that the optimal level of R&D investment is to conduct no R&D at all, the IP policy-maker might decide that the best policy is to have no patent system at all, even if there is a positive length of patent protection time that gives a local maximum to V^s, the total discounted net surplus to society.

One can analyse various other cases of inventions, patent protection and consumer and producer behaviour both from the point of view of the inventor firm and the patent policy-maker. Some examples of such cases are given below to put the preceding analysis in context.

1. Major output-expanding inventions (in his original work Nordhaus also analysed cost-reducing major inventions, which he called 'drastic' inventions).
2. Price discrimination by the patent holder.
3. Compulsory licensing (see, for example, Scherer 1977 and Tandon 1982 for economic analysis as well as Julian-Arnold 1992 and Merges 1996 for legal perspectives) and optimal licensing (see, for example, Gallini and Winter 1985; Shepard 1987; Kamien et al. 1992).
4. Patent races in stage I (see, for example, Tirole 1988).
5. Market structures in stages I and III other than perfect competition.
6. Market structures other than perfect monopoly in stage II (see, for example, DeBrock 1985).
7. Different shapes of market responses to a new product.
8. Different price and output responses when patent protection ceases.
9. Sequences of patents and innovations over time (see in particular works by Scotchmer, for example, Scotchmer 1991; Green and Scotchmer 1995; also Gallini 1992).
10. Clusters of interdependent patents and innovations.
11. Welfare distribution considerations by differentiating the weights put on producer and consumer surpluses.
12. Patent term restorations making up for increases in R&D time or time to market (see, for example, Grabowski and Vernon 1986).
13. Patent renewal fees (see, for example, Pakes 1986; Cornelli and Schankerman 1995).
14. Optimal breadth or scope of a patent (see, for example, Klemperer 1990, Gallini 1992 and Gilbert and Shapiro 1990 for optimization models, the latter also considering jointly optimal breadth and length of a patent for a given size of the resulting reward to the inventor. For a thorough qualitative analysis, see Merges and Nelson 1990).

15. Patent litigation (see, for example, Meurer 1989).
16. Patent valuation (see, for example, Schankermann 1989).

As can easily be imagined regarding technical inventions, the variety of behaviours and firm strategies, including both uses and abuses, which may be legally and economically inventive as well, make any comprehensive analysis exceedingly complex. As mentioned in the beginning of this section, practice has run ahead of theory as far as patents and IP are concerned. Considering the variety of firm behaviours and patent strategies exposed in the subsequent chapters, it is a safe bet to say that practice will continue to be ahead of theory for a long time, if not for ever. This is not a reason for abandoning formal economic analysis altogether. On the contrary, in order for theory and practice to go hand in hand (though sometimes requiring long arms), theory has to catch up further. Apart from giving approximate guidelines in specific situations, one of several additional advantages of such analysis is that it exposes relevant assumptions and conditions, which in principle can be used to predict further practices before they arise.

A few model variants from the inventor firm's point of view will finally be outlined. First consider a genuine product invention with perfect patent protection. As the product diffuses on the market, the firm's sales S build up with a stream of operating profits π. These profits are then gradually competed away, as IP protection weakens and competition builds up, for example, through successful invent-around activities, secrecy leakages and expiration of patents.

Now assume that π is a constant fraction ρ of sales S, that is, $\pi = \rho S$, as in the case where the product invention is licensed out with a constant royalty rate $\rho \cdot 100$ per cent, and let $S(t)$ correspond to a common pattern for diffusion and sales growth of innovations, for example, $S(t) = \hat{S}(1 - e^{-\lambda t})$ where $\lambda > 0$ is a variable determining the rate of diffusion and $\hat{S}$ is maximum sales. λ can be interpreted as the instantaneous probability that a consumer learns about the new product and adopts it. λ can be influenced by marketing investments and in particular by advertising, including the build-up of a trademark.

Assume, moreover, that ρ drops to zero after a period of L years of effective IP protection on the market, or the licence contract expires after L years. (A gradual decline of ρ and reduction of sales after L years can also be modelled, but is left aside here.) Then:

$$V = \int_0^L \rho S(t) e^{-rt} dt - DI = (1/r) \cdot \rho \hat{S}(1 - e^{-rL}) - \frac{1}{\lambda + r} \rho \hat{S}(1 - e^{-(\lambda + r)L}) - DI$$

$$(3.13)$$

The second term is a loss of discounted profits due to the limited market-penetration rate λ (in the Nordhaus type of modelling $\lambda = \infty$).

Now with a specification of how the market-penetration rate λ depends upon marketing investments M, the optimal M can be found, just as the optimal R can be determined from assuming an invention possibility function or an effort curve. Learning-curve reductions in variable unit costs could also be introduced into the model, which would correspond to a progressive royalty rate ρ.

Finally the value of secrets could be calculated. Suppose for simplicity that a cost-reducing invention, like the one in the Nordhaus model above, is guarded by a secret instead of a patent. The secret leaks out or diffuses in a manner that makes the secret-protection time uncertain. Thus, assume L is a random variable, for example, exponentially distributed with parameter $\mu > 0$, that is, the probability $P(L \leq x) = 1 - e^{-\mu x}$ and the expected value $E(L) = 1/\mu$. Thus, using (3.3), the expected discounted value of the secret (disregarding the investments as already sunk at the time of evaluation of the secret) is:

$$E(V) = \pi/r \cdot [1 - \mu/(\mu + r)] = \pi/(\mu + r) \qquad (3.14)$$

This is equivalent to discounting with an added risk premium to the discount rate. When $\mu \to 0$, the expected lifetime of the secret goes to infinity and $E(V)$ approaches π/r which equals the value of a patent with infinite lifetime. Now μ could be influenced by technology intelligence efforts made on both the innovator and the imitator sides (see Chapter 7). If the innovator's investment in secrecy protection is Y, one simple conceivable specification is $\mu = 1/(aY + b)$, where a and b are parameters, reflecting, for example, secrecy breaking efforts among competitors. If the product invention is covered by a patent and its process by a secret and the secret is still in force when the patent expires (an event with probability $e^{-\mu\hat{L}}$ of occurrence), its expected discounted value at time $t = \hat{L}$, conditional upon this event, is still $\pi / (\mu + r)$. Thus a secret under these assumptions, which is an 'exponentially lived secret' (or a secret without 'ageing'), does not lose its value over time as long as the secret is not lost. Hence, an exponentially lived trade secret should not be depreciated. At the time the invention is made ($t = 0$) and patent protection with length $\hat{L}$ starts to cover the product and secrecy protection covers the process, the total expected discounted value to the inventor firm of the total protection is:

$$EV = EV^{pat} + EV^{sec} - EDI \qquad (3.15)$$

The value of the patent V^{pat} can be calculated as earlier, and it can be assumed to be unaffected by the secrecy protection. The secrecy, on the other hand, has a value only in so far as it gives additional protection after the patent has expired. Thus

$$EV^{sec} = E[V^{sec} \mid L > \hat{L}] \cdot P(L > \hat{L}) = (\pi \cdot e^{-\mu\hat{L}} / (\mu + r)) \cdot e^{-r\hat{L}} \qquad (3.16)$$

The value of both patents, trade secrets and trademarks may be calculated in principle in simple cases by using this modelling approach. Copyrights and utility models ('petty patents', *Gebrauchsmuster*) can also be treated in this way in principle.

In summation, this section has illustrated, although briefly, how the economic value of the various IPRs can be calculated in principle in simple cases, and also how their combined value through 'multiprotection' (see Chapter 7) can be calculated, at least in simple cases.

3.7   SUMMARY AND CONCLUSIONS

A general framework for analysing patents and intellectual property has been presented as a textbook introduction to the topic. (A complementary framework for analysing patent information will be described in Chapter 9.) Innovations are fundamental not only to economic development but to cultural development at large. Various types of innovations in general were described (for example, technological, managerial, financial and legal) together with concepts (for example, invention, innovation and diffusion) and models related more specifically to technological innovations. Thus the product life-cycle model, the interactive innovation model and the buyer/seller-diffusion model were described.

In order to achieve economic development in a market economy it is crucial to ensure an adequate rate of innovation with an adequate rate of buyer diffusion producing an adequate rate of returns to innovators, buyers and society at large. Imitation in the form of seller diffusion and the resulting competition may hamper the rate of innovation, since innovators then may not be able to capture sufficient returns to cover their investments in innovation. At the same time seller diffusion may increase buyer diffusion and vice versa so that the resulting rate of returns to buyers and society for a given innovation may increase. Thus there is a problem when balancing or trading off the static efficiency for a given innovation and the dynamic efficiency for a stream of innovations. The patent system has been designed as an instrument or institution to deal with this balancing problem by offering restricted monopoly rights as an incentive to the innovator. The innovator can use these rights in turn to restrict seller diffusion and competition or to sell licences on the patented technology in order to make sufficient profits (capture sufficient returns).

The chapter described the nature and functioning of the patent system and dealt with the issue of who can patent what as well as why, when, where and how to patent from the point of view of an individual or a company. A simple, qualitative model for the valuation and pricing of patents and licences was presented. The pros and cons of a patent system from society's point of view were then discussed.

The chapter finally gave an overview of the growing literature on patents as well as an overview of the evolving economic theory of patents and IP. Some examples of economic modelling were also presented.

NOTES

1. In other words, economic success (or break-even) occurs when the total revenues exceed the total expenditures, compounded with the relevant rate of interest.
2. For an overview of PLC modelling, see Porter (1980).There is also a so-called international product life-cycle model, originated by Vernon (1966), which refers to different stages in terms of domestic or foreign location of production and markets. Briefly stated, the stages following upon each other are (i) domestic production for home market; (ii) domestic production for foreign markets; (iii) foreign production for foreign markets; (iv) foreign production for home market. This model has been criticized by various authors and was later revised by Vernon, see, for example, Cantwell (1989).
3. The so-called 'linear model of innovation' usually refers only to the case where innovations originate in S&T and then are developed, produced and marketed sequentially. This model, the origins of which may have been influenced by scientists seeking government support after World War II (see Bush 1945), has been strongly criticized; see, for example, Schon (1967), de Solla Price (1974), Kline and Rosenberg (1986), with an interactive type of model called the 'chain-linked model', and Rosenberg (1994). Another view, articulated early on by Schmookler (1966), is that successful innovations start from recognition of a market need (or demand pull rather than technology push). See further Phillips (1971), Mowery and Rosenberg (1979), Freeman et al. (1982) and Rosenberg (1994) for good reviews. As seen from Figure 3.4 the two linear views – technology push versus demand pull – pertain to what type of initial activity or institution constitutes the (major) source of innovations, while the view distinguishing between linear and interactive (non-linear) innovation pertains to the order, if any, of subsequent activities in the innovation process. Authors like Schon, Rosenberg and Kline have also criticized the view that activities have to follow upon each other in a neat sequential manner in an innovation process. The practice of concurrent engineering emerging in the 1980s has also shown the possibilities of compressing the innovation process through conducting activities more in parallel, thereby shortening the time to market (see further Chapter 6). For some further picturing of the innovation process see Rosenbloom (1985) and Imai et al. (1985).
4. Product innovation generally refers to a product that is new to the market, and therefore also new to the company, while product development in general refers to products that are new to the company but may not necessarily be product innovations. The line between what is new and what is not is difficult to draw.
5. Such discoveries are also called serendipities, that is, discoveries made while searching for something else.
6. There are similar definitions for a US patent as well as for a Japanese patent.
7. Extended protection may be granted for medicines covered by a patent if the period of registration for the drug consumed excessive time. (In Europe this legal title is called 'Supplementary Protection Certificate' (SPC).)
8. In other words, any technical invention that is industrially applicable, not known beforehand and not obvious is patentable. All these three requirements create legal debate, for example, over what is meant by technical. Also note that there is only a very weak requirement for usefulness. The requirement for level of invention is fairly low in practice, especially in certain countries. The novelty requirement could be seen as strong.
9. Neither living matter, such as genetically engineered plants or animals, nor computer codes in the form of strings of symbols could readily be considered technical inventions with a narrow interpretation of 'technical'. See Barton (1993) and Samuelson (1993).

10. Criteria for assessing the proper scope of a patent are not easily established. See Merges and Nelson (1990), NRC (1993) and Barton (1995).
11. For example, an application at the EPO essentially allows for the designation of all industrialized countries of western Europe for protection. However, on average only about seven countries are designated in European applications.
12. If Italian inventors do the inventive R&D work, the patent application will still be considered to be of Italian origin, although it may be written and filed in Germany.
13. Some major steps towards international cooperation and harmonization are noteworthy, however; in particular, the Paris Convention of 1883 and the implementation of PCT and EPC in 1978 (see Table 2.2).
14. There are other ways as well, for example, through prizes and contracts (see Wright 1983 for a theoretical analysis), or through tax deduction schemes (see Mansfield 1985 for an empirical analysis). Each way has a particular set of advantages and disadvantages and there is no way that is clearly recognized as superior overall. Usually, several ways are used at the same time in the hope that they complement each other.
15. The full cost of the patent system can be seen as a kind of large transaction cost for society, that is, a cost for improving and using market mechanisms in society.
16. This is the so-called 'information paradox' (Arrow 1962).
17. The burden of proof could, of course, be shifted to the other party, but to prove that one did know something at a previous time is also difficult in general. (See also Chapter 2.)
18. Patent systems do differ in their design of what and when to disclose to whom, and numerous variants are conceivable, even a system in which secrets are filed and registered and open only to authorized agencies in case of disputes. Such a non-public 'patent' system does not even have to be run by the state. However, dissemination of technical information would not be encouraged and infringement would be costly to police.
19. Not entirely, however, since a good portion of licence agreements are not pure patent licences, but are a mixture of complementary patent and know-how licences. In addition, there are pure know-how licences. (See also Anton and Yao 1994.)
20. Illuminating interpretations and some critique of Arrow (1962) are given in Cheung (1986) and Winter (1989).
21. Other subsequent works have argued that overinvestment in R&D may very well accrue, due to various factors, for example the tendency for firms to overinvest in R&D in order to win patent races and 'fish in common pools' of technological opportunities. See, for example, Dasgupta and Stiglitz (1980) and Dasgupta (1988). For an empirical and rather inconclusive work on this issue in pharmaceutical industry, see Cockburn and Henderson (1994).
22. Another way is through publicly financed R&D. For a theoretical analysis of patents versus alternative incentives like prizes and contracts, see Wright (1983).
23. Another expression for this type of right is 'licence to hunt' (or fish).
24. Overinvestment in R&D may of course occur as well, but it has seldom been perceived as the dominant tendency, especially not for countries trying to catch up technologically, for which purpose the patent system has historically often been used.
25. This is done in Wright (1983).
26. Here, as is common, the symbols for variables and functions are used with differing connotations. Thus, the function c is not the same in the cases $c(q)$, $c(q, T)$, and $c(q, R)$, but no misunderstandings are likely to derive from this convenient practice.
27. This latter alternative typically requires more investments P and M in production and marketing. Nordhaus disregards these; as long as they are independent of the optimizing variable R, it is not essential for the way the analysis is done.
28. It might of course happen, depending upon the coefficients in (3.5), that it does not pay at all to do research, that is, V is negative for any positive R, in which case the optimal solution is $R = V = 0$.
29. This simple calculation actually gives results that are of the same magnitude as the empirical results reported in Table 5.11 in Chapter 5. For example, the chemical companies (for which patents have traditionally meant most) in Japan reported in 1992 they would increase their R&D spending by 8.5 per cent in response to an increase of patent protection time of three years.

4. The technology-based firm: a general framework

CHAPTER CONTENTS

4.1 CHAPTER OUTLINE

The preceding chapter described intellectual property in general and patents in particular and put IP and the patent system in the context of technology-based innovations and their diffusion on a market. This chapter will put IP in the context of a firm, its resources and its intellectual (or immaterial) capital (IC). A firm's IC incorporates not only its IPR, but also its relations and competencies, including its technological capabilities. A special type of IC firm, the technology-based firm (TBF) is of particular interest here, and a general framework for such a firm is presented. The presentation is somewhat theoretical and compressed, and the reader interested in more empirical discussions can skip large parts of this chapter. However, it gives a framework for the following chapters regarding the resource structure of a company, the acquisition and exploitation of technology as a resource, and various corporate, technology and IP strategies. The term 'firm' will be used as it is commonly used in theories of the firm, and it is synonymous here with company, corporation and enterprise.

Chapter 1 described the basic notion of IC and its growing importance in an increasingly knowledge-based society. The emergence of the IC firm, with the TBF as a special but important case, is a reflection of this general long-run development, stretching over centuries. Many economic notions have centred around physical (land, capital) and manual (labour) human resources.[1] However, it may be argued that intellectual resources are becoming the most important and will remain so in the future, both in terms of expenditure and as a source of returns and wealth. For example, in large as well as small TBFs 'soft' investments in IC (for example, in R&D, education, training) nowadays often exceed 'hard' investments (such as machinery and buildings). The growing value of firm-specific competencies, patents, trademarks, goodwill and so on also often make the firm's intangible assets more valuable than its tangible assets, although the valuations are difficult to calculate and compare, as described in Chapter 1. The discrepancy between traditional physically oriented economic notions and the rise of IC creates problems, for example in accounting.[2] Thus the IPR system then also serves an important role as a means of 'tangibilizing' and codifying IC for purposes of economic analysis and accounting as well as for management. Intellectual property management in general assumes a much wider and more important role in the context of the rising IC firm (see further Chapter 8).

The TBFs as a group also become increasingly important as generators and accumulators of the world's technology and IC. The large TBFs typically become multinational, multiproduct and multitechnology as a result of diversification. This chapter also describes the nature and role of technology diversification and technology management.

4.2   CO-EVOLUTION OF TECHNOLOGY AND THE FIRM

In the history of institutions the modern business firm is a fairly recent innovation (emerging in 19th-century Europe), preceded by far by institutions like the church, the farm, the university (emerging in 12th-century Italy), the bank (emerging in medieval Italy as well), the patent system and also by the modern nation-state.[3]

As an institutional species, the modern business firm in market economies has developed a remarkable viability and variety.[4] In the 20th century, larger and more diversified MNCs and multiproduct corporations (MPCs) have emerged, typically internalizing their teaching, R&D and banking functions while at the same time forging links with universities and banks. These latter institutions have in turn increasingly adopted organizational features from business firms in advanced countries.

4.2.1 Super-markets

The viability of the firm as an institution partly stems from its possibility to recombine resources with other firms on the stock market, that is, the market for corporate control or the market for firms. This type of market is in fact a kind of 'super-market' since it works as a selection mechanism ('selection mechanism' in the sense of Nelson and Winter 1977, 1982) of a higher order, speeding up both variety generation and selection.

4.2.2 Standard Markets

Second, the viability of a firm also stems from its ability to combine, cumulate, and recombine resources through markets for resources (inputs) and products (outputs) and the firm's ability rapidly to respond to business opportunities and threats. Such abilities are fostered by competition and the legal framework around a firm together with alerting signals provided by a system of accounting. This, however, may in turn produce monopolistic as well as myopic behaviour, both potential dysfunctions of the firm as an economic institution.

4.2.3 Sub-markets

A third basis for the viability of the firm stems from the development of governance structures and managerial capabilities. From a transaction-cost perspective the emergence of increasingly large-sized, diversified and internationalized corporations could be interpreted as a sign of increasingly lower governance or management cost on average, compared to market transaction costs. However, the modern firm has also increasingly learned to utilize internal 'sub-markets' in order to reduce governance cost and/or raise innovativeness (for example, through the divisionalized so-called M-form of organization), as well as having learned to link up with external partners in networks. Thus, the modern firm has developed into a quasi-integrated hybrid form of organization, still possessing a considerable source of central power, however, thereby distinguishing it from a mere network.

4.2.4　Science and Technology

A fourth part of the viability of the firm stems from the long-run evolution of S&T, including the scientific 'revolutions' during the Renaissance (introducing, for example, the method of systematic experimentation) and the Age of Enlightenment. The S&T evolution has continually generated new business opportunities and new types of consequential needs. At the same time, basic human needs related to a fundamentally different biological evolution have remained much the same.[5] An increasing range of business firms has then in one way or another (product- or process-wise) become reliant or based upon technology in exploiting business opportunities, thus giving rise to the TBF as a growing sub-species of the modern business firm.

There is no need to operationalize here, through some cut-off point, when a firm is technology-based and when it is not. However, it is important to spell out that the concept of technology is used here in the narrow sense of natural science and engineering or technical knowledge, thereby sticking to an old tradition according to Cantwell (1994). More specifically, this book will equate technology with a body of knowledge of techniques that falls into areas containing, in principle, patentable knowledge. Operationalization of technology, in this way, is immensely aided by the international patent system, which provides a method for classification that is in turn important for codification. In the same spirit, a technology could be defined as new if it is less than 20 years old (20 years being the maximal patent lifetime), and a unit of technological advance could be defined as the minimum level of invention required for patentability. Thus, the patent system also offers an operationalization of novelty as well as of the size of a novelty in the form of a simple metric norm. In general, the patent system is underutilized as a way of operationalizing technology. It is far from error-free, but it is the best at hand, generally speaking.

As technology (engineering knowledge) has become an economic engine in TBFs, these firms have collectively become an increasingly important source of technology.[6] Thereby, firm-based technology has increased, absolutely as well as relatively. Thus, the increasing importance of TBFs and firm-based technologies is a perfect example of virtuous[7] co-evolution of an expansionary economic institution and S&T knowledge, concurrently independent of biological evolution in general.[8]

4.3　A GENERAL VIEW OF THE FIRM

A firm is a multifaceted phenomenon which theoretically could be viewed in many ways – as a nexus of contracts, as a special type of network, as a substitute for market mechanisms, as a self-organizing system interacting with an environment, as an input/output production system (epitomized by the smoke-stack factory), as a bundle of resources and so on. These different views are complements rather than substitutes for each other, as they emphasize different aspects of a firm with its many forms – small/large, national/multinational, private/public, manufacturing/service and so on.

In general, a business firm can be viewed as a legally identified, dynamic human system, consisting of a set of heterogeneous resources in an institutional setting (defining property rights, for example). The firm has an interior and an exterior (or environment), and it has management and business ideas with a dynamic goal (or incentive) structure having commonalities for coordinating purposeful action. The interior interacts with the exterior in various ways, in particular through business transactions (economic exchange) on a market, which consists of a network of meetings between buyers and sellers. The business transactions are essentially exchanges of resources between the firm and its environment, typically production factors and products (in a wide sense, including any services) for money. A business is defined here as a set of business transactions, which is coherent in some sense in terms of resources, products and markets.

As the system evolves, resources are transformed as a result of interior operations or activities as well as through interaction with the exterior. In particular, resources are acquired and exploited through both interior operations and business transactions. To the extent that resources are acquired and exploited by the firm through business transactions, one can speak of them as inputs and outputs of the firm, respectively. However, resources could also be classified as inputs and outputs of a resource transformation process (production process in a wide sense) inside the firm, not necessarily directly linked to business transactions with the exterior.

The environment must be recognized explicitly, since it provides business opportunities without which the firm would atrophy. At the same time, a firm faces environmental challenges or threats and may go bankrupt or disappear through merger, acquisition or liquidation. This normally results from interaction with the environment, which thereby provides not only opportunities but also threats. The opportunities and threats in the environment are changing, partly influenced by the firm, partly beyond its influence. The influence depends on the firm's management and (other) resources, which in turn are influenced by the environment and its past, current and anticipated interaction with the firm. The major strategic task for management is to position the firm in the stream of opportunities and threats, while creating a desired resource structure that can generate adequate rents and that can also be transformed over time to meet new opportunities and threats.[9]

In an IC-based firm (IC firm), the resources and business transactions of the firm are oriented around some type(s) of intellectual capital to a decisive degree that could vary from 'pure' IC firms to hybrid IC firms. In particular for a TBF, being a special case of an IC firm, the elements of the firm are technology-oriented. Thus, technologies constitute a vital part of such a firm's resources. A substantial part of the technology-based firm's interactions with the environment are moreover influenced by internal and external technical and technological changes, opportunities as well as threats, and the corresponding part of the environment is technology-oriented and constitutes the firm's technological neighbourhood. Moreover, technology management is a vital part of management, and technology-oriented ideas and goals are a vital part of the technology-based firm's business ideas and goal structure, although typically aligned to economic goals.

There is not much new about the general view of the firm as a system, which is dynamic, self-organizing, resource-transforming, interacting, human, purposeful and so on.[10] It is when the structure of the resource set and its associated processes of acquisition and exploitation are specified that something new and useful can hopefully be achieved. The TBF is, then, a particularly interesting case for further analysis here. This analysis will be made next, or at least forwarded a bit.

4.4   THE RESOURCES OF A FIRM

4.4.1   General Resource Structure

The resource set is considered as the firm's capital (or capitalized assets), and is decomposable into physical, financial and immaterial (or intangible or intellectual) capital (IC). Immaterial capital plays a key role and encompasses both disembodied IC (including business ideas) and embodied IC, the latter in the form of relational capital and competencies (or capabilities) possessed by humans. Disembodied IC is partly protectable by IPR, including trade secret protection (whether weak or strong) of business ideas. Table 4.1 gives an overview of the resource categories used here, which in fact is one way (out of several) to present a categorical structure of assets on a balance sheet.

The capital structure (resource structure) differs across companies and sectors and may be used for constructing taxonomies of companies, for example, classifying them into raw material-based, IC-intensive, knowledge-based, technology-based and so on. The capital structure of a company also is reflected in its culture and management style. Thus, organizational features and management skills are differentiated across sectors (forestry, banking, pharmaceuticals and so on), and management as an asset acquires a certain specificity to other assets, as well as to the local environment. Such adaptations of resources give rise to specific complementarities and concomitant difficulties

Table 4.1 Resource categories of a firm[1]

Material (tangible)		Immaterial (intangible) (IC)[2]		
Physical capital	Financial capital	Intellectual property[3] (disembodied IC)	Goodwill and power in internal/external relations[4] among	Human (embodied) competence[5] (capital)
Natural resources	Liquid capital	Patents	Employees	Managerial
Raw materials	Bonds	Databases	Customers	Technological
Buildings	Shares	Know-how	Suppliers	Commercial
Machinery	Securities	Licences	Competitors	Financial
Work in progress	etc.	Trade secrets	Universities	Legal
Inventories		Trademarks	Investors	Manual
etc.		Designs	Interest organizations	etc.
		Software	Societies	
		Copyrights	etc.	
		Concessions		
		etc.		

Notes
1. At this level of analysis, concepts such as resource, asset and capital could be used interchangeably.
2. Exactly what IC should encompass is debatable, but it should definitely include IPR as well as human competence (or capital or capability) and goodwill. For simplicity, IC will here be taken to comprise all immaterial or intangible resources or assets, admittedly with some conceptual borderline problems. Thus 'intellectual' is used roughly synonymously with 'immaterial' meaning non-material. (As distinct from insignificant. Unfortunately, the term 'immaterial' in English means both non-material and non-significant.)

   Needless to say, there are large problems associated with the valuation of IC. This is a contemporary subject for accounting research. The problems are not insurmountable and there are several approaches being tried to take a fuller account of IC. The traditional balance sheet in double-entry accounting could be extended, of course, but it could also be complemented by separate IC balance sheets, essentially with non-consolidated multiple-value concepts. The latter is probably a more viable approach. If nothing else, various balance sheets could be used continually in internal accounting, as well as for valuing the entire firm in connection with an acquisition on the stock market. See further, for example, Kaplan and Norton (1996) and Edvinsson and Malone (1997).
3. Intellectual property comprises exclusive as well as non-exclusive IPR, which could be both registered and unregistered. The firm's know-how in the form of trade secrets (like business ideas and plans) is an important part of unregistered IPR. Disembodied data bases, organizational routines and 'orgware' (called 'structural capital' in Edvinsson and Malone 1997) also belong to this category.
4. It is possible to distinguish the category 'relational capital' (including, for example, trust and internal motivation) as well as 'organizational capital' (or 'capability') from IC. Here we rather use these categories as sub-categories of IC.
5. Several terms are usable and distinctions could be introduced but, at this level of analysis, terms such as competencies, capabilities, abilities, skills, knowledge, information and so on can be used (roughly) interchangeably. For an overview of such terms, see EC (1997). The original concept of human capital, pioneered by Becker (1993), pertains to individuals. The results produced by the human capital typically become the property of the company when it is disembodied, however. For example, inventions made by R&D personnel and any associated patents may be stipulated in the employment contract to be the company's property. The embodied human competence is part of the company's IC, controlled through employment contracts. Thus, it has to be looked upon as rented human capital or IC rather than human capital owned by the company.

of resources give rise to specific complementarities and concomitant difficulties in transferring and trading the resources separately.

4.4.2   Acquisition and Exploitation of Resources

A firm's resources are continually being acquired, combined and exploited in various ways, as simply illustrated in Figure 4.1. The processes by which resources are acquired and exploited (including processes for generation, combination, transformation, regeneration and recombination of resources) vary widely across companies and sectors, of course, and give rise to variations in economic performance, in turn affecting further acquisition of resources. Resources by themselves, moreover, have different intrinsic economic properties that make their acquisition and exploitation processes different from each other, just as their transformations could be characterized in economic terms in various ways. We shall distinguish between four general types of process-related economies involved: static and dynamic economies of scale (in the ordinary sense of declining average cost, with dynamic economies of scale also in a broad sense of learning and increasing returns), scope (in a broad sense of synergies), speed (advantages of absolute and relative pace of a process) and space (advantages of location). These different types of economies contribute to different extents to a firm's growth, diversification and internationalization.

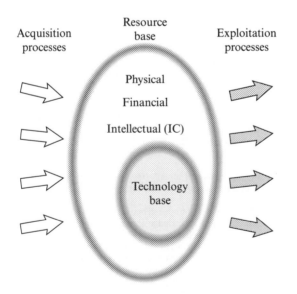

Figure 4.1   Acquisition and exploitation of a firm's resources

4.4.3 Management as a Meta-resource

It is not sufficient to view the firm simply as a set of resources without any reference to the way in which this set came into existence and evolved. In order to get a business firm started operationally (not only legally), there must be some business opportunity in the environment and a business idea in some person's mind of how to exploit this opportunity. The business idea, which may be treated as a piece of IC (for example, a patent or a trade secret), and the person as an entrepreneur (manager) constitute the initial necessary resources.

Managerial competence is also part of the firm's IC and is a decisive resource for reaping different types of economies for the firm's formation, sustained existence and development. Management[11] acquires, combines and exploits resources in response to business opportunities in the firm's exterior, thereby performing a control function (in a wide sense) in the system. In this sense, management could be viewed as a meta-resource. As such, managerial competence is a unique resource that is not substitutable in its entirety. The use of this resource takes time and is associated with a cost, which we can call management cost.[12] Such a concept of management cost can then be used as an alternative to a transaction cost concept when only two governance structures are used, that is, governance through markets and governance through hierarchies, and it can be used as a complementary analytical concept in a general case. What makes management so special as a resource is that it is a resource which is of unique decisiveness for any firm, as well as being 'self-sourcing' and 'self-allocating' in some sense. That is, management has to decide by itself (owners apart) how much effort to allocate to different tasks. This decision in turn requires some effort, and thus a theoretically difficult recursive problem of mental economy arises, usually resolved in practice by attending to time limits and corrective action rather than calculation.

However, management cannot be viewed as a meta-resource, incurring a resource cost, solely in a traditional, rational economic perspective. Various behavioural characteristics at individual and organizational level also have to be considered, just as is done in transaction cost theory (with bounded rationality and opportunism). To illustrate, an important behavioural characteristic among entrepreneurs can be called their 'entrepreneurial hubris', which gives them a bias towards overvaluing their IC, that is, their business idea and managerial competence.[13] This behavioural bias tends to keep the firm together as well as tending, within limits, to develop the firm, giving it more 'animal spirits' and 'sweat equity' in the pursuit of entrepreneurial goals. This type of bias among entrepreneurs, which in this sense is to be regarded as a managerial deficiency (or 'management failure'), increases corporate coherence and sustainability. (Although within limits, often there is too much entrepreneurial hubris, which risks disaster and dissolution of the firm.) Additional influence from any market failure, for example regarding market valuation of knowledge or complementarities, only serves to reinforce corporate coherence. Corporate coherence is thus explainable (at least partly) by reference to market failure or management failure (in the above sense) or both, each factor being in itself a favourable condition in principle for coherence, provided it is suitably biased.

Managerial competence is, moreover, to be regarded as a bounded, difficult to codify, non-protectable by patents, dynamically evolving, heterogeneous resource, especially in a large corporation with many sub-competencies pertaining to different managerial areas, tasks and functions (marketing management, financial management and so on). Technology management, then, is of particular concern in a TBF.

4.5.2 Knowledge Properties in General

Since knowledge (competence, capability) plays a key role as an IC resource, its intrinsic economic properties need to be recognized. This is often done, and there are various ways to characterize these properties, the characterization below being just one. However, it is important to make a fairly complete characterization of the properties of economic relevance in order to limit discussion of epistemological issues.

Thus, knowledge (competence) embodied in humans has the following characteristics:

1. It consumes much time and effort to acquire, especially at the individual level.
2. It consumes little time and effort to use, once acquired.
3. It improves and accumulates through use without deterioration (knowledge is limitlessly reusable or inexhaustible without wear, implying non-rivalry in consumption, and possibly with negative depreciation), but may deteriorate without use, creating a need for maintenance.
4. It is irreversibly transferable to others, if it is suitably codified and adapted to the recipients' knowledge, while still being kept by the knowledge-holder (and possibly even improved through 'learning by teaching'). Thus knowledge is cheaply cloned or reproduced if codified.
5. It is impossible to be dispossessed of, for an individual, and difficult to dispose of, that is, to unlearn or scrap. Machines are scrappable, but knowledge is not. Thus, knowledge advances are irreversible.
6. It often has strong complementarities with other knowledge.
7. It is easily rendered obsolete by new knowledge, appearing over time.
8. It is possible for an individual to keep in (almost) perfect control in form of secrecy but control is rapidly lost once secret knowledge is disclosed.
9. It is impossible to distribute equally among agents.

10. It is generally more expensive to generate than to regenerate or imitate (for example, knowing that something is possible, or exists, eases the search for it) and the generation of knowledge is uncertain and filled with surprises.

Compared to physical resources (capital), knowledge resources have some fundamentally different properties such as being inexhaustible, irreversibly producible and transferable (due to their dispossession impossibility) and reusable and reproducible at no or low cost. Economic and legal concepts and 'laws' for physical resources thereby could be expected to apply fundamentally differently for knowledge resources in some respects. (See Chapter 2.)

Acquisition and exploitation of knowledge are characterized by a large fixed initial investment cost with a small variable cost in application. The variable cost may even be negative sometimes due to the effect of 'learning by using'. The 'technical' lifetime of knowledge is infinite and, through learning by using, its depreciation is negative as long as it is not rendered obsolete by other knowledge.

Knowledge has strong economies of scale, both static and dynamic, and has increasing returns in use as long as it is not obsolete. Because of the scope of complementarities among its parts, knowledge also often has strong economies of scope. Moreover, it is not time-consuming to use, once acquired, and it is highly mobile if codified (although there may be multiple, incompatible codes). The codification (or disembodiment) process may be time- and effort-consuming, however, and the less the knowledge is codified (into one language), the more time and effort are needed to transfer it among humans.[14] Science and R&D are important in order to improve the codification process, but are by no means the only ways to do so.

Codification is important not only for facilitating transfer of knowledge *per se*, but also to enable its accumulation. Accumulation takes place within an individual and a group (through use of memories), among humans (through transfer) and between human generations, and results in a common pool or stock of knowledge.[15] This pool may partly be publicly available, and some knowledge may adopt a 'public good' characteristic.[16]

All in all, knowledge has properties that give it a great economic potential as a resource, even uniquely great in some respects. However, there are also properties that strongly limit the exploitation of this economic potential. As is well known, knowledge is difficult to value, price and sell. This is partly because knowledge is highly differentiated, which makes it difficult to match demand with a competitive supply, and partly because knowledge may easily be stolen with little chance of IPR enforcement (compare Arrow's information paradox, see Arrow 1962). New ideas and knowledge, which may be difficult to partially codify and specify without risking full disclosure, are especially vulnerable to theft and inadvertent diffusion. New ideas and knowledge can be kept perfectly secret by an individual for a 'cost-free eternity' (torture aside), but then the benefits from learning by using the new knowledge and complementarities from combining it with the knowledge of others are lost.

Thus, the intrinsic properties of knowledge create an economic potential, while at the same time they create limits to knowledge exploitation, especially to exploitation through market exchange mechanisms. This gives a natural rationale for having a system in an economy which stimulates knowledge exploitation without too many negative side-effects and costs. In fact, if a system could be designed that stimulates not only knowledge exploitation but also its acquisition, the system would be doubly effective. This is indeed what the IPR system is intended to accomplish regarding technical knowledge.

4.5   TECHNOLOGY AS A RESOURCE

4.5.1   Special Properties of Technology

Technology is a special kind of knowledge and as such has, in addition to the general properties of knowledge above, special properties, not all of which are shared by other types of knowledge. These properties include the following:

1. An artefact link, that is, technology is linked to artefacts (materials, products) or systems of artefacts and to the processes by which they are produced. These artefacts and their production processes are possible to characterize by physical design and performance parameters, which typically evolve over time as their underlying technologies develop. A certain technology may, moreover, be linked to many artefacts, that is, having a wide applicability or being multipurpose, just as a certain artefact may be linked to many specific technologies, that is, being multitechnological.
2. A science link, that is, technology is linked to natural sciences and their methodologies.
3. A relatively high degree of codifiability, partly stemming from the links to artefacts and the links to natural sciences, through the use of formulae in a formal language (mathematical, chemical, computational and so on), drawings, models, patent documents, textbooks and a scientifically-oriented language. Also the artefacts serve as codifiers of parts of technical knowledge, the embodied technology. However, in certain areas (for example, new and/or less science-based) there is an important tacit knowledge component as well. The tacit component is not static, since codification is a dynamic process, linked to R&D and scientification of technologies. On the other hand, R&D uncovers new technologies with, sometimes, a low degree of initial

codification. High codifiability facilitates the specification and transfer of technical knowledge as well as its accumulation.

4. A 'practical purpose' link, that is, technical knowledge is generated largely with the intention to have something working in practice or to achieve some level of technical performance.
5. Links to common globally-oriented systems for its operationalization (specification) and assessment, especially the patent system and the educational system but also systems for standardization, testing, regulation, classification and so on.

An implication of these idiosyncrasies of technical knowledge is that it is easier to have a system for registering technical knowledge, due to its higher codifiability and its artefact link. The patent system is such a system, and it also stimulates the codification of technology. At the same time, as its main purpose, it stimulates technology generation, diffusion (cloning) and technology cumulation.[17] The patent system thus reinforces some of the knowledge properties of technology, giving rise to economies of scale, scope and mobility (speed and space) of technology, although at the possible cost of some R&D and output market distortion plus the cost of administering the patent system. Thus there is still another special and unique property of technology, namely,

6. It is possible to protect it by patent rights.

The heterogeneity of technology must be emphasized, although this property is not unique to technology as a body of knowledge. Technology being heterogeneous means that different fields of technology and types of technology may be identified (not without difficulties) and combined, and that their economic properties typically differ. The economic properties of a specific technology, or combination of technologies, pertain to: (i) its genericness or degree of applicability; (ii) its impact on customer utility and/or production cost impacts which are mediated through the corresponding technical performance parameters; (iii) cost of acquisition; (iv) its complementarities and/or substitution effects upon other technologies; (v) potential for advancement; (vi) the excludability or appropriability (for example, through patents) of its related benefits or returns; and (vii) the state and rate of diffusion on the market.

Needless to say, new technologies are evolving dynamically in a cumulative and interactive manner. Technological changes that give rise to innovations, at a closer look, typically involve new combinations of partly old technologies, and partly new technologies, some of which render some other old technologies obsolete. An empirically important phenomenon is the increase in the range of relevant technologies, that is, technology diversification at the business level, giving rise to multitechnology products and processes, which in turn gives rise to multitechnology corporations such as the typical TBFs. At the same time, fundamental breakthroughs in S&T give rise to generic, multipurpose or multiproduct technologies. Together, these two phenomena of multitechnology products and multipurpose technologies create more and more technology/business couplings with associated economies of scale and scope. These economies are potential, however, and must be realized by an active and innovative management.

Finally, it is important to distinguish technology from management. Both technology and management are knowledge resources and as such are bounded, heterogeneous and dynamically evolving and, via their embodiments, both affect the transformation of other resources. However, management has links primarily to human resources, behavioural characteristics and social sciences. Compared to technology, managerial knowledge is less codifiable, more localized and non-protectable by patents.

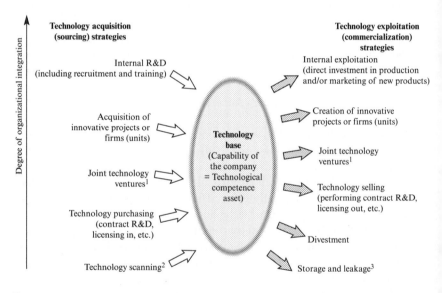

Notes
1. Joint technology ventures refers to ventures involving some form of technology-related external cooperation in general, for example joint R&D with subcontractors.
2. Scanning includes legal and illegal forms of acquiring technological know-how from the outside without any direct purchasing from its original source.
3. This is not a strategy for exploitation but a kind of residual of unappropriated technology, possibly leaking to competitors through their technology scanning efforts.

Source: Adapted from Granstrand and Sjölander (1990a).

Figure 4.2   Generic strategies for acquisition and exploitation of technology

4.5.2 Acquisition and Exploitation of Technology

From the point of view of a company, technology as a resource or asset can be acquired and exploited in various ways (see Figure 4.2). This asset or technology base is embedded in the general resource base of the company, as depicted earlier in Figure 4.1. At the same time the firm's technology base is embedded in the collective technical knowledge in the firm's industry and in society in general, as illustrated in Figure 4.3. It should also be noted that acquisition and exploitation of technology using various strategies or modes give rise to corresponding markets. In particular, external acquisition of technology gives rise to technology

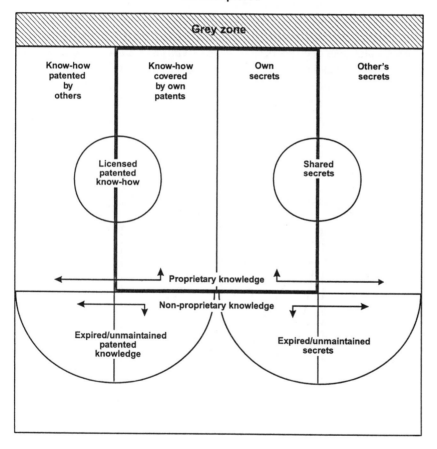

Figure 4.3   IPR status in various parts of a new technology or research field

markets, which are a particular form of IC markets. There are various types of such technology markets, corresponding to company acquisitions, licensing, contracts and so on.

4.6   DIVERSIFICATION

4.6.1   Types of Diversification

A firm can be viewed as being composed of one set of businesses (or product/market combinations), constituting its business base, and one set of resources, constituting its resource base. Between these two bases there is a many-to-many correspondence between resources and businesses (with a standard production function as a very special case), subjected to environmental changes and management and organizational behaviour. A firm may engage in two fundamental types of diversification – *business diversification*, that is, increasing its range of business types (with product, service and market diversification as special cases) and *resource diversification*, that is, increasing its range of resource types (with, for example, technology diversification as a special case).[18] Resource and business diversification corresponds to input and output diversification, from the point of view of the firm as a whole. Note that 'business

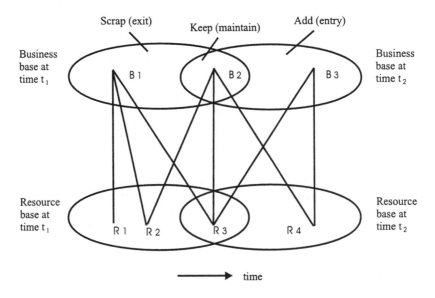

Figure 4.4   Shifts in the resource and business bases over time

diversification' here typically refers to business on the firm's output markets, while diversification on the firm's input markets is subsumed under resource diversification. This is an essential distinction in the argument below, which states that the interaction between these two diversification processes is one important source of dynamics in the evolution of the firm.

Each business of a firm has in turn a resource base, and each type of resource may be exploited in several businesses. These links can be summarized in a resource/business matrix (see below), analogous to the product/market matrix commonly used in describing diversification.[19]

As the firm evolves over time, its resource base and business base may shift, with some resources R_i, businesses B_i, and mutual BR-couplings scrapped (or substituted), and some kept (conserved) and some added. See Figures 4.4 and 4.5 for two graphic representations of this phenomenon.

Strictly speaking, the concept of diversification refers to the 'added part' in these shifts. We can then distinguish between the processes of substitution or exit, conservation, and diversification or entry, pertaining to both businesses and resources. Any change in the business base as well as in the resource base, then,

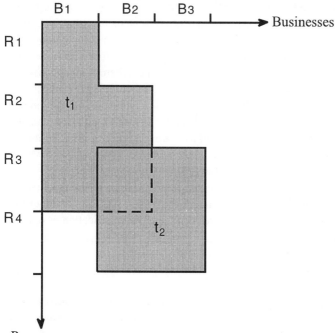

Figure 4.5   Shifts in the resource/business matrix over time

involves some or all of these processes, which gives a number of possible types. For example, over long periods of time the resource and/or business base may shift entirely and become disjoint from what it was originally. This may particularly happen to raw material-based firms and chemical firms, while invention-based firms in mechanical and electrical engineering sectors can rather display 'rooted' diversification, with the original business and product area remaining at least for a long period of time before it is scrapped. Sometimes a stage of resource diversification, driven by 'demand pull' and economies of scope, is followed by a stage of business diversification, driven by 'resource push' and economies of scale, which is then followed by a stage of business and resource scrapping. However, different types of diversification in a firm do not necessarily have to evolve in a stage-wise or sequential manner but can instead be conducted concurrently. Concurrent diversification puts larger demands on managerial resources, though, and sequential diversification has historically been more common.[20]

An innovation typically leads to changes in the resource and/or business base, and to the extent that resources and businesses are kept compared to those that are scrapped and added due to the innovation, the change is gradual rather than radical. Tushman and Anderson (1986) make the distinction between competence-destroying (that is, scrapping) and competence-enhancing (that is, adding) technological innovations. Many, if not most, technological innovations shift the competence base (including the technology base) into a new base which overlaps the old one to some extent. Typically, then, there is an enhancement (diversification) bias, that is, with more adding than scrapping of competencies (see Granstrand 1994, Ch. 7). In addition, several technologies in the technology base are usually retained or conserved. Thus, to the extent that technology conservation and diversification dominate over technology substitution, the resulting change becomes more gradual than radical, which is in line with the cumulation and continuity view of the firm.

Generally speaking, then, the size and rate of change in the resource and business base implied by any diversification provide a basis for distinguishing between different types of related and incremental diversification as opposed to unrelated diversification.[21]

4.6.2 Diversification Dynamics

As commonly perceived, a firm derives its dynamic features primarily through interaction with its environment. There are other sources of dynamism as well, which are fairly well recognized. One is management (in a broad sense, including entrepreneurial acts in the organization as a whole) to the extent that it is not entirely adaptive to environmental changes. Another is endogenous innovations, rather than adaptations. However, two additional sources of dynamism need to be recognized as well.

The first is the increasing returns that accrue in the resource acquisition and exploitation processes *per se*, in particular learning (in a broad sense, including learning in recurrent contracting, leading to reduced transaction costs). The second source is the interaction between resource and business base shifts, diversification in particular. As resources are acquired to support a specific business, some of these resources may have multiple uses with properties that improve the economic prospects of going into a new business, for example, through the provision of economies of scale and scope.[22] This in turn may require that new resources are acquired as well. Moreover, resources already acquired for a business that are later scrapped may be difficult to dispose of in the market in the short term, possibly leading to sunk fixed costs, which in turn creates an incentive to use surplus resources for business diversification.[23]

A resource may also be lost or scrapped for other reasons (for example, loss of key people or concessions), leading to the scrapping of a business, thereby possibly releasing other resources with alternative uses and so on. These dynamics in scrapping/keeping/adding businesses and resources with alternative uses are in reality influenced by the firm's interaction with its environment, of course, but it is important to note that external dynamics is a sufficient (at least in the long run) but not a necessary condition for internal dynamics. That is, a firm could in principle go on scrapping (substituting) and adding (diversifying) even in a static (let alone stable) environment.[24]

The internal diversification dynamics is driven by the economic properties of resources and their transformation, notably of the four types considered here: economies of scale, scope, speed and space. These economies derive from the physical or intrinsic properties of resources in conjunction with the many-to-many transformation or production (in a wide sense) correspondence between resources and businesses. Different diversification patterns put different requirements on management in reaping the relevant economies involved. Too much unrelated resource and business diversification, as in conglomerate diversification, as well as too much diversification in a short period of time may then overtax management as well as other resources. Commonly observed sequences of corporate evolution such as internationalization (market diversification) followed by resource diversification, spurring subsequent product diversification, can then be explained by dynamically changing mixes of economies of scale, scope, speed and space. Concurrent diversification, for example, with more or less simultaneous internationalization and product diversification, may then be achieved through: (i) complementarities, giving rise to economies of scope; (ii) resource-sharing, giving rise to economies of scale; (iii) managerial learning, removing certain diseconomies of scale; (iv) a premium on time to certain markets; and (v) locational economies (economies of space).

Knowledge resources in general and technology in particular have properties, many of which are unique, that form a strong dynamic interaction between the different diversification processes within the firm.

4.6.3   Technology and Product Diversification

Technology diversification can lead to growth in the TBF, while at the same time leading to growth in the firm's R&D expenditures. Theoretically, in the process of taking advantage of technological opportunities, technology diversification at the corporate level may lead to increased sales in five different and partly complementary ways.

1. *Static economies of scale* There are static economies of scale to the extent that the same, or close to the same, technologies could be used in several different products with minor adaptation costs. Because exploiting knowledge in various applications is characterized by relatively smaller variable costs per additional application in relation to the fixed cost of acquiring the knowledge, the static economies of scale are significant when a technology has a wide applicability to many different product areas in a corporation. This is the case for generic technologies by definition.
2. *Dynamic economies of scale* Knowledge is not consumed or worn out when applied, but is typically improved by the learning process when applied repeatedly, which allows for dynamic economies of scale.
3. *Cross-fertilization (economies of scope)* Different technologies have a potential to cross-fertilize with other technologies, yielding new inventions, new functionalities and increased product and/or process performances when combined, regardless of whether the technologies in question have a wide applicability to many product areas or not. This cross-fertilization, then, yields what could be called true economies of scope, which are not the kind of economies of scope that arise from shared inputs, and are considered special cases of economies of scale. This third type of economy, associated potentially with technology diversification, depends on specific technologies which could be combined or integrated. The economics of this type also vary over time, depending upon the intra-technology advancements.
4. *Economies of speed* Combining technologies most often requires some technology transfer, and (under certain conditions) intrafirm technology transfer is faster and more effective than interfirm, giving rise to speed and timing advantages, that can be labelled as economies of speed.
5. *Economies of space* A technologically diversified company with diversified absorptive capacities can reap economies of space by locating operations in regions with a concentration and high diversity of technologies that yield spill-overs (that is, 'multitechnology' regions).

The growth of R&D expenditures resulting from technology diversification derives from the cost of new technologies plus the cost of overcoming difficulties in combining various technologies. Increasingly expensive R&D needed to support existing businesses thus gives an incentive for technology-related business diversification to economize upon the (quasi-fixed) R&D investments, be it through product diversification or market diversification or both. The relative failure of multiproduct companies versus MNCs observed in literature could then be hypothesized to result from a higher degree of technology-relatedness (implying scale, scope as well as speed economies) in MNCs, everything else being equal. In addition, internationalization may provide locational economies[25] (or 'economies of space') in relation to R&D. Since diverse S&T activities tend to agglomerate in various regions of the world (Cantwell 1989, 1994) a multitechnology company gains further locational advantages by locating R&D and technology-sourcing activities in such 'multitechnology regions', as mentioned above.

Sceptics of business diversification, of whom there are many, might submit that technology diversification does not necessarily have to lead to technology-related business diversification. The need for technology diversification is largely generated by forces exogenous to the firm. As empirical studies have shown, many firms also grow through technology diversification without engaging in business diversification. However, as R&D expenditures grow through technology diversification, a need arises to recover those expenses through expanding the business base. Many firms have in the past responded to this through market diversification, especially internationalization, thereby becoming MNCs.

Technology-related product diversification

An alternative, sometimes complementary, depending on the limits of managerial capabilities, is to engage in technology-related product diversification and spread R&D costs over several product areas. Compared to internationalization, however, this puts other and seemingly larger demands on management.

Division of R&D labour

Another general response to rising R&D costs in TBFs is the development of markets for technology with increasing division of R&D labour among TBFs. Rising R&D costs, in conjunction with the genericness of new technologies, increase both supply and demand on a technology market. Empirical studies have shown an increase in external sourcing of new technologies in TBFs. More general rationalization of R&D work is also possible, for example through cost-reducing innovations in the R&D process itself (for example, in software development).

Technology-related partnering

Still another possibility for mitigating the rise in R&D costs so common to TBFs is to engage in technology-related partnering, either pure R&D partnering or technology-related business partnering. In fact the growth of partnering among TBFs of all sizes is to a considerable extent motivated by rising R&D costs, influenced by technology diversification. Again technology-related partnering puts special demands on management, general management as well as technology management, but in this case, it relates to management links among several firms, which requires a quite different type of quasi-integrated governance structure.

In summary, the economic properties of technology as a resource create, through technology diversification and technology-related business diversification, an economic potential for the firm. Other physical and intellectual resources may also provide an economic potential in similar ways, of course, but it is argued here that technology has some unique and particularly strong properties in these respects, including the associated tendencies towards costly (and risky) R&D. The fact that physical capital and intellectual capital have some fundamentally differing economic properties is clear, but how then does technology differ from other IC resources? Don't other competencies or knowledge resources provide economies of scale and scope much as technology does? Yes, they do, but as described above, technology has some unique properties which lead to a particularly strong economic potential. For example, it is possible to embody ('productify') technology in artefacts to decrease transactional hazards, and more so than in the case of pure knowledge-based services. The possibilities to codify can be argued to be larger on average for technology than for other competencies, which improves the prospects of accumulation and transfer, which in turn improves the prospects of reaping economies of scale, scope, speed and space.[26]

S&T discoveries and inventions (for example, radio waves, photoconductivity and the laser) have a feature of indivisibility, in the sense that the magnitude with which they are made is far from fully determined by the need for them in a particular situation of resource utilization. This property they share with discoveries in other knowledge areas in general (compare the discovery of the American continent by explorers and exploiters). Mother Nature simply has a way of revealing herself in bits and pieces, not always proportional to the effort or need of her explorer. The patent system is directed to technology and technical inventions (not science), and by design gives indivisibilities in the form of a unique economic potential to technical advances beyond a certain technical (as opposed to economic) size or level of invention. The indivisibilities induced by the patent system yield possible slack and economies of scale. This may, however, be a minor consideration compared to the role of the patent system in providing potential economies for the patent holder relative to competitors, through the temporary, restricted input monopoly protection associated with patent rights.[27]

The role of patents in firms (and economic development in general) is an issue which could be elaborated at great length. Most authors do not regard the role of patents as very important, however. For example, Chandler (1990) attributes a secondary role to them in firm formation historically. On the other hand, there are not many studies with this focus. At the same time things are changing. A 'pro-patent' era has emerged in the 1980s as IC has become generally more important. (See Chapter 2.)

4.7 THE MANAGEMENT FACTOR

Abstaining from further elaboration here, we may infer that technology has properties with an enormously strong economic potential. Some of these properties are shared by other resources, in particular by other competencies, while some properties are unique. Some properties are intrinsic to technology; some are man-made. The IPR system in particular is part of the institutional setting that by design endows technology with unique economic properties, although it is debatable how strong they are.

However, the general economic potential of technology is not realized automatically, nor are its returns automatically appropriated, not even by a firm which has invested in acquiring it. In order to accomplish that, management (in a broad sense, including organizational capabilities) is a necessary but not sufficient competence. This is not the proper place to elaborate upon how it can be achieved, more than to indicate a few challenges to current managerial thinking based on the analysis above. First, a specialization strategy of 'sticking to the knitting' could be severely criticized on the above grounds (see Granstrand et al. 1992a). Second, in order to reap technological economies of scale, scope, speed and space, technology transfer and technology integration are of decisive importance in acquiring and exploiting technology, often with in-house R&D as a dominant mode of acquisition. This challenges to some extent the current approach (at least in the West) that favours one-sided decentralization of R&D and technology management. Moreover, down-sizing middle technology management in that connection may jeopardize critical integrative functions for reaping the economic benefits of technology diversification.

The management factor must enter explicitly into a theory of the TBF and its diversification processes as a variable intermediate between technological and economic changes at the firm level. Management should not only be represented by its embodiment in humans, expressing itself in managerial strategies and performance (of which the yardsticks are much poorer than for technical performance), but should also be represented by a knowledge area,

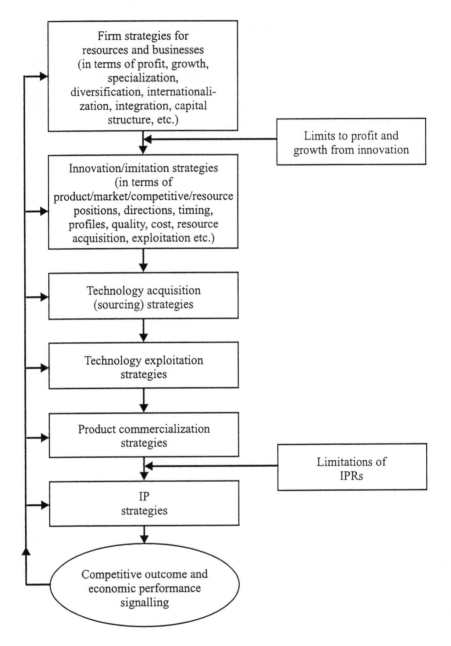

Figure 4.6   Types of strategies for the technology-based firm

subjected to evolution through learning, accumulation and innovations just as for technological evolution. At the same time, managerial knowledge and practices co-evolve with new technologies (for example, new computer and communication technologies) with an interplay between technological and managerial innovations. Management serves as an explanatory factor together with the technology factor not only behind the formation, sustained existence and diversification of the TBF, but also behind differences in economic performance of firms (exogenous factors apart). In an even wider perspective the management factor could be seen as a partial explanation of the strength in the co-evolution of S&T and the firm as an institution.

Unfortunately for many economic theorists, management has paradoxically been somewhat of a big, dark box, perhaps even bigger than the black box of technology. An important way to explore this box is to represent the management factor by the formulation and execution of management strategies in a broad sense of target-related controlled courses of organizational action. Strategies can be formulated at various managerial levels for various sets of activities, and needless to say there are many general typologies of company strategies. Figure 4.6 gives an overview of some general types of strategies for a TBF. These strategy typologies also serve as a frame of reference for the empirical chapters to follow.

4.8   SUMMARY AND CONCLUSIONS

The modern firm is a very viable economic institution, drawing strength from several layers of competitive markets, as well as from the development of management capabilities and a powerful co-evolution with science and technology. As a result of this co-evolution, TBFs have grown so as to altogether control most of the world's technologies, thereby also increasingly giving rise to proprietary firm-based technologies. TBFs are a special but important case of IC-based firms. The IC base of a company can be decomposed into various types of IPR, inter- and intrafirm relational capital and competencies, which can be acquired and exploited on various types of IC markets. The function of management is a defining characteristic of a firm and therefore could be viewed as a meta-resource. For a TBF, technology is also a defining characteristic. Technology has a number of specific properties in addition to the general properties of knowledge. In particular, technology is possible to codify and protect by patents.

Through notably strong economies of scale, scope, speed and space associated with the combination of different technologies and other resources, the TBF is subjected to specific dynamics in its growth and diversification and shifts in businesses and resources. In particular, a TBF tends to engage in technology diversification, thereby becoming multitechnological. As such, the TBF has incentives to economize on increasingly expensive new technologies by pursuing strategies of internationalization on both input and output markets, technology-related business diversification, external technology sale and sourcing, R&D rationalization and technology-related partnering.

In order to realize the potential economies associated with new technologies, management is crucial. An important function of management, then, is to formulate and execute strategies at corporate, technology, product and IP levels, for which there are a number of general types and options. These options are explored in subsequent chapters in more empirical detail.

NOTES

1. This does not mean that non-physical or intellectual resources and activities such as inventive work were ignored altogether by classical economists. Adam Smith, for example, dealt with the role of inventions and the division of inventive work. Nevertheless, such issues do not take up a major part of his works.
2. This is also true for a country like Japan. See Fujita (1991) for the historical developments of accounting in Japan.
3. Inserting a qualifier like 'modern' obviously opens the door for vagueness in dating. Here 'modern business firm' refers to a joint-stock limited-liability firm and 'modern nation-state' to the type emerging in connection with the American and French revolutions in the late 18th century.
4. Despite the terms used here no biological analogies are intended. On the contrary, such analogies are often more misleading than helpful when applied to firms and technologies; see Penrose (1952) and Granstrand (1994, Ch. 19). The (admittedly biology-inspired) terminology is used here as a language of general evolution, not necessarily confined to its application in biology (see von Bertalanffy 1968).
5. Humans have not, for example, developed three arms for cocktail parties, separate talking and eating organs or entirely new senses with new forms of stimulation and entertainment.
6. See, for example, Pavitt (1991).
7. In some sense the Christian church as an institution on the one hand and S&T on the other hand would rather be an example of adversary co-evolution, at least in the Middle Ages.
8. Biology and genetic engineering develop as an S&T field and biotech-based firms increase in numbers. New evolutionary patterns in nature may take root as a result, desirable or not. Incidentally, this may open up possibilities for new analogies between biology, firms and S&T.
9. This formulation does not imply that opportunities are fully exogenous to the firm. For example, a firm that comes up with an innovation may create entirely new opportunities, some of which also spill over to other firms.
10. This does not mean that there is nothing disputable about such a view.
11. No essential distinction is made at this level of the analysis between management, entrepreneurship, leadership, administration and so on. Nor is a distinction made here between ownership and management. Ownership can rather be viewed as management at a higher managerial level, when need arises to make this admittedly important distinction (as in principal–agent theory).
12. The occurrence of managerial evolution, managerial innovations and managerial learning serves to lower this cost, just as new technologies can (for example, new information and communication technologies).

13. There are other dimensions of entrepreneurial characteristics of importance for the formation and existence of a firm, such as need for achievement, need for autonomy and need for power.

14. Throughout the text here, both time and effort are emphasized. This is because there are very limited possibilities to make trade-offs between time and efforts (or costs). That is, in learning and teaching you can buy time through increased efforts only up to a point.

15. The terms 'pool or stock of knowledge' are deceptive since they are often used together with the term 'flow' which indicates a physical transfer rather than diffusion or cloning of knowledge.

16. This does not mean it is a free good in the sense that it is 'costless' to acquire and use (see Nelson 1992).

17. Sometimes, however, complementarities are not gained since technology exploitation may also be hindered rather than fostered by a fragmentation of IPRs among agents that raises transaction costs to the point of hindering exchange through market transactions. One example of this is the digital audio tape technology; another may occur in what is termed multimedia, in which numerous interests in media, telecommunications and computing industries converge and conflict.

18. Such a firm could be labelled multibusiness, multiresource, and corresponds to the multiproduct, multifactor firm in neoclassical theory.

19. In fact, a key contribution by Wernerfelt (1984) was to emphasize the resource perspective in strategy-making, which previously had commonly focused only on product/market diversification (with internationalization as a special case).

20. Cantwell and Piscitello (1996) argue that, for the largest European and US firms, technological diversification and internationalization of technological activity have historically occurred sequentially, while a new contemporary complementarity between them has been emerging since the 1980s.

21. This latter type is also referred to as conglomerate diversification. As is well known, most studies show the poor economic performance of such diversification, although it could be argued that perfect capital markets should lead to neither economies nor diseconomies. However, conglomerate or unrelated diversification is in practice related to some extent through the use of common managerial resources. Management failure in the form of managerial or entrepreneurial hubris mentioned earlier can easily come into play, as does the principal–agent problem arising from management seeking job security in corporate diversification.

22. This case has been well recognized in literature. Penrose (1959) is definitely a pioneering work, followed by Teece (1982), Chandler (1990) and others. Normally, reference is made to resource slack, indivisibility and underutilization.

23. One example being diversification induced by life- (or long-) time employment, for example, in Japan.

24. Of course, there are environments that would not allow this to happen, but the point is that, if there are admissible environments, they do not need to be dynamic.

25. This corresponds to the L factor in Dunning's OLI-paradigm (see, for example, Dunning 1988).

26. The whole issue of codifiability could be elaborated at length, but must be omitted here (see above and also Arrow 1974 and Nelson 1992). Suffice it to say that codification is a dynamic (evolutionary) process, driven partly by R&D (compare the importance in this respect of contributions by Lavoisier and Mendelejev in chemistry). As a technology matures, it becomes more codified – in fact the level of codification could even be taken as a defining characteristic of maturing, until new discoveries challenge the accepted code, thereby temporarily disrupting cumulation (compare Kuhn 1970; Lakatos and Musgrave 1970; Popper 1968).

27. If the indivisibilities are small they could be taken to 'convexify'. The number of patents related to a product is often large and also tends to increase with new product generations. At the same time, it may be claimed that the genericness or range of application of many patents increases.

   The timing properties induced by the patent system are notable. First, there is a 'winner takes all' race to get a patent granted; second, (single) patent protection expires fully after a fixed time interval.

5. Japanese patenting – an overview

CHAPTER CONTENTS

5.1 CHAPTER OUTLINE

As a continuation of the historical overview in Chapter 2, this chapter will give a brief history of patenting in Japan. Against this background of patent systems in the East and West, we shall then compare the different patent systems in Europe, Japan and the USA. A sample of 24 large Japanese corporations will provide further comparisons, adding statistics and trend assessments as a basis for subsequent chapters. In particular the high propensity to patent in Japan will be explored.

5.2 BACKGROUND

Japan's techno-economic developments since World War II have caught the whole world, including Japan, with stunning surprise. This is so, even in light of the crisis of the late 1990s. Japan's rise to a leading nation in many technological and business areas has sent great technological and economic, as well as political and psychological, repercussions around the world. This is not the place to elaborate in any depth upon the causes and effects of Japan's successful techno-economic developments, but a few reflections are in order.[1]

The 1990s seemed to be a period of crossroads and confusion in Japan. Having by and large completed the catch-up process in many areas, new challenges arose increasingly as competitiveness became more dependent upon innovativeness. Moreover, a long period of stable prosperous growth was seriously disturbed by a deep and prolonged recession after the collapse of the bubble economy. However, in a longer time perspective, Japan's success is indisputable and the recession in the 1990s may very well be seen in retrospect as having strengthened her industry.[2]

Japan herself cannot explain her success clearly. To what extent Japan's success can be attributed to a small set of explanatory factors, as some analysts claim, or to a large eclectic set of factors related to Japanese culture, institutions, government policy, technology, management capability and so on is unknown and will probably remain so. Moreover, Japan has not been accustomed to being in a leadership position (just as the USA is unaccustomed to not being in one). There still seems to be some lack of self-confidence in Japan, not the least among the older generation, for example regarding Japan's possibilities to make significant progress in basic science and radical creative and innovative work. On the other hand, there has been a significant generation shift among managers in Japan, as in all countries damaged by World War II, and changes in life-styles and values in the Japanese elite could lead the relatively collectivist and homogeneous Japanese society in new directions. This shift could create self-content and hubris.[3] On the other hand, a sense of insecurity (*fuan*) is deeply ingrained in Japanese society.

It has not become clear, at least not to an outsider, how Japan, with the world's second-largest economy, will use her economic surplus, which at some point became the largest that was ever amassed by a single country in history. The choice of different investment strategies in industry and government will also push the country in new directions. Despite the long-run appreciation of the yen with some periods of strong appreciation in the 1980s and 1990s, there was no correspondingly strong wave of outward foreign direct investments, although Japanese FDIs certainly have grown considerably in the past few decades.[4] An inhibiting factor here may have been Japan's self-perceived lack of experience in managing international relations. However, over the long run, there have been strong investments in education and R&D at many levels, including a build-up of substantial R-capabilities (rather than only D) since the 1980s. This build-up within Japanese industry has created a 'research industry' with the world's largest civilian R&D community, which at some point owned almost half of the world's patents.[5] At the same time, almost every major company has invested in the diversification of both products and in-house technology. Moreover, Japan has been and still is significantly acquiring inputs from the world's S&T system by various means, not only through technology intelligence and licensing, as was done traditionally, but increasingly through acquiring stakes in small innovative companies in the West, joint ventures and utilization of Western universities. Japan's industrial R&D is therefore becoming increasingly internationalized (see further Granstrand 1999).

It remains to be seen whether Japan will follow the all too common pattern of Western *nouveaux riches* – to make bad investments, thereby breeding failure from success. In one way this has already happened in the Japanese 'bubble economy' of the late 1980s and early 1990s with financial and real estate speculation. Conceivably, there is even a risk of overinvestment in R&D, at least in certain areas – given the nature of Japan's science and technology system with research-weak universities, semi-public governmental R&D and large, fiercely competing corporations. These corporations, through long-time employment, employee loyalty, special norms of communications and other means, have been in a position to appropriate returns from investments in R&D, perhaps to a larger extent than Western corporations. At the same time as the corporate innovation systems have become strong in some key sectors, there remain substantial weaknesses in the Japanese innovation system as a whole, for example, a weak entrepreneurial function with weak financial markets for risk capital and various strong rigidities in the educational and political systems.

Japan, with her lack of natural resources, is economically dependent upon her R&D and innovativeness, perhaps more than any other country in the world, and is becoming increasingly so. Moreover, since her R&D is predominantly civilian and concentrated in large corporations, protecting and commercially exploiting this R&D effectively becomes of utmost concern; in fact, it is an issue of national economic security.[6] Consciously building and exploiting intellectual capital requires suitable economic institutions, such as industrial corporations (especially multinational and multiproduct corporations), national R&D institutes and projects, and a strong IPR system. Against this background it is quite natural that patenting and IPR are of importance for Japanese industry, not only for large companies, but also for small ones which will become increasingly necessary in the future as an instrument to bring out innovations.

5.3   HISTORICAL OVERVIEW OF JAPANESE PATENTING

We have looked to see what nations are the greatest, so that we can be like them. We asked ourselves 'What is it that makes the United States such a great nation?' We investigated and found that it was patents, and we will have patents. (K. Takahashi, First Director General of JPO, appointed 1885)

In the era since industrialization took off in Europe, Japan, like no other major country, has swung from extreme isolationism under the Tokugawa military rule to extensive international engagement. The turning point was the proclamation in 1868 of the Meiji Restoration (or rather 'renovation' in Japanese). Although Japan's transformation and techno-economic achievements since World War II are remarkable indeed, the pendulum's momentum and pace of change were probably higher a century earlier. The long preceding period of isolationism, which lasted for more than two centuries, probably also paved the way for its contrary movement to some extent. The foundations of many current practices in Japan were in fact laid in the decades after Meiji (for example, wearing Western suits,[7] competing fiercely in industry). Japan's willingness and ability to absorb foreign things without being culturally subdued has been remarkably high ever since. This has indeed been the case regarding foreign technology. While the Tokugawa dynasty tried to perpetuate its power by preserving the status quo – including forbidding technical innovations[8] – the absorption, development and control of new technologies are at the heart of modern Japan's policies for establishment of her power and economic security in the world economic order. Thus, the course of isolationism and technological stagnation has been reversed, with Meiji as a turning point.[9] To a considerable extent, new technologies also brought about the Meiji Restoration. The superiority of US military technologies, dramatically demonstrated by Commodore Perry when his naval ship prompted Japan to open up in 1852, had a profound effect on Japanese leaders,[10] just as the superiority of US military and industrial technology had on the formation of Japanese post-war policies.[11]

Japan has centred her economic development around intellectual resources (intellectual capital), especially in science and technology. Thus, in the Ministry for International Trade and Industry (MITI) vision of the 'Strategy for Trade and Industry' in the 1980s, it was proclaimed that Japan should now establish herself as a Technological State, having succeeded in establishing herself first as a trading nation and later on as an industrial nation. Japan has become a symbol of what some authors label 'techno-nationalism'. (For this concept see Nelson and Rosenberg 1993, p. 3; and Ostry and Nelson 1995).

It is to be expected that a nation lacking natural resources but aspiring to modernize will sooner or later emphasize intellectual resources and their property protection as indigenous S&T achievements start to become relatively more important. Concomitant with Japan's techno-economic developments since the Meiji Restoration has been the introduction and development of an IPR system, including a patent system, patterned on those in the West. An excellent account of these developments is given in Rahn (1983). A chronology is given in Table 5.1. One may note the early introduction of an IPR system and the continual developments of it in compliance with international legal developments as well as with domestic industrial developments. Certain asymmetries with other countries have been kept from time to time in order to favour domestic industry and its build-up of a technology base. However, a large number of licensing contracts were signed after World War II, which in retrospect proved to be a considerable bargain for the Japanese (by some called 'the greatest bargain ever').[12]

Table 5.1   Chronology of the evolution of the Japanese IPR system until 1980

Year(s)	IPR-related event
1603–1868	The Tokugawa period with military rule and feudal system under the Tokugawa family.
1633	Adoption of a policy of national seclusion.
1718	The proclamation of a new law, which forbade 'new things', that is, technical innovations (*Shinkihatto no Ofuregaki* – 'Ordinance Prohibiting Innovations').
1852	Commodore Perry visits Japan, leading to the re-opening of the country.
1867	Yukichi Fukuzawa[*] reported on the existence of patent laws in the USA and Europe.
1868	Proclamation by Emperor Meiji of the modernization of Japan (*Meiji Ishin* – Meiji 'Renovation').
1871	Promulgation of the first Japanese Patent Law. Failed in the absence of applications for a whole year and was abrogated.
1884	Promulgation of the first Japanese trademark law.
1885	Promulgation of the Patent Monopoly Ordinance, modelled on American and French law, after extensive preparations by Korekiyo Takahashi (who later on served as Finance Minister (twice) and Prime Minister). However, foreigners were barred from obtaining patent rights.
1885	Establishment of the Japanese Patent Office. K. Takahashi became its first Director General.
1886	1384 applications were filed and 205 patents granted.
1888	Improved patent and trademark laws replaced the first ordinances. Promulgation of a design ordinance, modelled on English law.
1899	Japan became a member of the Paris Convention for the Protection of Industrial Property, which had come into force in 1883. Foreigners were admitted to the Japanese industrial property system.

1905	Enactment of a Utility Model Law, inspired by German law.

1909   Revision of the four industrial property laws: the Patent Law, the Utility Model Law, the Design Law and the Trademark Law. A new section on employee inventions stated that the patent right belonged to the employer.

1921   Grand-scale revision of IPR laws, introducing novelties, such as first-to-file priority instead of the first-to-invent priority, employee ownership of patent rights instead of employer ownership, and an opposition system.

1935   Law for the Prevention of Unfair Competition came into force, together with the ratified Hague revision from 1925 of the Paris Convention.

1938   Establishment of Japan Patent Association, an organization of leading Japanese companies.

1950   'Foreign Investment Law' and the 'Foreign Exchange and Foreign Trade Control Law' were enforced to regulate technology imports and foreign exchange for the reconstruction and renovation of Japanese industry. A period of substantial technology imports started, mainly from the USA, but also from Europe.

1958   Japan becomes the leading country in terms of number of patents and utility model applications filed per year. (A position retained since, as of 1995.)

1960   Enactment of revised IPR laws. Special injunction and damages as remedies for infringement were introduced.

1971   Revision of the Patent Law, allowing seven years for the request for examination and laying-open of the application.

1974   Liberalization of technology imports.

1976   Adoption of the product patent and the multiple claims system (although allowing only dependent sub-claims).

1978   Japan acceded to the PCT, and JPO became one of the international searching authorities under the PCT.

Note: * See a 10 000-yen bill for his portrait.

Sources: Compiled from Doi (1980), Rahn (1983), with the assistance of A. Mifune and K. Norichika.

In general, the IPR system in Japan came into extensive use in the post-war period as one of the means for catching up and forging ahead. This was accomplished through the analysis of existing patents, licensing in and improving imported technologies, mostly through many small improvements that were readily and extensively patented.[13] Throughout this process, patent managerial skills, resources and methods were developed, as will be described in later chapters. Also, Japan has in various governmental and private ways supported the ongoing international harmonization of IPR laws. However, while one may say that large parts of Japan's industry have become leaders in patenting and IP management, Japan has not been a leader in developing the basic IPR legal framework.[14]

Around the turn of the millennium, Japan has amassed substantial financial resources by world standards and also controls considerable physical resources through FDIs, foreign holdings and other means. Still, she is more dependent on her intellectual capital (including goodwill and 'relational capital' in relations with her neighbours) than most countries and regions of the world. IP has also become recognized as an issue of economic security at the national level in the same way as it has been recognized as an issue of corporate economic security in several large corporations.

The developments in IPR systems and IPR relations between Japan and the USA are summarized in Table 5.2.[15] In the 1980s, patent-related trade friction between the USA and Japan grew into what some observers later termed a 'patent war'.[16] The following citation illustrates the kind of patent and litigation strategies advocated by a major Japanese newspaper in this patent war:

> What should our attitude be towards the raging patent war between Japan and the U.S.? First, in the light of the history of patent wars, there is no alternative but to fight patent with patent. Needed in this process are expediting technological development, establishing as many patents as possible and securing cross-licensing contracts to offset patent royalty payments. To these ends, joint technological development may be considered by leading manufacturers of this country, the U.S. and Europe.
>
> Second, in its patent wars with the U.S., Japanese industry should openly seek court decisions on the rights and wrongs of each case and avoid out-of-court settlements as much as possible.
>
> Third, the Japanese government should strive to reconcile institutional differences in patent applications that exist among Japan, the U.S. and Europe. (Editorial, *Mainichi Daily News*, 31 March 1992 (excerpts))

It is particularly noteworthy that this editorial advocates the avoidance of out-of-court settlements, which traditionally have been the preferred mode of patent conflict resolution in Japanese industry for cultural reasons. To some extent, Japanese corporations became reactively litigious and aggressive in court (with the aid of US lawyers). Goals were set up in some cases to win patent disputes with US companies in order to win demonstration effects, prestige and self-confidence. All in all, however, the warfare aspect was overplayed by the popular press[17] and gradually the feelings of animosity abated somewhat after a peak in the early 1990s.

Table 5.2   Chronology of the evolution of the IPR system in Japan and the USA, 1980–1995

	Japan	USA
1980		US Copyright Law amended Chakrabarty case (micro-organism patent)[1]
1981		Diehr case (computer program)[2]
1982		CAFC[3] established
1983		Patent Commissioners' trilateral conference started
1984	JPO 'paperless project' initiated	
1985	Maskwork Law enacted Copyright Law amended (computer program)	WIPO Harmonization Conference USITC litigations increased
1986	TI semiconductor patent litigation initiated at USITC.[4] Kilby patent granted[5]	GATT TRIPs started
1987	Patent Law amended (refined multiple claims system introduced)	
1988		US Trade Act (Special 301) US Tariff Act 337 amended
1989	Copyright Law amended (fair use)	Japan on Watch List of Special 301
1990	Unfair Competition Protecting Law amended (trade secret)	
1991	Trademark Law amended (new service mark registration system introduced)	
1992	Honeywell won patent litigation against Minolta	US Patent Law reform report
1993	Patent Law and Utility Model Law amended; Unfair Competition Protecting Law amended	GATT TRIPs completed
1994		US–Japan Patent Commissioners' Understanding signed

Notes
1. The patentability of a bacteria genetically engineered by A.M. Chakrabarty was finally decided by the US Supreme Court, overruling the USPTO's rejection of the patent application. This decision opened the possibility to grant patents for living organisms.
2. A US Supreme Court decision, which through its interpretation by the USPTO opened the possibility to grant patents to computer software.
3. CAFC = Court of Appeals for the Federal Circuit.
4. Texas Instruments claimed eight Japanese and one Korean company infringed on ten of their patents for DRAMs (see Warshofsky 1994).
5. In 1961, Texas Instruments had filed the patent in Japan for the integrated circuit, called the 'Kilby patent' after its inventor Jack Kilby. JPO required the application to be divided into several parts, the first of which was granted in 1977.

Source: K. Norichika and the author.

5.4   PRESENT (1995) JAPANESE PATENT SYSTEM IN INTERNATIONAL COMPARISON

As described in Chapter 3, the basic design idea of any patent system is that society promises an individual or organizational inventor enforcement of limited but transferable monopoly rights in exchange for disclosure of the invention, provided it fulfils certain requirements (being technical, novel and non-obvious). Society's purpose for providing such a transaction possibility is to stimulate both the development, commercialization and disclosure of new technologies.

This design idea is fairly simple but nevertheless opens up numerous national variations of patent systems in practice. Nations strike different balances between societal interests and individual interests (see Chapter 2), depending upon cultural and economic traditions as well as upon their stage of development. Certainly in Japan the IPR system and its enforcement practices were adopted and modified in the interest of catching up technologically with the West. The determination with which the Japanese IPR system has been used for the purpose of catching up has apparently been much stronger in the past than the determination in the USA and Europe to use their IPR systems to preserve their once undisputed leading roles in technological development and commercialization.[18]

The question now arises of what will happen with the IPR system in Japan and elsewhere when Japan adopts the role of one of the leading nations in a wide range of technologies. At the same time, the USA, to a certain extent, and particularly Europe have been falling behind in several areas, although the USA has forged ahead in some broad areas as well as regained some leads in the 1990s. All in all, everyone has to realize that a mix of catch-up and innovative behaviour is needed to compete, based on increasingly interrelated and expensive technologies in an increasingly integrated international economy. There is much pressure for international harmonization of IPR systems, but the national differences in the leading triad are still substantial, as evidenced by Table 5.3. Moreover, there are deep cultural differences underneath, for example a higher emphasis on individual rights and court resolution of conflicts in the West as opposed to more collectivist thinking and concern for harmony and consensus-seeking in Japan (see, for example, Helfgott 1990). Nevertheless, the business forces for international harmonization are strong, and it is likely that they will succeed as internationalization of S&T in general proceeds. This is highly desirable for the efficiency and promotion of S&T, as well as for internationalization in general (see Chapter 10). It may also be argued that for Japan's catch-up the IPR system has worked well, partly because of the lackadaisical use of it in the West. However, it may not work equally well for other countries wanting to catch up in future technologies, including Western countries that are behind or have fallen behind. The Japanese success has led the USA to strengthen its IPR system to make similar successes harder to achieve. At the same time other leading countries, including Japan, share such interests, as illustrated by Japan's tough attitudes towards South Korean requests for Japanese licences. Some even argue that the Japanese success has 'closed the window' for those developing countries that want to catch up.

5.4.1 Problems with International Patenting

As Table 5.3 shows, the Japanese patent system is more similar to the European system than to the US system. Some observers also believe the US system is the one that will change the most in the harmonization process. However, the present assertiveness in the USA regarding patents leaves some doubts about this. The adoption and development of an IPR system in China and in the former USSR will of course be important in this context.

First to file versus first to invent
Differences in national patent laws as illustrated in Table 5.3 create various problems in international patenting, sometimes resulting in friction in international relations as well. In particular, the 'first-to-invent' priority rule in the USA creates problems when confronted with the 'first-to-file' priority rule in Europe and Japan. Naturally, the one who is first to invent may differ from the one who is first to file a patent application, so problems to determine who has priority to an invention may occur in international patenting.[19]

Submarine patents
The previous absence of a laid-open publication (that is, an open, pre-grant publication) of patent applications in the USA has created problems in the past with so-called 'submarine patents', that is, inventions made early that show up unexpectedly at a much later date when finally granted patent rights.[20] This possibility in the USA for keeping an invention secret while it is being processed by the USPTO has been notoriously exploited by a few inventors who by various means have been able to prolong the patent examination process.[21] Meanwhile, other companies may think the area is clear from patents, and some company may even come up with a related invention, for which a patent is granted in some other country. Thus, other companies are inclined to go ahead with R&D, production and marketing in the area.[22] Finally, the submarine patent surfaces and, to the extent that infringement is feared or has occurred, it enables the patent holder to collect royalties or damages.[23] It should be noted, however, that cases like these have been rare (although notorious), and that inventors blatantly exploiting this opportunity could lose the patent rights or the

Table 5.3   Comparison of patent laws in Japan, Europe and the USA (as of 1997)

	Japan	Europe (EPO, EC)	United States
Priority ground[1]	First to file	First to file	First to invent
Filing	Inventor or assignee	Inventor or assignee	Inventor only[2]
Grace period[3]	Limited to 6 months prior to national filing date	No	One year prior to US filing date
Whole contents prior art effects[4]	From convention filing date[5] a. Secret prior art for novelty b. No secret prior art for obviousness	From convention filing date[5] a. Secret prior art for novelty b. No secret prior art for obviousness	From national filing date a. Secret prior art for novelty b. Secret prior art for obviousness
Patent lifetime	15 years from publication date but not exceeding 20 years from filing date	20 years from filing date	20 years from filing date
Laid-open publication	18 months from filing	18 months from filing	
Subject matter excluded from patenting	– Substances manufactured by the transformation of the atom – Inventions liable to contravene public order, morality or public health	– Plant or animal varieties[7] – Essentially biological	No[6] – Nuclear weapons – Inventions liable to contravene public order, morality or public health
Patent term extension or restoration[8]	Patent term extendible for some products subject to approval at most 5 years	Patent term extendible for some products subject to approval at most 5 years	Patent term extendible for some products subject to approval at most 5 years
Opposition[9]	Post-grant opposition (within 6 months after the publication of granted patent. Evidence added within 3 months after filing opposition)	Post-grant opposition (within 9 months after the publication of granted patent)	No opposition system Post-grant re-examination (without argument)
Deferred examination[10]	7 years from filing date	6 months from publication of search report	No deferred examination
Allowance for amendment[11]	Restrictive amendment practice (more severe under the latest revised Patent Law)	Most strict amendment practices (although applicants can oppose their own applications to amend them)	Liberal amendment even after final rejection and final allowance
Claiming practices[12]	Limitation in claiming practices	Strict claim form, but liberal claiming including dependent claims referring to other dependent claims	Permit any number of independent and dependent claims, separately enforceable. Permit means plus function claims
Claim interpretation	Comparatively narrow interpretation	Leaning to broad interpretation	Broad interpretation
Language of application[13]	Japanese or English	English, French or German	Any language acceptable, formal specification in English requested later

Notes

1. That is, the ground for deciding who is first and therefore has priority to an invention.
2. Assignee in certain limited situations. However, assignees do a large part of the filing work in general.
3. That is, the period before patent filing date, during which the invention may be publicized without violating the novelty requirement.
4. That is, whether prior art in information in submitted, but not yet published patent applications, can be taken into account when assessing whether the novelty and non-obviousness requirements are fulfilled. Secret thus refers to non-published information in patent applications.
5. That is, the date for filing in a country which is a member of the Paris Union, comprising all countries which have signed the Paris Convention.
6. Laid-open publication was adopted in 1995 in the context of GATT, but the final adoption has been delayed.
7. A change has been proposed and the nature of the requirement is unclear.
8. This is of particular importance for the pharmaceutical industry.
9. That is, of third party.
10. This refers to the possibility of the patent applicant to request a postponement of the patent examination procedure of the patent office.
11. That is, possibility for the applicant to make amendments to the application after filing date.
12. That is, to what extent the inventor can make different claims in the same patent application regarding the functionality and performance of the underlying invention and its possible sub-inventions.
13. Most signatory nations require a patent to have its document finally written in their own language to be valid.

Source: Original material for this table has kindly been provided by Professor A. Mifune. The table has been updated to be valid as of 31 December 1997. Minor qualifications and exceptions may apply.

inventors blatantly exploiting this opportunity could lose the patent rights or the right to sue.

Kilby patent

A related type of problem arises from old inventions that are finally granted patent rights. The delay may be due to excessive nursing of the patent application as described above or some other procedural matter, such as deferred examination in Japan. A case in point is the Kilby patent,[24] which was used by Texas Instruments in their offensive move initiated in the mid-1980s to enforce their patent rights through drastic royalty increases and litigation.[25]

International friction

Problems like these and other types naturally occur as a result of incompatible and/or imperfect patent laws. As the pro-patent era has emerged, these problems have become more serious and visible and soured relations not only among companies, but also among countries, notably between the USA and Japan.

Seen in a historic perspective, such international friction arising in connection with the patent system is not surprising. Patent laws were originally adopted and adapted to suit national interests, such as the stimulation of technological catch-up with other more advanced nations at the time. Foreign discrimination was partly built into the patent system and its operations, and is still present to some extent.[26] International cooperation and treaties have served to eliminate foreign discrimination[27] and increase international harmonization, but this process is painstakingly slow as technical gaps proliferate, leaving much to be done.

5.4.2   Strengths and Weaknesses of Patent Systems

In viewing the effectiveness of the patent system, one must consider all of its constituent parts in a society. These parts are considered to be: (i) legislation *per se*, including provisions for change in legislation; (ii) law adherence by the public at large in the society; (iii) law enforcement provisions (which may be unsatisfactory) by policing and prosecuting functions; (iv) court practices; and finally (v) penalty provisions or a corrective and preventive system in general. Public bodies perform legislation and court practices, while companies must carry out the policing and prosecution by themselves. This does not need to be the case, however. Subject to the law in general, private companies could form associations for IPR protection with their own additional rules, and policing and prosecution could conceivably be carried out by public or semi-public bodies.[28] The question of how to mix public and private functions for upholding an effective IPR system as a whole is important and interesting, but nevertheless must be left aside here.

Table 5.4   Strength of patent system in Europe, Japan and the USA as perceived by large Japanese corporations, 1992

(Scale: False = –2, –1, 0, +1, +2 = True)

(Code) Proposition[1]	Chemical ($n = 9$)	Electrical ($n = 10$)	Mechanical ($n = 5$)	Total[2] ($n = 24$)
(F12a) The patent laws in Europe, Japan and the USA provide adequate protection through:[3]				
Legislation in Europe	1.25	0.86	0.50	0.95
Legislation in Japan	1.11	0.88	0.00	0.77
Legislation in USA	0.50	–0.38	0.60	0.19
Law adherence in Europe	1.00	1.00	1.25	1.05
Law adherence in Japan	0.89	0.63	0.40	0.68
Law adherence in USA	0.63	0.13	1.20	0.57
Law enforcement in Europe[3]	0.50	1.00	1.25	0.84
Law enforcement in Japan	0.33	0.75	0.40	0.50
Law enforcement in USA	0.88	0.00	0.80	0.52
Court practices in Europe	0.50	0.57	0.25	0.47
Court practices in Japan	0.56	0.63	0.00	0.45
Court practices in USA	1.00	–0.63	0.75	0.33
Infringement penalties in Europe	0.63	0.86	0.50	0.68
Infringement penalties in Japan	0.33	0.63	0.00	0.36
Infringement penalties in USA	1.00	–0.25	1.00	0.52
(F12b) The patent protection has grown stronger over the last decade as a means of protecting new technology on:				
European market	0.88	1.00	0.60	0.87
Japanese market	1.00	1.10	0.60	0.96
US market	1.56	1.80	1.80	1.71

Notes
1. The proposition roughly as it appeared in the survey questionnaire together with its question or variable code. (See Appendix 2 for the complete questionnaire.)
2. The sample of 24 large corporations consists of nine mainly chemical ones, ten mainly electronic ones and five mainly mechanical ones. See Appendix 2.
3. Enforcement here refers primarily to enforcement through policing and prosecution.

Table 5.4 shows the perceptions in large Japanese companies of the strength of the different constituent parts of the patent system in Europe, Japan and the USA. As seen in the table, the perceptions of the protective strength differ widely for these three regions, and the perceptions differ across industries as well. In general, Europe ranks highest, showing significant differences with the USA regarding legislation and law adherence, but insignificant differences regarding court practices on average. However, the industry differences are large, especially for the USA, with the electrical industry deviating the most. The most likely reason for this is the wave of litigation from US firms, or the 'patent war'. This has particularly struck the large electronics companies in Japan, creating many hard feelings against US firms and the way the patent system functions in the USA. Court practices that are perceived as discriminating against Japanese companies, for example through jury verdicts, naturally lead to a feeling in Japan of inadequate protection in the USA. That is to say, Japanese companies feel they have inadequate protection against US patentees claiming infringements rather than inadequate protection of Japanese patentees against their infringers. Thus the table's subjective perceptions must be interpreted very cautiously. The answers to the second question (coded F12b, see Appendix 2) in the table could, however, be taken to indicate the emergence of a pro-patent era across regions and industries in the 1980s, especially in the USA, and especially felt in the electronics industry.

5.5   JAPANESE R&D AND PATENTING IN INTERNATIONAL COMPARISON

5.5.1   Growth of R&D and Patenting[29]

In most industrialized countries industrial production and R&D have grown and become steadily more internationalized, especially since World War II. In the last decade or so, it has also become more common among advanced industrial companies worldwide that their R&D investments surpass their physical investments. Since patenting is closely linked to R&D (which in turn is linked to company sales), one may also expect that patenting has grown on average and become more internationalized. Table 5.5 shows this to be the case. On average the growth rate is highest for external or foreign outward patenting (that is, patents extended to foreign countries by domestic residents), followed in falling order by inward foreign patenting (that is, domestic patents taken out by foreign residents), R&D expenditures, industrial production, and finally domestic patenting with the lowest growth rate. Thus international patenting has grown faster than R&D and production, while domestic patenting shows only a modest growth on average. Among the countries in the table, Japan's growth rates are highest overall, except for inward foreign patenting which actually ranks among the lowest. Sweden has the second-highest growth rate in R&D and also has the largest difference between growth rates for R&D and domestic patenting. The USA has the second-highest growth rate in industrial production and ranks highly in the other categories.

Table 5.5   The development of international patenting in various countries (average annual percentage change)

Country	Industrial production 1979–88	R&D expenditures 1979–88	Domestic patenting 1979–88	Foreign patenting 1979–88	External patenting 1979–88	External/domestic 1979	1988
USA	2.66	5.30	2.44	6.30	7.50	1.73	2.67
Japan	3.84	8.15	8.30	' 3.85	11.53	0.25	0.33
Germany	1.70	3.58	0.54	4.87	6.79	2.28	3.93
France	1.82	4.86	1.16	5.95	7.64	2.41	4.22
UK	1.44	2.43	0.64	5.49	8.34	1.37	2.65
Netherlands	1.50	3.83	2.00	10.17	6.91	5.18	7.90
Switzerland	2.21	4.75	–2.21	9.87	3.38	4.60	7.58
Sweden	1.98	7.71	–2.39	10.12	8.56	2.51	6.52
Austria	1.82	3.95	–0.75	13.51	7.44	1.66	3.39
Canada	2.39	5.60	6.28	2.88	8.31	2.83	3.35

Notes
Domestic patents are patents granted in the country to residents of the country. Foreign patents are patents granted in the country to foreigners. External patents are patents extended to foreign countries by domestic residents.
The highest and lowest values for each column in the table are overlined and underlined, respectively.

Source: Archibugi and Pianta (1992).

Table 5.6 further shows the growth of patents granted in the USA in 1978–91, broken down by country of origin and sector. Industries that are associated with a high growth in patenting on average are fine chemicals (including drugs), mechanical engineering, electronic capital goods and components and telecommunications.[30] Japan again stands out with the highest growth rate in all of the specified industries, except in telecommunications, raw materials and defence. In these three industries the USA ranks highest. Surprisingly, the USA ranks lowest in other chemicals and motor vehicles. On average, however, two small countries, Sweden and Switzerland, rank lowest, with negative growth in a number of industries.

As with all comparisons of growth rates, differences in absolute levels must be kept in mind. Table 5.7 further shows for a few countries and industries the number of US patents held by a country divided by the total number held by a set of 18 OECD countries. Except for pulp and paper, the patent shares (defined in this way) have increased considerably for Japan, while they have decreased for the USA as well as for Germany, Sweden and the UK.

Table 5.6 The average annual percentage change in the USA of patenting by different countries and industries, 1978–1991

Industries	Austria	Canada	Switzerland	Germany	France	UK	Italy	Japan	Netherlands	Sweden	USA
Fine chemicals	0.78	2.07	-1.36	9.64	6.28	2.21	5.21	47.7l	0.21	0.00	29.9
Other chemicals	1.57	5.71	-0.83	7.21	2.71	-4.61	1.35	85.9l	4.85	-1.50	-20.7
Composite materials	0.64	0.78	-0.07	6.91	1.28	-2.14	1.57	48.2l	0.57	-0.36	25.7
Mechanical engineering	0.41	19.7	5.64	55.9	20.8	-1.28	15.5	285.2l	6.64	-7.78	156.6
Motor vehicles	0.35	2.00	-0.64	4.71	-0.42	-0.85	0.50	28.1l	0.07	0.21	-5.1
Electrical machinery	0.36	3.78	-2.21	4.64	5.28	-2.42	1.64	64.1l	-0.92	-0.57	26.2
Electronic capital goods and components	0.67	1.85	-2.42	7.00	3.78	3.78	1.85	177.3l	4.14	0.57	125.7
Telecommunications	0.71	2.28	-1.42	5.35	6.07	3.50	0.21	54.3	2.21	-0.71	75.6l
Electronic consumer goods	0.14	2.64	0.28	3.64	2.28	2.78	0.50	169.5l	-0.28	-0.14	38.7
Technologies for extracting and processing raw materials	0.64	2.71	-2.78	4.21	4.21	0.86	1.64	11.3	0.57	0.21	13.2l
Defence-related technologies	0.21	0.14	0.14	4.41	2.35	1.71	0.21	0.85	0.07	0.28	16.7l
Others	0.14	13.7	2.64	12.8	7.07	2.14	4.28	34.3	3.78	1.92	222.1l

Note: The highest and lowest values for each country are overlined and underlined, respectively. The highest value for each industry is marked l.

Source: Deiaco (1993).

Table 5.7   The share by different countries and industries of the amount of US patents granted in 1978 and 1991

Industry	USA 1978	USA 1991	Japan 1978	Japan 1991	Germany 1978	Germany 1991	UK 1978	UK 1991	Sweden 1978	Sweden 1991
Mechanical engineering	62.8	56.9	10.5	20.4	10.8	10.6	4.2	3.3	2.0	1.1
Electrical machinery	64.5	55.5	14.6	26.0	8.7	7.3	3.5	2.4	1.4	0.0
Motor vehicles	39.2	30.7	28.9	44.7	15.6	12.9	3.3	2.6	—	—
Pharmaceuticals	30.8	21.3	17.6	28.6	18.2	16.5	13.1	12.6	1.8	1.3
Pulp and paper	50.6	51.7	7.8	5.2	—	—	—	—	10.8	12.6

Note: The shares have been calculated for 18 OECD countries. The highest and lowest values for each column in the table are overlined and underlined, respectively.

Source: Deiaco (1993).

The patent statistics show the growth of patenting, particularly international patenting, as well as the outstanding growth of Japan's patenting. Japan's patenting has also grown faster than other countries in a broad range of industries with respect to patents granted in the USA. However, the present purpose is not to make a detailed benchmarking of different countries using patent statistics. This is a special topic in itself, which has been treated in a number of studies.[31]

5.5.2   Quality of Patents

First, a reminder of the general warning against interpretations based only on patent statistics is in order. Simple patent counts do not account for the large variations in the technical and economic qualities of patents. A popular quality indicator of patents is the number of times a patent document is cited in other patent documents.[32] However, patent citation counts per patent issued can vary greatly across industries, countries and years due to skewed distributions and averages over a small number of patents.[33] Comparisons of trends are a little less dangerous. Keeping this warning in mind, we proceed boldly to Figures 5.1a–e, which show time trends for average patent quality.

Figures 5.1a–e show how patent quality has improved over time.[34] The general trend is that, except for pharmaceuticals, Japan has upgraded the quality of her patents, just as she has upgraded the quality of her products. There is also another possible parallel between Japan's patent quality and product quality. The quality of Japanese products was once low by Western standards, and therefore many Western companies in the 1960s and 1970s thought Japanese products

(a) Iron and steel

(b) Pharmaceuticals

(c) Electrical equipment

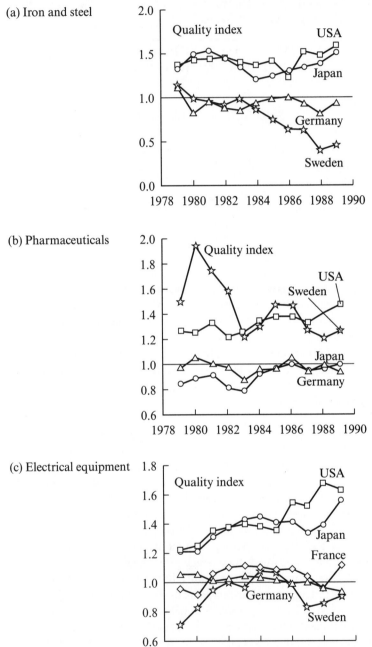

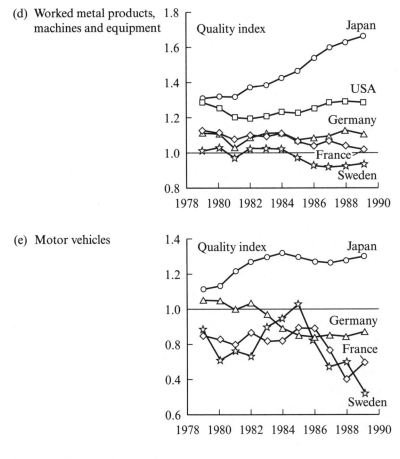

(d) Worked metal products, machines and equipment

(e) Motor vehicles

Source: Deiaco (1993).

Figure 5.1   Patent quality in different industries and countries, 1978–1990
(three-year moving average)

would not present future competitive threats, thereby ignoring any upward trend. Similarly, many Western companies today view Japanese patents as being of low quality. Figures 5.1a–c show that this view is no longer justified in general (although Japanese pharmaceutical patents are cited below average, as shown).

As was shown in Table 5.5, Japan, for the period 1978–88, ranked highest among a number of OECD countries regarding growth of industrial production, growth of R&D expenditures, growth of domestic patenting and growth of international patenting (while the growth of foreign patenting in Japan ranked next to the lowest). International patenting also grew considerably in other countries in this period. At the same time, however, in most OECD countries domestic patenting grew poorly or even negatively. What, then, explains the continued high levels of patenting in Japan? Large Japanese corporations take out a great portion of Japanese patents and much of the growth in Japanese patenting is attributable to the growth of patenting in these corporations. We shall therefore take a closer look at these corporations in the next sections and then turn to explanations for the high patenting propensity in Japan in Section 5.8.

5.6   SURVEY DATA ON R&D AND PATENTING IN LARGE JAPANESE CORPORATIONS

In this study a sample of 24 large Japanese corporations, drawn from chemical, electrical/electronic and mechanical industries, has been surveyed through a mail questionnaire. (The sample and questionnaire are described in more detail in Appendix 2.) Tables 5.8, 5.9a, 5.9b and 5.10 give some R&D and patent statistics, as reported by the IP departments of the corporations in the survey questionnaire.

As can be seen in Table 5.8, R&D expenditures grew 53 per cent in the period 1987–91 with an even greater growth in international R&D.[35] Moreover a substantial portion of R&D was devoted to research although product development dominated, a larger portion of which went into development of new rather than existing products. Although the difficulty of upholding a common distinction between R and D as well as between new and existing products and processes makes the figures very uncertain, the data are in line with the generally acknowledged emphasis in Japan on research and development of new products initiated in the 1980s. Moreover, licensing in grew substantially and exceeded licensing out.

Table 5.9a shows that domestic and international patenting also grew but at a more modest rate. The growth of patent portfolios was fairly consistent (about 10 per cent) across sectors. The dominance of electrical corporations in patenting, for example in the USA, is also clear from the table data. The length of time patents are kept in force is, moreover, fairly equal across industries, while the share of patents that are kept in force the maximal length of time varies across industries. Table 5.9b shows the fairly low shares of patent applications in Japan that led to patents, and the low share of patents that were commercially and economically successful. The industry differences in this respect are noteworthy, however. The long time between patent application and market introduction, particularly in the chemical and pharmaceutical corporations, is also noteworthy.

Table 5.8   R&D structure in large Japanese corporations

(Code) Variable	Chemical ($n = 9$)	Electrical ($n = 10$)	Mechanical ($n = 5$)	Total ($n = 24$)
(B1) Total R&D expenditures worldwide in your company 1991				
(US$ million)	255	1984	1285	1190
Growth ratio 1991/1987	1.38	1.56	1.50	1.53
(B2) Percentage of R&D conducted				
abroad in 1991	5.57	3.86	5.80	5.00
Growth ratio 1991/1987[1]	7.85	3.39	1.71	3.16
(B6) Percentage of company's total R&D expenditures that were:[2]				
Related to development of new				
products, 1991	44.40	22.80	32.50	35.50
Growth ratio 1991/1987	1.04	1.00	1.13	1.06
Related to development of existing				
products, 1991	21.20	47.80	30.50	31.40
Growth ratio 1991/1987	1.00	1.00	0.88	0.97
Related to development of new				
production processes, 1991	15.10	13.80	11.80	13.80
Growth ratio 1991/1987	0.96	1.00	1.09	1.04
Related to development of existing				
production processes, 1991	15.30	6.30	16.00	12.90
Growth ratio 1991/1987	0.91	0.83	1.36	0.94
Unrelated to specific products or				
processes, i.e., research, 1991	11.70	9.50	9.30	10.40
Growth ratio 1991/1987	1.04	1.21	0.65	0.91
(B8a) Total licensing receipts, 1991				
(as % of total R&D)	9.20	5.20	7.33	7.50
Growth ratio 1991/1987	1.51	1.53	1.38	1.47
(B8b) Total licensing expenditures, 1991				
(as % of total R&D)	3.20	3.60	8.30	4.40
Growth ratio 1991/1987	0.74	1.00	0.86	0.85

Notes
1. The growth is from low absolute levels, which gives a high growth rate.
2. The figures do not add up exactly to 100 per cent due to partially missing data, particularly from the electrical corporations.

Table 5.9a   Patenting in large Japanese corporations

(Code) Question	Chemical $(n=9)$	Electrical $(n=10)$	Mechanical $(n=5)$	Total $(n=24)$
(D2a) Total number of priority applications filed in 1991[4]	393	5 285	2 100	2 678
Growth ratio 1991/1987	0.96	1.05	0.79	0.99
(D2c) Total number of patents in force in your company's patent portfolio, 1991[4]	4 022	22 857	9 380	11 954
Growth ratio 1991/1987	1.09	1.10	1.10	1.10
(D2d) Total number of patents granted to your company in the USA in 1991	53	495	123	230
Growth ratio 1991/1987	1.36	1.12	0.57[1]	1.02
(D6a) Company's average number of years for keeping a patent in force	10.5	11.4	9.2	10.5
(D6b) Percentage of patents that are kept in force for the maximum patent protection time	4.9	36.1[2]	3.8	16.1
(D7) Percentage of patents with domestic priority for which a foreign application was filed in 1991	33.0[3]	13.6	17.2	23.2
Growth ratio 1991/1987	1.06	1.36	1.13	1.12

Notes
1. This figure is highly influenced by Honda and Toyota.
2. This figure is large due to the high patent retention (that is, different patenting strategies) reported by a few electrical companies.
3. Chemical corporations have a longer tradition of foreign patenting, especially for licensing purposes.
4. In some instances, contradictions between the responding data and data from other sources (that is, JAPIO) have been observed. The data in this table represents that which was received by questionnaire and portrays an accurate representation of the magnitude of patenting by sector.

Table 5.9b   Patenting in large Japanese corporations

(Code) Question	Chemical ($n = 9$)	Electrical ($n = 10$)	Mechanical ($n = 5$)	Total ($n = 24$)
(D4) Share of patent applications for which a patent is granted in:				
Europe	85.0	78.8	89.0	83.7
Japan	55.0	64.3	58.0	59.6
USA	88.3	85.3	89.0	87.3
(D5a) Percentage of patents granted that are exploited commercially through own production	20.7	31.7	25.7	26.1
(D5b) Percentage of patents granted that through own production have led to economically successful new products or processes[1]	12.3	20.3	6.5	14.7
(D5c) Percentage of patents granted that are licensed commercially	4.5	22.7[2]	3.0	11.3
(D12) How many years on average before market introduction of a new product a key patent is applied for in the R&D process[3]	7.0	4.8	4.3	5.7

Notes
1. Assuming patents are applied for in Japan in the first place, this means that only 6.8 per cent (D4 × D5b) of patents applied for by chemical corporations lead to economically successful new products or processes, while the corresponding figures for the electrical and mechanical corporations are 13.1 per cent and 3.8 per cent respectively. However small samples and missing data make these compound figures uncertain. The low value for the mechanical sector is noteworthy, however. This figure apparently illustrates the 'patenting paradox' mentioned in Chapter 3, which illustrates the fact that some companies continue to patent without considering patents as particularly important on average.
2. This high figure is probably due to more widespread block-licensing among electrical corporations, which in turn is an indication of higher patent interdependencies.
3. There was a high variation in the data received, with some companies responding that patent protection was not sought until some time after market introduction as opposed to before.

Table 5.10 shows the detected infringement propensity and which industry was most involved in litigation. An indication of litigious propensity is given by looking at the ratio of the number of litigated patents to the number of infringed patents (D10/D9 × D2c), as detected by the companies. However, the sample is small, and some data are missing and the collected data refer only to one year. Thus the results cannot be taken as representative. A downward bias could perhaps also be expected regarding outward litigation in Japanese corporations that traditionally are not litigious and do not want to appear as litigious. On the other hand the propensity to litigate has increased among large Japanese corporations as a response to the increasing propensity to litigate among US corporations, and the Japanese corporations do wish to make this signal clear to their competitors. One can also note that chemical corporations in the sample have a high ratio of outward litigation to inward litigation.

Table 5.10   Infringements and litigations in large Japanese corporations

(Code) Question	Chemical ($n = 9$)	Electrical ($n = 10$)	Mechanical ($n = 5$)	Total ($n = 24$)
(D9) Percentage of own patents for which infringements were detected in 1991(approx. no. of detections)	1.22 (62)	2.00 (241)	0.13 (18)	1.12 (103)
Growth ratio 1991/1987	1.20 (1.29)	1.33 (1.35)	1.63 (1.80)	1.27 (1.36)
(D10) Number of patent litigations filed from your side against other firms or parties in 1991	3.10	0	0.25	1.40
Growth ratio 1991/1987[1]	3.10	n.a.[2]	n.a.[2]	3.50
(D11) Number of patent litigations directed against your firm in 1991	0.30	1.50	1.70	1.00
Growth ratio 1991/1987[1]	n.a.[2]	8.82	5.00	7.70
(D10/(D9 × D2c)) Litigious propensity 1991 (%)[3]	5.00	0	1.40	1.40

Notes
1. Growth rates are high since growth takes place from low levels.
2. Not applicable since 1987 value is zero.
3. That is, the number of litigated patents divided by number of patents with detected infringements. Small samples and missing data make this compound figure uncertain, however. The zero value for electrical corporations is not representative for other years.

Table 5.11 shows that patent protection actually stimulates R&D investments as intended, especially in the chemical industry. The industry differences are large, however, depending upon differing technological and patenting opportunities, differing product market lifetimes and the different relevance of alternative appropriation mechanisms or commercialization strategies (see Chapter 6). Taylor and Silberston (1973) found, based on a sample of 27 UK firms, that R&D budgets would be cut by 5 per cent if patent protection was removed, except in speciality chemicals firms and pharmaceuticals who would cut their budgets by

25 per cent and 64 per cent, respectively. Thus the sensitivity of R&D budgets in the UK in the late 1960s was much lower on average than in Japan in the early 1990s. Mansfield (1986) also indicates a fairly low sensitivity of the rate of invention to the removal of patent protection. Chapter 3 also gives some theoretical calculations of company responses to changes in the maximum patent protection time. These calculations are surprisingly consistent with the data for the chemical corporations. The chemical industry is also traditionally most dependent upon and sensitive to the strength of patent protection. On the other hand, the low sensitivity to patent protection time among mechanical corporations is surprising, also when compared to the share of patents they maintain for the maximum patent protection period (see question D6b in Table 5.9a). Similarly the electrical corporations keep a large share of their patents in force for the maximum time while they are rather insensitive to a reduction of this time by ten years. Whether this is due to small samples, the skewed nature of patent values, deficient patent management or something else must be left as an open question. However, the results for the total sample are roughly in line with expectations. The figures indicate a lower sensitivity than a simple theoretical calculation, as done in Chapter 3, would yield. Since there are other appropriation mechanisms for R&D investments, this is a reasonable result.

Table 5.11   Sensitivity of the R&D investments of large Japanese corporations to patent protection time, 1992

(Code) Question	Chemical ($n = 9$)	Electrical ($n = 10$)	Mechanical ($n = 5$)	Total ($n = 24$)
(F13) What would the effect be on your company's total R&D budget as a rough percentage, if the maximum patent protection time was:				
(a) Increased by 3 years	+8.5	+2.8	+0.3	+4.8
(b) Decreased to 10 years	–21.2	–3.7	–0.3	–10.7
(c) Decreased to 0 years (i.e., patent protection ceases)	–59.2	–40.0	–5.5	–38.2

5.7   PATENTING TRENDS IN LARGE JAPANESE CORPORATIONS

As mentioned several times, a strong basic trend towards an increased role of and attention to patenting appeared in the 1980s. This is corroborated and detailed in Table 5.12.

Table 5.12   Patent trend assessments in large Japanese corporations,
1987–1992

(Scale: False = –2, –1, 0, +1, +2 = True)

(Code) Trend proposition	Chemical ($n = 9$)	Electrical ($n = 10$)	Mechanical ($n = 5$)	Total ($n = 24$)
(D15) In your opinion have any essential changes on an average occurred in your company during the period 1987–92 with regard to the following:				
(1) Patents are sought earlier in the R&D and innovation process	0.89	0.60	1.40 (5)	0.88
(2) The use of patent literature as an information source has increased	1.11	0.90	1.60 (2)	1.13
(3) The resources for the firm's patent activities have increased	1.22 (5)	1.60 (2)	1.00	1.33 (5)
(4) Hiring patent agencies or similar outside assistance has increased	0.56	1.30 (4)	0.80	0.92
(5) The status of patent activities within the firm has increased	1.11	1.50 (3)	1.80 (1)	1.42 (2)
(6) The cost of licence negotiation has increased	0.78	1.30 (4)	1.20	1.08
(7) Licensing is becoming increasingly broad-based	0.56	1.20	1.20	0.96
(8) Patent pooling has increased in importance	0.22	0.50	0.80	0.46
(9) The average number of years for keeping a patent in force has increased	–0.22	–0.10	0.20	–0.08
(10) The number of countries in which patents are sought has increased	0.75	0.50	1.00	0.70
(11a) The frequency of patent infringements has increased	0.67	1.10	1.40 (5)	1.00
(11b) The frequency of competitors' patents blocking your activities has increased	1.00	0.60	1.00	0.83
(11c) The frequency of your patents blocking the activities of your competitors has increased	0.56	0.50	1.00	0.63
(11d) The frequency of patent litigations has increased	0.67	0.70	1.20	0.79
(12a) The possibility of finding generic patents has increased	0.33	0.60	0.40	0.46
(12b) Your company's propensity to patent has increased	1.33 (3)	1.11	1.20	1.22
(13a) Your company's propensity to license out has increased	0.33	0.60	0.60	0.50
(13b) Your company's propensity to license in has increased	0.63	0.60	0.40	0.57
(13c) The role of patents in joint ventures				

and cooperative R&D has increased	0.89	0.80	1.20	0.92
(13d) Patents are increasingly sought in order to generate licence incomes	0.44	0.70	1.60 (2)	0.79
(13e) Increasing R&D costs have increased your propensity to license out	0.33	0.40	0.60	0.42
(13f) Royalty rates have increased when licensing out	0.44	0.60	0.40	0.50
(13g) Royalty rates have increased when licensing in	0.67	1.30 (4)	0.80	0.96
(14) The strategic role of patents in your company has increased	1.56 (1)	1.30 (4)	1.20	1.38 (3)
(15) The strategic role of licences in your company has increased	1.33 (3)	1.30 (4)	1.60 (2)	1.38 (3)
(16) The role of patents in standard-setting has increased	1.13	1.00	1.00	1.05
(17) The role of cross-licensing has increased	1.11	0.67	1.00	0.91
(18) Top management attention to IPR and patenting matters has increased	1.44 (2)	1.70 (1)	1.40 (5)	1.54 (1)
(19) The importance of trademarks has increased	0.89	1.10	1.25	1.04
(20) The importance of prophylactic publishing has increased	–0.33	0.10	1.00	0.13
(21a) New products are related to an increasing number of patent classes	1.11	0.80	0.80	0.92
(21b) New production processes are related to an increasing number of patent classes	0.67	0.70	1.00	0.75
(22) New patents are related to an increasing number of product areas	1.00	0.20	0.80	0.63

Note: The top five ranks of values in each column are shown in parentheses.

Some summary observations from the table are:

1. Patenting and licensing have taken on a wider variety of roles and especially a greater strategic role in the corporations studied, regardless of industry. The role of patents in standard-setting, which is also a new kind of role for patents, has moreover increased in importance. Infringements and litigious activities in connection with patents have also increased. This will be further elaborated in Chapters 6 and 7.

2. The cross-linkages from patents to products/processes and vice versa have also grown in both directions. This is to say that new products and processes are becoming increasingly multitechnological (see D15(21) in the table). This is in line with a general trend towards more 'mul-tech' products and processes in industry. At the same time, new patents are becoming more widely applicable to different product areas, that is, inventions become

more multiproduct-related or generic in that sense (see questions D15(12) and D15(22)). This will also be dealt with further in Chapters 6 and 7.

3. Across industries, patenting has been significantly upgraded in the corporations as indicated by increased top management attention, increased resources and increased status. This will be further elaborated in Chapter 8.
4. Patent literature is more intensely used as a source of information about new technologies and other companies. This will be dealt with further in Chapter 9.
5. Patenting propensity has increased among the companies (see further next section) and the 'speed to patent' in the R&D process has increased (see further Chapter 7).

Naturally, one cannot be very conclusive about simple trend perceptions pertaining to a sample of companies as shown in Table 5.12 over a relatively short period. However, the statistical evidence supports the trends indicated above as well as the case interviews pointed out in this study.

5.8   THE PROPENSITY TO PATENT IN JAPAN

5.8.1   Quality and Quantity of Patents

As seen above, Japan's industry has an outstanding post-war record of patent growth, abroad (especially in the USA) as well as at home. This is corroborated by data over several indicators, such as patent numbers (number of patent applications and patents granted in Japan, the USA, Europe and so on over the last few decades); patent shares (regarding both applications and patents granted); patent intensities (for example, number of patents per R&D worker or R&D dollar); and patent citations.[36]

What accounts for this record?[37] The relevance of the question is underscored by the fact that the growth of patenting in many countries declined in the 1970s and in some cases even turned negative (see Griliches 1984).[38] The survey study here cannot give an answer to this question on the basis of cross-national comparisons. However, some suggestions will be made on the basis of the sample of corporations studied.

As seen in Table 5.1, Japan had already taken the worldwide lead in 1958 in the number of patent and utility model applications. The dramatic increase in patent application filings in Japan even before the pro-patent era of the 1980s has to a large extent been attributed to efforts by leading electrical and electronics firms. In the early 1980s, Hitachi, Toshiba, Matsushita, Mitsubishi Electric, NEC and Fujitsu were reported to account for about 25 per cent of all applications filed with the JPO (Rahn 1983, p. 485). In a report from 1976, the JPO enumerated the following concrete causes for the rise in patent applications (as described in Rahn 1983, pp. 486–8):

1. Causes on the enterprise side
   a. utilization of applications for enterprise strategies (for example, for propaganda purposes);
   b. omissive preliminary search activities;
   c. increase in defensive applications.
2. Causes on the patent administration side
   a. quality of the examination (inconsistent and sometimes low requirements on the level of inventiveness);
   b. low application fees and requests for examination fees.
3. Causes on the service organization side
   a. the situation of the patent attorney business (with a tendency to file inadequate applications);
   b. incomplete organization of search services and inspecting systems.

With the emergence of the pro-patent era in the 1980s, IPR activities and status have increased considerably in Japan. However, it is fair to say that IPR is still an issue with limited attention from the public at large.

The higher propensity to patent in Japan's industry compared to US industry was singled out by Westney (1993) as one of nine key characteristics distinguishing technology management and behaviour in Japanese firms from US firms (see further Chapter 6). Westney presents two sets of explanatory factors, likely to complement each other. The first set refers to strategic motives of three kinds: (i) to access others' technology breakthroughs by surrounding them with patents, thereby forcing the other party to cross-license; (ii) to conceal one's own R&D priorities by patent flooding (see Chapter 7); and (iii) to offset licensing expenditures. The second set of explanatory factors refers to organizational factors, especially the internal incentives R&D personnel in Japanese companies receive for patents.

In addition to these types of explanations, Westney refers to factors such as the fact that the Japanese patent system, compared to the USA, has lower requirements on the level of invention needed for a patent application to be granted (approved), and that – despite this[39] – Japanese patent applications have a lower rate of success for approval. The latter factors would to some extent account for a higher volume of patents granted in Japan and a higher volume of Japanese patent applications in general. Historically this may have been the case, as is indicated in the JPO report from 1976 (see above).[40] A contributing factor has been Japan's legal framework in the past, with a utility-model law and a narrow scope of protection with basically a single-claim system until 1987.[41]

An important overall factor behind Japan's large volumes of patent applications for mostly minor inventions has been the catch-up process described earlier. However, when discussing quality of patents, several distinctions must be made. First there is the *legal quality* of the application in terms of formulating its wording, supporting it with evidence of novelty and aligning it with the legal framework.[42] Second, there is the *technical quality*, roughly expressible in terms of level of invention. Third, there is the *economic quality* in terms of potential economic value for the rights holder. Unfortunately, the correlation between the legal, technical, and economic qualities of patent applications and patents is not strong.[43] Minor technical inventions may have major economic value and vice versa. The common attitude among Western engineers of frowning on minor 'junk patents' or 'petty patents' is often economically questionable from a corporate point of view. Just as questionable is the behaviour, also common among Western engineers, of seeking technically major patents and then neglecting to support them with subsequent patents, minor as well as major. Many companies can certify that it is costly to have an engineering culture that gives priority to technical qualities with little regard to economic values (see further Chapters 7 and 8).[44]

Still another distinction to be made is between domestic and foreign patent applications and patents. In most cases the domestic application is the priority application, and only the 'best' applications are followed up by foreign applications.

Table 5.13   Approval rates of patent applications (per cent)

	Approval rate in		
	Europe	Japan	USA
Japanese companies[1]	83.7	59.6	87.3
Swedish companies[1]	87.5	80.0	85.4
Average approval rate in 1983–87[2]	87.2 (UK)		
	58.6 (WG)	16.8	59.4

Notes
1. As estimated by the companies in 1992 for the period 1987–91. The samples are described in Appendix 2.
2. These data, published in Westney (1993, p. 42) as well as in Westney (1994, p. 162), apparently refer to the ratio of gross number of approvals to applications received by the patent office in the respective countries during the period 1983–87. Europe is represented by the United Kingdom and what was then West Germany. Such a ratio is also influenced by patent office capacity constraints (resulting in delayed approvals) and by differences in the legal framework with respect to whether requests for examination are needed or not.

Regarding the technical quality of Japanese patents, several studies have shown, based on number of citations, that Japanese patents in general in the 1980s were not inferior. (See, for example, Narin et al. 1992, and also Section 5.5 as well as the repeatedly published Patent Scoreboards in *Business Week*.) There were significant sector differences, however. The number of citations of Japanese patents in pharmaceuticals was low while it was high in electronics (see Figure 5.1).

The technical and legal quality of patent applications reflects on their approval rate.[45] There is reason to believe that this approval rate is increasing, at least among large, leading companies in Japan (see Table 5.13). The technical and economic quality of patents is also indicated by the share of commercially exploited patents and share of patents supporting economically successful products, as well as by the maintenance profile (or vintage structure) of the company's patents, that is, how long patents are kept in force by the company. Table 5.14 gives an overview of these indicators.

Table 5.14   Quality indicators of Japanese and Swedish patents[1]

	Share of commercially exploited patents[2]	Share of patents leading to economic success	Share of patents licensed commercially[3]	Number of years patents are kept in force	Share of patents kept maximally[4]
Japanese companies	26.1	14.7	11.3	10.5	16.1
Swedish companies	60.5	38.1	4.9	11.4	21.6

Notes
1. Estimated by the companies in 1992. The samples are described in Appendix 2.
2. Through own production.
3. This figure is biased upwards due to block licensing and broad cross-licensing agreements.
4. More detailed data on maintenance profile were collected as well, but are not shown here.

All in all, there is insufficient reason to believe in low quality levels of Japan's patents as a dominant explanation behind its large quantity of patents.

5.8.2   Reasons behind Japan's High Patenting Propensity

Legal, economic and historical factors in a company's environment influence its patenting behaviour, as do internal factors related to the company's economics, management, strategy, organization, culture and so on. These factors interact over time. For example, as mentioned several times, the lack of natural resources in Japan yielded emphasis on intellectual capital with a concomitant build-up of R&D resources and IPR resources. The role of the historical catch-up process

Table 5.15   Most important factors behind increased importance of patenting

	Three most important factors behind increased importance of patenting		
Company	Factor (1)	Factor (2)	Factor (3)
1	Patent litigation and mediation system	Increase in patent licensing	Expedition of patent examination period
2	Prevailing competitors	Prevailing patent infringement	Cross-licensing with competitors
3	Increase in royalty	International harmonization of patent laws and practices	Increase in patent infringement suits
4	To prevent competitors from copying	To keep strong shares of market	To encourage engineers to create new technologies
5	The business of functional products has increased	The business has become worldwide	The case of cross-licensing in some areas has increased
6	The competition for developments of new technologies has increased	Intensification of patent protection, especially in the USA	Markets and/or firm activities have become borderless
7	Specialization and concentration in technical strategy	Tie-up with technologically advanced corporations	Acquiring exclusive possession legitimately
8	Competition in R&D has grown more intense	Evaluation of patent has been changed (becoming more effective weapon)	USA's policy for patenting
9	Market globalization	R&D cost increases	Short life cycle of new products
10	Trend in the USA that patents produce money	Growing numbers of technology transfer cases	—
11	Increased need for high value-added products	Stricter earth environment protection policies	More severe competition in development as the technological gap between companies is narrowed

Note: The wording of question F6b was: 'In case the importance of patenting for commercialization of new technologies in general has increased, which are the three most important factors behind this increase in your opinion (please specify briefly)'. A selection of answers is presented here, with the original wordings (with some minor exceptions).

in Japan has also been noted repeatedly. The patent culture and top management attention to patenting in companies like Canon is described in Chapter 8. This in turn has led to a build-up of substantial IP departments and resources with strong IP management which in turn has further boosted the quantity and quality of patenting.

In the questionnaire survey of large Japanese corporations, data on R&D and patenting facts was collected together with perceptual and qualitative data. Stepwise, linear regressions on the questionnaire data were then run to determine which variables reduced most of the variance in the number of patent applications and patents granted (in the USA) in the Japanese corporations in the sample. Not surprisingly, IP resources were most important in this respect; that is, the number of patent personnel was the primary explanatory variable, followed by the total amount of patenting expenditures.[46] Variables of much less importance were the total amount of R&D and the percentage of sales based on patents, that is, question F1 in the questionnaire (see Appendix 2).

Table 5.15 summarizes the factors believed by the Japanese companies in the study to be behind the increased importance of patenting as expressed in the questionnaire survey (question F6b), company by company (not all of them). The factors pointed at in the table give a rough idea of the inside-out perspectives in the corporations. As indicated, there are a few general reasons related to US policy changes, intensified international competition, growing technology interdependencies and institutional changes. These kinds of answers have then been complemented by answers given in in-depth interviews. Essentially the answers confirm the emergence of the pro-patent era with its various features. However, it must be kept in mind that Japan's patenting propensity was high already before the pro-patent era, indicating more deep-running historic, institutional reasons.

5.8.3 Reasons behind a Low Patenting Propensity in some European Corporations

The high patenting propensity in Japanese companies is outstanding, and the reasons behind it have been elaborated above. But what reasons lie behind the often low patenting propensity in many Western firms? We may shed some light on this question by looking at the large Swedish corporations in the sample, which mostly have had significantly lower patenting propensity than their matching competitors in Japan. First, some illustrative anecdotal evidence has been collected in interviews, and we shall give two examples.

In the 1960s and 1970s the white-goods company Electrolux (with global operations, employing more than 100 000 people) emphasized market lead times rather than patenting. Acquisition of companies was a dominant growth strategy. In connection with the acquisitions of foreign companies like Zanussi in Italy and White in the USA, corporate management in Electrolux later became alerted to the importance of patenting, since these companies, especially White, had a much more pro-patent culture. The subsequent need to find patenting personnel has then forced Electrolux to internationalize patenting operations to some extent.

For the telecommunications equipment manufacturer, Ericsson, patenting was almost never considered a strategic issue until the late 1980s and early 1990s.[47] During the 1960s and 1970s Ericsson's patenting work was considered of high technical and legal quality but was nevertheless of minor importance. In the 1980s, in connection with a management and policy shift in patenting and R&D, patenting operations deteriorated. Although patenting was not considered unimportant, for example in licensing and pricing, R&D people were usually too busy with R&D to spend much time on patenting, and top management did not do much to change this, beyond lip-service. A turnaround in efforts and management attention to IP in Ericsson, as well as in many other telecommunications companies, took place in connection with Motorola's push of their standard blocking patents in mobile communications in the late 1980s, as described in Chapter 6.6. This triggering event was like a 'wake-up call', although it did coincide with several other conducive event streams. First, Ericsson appointed a new CEO with hands-on experience in patenting from outside the telecommunications sector. Patent issues now did not experience the traditional difficulties in getting top management attention. On the contrary, the agony in Ericsson over Motorola's behaviour was shared and fuelled by top management. Considerable resources for patenting were set aside, ambitious targets were set, extensive recruiting was done, attitudes were changed and so on. This created a sudden turnaround in IP practices. Second, the mobile communications business was beginning to thrive, which involved Ericsson in the business climate of consumer electronics, including its stronger emphasis on IPR. The mobile communications division in Ericsson thereby became a kind of lead-house for IPR issues in Ericsson. Third, the telecommunications service sector was further liberalized with the break-up of AT&T and the Bell system in 1983,[48] and became subjected to technology-based competition with an increased role for IPR. Fourth, the awareness of the emerging pro-patent era had grown in general, signalling a need for change throughout Swedish big industry.[49]

In summary, general reasons behind a low patenting propensity were:

1. Emphasis on other strategies for technology exploitation, for example, secrecy and/or market lead times.
2. Lack of competition.
3. Lack of a patent culture in a company or a whole industry.
4. Disappointing experiences from trying to enforce patent rights in the past, with low probability of winning in court, low damages and so on.

5. Engineering attitudes, overly emphasizing the technical quality of patents and snobbishly frowning on small, 'petty patents' or 'nuisance patents'.
6. Lack of management attention and mismanagement.[50]
7. Absence of litigation, large damage claims, injunctions and so on.
8. High costs of patenting.
9. Self-fulfilling attitudes in an industry.[51]

Several variables used to explain the low patenting propensity in Sweden are similar to variables used to explain the high patenting propensity in Japan. There are differences in the weight attached to these variables, which are likely derived in turn from historical and cultural differences. However, some institutional and general business conditions have become more similar between East and West in the post-war period, such as increased internationalization, increased technology-based competition, increased R&D costs and increased privatization of R&D results. One must also keep in mind that before the pro-patent era in the 1980s, incentives to patent were much weaker, except for a few industries such as chemicals and pharmaceuticals, where invent-around possibilities could be limited (see Chapter 6). Patenting, paradoxically, seems to have been of less importance for companies accustomed to being on the technological forefront than for companies trying to catch up.

Thus, one might expect that companies in the West would increase their patenting propensity, but with varying time lags, as a reaction to the pro-patent era and to Japan having caught up and having continued to pursue patenting aggressively, as well as a result of the self-reinforcing nature of patenting. Many large Swedish corporations have indeed increased their patenting propensity in the 1990s, sometimes slowly, sometimes abruptly. Several factors have acted as 'alarm bells' or alerting events, for example:

1. recognition of weak bargaining power;
2. acquisitions of companies with a patent culture;
3. new entrants on the market with aggressive patent strategies;
4. litigation and large damage claims;
5. missed business opportunities;
6. severe blockages encountered; and
7. alarming patent statistics coming from benchmarking projects or public ranking lists.

Most importantly, however, the uncertainty arising from the frequent patenting of competitors triggers increased attention to and efforts in patenting, leading to increased patenting propensity. The hike in patent values since the 1980s, with some specific widely publicized examples, seems to be of much less importance than the insurance value of patents, or the expected cost of not taking out patents (that is, less aversion). This is especially true, since the insurance value of a patent increases when others insure themselves as well through patenting.[52] In contrast, the lottery value of a patent (that is, the value of a patent as a lottery ticket), is decreased as others increasingly participate in the lottery.

5.9   SUMMARY AND CONCLUSIONS

This chapter started with a review of the history of the patent system in Japan. The Meiji Restoration in the mid-1860s, inspired in no small measure by the perceived importance of technology, was of course a major turning point in Japan's general development towards an industrial state. Shortly thereafter a patent system was tried in Japan, inspired by the perceived importance of patents for the development of industry in the West and in the USA in particular. Thus Japan's patent system was installed right at the beginning of her industrialization. However, one cannot infer that the patent system was of decisive importance for Japan's industrialization. The ability to catch up by absorbing and modifying technology from the West, and particularly from the USA after World War II, was much more important. The patent system was, however, widely used in the catch-up process. Since the end of World War II, Japanese corporations have accumulated very large patent portfolios and substantial patenting capabilities. Concomitant to the post-war growth of industrial production and R&D, Japan has developed an outstanding patenting record in the world, with large electrical corporations at the forefront.

The modern Japanese patent system is more similar to the European patent systems than to the US one, but there are also some features specific to Japan, in particular regarding the way cultural factors and the catch-up process have influenced the use of the patent system. Thus the symbolic value of patents as rewards is important, as is technology diffusion and the use of patent information for technology intelligence. The individual inventor's right is downplayed in relation to the company and the nation, and harmony and non-litigious forms of conflict resolution are emphasized.

Survey data from 24 large chemical, electrical and mechanical corporations further indicate the growth of R&D, foreign R&D, licensing out, domestic and international patenting, and patent portfolios. The emphasis in R&D on research and new product development is significant in the 1980s, as is the sensitivity of the size of R&D investments to the length of patent protection. The survey also indicates a wide array of consistent trends, the most important of which are the increasing strategic importance of patents and top management attention paid to patents, the increasing resources for patenting, the increasing interdependencies between patents and products, the increasing propensity to patent, infringe and litigate, and the increasing use of patent information for technology intelligence.

The extraordinarily large quantities of Japanese patents in international comparison need to be explained. A traditional explanation is that Japanese patents are of low quality. This may have been true in the past, as was the case for Japanese products, but it is no longer true. If the quality of a patent is broken down into legal, technical and economic quality aspects, each of which can be indicated in various ways, this study shows that Japanese patents are no longer inferior, on the contrary, as is the case with Japanese products.

The chapter has analysed various explanations for the high patenting propensity in Japanese corporations. In summary, the different types of (non-conflicting) explanations for the high quantities of Japanese patents are (where 1, 2 and 3 are derived from the current study):

1. Historical/institutional explanation, referring to
   a. catch-up effects;
   b. lack of natural resources;
   c. patent culture (see further Chapter 8);
   d. legislation (single claim, narrow scope, utility models);
   e. JPO behaviour.
2. Strategic/managerial explanation, referring to
   a. response to pro-patent era and US litigation;
   b. increasing economic value of patent portfolios;
   c. R&D strategies and effectiveness (*kaizen* – literally 'improvement', in an industrial context it translates as continuous improvement, related to quality control – exploratory R&D and so on, see Chapter 6);
   d. patent strategies (with emphasis on continuous patenting, flooding, fencing, licensing, bargaining power, technology acquisition);
   e. internal incentives.
3. Regression-based explanation, referring to the most important company variables explaining the number of patent applications which were
   a. amount of patent personnel and resources;
   b. amount of R&D expenditures and patent-based sales;
4. Explanation in Westney (1993), referring to
   a. strategic motives (technology access, offset royalties and so on);
   b. organization (incentives and so on);
   c. legislation.
5. Explanation by JPO in 1976, referring to
   a. enterprise causes (patent strategies, omissive search, defensiveness);
   b. JPO causes (low requirements and fees);
   c. patent attorney causes.

In order to contrast and enrich the various explanations offered for the high patenting propensity in Japan, the chapter finally presented some possible reasons for the opposite phenomenon of a low patenting propensity, which was the case for Swedish industry up until the early 1990s.

NOTES

1. Needless to say, numerous scholars have elaborated on the causes of Japan's techno-economic success, especially in the post-war period. For some references, see Chapter 6.
2. The recession was no doubt the most serious one in the post-war period, and caused a great deal of soul-searching, analysis and attempts to reform. Many possible causes (such as the financial system, the political system) and consequences have been pointed out, ranging from ultimate decline to radical crisis-induced renewal.
3. 'Hubris' was a deadly sin in Greek mythology, severely punished by the gods. This is a variant of the 'success-breeds-failure' syndrome.
4. For an interesting analysis of the causes of this appreciation, see McKinnon (1996, 1997), attributing a substantial role to self-serving interventions in the USA.
5. For an account of the build-up of R&D in industry, see Kodama (1995), who also describes how investments in R&D surpassed capital investments in large Japanese corporations in the mid-1980s. See also Chapter 1. The severe recession or crisis in the late 1990s does not seem to have led to severe cuts in corporate R&D, while businesses have been divested and diversifications have been reconsidered. The crisis calls forth structural changes, that very well may strengthen large parts of the corporate sector in the long run. Some observers even refer to the crisis as a 'happy crisis', although incurring substantial sacrifices.
6. Some would also argue that economic strength tends to lead – by design or default – to the build-up of military strength in one way or another (see Samuels 1994).
7. Ueda (1994, p. 111).
8. One may observe that the Tokugawa perception of the power-disrupting effects of new technologies was correct, although not their hopes for eternal control of technological change in a small part of a world that was after all essentially an open, globalizing system.
9. This is not to suggest a simple 'open-the-lid' kind of explanation, saying that the catch-up would owe its rapidity to the release of pressures for change built up during a long period of stagnation.
10. See, for example, Francks (1992, pp. 25–6).
11. A recent, and so far history's perhaps largest, example of the disruptive effects of technological change upon political structures is the downfall of the Soviet empire, following on a short period of desperate high-level attempts to catch up through reconstruction from within (*perestroika*). It is interesting to speculate over why the technological and industrial catch-up process of the former USSR (it was in fact a catch-up process) initiated in the mid-1980s was derailed and did not succeed while catch-up processes in other regions and periods have succeeded (for example, Japan and 19th-century USA). For example, *glasnost* (that is, openness, no secrets) was a radical shift away from an extremely secretive regime and perhaps counteracted its purpose of serving *perestroika*.
12. This does not mean that all technology has been acquired by Japanese industries in ways that could be called proper and fair by Western industries. However, much of the subsequent resentment and bashing of Japan for stealing Western technology has been exaggerated. Western industry has, in fact, had a weak protection of its technology by patents and secrecy in the post-war decades. There are many stories of Western companies opening their doors for Japanese visitors, proudly showing them their technologies; companies fumbling with their secrets and companies with weak or no enforcement of their patent rights, and so on. (Motorola, for example, prior to the mid-1980s, was called 'the sleeping giant' in Japan since it had many good patents but did not enforce their rights.) Some US technology was also diverted to Japan through anti-trust action, forcing US companies (for example, Xerox) with a strong patent-based monopoly to sell licences cheaply. The latter had more to do with US concern over potential cartels cheating US consumers than concern over Japanese companies potentially

cheating US industry. (According to Professor F.M. Scherer at Harvard, who was involved in the Xerox patent licensing decree, US authorities had no idea that Japanese firms would enter the copying business so quickly, but had they known, they would probably not have changed policy.) Nevertheless, there is evidence of Japanese misbehaviour as well (for example, the case of Hitachi spying on IBM in the 1980s) and any verdict must be mixed.

13. For some further readings, see Borrus (1990), Odagiri and Goto (1993), Foray (1994), Yamaji (1997) as well as Ordover (1991), pointing at the conduciveness of Japan's patent system to licensing and cross-licensing, and Aoki and Prusa (1995) pointing at the conduciveness of Japan's patent system to smaller quality improvements.

14. Some efforts have been made, however. For example, a Japanese proposal was made in the 1980s for a new (*sui generis*) law for protecting computer software, a proposal that was dismissed by the USA. (See Samuelson 1993 for more details.)

15. See Chapter 2 for the background developments in the USA. See also Collins and Bosworth (1994) and NAS (1994).

16. See Warshofsky (1994).

17. Nevertheless, it should be noted that US litigation language traditionally contains war terms and metaphors, just as the management field has borrowed concepts as well as methods from the military field. Compare the expressions 'to wage a battle', 'defendant', 'business intelligence' and 'competitive strategy'.

18. Developing countries have been criticizing Western patent laws for overly favouring countries which are technical leaders. This may be a valid criticism, but nevertheless Japan presents a case of catch-up, being nurtured by an IPR system aligned to – but not identical with – Western patent laws. At the same time it should be kept in mind that the IPR system in Japan has been used in conjunction with various national protectionist measures.

19. From time to time it has been hypothesized that the USA would sooner or later yield to the pressure to adopt the first-to-file priority rule while retaining some other unique feature as a compromise. However, there are no signs at present (1998) that this will take place in the near future. For a qualitative comparison of the first-to-file and the first-to-invent rules and an advocacy of the latter, see Kingston (1992), and for a theoretical comparison with a certain advocacy of the first-to-file rule, see Scotchmer and Green (1990). Systematic empirical research on the issue is lacking, however.

20. A further step towards international harmonization has been taken in the context of GATT, as the USA has agreed to adopt laid-open publication, thereby eliminating 'submarine patents' (although not yet enacted in 1997).

21. One way to do this is to withdraw the application temporarily in order to modify and/or add patent claims in it.

22. This is sometimes referred to as 'letting the pig grow' from the point of view of the 'submarine patentee'. One way to limit this possibility is to have a limited time for litigating against a clearly detectable infringer.

23. An often quoted example of a submarine patent is the Lemelson patent. This patent, covering some methods and devices for automatic analysis of electronic images to detect product defects, for instance, was filed on 24 December 1954 and granted on 1 September 1992, thus being 'hidden' for 38 years. Other examples are the Gould patents (for lasers, being used in semiconductor manufacturing), filed in 1959 and granted in 1987, and the Hyatt patents (for microprocessors), filed in 1969 and granted in 1990. In total 109 728 patents were issued in the USA in 1992, and of these 623 had been filed at least ten years earlier, that is, about half a percent.

It must be kept in mind, however, that on the surface this practice of creating submarine patents was legal in the USA, although not clearly in the spirit of patent laws. As a patent strategy, it has presumably paid off well in several cases and it has also been used by companies for a long time (see, for example, Vaughan 1925). The new amendments to the US patent statute in connection with GATT agreements will provide for publication of pending US applications and thus make the submarine patent strategy less effective. Nevertheless claim refinements or new claims within the scope of the patent application could be filed at a later date before issuance of the patent. Thus, time limited submarine claims are still possible (Glazier 1995).

24. The Kilby patent concerned the invention of one version of the integrated circuit made by Jack Kilby in the late 1950s at Texas Instruments. Almost at the same time, Robert Noyce, later co-founder of Intel, invented another version of the integrated circuit, solving the problem of interconnection (see Warshofsky 1994, pp. 112–13).
25. See Warshofsky (1994) for details.
26. See, for example, Kotabe (1992) who found discriminatory practices in Japan, as well as in the USA and Europe against foreign patent applications. US patent laws have also discriminated against foreign inventors to some extent.
27. An example is the Paris Convention of 1883.
28. A case could develop for fighting intellectual piracy in parts of Asia.
29. A general warning should be mentioned here regarding the use of patent statistics. Simple comparisons of patent counts across countries must be treated with much caution since the patent systems differ (see Rahn 1983, p. 485 and also Chapter 9). Still some results, like the Japanese record growth in number of patents, are too robust to be explained away by the incommensurability of patents across countries. For further readings, see Frame and Narin (1990), Chakrabarti (1989), IIP (1994).
30. Growth in patenting is associated with growth of R&D. The relative (percentage) growth of R&D in turn is not necessarily highest in R&D-intensive industries (the growth rates may, for example, be independent of size, that is they follow Gibrat's law, see, for example, Scherer 1980).
31. For some methodological discussions, see Chapter 9 and Appendix 1 and references given there.
32. In the prior art search performed by a patent examiner in order to establish the novelty of an invention for which a patent has been applied, previous patents appear as relevant. Such information is sometimes supplied by the applicant as well. Other relevant patents may therefore be cited in the final document of a specific patent, just as a published article may cite previous publications. Apart from variations and arbitrariness in citing behaviour, the assumption is that the more a patent becomes cited by subsequent patents, the higher its technical quality, analogously to the use of citation counts in scientific literature.
33. Skewness is also a prevalent feature in the patent world. A small number of patents account for a large number of citations and just a few patents may yield high pay-offs. In other words, technical as well as economic qualities of patents show high concentration. Only a weak correlation between technical and economic quality of a patent has been indicated, based on just a few available studies (see in particular Trajtenberg 1990; see also Chapter 9.)
34. The indicator used is based on the ratio between the average citation intensity (that is, the number of citations per patent) for a country's companies in an industry and the average citation intensity in the industry across countries, so that a value above one indicates a higher patent quality than average. The indicator time series is then smoothed by using a three-year moving average.
35. Growth rates in absolute as well as in relative terms must be interpreted and compared with caution, of course, especially when size increases from low levels. The share of foreign R&D to total R&D grew by as much as 216 per cent from 1987 to 1991 as shown in Table 5.8, while the share only increased from 1.6 per cent to 5.0 per cent.
36. Note that patent numbers, patent shares, patent intensities and patent citations are four general categories of patent-related indicators for comparing (benchmarking) nations as well as companies (see Chapter 9). Additional ones are conceivable as well, for example, utilizing the age of cited patents to indicate newness of related technologies (see Narin 1993).
37. The question about possible effects of this record will be addressed further below.
38. One explanation forwarded by Professor Griliches is that the USPTO has had a shortage of patent examiners. In fact, the number of patents granted correlate well with the number of patent office examiners.
39. Or perhaps because of this. It could very well be the case that a lower requirement could lead to lower level of quality of applications, and then even to a lower success (approval) rate.
40. The JPO has been criticized repeatedly in the 1980s and early 1990s for having long examination times and large back-logs. The JPO has responded that it has capacity problems and that industry has to raise the quality of applications and to decrease the quantity. It has also launched a computerized system for paperless patenting in order to increase efficiency.

41. That is, a patent system in which only one claim is allowed in a patent application. (Europe and the USA have had a multi-claim system for many years.) Also, Japan did not have a doctrine of equivalents allowing for an extended interpretation of the patent claim to technically equivalent claims. Thus, each patent gave a narrow scope of protection. This behaviour of narrow rights-granting was in line with Japanese culture, in which granting strong rights to individuals was not considered as fundamental as in the USA, for instance.

42. An omissive or incomplete search of state-of-the-art or prior art may lead to many disapproved patent applications, for example.

43. There is no scientific empirical evidence for this proposition, however, but only evidence based on the impressions of the practitioners interviewed.

44. The same may be said regarding one-sided emphasis on legal quality, of course. This may not be as prevalent as one-sided technical emphasis, at least in patent application work. However, in a more general context there are several anecdotes about how legally 'good' contracts, for example in joint ventures and licensing, have stifled cooperation and efficiency.

45. The economic-quality dimension of patents should in principle not influence the approval decisions (apart from a general but weak requirement of usefulness of the invention). (See Merges 1988 for a good review of this issue.)

46. 'Explanatory' here means reducing the sample variance in the dependent variables number of patent applications and patents granted, for the corporations in the sample. Primary explanatory variable refers to the variable that reduces most of the variance for a given number of variables in a regression run. Exploratory variations of dependent and independent variables and various lag structures for the years 1987 and 1991 were tried in the regression runs. The significance of IP resources (that is, variables E6a and E7 in the questionnaire) as primary explanatory variables was robust under these variations. (Strictly speaking, ordinary significance levels are unreliable for exploratory regressions performed on the same data set.) However, different variables with far less significance appear in the third place depending upon which dependent variable is used to indicate the volume of patenting.

47. One can note here that Ericsson's start-up phase in telephony from its foundation in 1876 was facilitated by the omission of Bell to take out a patent in Sweden on his invention of the telephone, plus the fact that the Bell companies used a high-price strategy in Scandinavia.

48. The liberalization of the US telecommunications sector started in the late 1960s with the so-called Carter-phone decision, allowing non-Bell companies to attach certain equipment of their own to the Bell system.

49. Some rough figures indicate the magnitude of Ericsson's turnaround regarding patenting. In a period of about seven years, Ericsson increased the number of patenting employees more than ten times and the number of priority applications more than 20 times, with 50 priority applications in 1987, 145 in 1991, and 1200 in 1997.

50. It is partly in the nature of patenting that business managers can largely escape any blame for mismanagement of IP in the absence of an enforced corporate IP policy, unless high damages and injunctions occur.

51. If every competitor thinks patents are unimportant and therefore does not apply for patents, patents do become unimportant. No one then has an incentive to change this situation, which thus becomes an equilibrium, although an unstable one, since if someone starts to patent effectively, others have to follow (compare the expression 'there is no way to fight a patent but with a patent'; see Chapter 5).

52. In principle this is not in contrast to normal insurance, for example, of homes against fire or cars against collisions or bodies against illness. The probability of a fire in an insured house may increase due to adverse selection of insurance holders and their moral hazards. The probability of a house fire may also increase for a specific house as other houses nearby become insured, because of adverse selection and moral hazards among their insurance holders and the possibility of a fire in one house spreading to other houses. Similarly the probability of an insurance holder being subjected to collisions or illness may increase as more people take out insurance, due to bad driving on roads or infectious diseases. What does differ between a normal insurance and a patent as an insurance of freedom of action in a business (that is, insurance against blockage or imitative entry) is the possibility of a patent holder to inflict one-sided damages on others on purpose, which is a strong form of moral hazard.

6. Technology and commercialization strategies

CHAPTER CONTENTS

6.1 CHAPTER OUTLINE

This chapter will deal with the commercialization of new technologies in Japan as seen at the national level, the corporate level and the level of individual product businesses. Various strategies and common features for technology exploitation will be elaborated upon. This will also provide a broader context for subsequent chapters, which will deal specifically with IP strategies and IP management.

6.2 TECHNOLOGY POLICY AND MACRO FACTORS

There is an old saying, that stated roughly says Europe makes science, the USA innovates and Japan commercializes. This is obviously a sweeping statement, which is no longer true, but to a certain extent it has been true in the past. Europe has been providing an essential scientific base for the spur of US technological innovations from the late 19th century on, and the USA in turn has been providing much of the technological base for Japan's commercial achievements since World War II. Scholars have also pointed to the numerous innovative skills in the USA coupled with a certain lack of imitative and commercialization skills compared to Japan (see, for example, Mowery and Rosenberg 1989; Rosenberg and Steinmueller 1988). A number of reasons behind Japan's skills in commercializing new technologies can be found at the macro and policy levels.[1] For example, a strong pragmatic technology orientation in government and industry, a low level of government spending on military R&D, a high level of privately financed industrial R&D under conducive macro policies (for example, technology, fiscal and trade policies providing features such as low cost of capital and instrumental protectionism) and fierce domestic competition have created a technology-driven economy with a strong market orientation.

The process of catching up may generate dynamic advantages relative to the process of sustaining a lead (see Abramovitz 1986). Table 6.1 gives an overview of the pros and cons for a country's industry when operating as an early or late mover in a market. Japan has certainly been able to develop late-mover advantages. The catch-up process has also created a culture and a momentum conducive to further progress, based on skills or competence cumulated in the catch-up process. These skills are also highly useful in the process of sustaining a lead as well, at least for a time. Important examples of such skills are the ones acquired in connection with patenting and the use of patent information, as will be seen in this and the following chapters. At the same time, attitudes and competencies acquired by innovators and early market leaders often seem to threaten the sustenance of their leading positions, for example, through the 'not invented here' (NIH) syndrome, which could be seen as part of a larger 'success breeds failure syndrome' common among innovators.[2] A successful catch-up also tends to build in risks associated with rapid but unbalanced growth, allowing progressive and backward parts to coexist in the economy, possibly to the point where the backward parts become bottlenecks seriously limiting further aggregate growth until structural change is called forth.

Of course, it is also possible that some attitudes and competencies nurtured by a catch-up process are not conducive to reaching and sustaining an innovative position. One example is what can be called the 'foreign is better' (FIB) syndrome, which deters companies from venturing into a technological lead. To overcome this syndrome, MITI has played an important role through its collective R&D projects, such as the very large scale integration (VLSI) project. Much has been written about the importance of MITI in engineering these collective R&D projects in 'pre-competitive' stages as an instrument for catching up (see, for example, Fransman 1994, 1995; Sigurdson 1995, 1996). However, forging ahead in addition to catching up also requires overcoming the

Table 6.1   Advantages and disadvantages of early and late movers on markets

Early mover	Late mover
Advantages	
• Economies of scale and learning and increasing returns in general	• Economies of speed and timing
	• Reduction of basic R&D costs compared to firstcomers
• Firstcomers have first crack at emerging technologies and markets and the opportunity to establish unchallenged, dominant market share	• Lower initial start-up costs
	• Reduction of aimless groping
	• Technological leapfrogging is possible
• Possibility of using preemptive and foreclosing strategies or otherwise building up barriers to entry	• Learning from early movers
	• Reduction of NIH effects
• Reputational advantages	• Aggregate growth rates tend to be faster
• Possibility of building up exclusive IP positions	• Cumulation of catch-up competencies
• Possibility of setting standards	
Disadvantages	
• Build-up of physical and intellectual capital which becomes obsolete	• Lag in technology
	• Resource scarcity due to early mover preemption
• Build-up of inertia, rigidities and hubris	• Forced to concentrate on low value-added products
• Build-up of the NIH syndrome and the success breeds failure syndrome	• Lacking economies of scale in production
	• Threat by foreign imports from firstcomers
	• Competition from foreign subsidiaries operating in home markets
	• Threat of being overwhelmed (the FIB syndrome)
	• Lack of large companies which can invest in product improvements, appropriate innovations and pursue second-to-market strategies
	• Tendency towards unbalanced growth and a polarized economy

Note: In principle, categories diagonal to each other in the table would be logical negations of each other if the table had contained exhaustive lists of relative advantages and disadvantages. However, as a matter of emphasis the table shows mainly different factors in all four early/late pro/con categories without being exhaustive.

Sources: Compiled and selected from Abramovitz (1986), Ames and Rosenberg (1963), Conrad (1984), Gerschenkron (1962), Kerin et al. (1993), Leonard-Barton (1995), Lieberman and Montgomery (1988), Okimoto (1983), Schnaars (1994), Utterback (1994) and the author. The works represent a mixture of country and company perspectives.

FIB syndrome and the setting of actual R&D targets for the purpose of taking a technological lead in a dynamic race. When MITI proposed such targets, there was a large degree of initial hesitation among Japanese companies who were sceptical that such targets could be met, creating responses such as 'IBM will always be ahead'.[3] Naturally, collective R&D with government support has been instrumental in smoothing financial risks, but in addition, MITI, along with some progressive companies and industrialists, has been instrumental in overcoming the FIB syndrome in more and more parts of Japanese industry.

For further readings about Japan's economic and technology policies, see, for example, Calder (1993), Fransman (1994, 1995), Freeman (1987), Gerlach (1992), Johnson (1982), Johnson et al. (1989), Odagiri and Goto (1993), Okimoto (1989), Porter (1990), Sigurdson (1995, 1996), Tyson (1992).

6.3   TECHNOLOGY MANAGEMENT IN JAPAN

A number of reasons behind Japan's success in commercializing new technologies can also be found at micro levels and in the fine structure of society and corporate life. A particularly important factor is the management skill developed in large parts of industry, especially for managing large corporations.[4] Since technology has been the engine of Japan's developments, skilful technology management has been crucial. As is well known, Japanese management has drawn considerably upon Western management but has at the same time developed unique features and a considerable range of managerial innovations (TQM, JIT, *kanban* and so on), which in turn have been emulated in the West.[5]

There are several good writings available in English on Japanese technology management and related matters. See for example, Bowonder and Miyake (1993), Branscomb and Kodama (1993), Eto (1993), Florida and Kenney (1992), Fransman (1995), Funk (1993), Imai (1986, 1992), Kodama (1995), Miyazaki (1995), Nonaka (1990), Nonaka and Kenney (1991), Okimoto and Nishi (1994), Sigurdson (1996), Urabe et al. (1988), Woronoff (1992), Yamaji (1997).

What, then, characterizes Japanese technology management? According to Westney (1993, p. 37), commonly recognized characteristics of the technology behaviour of Japanese firms, compared to US firms, are as follows:

1. shorter development times;
2. more effective identification and acquisition of external technology, on a global scale;
3. more effective design for manufacturability;
4. more incremental product and process improvement;
5. innovation dominated by large rather than small firms;
6. greater propensity for competitive matching of products and processes;

7. greater propensity for interfirm collaboration in developing technology;
8. greater propensity to patent;
9. weakness in science-based industries, for example, pharmaceuticals, chemicals, biotechnology.

Several of these general characteristics have been corroborated in the present study, such as shorter development times, skills in acquiring external technology (including using interfirm collaboration), incremental and coordinated product/process improvements, high patenting propensity and skills, and the remaining weakness in certain science-based industries.

When specifically considering the commercialization of new technologies, or what we will also refer to as technology exploitation, a number of common features in Japan are indicated by the present study. These will be dealt with in Sections 6.4 and 6.5.

6.4 STRATEGIES FOR ACQUIRING AND EXPLOITING NEW TECHNOLOGIES

There are various means for a company wishing to acquire and commercialize new technologies and innovations. These means are mostly complementary and interact with varying importance over time in developing technology-based businesses. Simply to list and weigh these means through a snapshot survey is not sufficient for their understanding and application. In this study, survey data have therefore been complemented with extensive interviews. The survey data are first presented in Tables 6.2–7 below.

6.4.1 Technology Acquisition

Table 6.2 shows how Japanese corporations put emphasis on various strategies for acquiring technological capabilities. These strategies represent, in descending order, different levels of organizational integration from fully integrated in-house R&D to technology scanning (see Chapter 4).[6] External technology sourcing or acquisition by various strategies was found to be increasingly important, although in-house R&D definitely remained as the main strategy, regardless of sector. Collaborative R&D and technology scanning was shown to be especially important on average. For a similar but smaller sample of Japanese large corporations, external technology sourcing also increased during the 1980s (Granstrand et al. 1992a). To a considerable extent regarding Japan, external technology has traditionally come from foreign sources. Technology scanning has always had an international outlook, international technology licensing has had a long history and international joint ventures and other forms of cooperative R&D have grown rapidly in recent decades (Mowery 1992; Niosi 1994). Less is known, however, about how corporations view collaborations with universities at home and abroad.[7]

Table 6.2   Strategies for acquisition of technological capabilities in large Japanese corporations

(Scale: Of no importance = 0,1, 2, 3, 4 = Of major importance)

(Code) Question	Chemical (n = 9)	Electrical (n = 10)	Mechanical (n = 5)	Total (n = 24)

(C1) For your corporation as a whole, please indicate roughly the relative importance of the following strategies of building up your technological capabilities in 1987 and 1992:

In-house R&D 1992	3.89	3.70	3.80	3.79
Growth ratio 1992/1987	0.97	0.98	0.95	0.97
Acquisition of innovative companies (or business units) 1992	1.88	1.40	2.40	1.78
Growth ratio 1992/1987	1.57	1.19	1.33	1.38
Joint venture and other forms of cooperative R&D, e.g. with subcontractors 1992	2.89	2.40	2.80	2.67
Growth ratio 1992/1987	1.26	1.42	1.07	1.27
Purchasing of licenses 1992	2.75	1.90	2.40	2.30
Growth ratio 1992/1987	1.13	1.04	1.10	1.09
Other forms of technology purchasing, e.g. contract R&D 1992	2.25	1.70	2.20	2.00
Growth ratio 1992/1987	1.06	1.13	1.10	1.10
University collaboration 1992	3.00	2.56	2.00	2.60
Growth ratio 1992/1987	1.26	1.23	1.25	1.25
University collaboration with universities in:				
Japan 1992	2.78	2.56	2.80	2.70
Growth ratio 1992/1987	1.04	1.11	1.20	1.10
USA 1992	3.13	2.67	3.20	2.95
Growth ratio 1992/1987	1.48	1.22	1.27	1.33
Technology scanning (incl. monitoring and intelligence) 1992	2.88	2.70	3.00	2.83
Growth ratio 1992/1987	1.04	1.00	1.17	1.05

Note: The highest and lowest values for each industry are overlined and underlined, respectively. Appendix 4 gives numbers by which the statistical significance of observed differences in the perceptual data can be approximately calculated. The growth ratio under each variable is the ratio between the value of the variable in 1992 and 1987.

As Table 6.2 shows, Japanese corporations put the importance of collaborations with US universities second only to in-house R&D, regardless of sector. Collaborations with their domestic universities during 1987–92 have fallen behind US universities in importance, as perceived in 1992. Although this study provides only perceptual data rather than factual data on the foreign share of university collaborations in Japanese industry, it can be expected that this foreign share is quite high and will increase in the future.

6.4.2   Technology Exploitation and Complementary Assets

New technologies can be commercialized in various ways, some of which are innovative in themselves, and some of which are commonly recognized and classifiable into various strategy taxonomies. Two such taxonomies for technology commercialization (or exploitation) will be used here, corresponding to Tables 6.3 and 6.4. The first taxonomy is based on contractual ways of linking a new technology to complementary assets inside or outside the company for production and marketing, typically of a new product (see also Chapter 4). The strategies are then arranged in falling order of organizational integration, from full integration through internal exploitation over various quasi-integrated forms to complete disintegration through divestment, that is, selling the assets. (For details, see Granstrand et al. 1992a; see also Teece 1987 for a related taxonomy.) Table 6.3 thus shows the preponderance across industries of internal exploitation, with no significant growth in importance attached to it between the years 1987 and 1992. Divestment is at the other extreme, dismissed across industries with little change between 1987 and 1992. The quasi-integrated intermediate strategies are employed fairly equally across industries and with growing importance attached to them, particularly in the mechanical industry for technology selling.[8]

To create innovative firms is one way for a large company to package technology together with complementary resources or assets for production and marketing, usually under semi-autonomous management but with retained ownership and control. This may be an effective way of combining large and small company advantages in commercializing new technologies at some stage, especially for products and processes that fall outside the company's existing business areas.[9] This strategy can also be used for radically new technologies when their commercialization would be jeopardized by integration with some operating business division, entrenched in a current, well-proven technology. This strategy has not been used much by Japanese companies in the past, at least not for the purpose of potentially spinning off a new, innovative firm. However, the urge to become innovative prompts many Japanese companies to search for and experiment with new organizational forms. Another expression of this along similar lines is to endow the corporate R&D laboratory with responsibilities for the initial marketing of radically new products in certain situations, something that was tried in several companies with promising results.

Table 6.3   Strategies for commercializing technological capabilities in large Japanese corporations

(Scale: Of no importance = 0,1, 2, 3, 4 = Of major importance)

(Code) Question	Chemical ($n = 9$)	Electrical ($n = 10$)	Mechanical ($n = 5$)	Total ($n = 24$)
(C1) For your corporation as a whole, please indicate roughly the relative importance of the following strategies of building up your technological capabilities in 1987 and 1992:				
Internal exploitation 1992	3.89	3.50	4.00	3.75
Growth ratio 1991/1987	1.00	1.01	1.07	1.02
Creation of innovative firms 1992	2.00	2.00	2.40	2.09
Growth ratio 1991/1987	1.25	1.04	1.50	1.19
Joint ventures 1992	2.44	2.50	2.60	2.50
Growth ratio 1991/1987	1.40	1.33	1.40	1.37
Technology selling 1992	1.89	2.50	2.40	2.25
Growth ratio 1991/1987	1.24	1.43	1.90	1.46
Divestment 1992	1.00	0.33	0.25	0.59
Growth ratio 1991/1987	0.89	1.00	1.00	0.93
What is the magnitude in your company of:				
(C3a) Uncommercialized technology 1992	2.13	2.44	1.50	2.14
Growth ratio 1991/1987	1.27	1.33	1.17	1.28
(C3b) Loss and leakage of proprietary technology	2.29	2.56	2.33	2.42
Growth ratio 1991/1987	1.14	1.31	1.50	1.29

Note: The highest and lowest values for each industry for question C2 are overlined and underlined respectively.

It is also interesting to note in Table 6.3 that a significant and growing amount of a company's technology is not commercialized within reasonable time limits (especially in electrical companies), something that is also shown by the fraction of uncommercialized patents, as seen in Table 5.14. Uncommercialized technology results from a number of factors: for example, a time lag till commercialization, serendipities, a recent shift towards specialization, exploratory

R&D or simply commercially unsuccessful R&D.[10] There is also a significant and growing amount of loss and leakage of proprietary technology. Both this and the amount of uncommercialized technology are in fact around the same magnitude as technology selling, although one should be very cautious when comparing assessments based on the scales used across questions.

6.4.3   Internal Exploitation

From a company's point of view, the main function of a patent should be to help the company recover sufficient returns from its investment when commercializing a new technology.[11] However, there are other ways to perform this function, for example, by means of secrecy, efficient production or efficient marketing. Mostly these other ways are complements rather than substitutes for using patents. Moreover, there are other advantages of a patent to a company, as well as disadvantages (see further Chapter 7). Thus, a company might apply for patents even if they are not important in commercializing new technologies, just as a company could refrain from patenting even if it is important. The questionnaire survey tried to assess the effectiveness of patents in fulfilling their main function relative to alternative methods, as well as the advantage of patents in this respect relative to other advantages and disadvantages.[12]

Table 6.4 shows the survey results at country level, where the data for the USA are derived from Levin et al. (1987).[13]

Table 6.4   Means for commercializing new product technologies

(Scale: No importance = 0, 1, 2, 3, 4 = Major importance)

Means	Japan[1]	Sweden[1]	US[2]
(a) Taking out patents to deter imitators (or to collect royalties)	3.4	1.9	2.0
(b) Exercising secrecy	2.4	2.0	1.7
(c) Creating market lead times	2.9	2.4	2.9
(d) Creating production cost reductions	3.1	2.7	2.7
(e) Creating superior marketing	2.9	3.0	3.1
(f) Creating switching costs at user end	2.3	1.7	n.a.

Notes
The highest and lowest values are overlined and underlined, respectively.
1. Current sample of 24 large corporations. Perceptions for 1992.
2. As reported in Levin et al. (1987). Perceptions for the mid-1980s, rescaled to the scale used in the current study.

Table 6.5   Means for commercializing new product and process technologies in large Japanese corporations, 1992

(Scale: No importance = 0, 1, 2, 3, 4 = Of major importance;
Tend. = Tendency 1987–92: Decreasing = –1, 0, +1 = Increasing)

(Code) Question	Chemical (n = 9) Tend.	Electrical (n = 10) Tend.	Mechanical (n = 5) Tend.	Total (n = 24) Tend.
(F6) How important to your company are on an average the following means for commercializing new *product* technologies?				
Taking out patents to deter imitators	3.89 (0.5)	3.40 (0.6)	2.60 (0.6)	3.42 (0.6)
Exercising secrecy	2.38 (–0.1)	2.50 (0.3)	2.40 (0.8)	2.43 (0.3)
Creating market lead times	3.00 (0.2)	3.00 (0.3)	2.40 (0.4)	2.87 (0.3)
Creating production cost reductions	3.13 (0.3)	3.00 (0.4)	3.40 (0.4)	3.13 (0.4)
Creating superior marketing and after-sales service	2.75 (0.3)	3.11 (0.6)	2.80 (0.4)	2.91 (0.4)
Creating switching costs*	2.13 (0.1)	2.75 (0.3)	2.00 (0.2)	2.33 (0.2)
(F7) How important to your company are on an average the following means for commercializing new production process technologies?				
Taking out patents to deter imitators	3.33 (0.1)	3.30 (0.4)	2.40 (0.6)	3.13 (0.4)
Exercising secrecy	2.67 (0.1)	2.60 (0.2)	2.80 (0.6)	2.67 (0.3)
Making implementation rapid	3.00 (0.2)	2.70 (0.2)	2.60 (0.6)	2.78 (0.3)

Notes

Highest and lowest values for each industry are overlined and underlined, respectively.

* That is, costs for a customer to switch to another supplier.

A few observations deserve to be pointed out:

1. Patenting ranked highest in Japan, while close to the bottom in Sweden and the USA, and was the means of commercialization differing most among the countries.
2. Superior marketing ranked highest in Sweden and the USA, while it fell in the middle range in Japan.
3. Creating switching costs ('lock in' of customers) ranked lowest in both Japan and Sweden (data missing for the USA), and thus to 'lock out' competitors from the market through patents and other means was perceived as more important.
4. Sweden and the USA were fairly similar in their average responses, while Japan deviated most.

Thus, the data indicate a difference between Japanese and Western companies, in particular regarding the role of patents.

Table 6.5 shows a breakdown of industrial sectors in Japan. One may observe that:

1. Patenting ranked highest for both products and processes in chemical and electrical companies, with secrecy close to the bottom.
2. Mechanical companies deviated from the chemical and electrical firms for both products and processes, with the highest emphasis on production cost reductions and production process secrecy.

The country and sector differences challenge some notions commonly held, at least in the past. One is that patents play a secondary role overall compared to marketing and production efforts. This is certainly not true for Japan.[14] Another common notion is that secrecy plays a larger role than patenting in the protection of process technology. This is not true for Japan either, except for mechanical companies.

Exercising secrecy
There may be a changing role regarding secrecy in the chemical and electrical companies in general, due to technological changes facilitating reverse engineering. For example, new types of chemical analysis can trace minuscule amounts of a wide range of substances in a product, from which the production process can be inferred. This not only helps competitors to reverse engineer, but it also helps patent holders to detect infringement through reverse engineering of the suspicious products of their competitors. Thus, a weakening of secrecy protection by more cost-effective tools for reverse engineering increases the propensity for patenting (everything else being equal) in two ways. First, the

innovator's secrecy barrier is more easily penetrated by imitators. Second, the imitator's secrecy barrier is more easily penetrated by the innovator's ability to detect infringement. This also holds true if secrecy protection is generally weakened for other reasons, for example, outsourcing of process equipment and process engineering services to leaky suppliers, although the incurred savings in intelligence operations may differ substantially among competing companies. Chapter 7 further discusses secrecy protection and secrecy penetration.

The changing role of secrecy protection is further illustrated by Table 6.6. Although some new technologies make it easier to overcome secrecy barriers, such barriers on the other hand might become easier to erect as products and processes become more complex and multitechnological in character. For this and other reasons, complexity would raise imitation costs, making patents relatively less useful. However, this is not the case but rather the contrary as Table 6.6 indicates.[15]

Table 6.6   Means for protecting new product technologies from being copied as perceived by large Japanese corporations

(Scale: Not effective = 0, 1, 2, 3, 4 = Very effective;
Tend. = Tendency 1987–92: Decreasing = –1, 0, +1 = Increasing)

(Code) Question	Chemical ($n = 9$) Tend.	Electrical ($n = 10$) Tend.	Mechanical ($n = 5$) Tend.	Total ($n = 24$) Tend.
(F4) For your company on an average, how effective is each of the following means in preventing or deterring competitors from copying your new product technologies?				
Patents	3.44 (0.9)	3.70 (0.8)	3.60 (0.8)	3.58 (0.8)
Secrecy	2.44 (0.3)	2.70 (0.4)	1.80 (0.6)	2.42 (0.4)
Complexity of product design making copying very costly	1.67 (–0.1)	1.78 (–0.2)	1.40 (0.2)	1.65 (–0.1)
Lead-time advantages of the innovator making attempts at copying unprofitable	2.00 (0.1)	2.00 (0.1)	2.00 (0.2)	2.00 (0.1)

Note: The highest and lowest values for each industry are overlined and underlined, respectively.

Patenting

Numerous studies have confirmed the prevalence of differences among industries in their amenability towards patenting as well as the leading role of chemical and especially drug companies in patenting.[16] The issue of how the patent system relates to, or ought to relate to, the intrinsic features of different technologies and industries is complex.[17] Many pending questions cannot be dealt with here, except for a few aspects. As science and technology evolve, codes develop, for example mathematical or chemical formulas, models, drawings and circuit schemes. A patent system puts certain requirements on the codification of an invention and its functionalities. Since, in different fields and stages of technological development, different codes are developed, one might expect differences in the way these codes meet the coding requirements of the patent system among technological fields. Moreover, there is reason to believe that these differences among technological fields are in the nature of nature so to speak, and that the differences may change over time. In fact, much of the essence of R&D is to make new discoveries, for which a descriptive language often is initially rudimentary, thus requiring an advance in the codification of new knowledge into operational language and symbolism. Chemical formulas constitute a type of structural, discrete code for describing matter that often enables fairly precise and preemptive linking of patent claims to discrete functionalities and performance. This does not preclude the possibility that codes develop (for example, in electronics) that are similarly amenable to patent requirements and preemptive patenting. Also, patent applicants and examiners adopt and develop new codes and practices over time. After all, the patent system existed long before the current symbolism in chemical formulas or electronic circuit schemes. This is to say that some (but not all) industry differences in the appreciation of patenting pertain to the exogenous and changing nature of the technologies involved.

Creating competitive advantages
Finally, the importance of competitor lock-out relative to customer lock-in, when commercializing new technologies, should be recognized in the table data. In fact, one can talk about four ways of commercializing new technologies in everyday terms: to create a temporary monopoly or dominant position through *run-in* (first on the market); *lock-in* of customers (by raising their costs of switching suppliers); *lock-out* of potential competitors (deterring or preventing them from imitating by raising their costs of imitation); or *squeeze-out* of existing competitors (by superior production or marketing and also by non-conventional as well as illegal methods such as bribing and threatening). These ways may be used together but with different emphasis in different stages of commercialization. They all aim at reducing competition or creating competitive advantage up to the point of creating a monopolistic position.[18] Needless to say, commercial success does not necessarily entail economic success in terms of sufficient total rate of return on the relevant investments.

In view of the primary importance attached to patents in Japan as means of profiting from innovation through protection, it is interesting to look at conditions limiting their effectiveness as well as conditions limiting the possibility of profiting from innovation in general. As for the latter, Table 6.7 shows that most of the limitations to profit from innovation apply on average across industries without significant differences.[19] On the whole it appears that mechanical companies are the least restrained in profiting from innovation. Lack of suppliers is least limiting in every industry, while conditions pertaining to technology acquisition, production and marketing were most limiting and more limiting than competition from imitators. This must be kept in mind when discussing the role of patents, a main function of which is to enable the innovator to reduce the competitive pressure upon him- or herself during commercialization. The difficulties encountered in marketing innovations rank very high, which is perhaps not surprising, considering that many Japanese corporations have fairly recently moved from a catch-up stage to a more innovative stage.

Table 6.7   Limitations to profit from innovation (commercializing new technologies) in large Japanese corporations

(Scale: No importance = 0, 1, 2, 3, 4 = Of major importance;
Tend. = Tendency 1987–92: Decreasing = –1, 0, +1 = Increasing)

(Code) Question	Chemical ($n = 9$) Tend.	Electrical ($n = 10$) Tend.	Mechanical ($n = 5$) Tend.	Total ($n = 24$) Tend.
(F3) To what extent does each of the following limit the ability of your company to profit from innovation?				
Inability to prevent other firms from copying the technology	2.75 (0.4)	2.50 (0.3)	2.00 (0.4)	2.48 (0.3)
High cost or limited access to capital	2.50 (0.1)	2.14 (0.3)	1.80 (0.4)	2.20 (0.3)
High cost or limited access to technology needed	2.75 (0.3)	2.88 (0.4)	2.00 (0.2)	2.62 (0.3)
Lack of access to competent suppliers of needed equipment, or of specialized inputs	2.00 (0.0)	2.00 (0.3)	1.20 (–0.2)	1.80 (0.1)
Problems of getting a product into production in a timely way	2.38 (0.3)	3.00 (0.5)	1.80 (0.6)	2.48 (0.4)
High costs or other difficulties in marketing	3.13 (0.4)	2.38 (0.1)	2.00 (0.4)	2.57 (0.3)

Note: The highest and lowest values for each industry are overlined and underlined, respectively.

Limitations of patents

A few limitations to profit from innovation could be alleviated by patents. Patents could be used directly to prevent copying, which is their main purpose, but could also be used indirectly to get access to technology needed through cross-licensing (see further Chapter 7). It is therefore of interest to find out about the limitations of patents in turn. Table 6.8 shows that in every industry the main limitation of patents is their inability to prevent the competition from finding ways to get around a patented invention by finding a substitute invention, that is, to invent around.

Table 6.8   Limitations of patents for technology protection in large Japanese corporations

(Scale: Not true = 0,1,2,3,4 = Very true)

(Code) Question	Chemical (n = 9)	Electrical (n = 10)	Mechanical (n = 5)	Total (n = 24)
(F5) To what extent does each of the following statements apply in describing the limitations of patents as protection of your firm's technology?				
New products are not patentable	1.89	1.20	0.80	1.38
New processes are not patentable	1.88	1.60	0.80	1.52
Patents are probably not valid if contested	2.11	1.80	1.00	1.75
Firms do not try to enforce their patent rights	<u>1.11</u>	<u>1.00</u>	1.40	1.13
Competitors can legally circumvent patent rights or invent ways around them	2.44	2.80	2.40	2.58
Technological development is so rapid that patents become irrelevant	1.78	2.00	2.20	1.96
Patent proceedings require a firm to disclose too much of its information	1.78	2.00	1.00	1.71
Compulsory licensing can be imposed by court decisions or regulations	1.22	1.20	<u>0.20</u>	<u>1.00</u>
Firms engage in cross-licensing with competitors	2.00	2.56	1.20	2.04

Note: The highest and lowest values for each industry are overlined and underlined, respectively.

Another major limitation of patents, which applies fairly equally across industries, is their limited functionality in a world of fast-moving technology. With more fast-moving patent offices as well, this limitation is partially negated. Other limitations differ more from industry to industry. Since most of these limitations are influenced by policy decisions, this observation could to some extent be used to support more industry-specific policies regarding the patent system. This is also in line with the findings and arguments by Levin et al. (1987). The deviation regarding the mechanical companies' perceptions of limitations should again be noted.

One should also note that the limitations of patents in Table 6.8 are, on the whole, perceived as less severe than the limitations to profit from innovation in Table 6.7. However, one has to be careful in comparing averages of responses across tables. One can further note that the inability to prevent copying is perceived (in Table 6.7) as about equally severe as the corresponding limitation of patents to prevent invent-around (in Table 6.8). As mentioned, patents are aimed particularly at reducing the limitation to profit from innovation that arises from copying.

To prevent or aggravate inventing-around through the broad scope of a patent therefore becomes critical. This in turn speaks in favour of using patenting strategies such as blanketing and fencing, strategies for which Japanese companies have become renowned (see further Chapter 7).

6.5   COMMON FEATURES OF TECHNOLOGY EXPLOITATION IN JAPAN

At the company level, the interviews in the study suggest that the features in Table 6.9 are characteristic for the sample of Japanese companies in their commercialization (exploitation) of new technologies. Each of these features will be dealt with in the subsequent sections.

Table 6.9   Common features of technology exploitation in Japan

---

1. Synergetic product/technology diversification (reaping economies of scale, scope and speed).
2. 'Speed to market' through
   - exploratory R&D;
   - incremental development and learning;
   - concurrent engineering, coordination and communication;
   - sense of urgency (stimulated by domestic competition);
   - global marketing.
3. 'Speed to technology' through
   - technology scanning;
   - will to explore and experiment (often early on and with patience);
   - technology acquisition (for example, from Western firms and universities and through internal and external technology supply and licensing networks);
   - large central R&D;
   - technology transfer and communication internally and externally.
4. Dynamic application orientation and user cooperation.
5. IP protection, licensing and monitoring.

6.5.1   Synergetic[20] Diversification

Japanese companies at large have long been engaged in product diversification processes, usually resulting in a considerable diversity of product businesses (see, for example, Kodama 1995; Granstrand et al. 1989; Granstrand and Oskarsson 1994). As is well known, many Western companies also engaged in product diversification as a strategy for balanced growth and risk dispersion, especially when this strategy came into vogue in the 1960s and 1970s in the USA. Product diversification in the West has often resulted in economic failure, as in ITT, although there have been some striking successes too, as in General Electric.[21] As is also well known, diversification failures in the West have then resulted in a pendulum swing towards product specialization, under labels such as 'back to basics', 'stick to the knitting', 'do what you do best' and so on.

In contrast, Japanese companies have on average been successful in product diversification. They also engage, not in unrelated or conglomerate diversification as was often the case in the West, but in related diversification and especially in technology-related diversification. Most companies interviewed in this study and related studies judged that most of their successful diversifications have been 'technology-driven' (for example, Canon, Toshiba, Hitachi, Teijin, Toray, Yamaha, Seiko, NEC).[22]

As a rule, Japanese companies have diversified through internal development, while US companies have typically diversified through mergers and acquisitions. In Japanese companies, there is in fact an ongoing evolutionary process of diversifying the technology base together with diversifying the product base of the company. This is a process comprising several sub-processes in parallel: refinement of existing technologies, refinement of existing products, technology diversification related to the company's existing products, and finally product diversification related to the company's existing technologies. The company's existing technologies are refined at the same time as technologies new to the company, but possibly relevant to its existing product areas, are incorporated in the company by various means and are then tested and further improved upon. Ultimately, the new technologies may be incorporated in a new product or in an existing product area with increased performance-to-cost ratios or new functionalities for the customer. This product and its technologies, including its production technologies, are then further improved upon.

As in-house competence in new technologies is built up, a search for new applications of these technologies is initiated, which after some time – occasionally a considerable time – may result in a venture into a new product area. Thereby, the product base of the company is expanded but in a way that is related to the existing technologies in the company. This *technology-related product diversification*, in interaction with *product-related technology diversification*, takes advantage of economies of scale, since the same technology may be utilized in several products, possibly with an adaptation cost, which is sometimes considerable but more often is minor (see Chapter 4). It must be noted that these types of economies of scale derive from the commonly held fact that technical competence in an area is built up at a considerable fixed cost but with a low variable cost when applied over a number of applications. That is, as with any body of knowledge, the cost of technology is not very dependent upon the scale of its use. In addition, adapting the technology to different applications further enhances competence, which usually gives some kind of learning revenue.

Thus, new technologies often become a shared input in the development and production of several products, and are thereby subjected to economies of scale. This is especially true for generic technologies by definition. (Note the indications in Chapter 5 that the possibilities to find generic technologies may have increased.) These *technological economies of scale* must be distinguished from traditional static and dynamic economies of scale in physical production, as well as from traditional economies of scale in R&D derived from surpassing critical thresholds in the size of laboratories and so on. Reaping these latter traditional types of economies of scale also plays a considerable role in commercialization of new technologies in Japanese companies, for example, through creating a dominant market share and driving down the learning curve, as is fairly well known.

When new technologies are complementary to old ones in the technology base of a product – which they often are – technological economies of scope or technology-related synergies arise from cross-fertilization. However, incorporating more technologies in a new product or process also leads to progressively increased R&D costs, since integrating more technologies requires more coordination and communication (see Chapter 4).

As also described in Chapters 4 and 5, new products and processes tend to become increasingly multitechnological. A diversified company with a broad technology base, which involves a new technology needed for a new product, also has what can be called speed advantages in addition to scale and scope advantages. The company can then incorporate this technology not only more cheaply but also faster, by transferring it internally (possibly with some modification). Usually technology transfer is slower for a company which has to acquire the new technology through external sourcing instead of in-house R&D, although barriers to intrafirm technology transfer (such as NIH barriers) may sometimes be significant. Hence, new proprietary technologies constitute intellectual capital with attractive economies of scale, scope and speed, which can be reaped through technology-based product diversification. However, trademarks can also offer economies of scale, scope and speed, in connection with technology-based product diversification through the use of trademark extension and the building of combined corporate images and business images. This will be dealt with in Chapter 7.

Figure 6.1 depicts the type of diversification processes just described. The corporate evolution could be seen in principle as stepwise over time (time points t_1 to t_6), although the steps may be more or less concurrent, and the combined technology/product base shifts over time, as may the customer base in concordance. The speed of technology diversification and product diversification differs between companies and industries. The figure shows a company that at time t_6 has left its historical origins completely. As described in Chapter 4 this general kind of moving or 'floating diversification' is common for a raw material-based company or a chemical company over long periods of time, in which case physical byproducts in extraction and processing also play an important role. Product invention-based companies in electrical and mechanical engineering, on the other hand, often display a kind of 'rooted' diversification, sticking to the original product business area, at least for a longer time, while

Product business

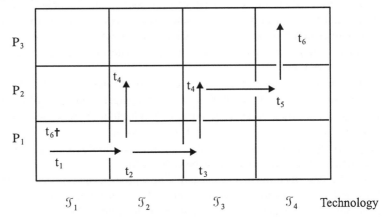

Legend

$\mathfrak{I}$ = technology

P = product business

t = time

† = discontinuance (exit)

Figure 6.1   Diversification processes utilizing technological economies of scale and scope

diversifying into others. Of course, by speeding up the diversification process, for example with acquisitions, the time points t_1 to t_6 can be compressed, possibly yielding economies of speed. Figure 6.2 summarizes different diversification patterns in general.

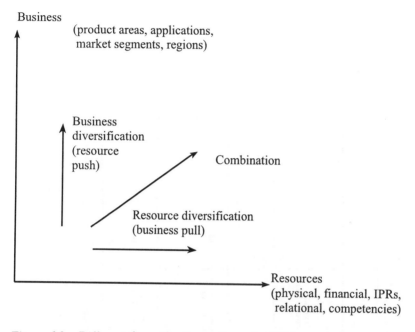

Figure 6.2   Different diversification patterns (paths) in general

In summary, there is an interplay between market-pull and technology-push forces or more generally between business-pull and resource-push forces concerning diversification. Different mixes and sequences of these forces over time yield different patterns of input–output diversifications, for example, 'first pull then push' or vice versa, or pull–push–pull and so on.

The Canon case is illustrative as an example of the diversification processes described; (see Figures 6.3 and 6.4). Canon's diversification move from the camera business into the copier business was actually without synergies and thus unrelated to existing technological and marketing capabilities. The diversification moves from copiers to laser printers to bubble jet printers on the other hand were technology and market related enough to provide significant economies of scale and scope, which also implied less risk. However, the success of these latter diversification moves was contingent upon the first, non-synergistic and more risky diversification.[23]

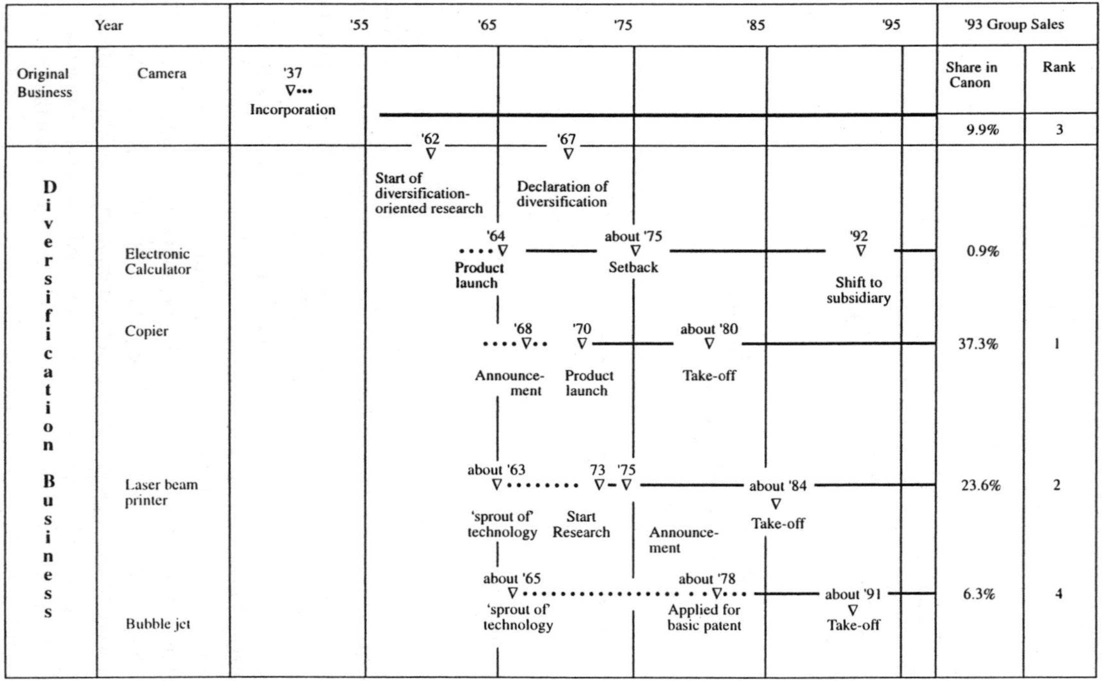

Figure 6.3: Progress of Canon's diversification — timeline chart with columns for Original Business/Diversification Business, Year, timeline decades ('37, '55, '65, '75, '85, '95), and '93 Group Sales (Share in Canon, Rank).

Original Business / Business	Year	Timeline milestones	'93 Group Sales — Share in Canon	Rank
(Original Business)	Camera	'37 ▽ Incorporation	9.9%	3
Diversification	Electronic Calculator	'62 ▽ Start of diversification-oriented research; '64 ▽ Product launch; '67 ▽ Declaration of diversification; about '75 ▽ Setback; '92 ▽ Shift to subsidiary	0.9%	
Diversification	Copier	'68 ▽ Announcement; '70 ▽ Product launch; about '80 ▽ Take-off	37.3%	1
Business	Laser beam printer	about '63 ▽ 'sprout of' technology; '73 ▽ – '75 ▽ Start Research; Announcement; about '84 ▽ Take-off	23.6%	2
Business	Bubble jet	about '65 ▽ 'sprout of' technology; about '78 ▽ Applied for basic patent; about '91 ▽ Take-off	6.3%	4

Source: Yamaji (1994).

Figure 6.3   Progress of Canon's diversification

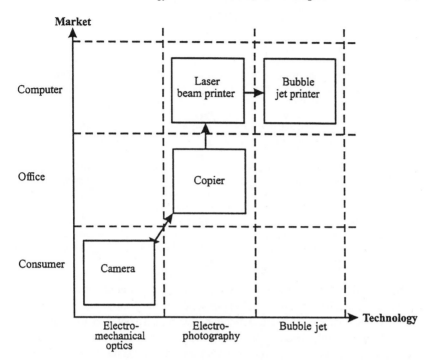

Source: Yamaji (1994).

Figure 6.4 Technology-related product diversification in the Canon case

Several concepts and procedures observed in the studied corporations were created in connection with commercializing new technologies through diversification. For example, in Hitachi one talked about the need for two types of management: synergistic management and concurrent management. Concurrent management refers to managing various processes concurrently rather than sequentially. Concurrent engineering is a related concept, specifically referring to the considerable overlapping in time of the production and marketing preparations for a new product with R&D operations, (see further below).

A similar emphasis on synergy and speed was found in Canon. Canon had five major strategies (as of 1992):

1. new corporate philosophy of mutual prosperity, *kyosei*;
2. strengthening of R&D;
3. diversification (which must be *synergetic*);
4. globalization;
5. new organization.

The special features of Canon's R&D were in turn:

1. Development of original products based on an unexplored technology for new business creation;
2. Revolutionize the organizational behaviour in the R&D division, particularly the improvement of R&D process management, R&D engineers and the organizational culture;
3. Continuous upgrading of core technologies to support new businesses;
4. Market-minded product planning to secure successive delivery to the marketplace of the best and long sellers as identified by strategic R&D planning.

Feedback from the marketplace is a continuous process in which virtually the entire organization, at all levels, is involved. To attain maximum efficiency in the management of R&D processes, emphasis is given to time-saving in all aspects. This, ultimately, requires a persistent effort beginning with the individual in order to improve engineering skills. Canon's increased emphasis on efficiency in R&D, including bringing new innovative products to market in record time, accelerates the process of diversification and at the same time improves the usefulness of existing products. (Documentation provided by Canon in 1992)

NEC used the term trunk technologies, referring to technologies that give rise to many applications and product businesses (see also Branscomb and Kodama 1993). Other concepts related to technologies with such a potential for economies of scale are mainly wide application technologies, generic technologies, pervasive technologies and core technologies (see Miyazaki 1995, p. 23).[24]

Concepts related to technological economies of scope are: winning technology combinations (Canon), technology 'blocs' or 'families', technology fusion (Kodama 1995), technological convergence (Rosenberg 1963), technology confluence (Jantsch 1967) and also technology diversification.[25]

Some additional features in connection with technology and product diversification must be mentioned as well. First, diversification was often guided by a general vision, a well-known example being the C&C (Computers & Communications) vision of NEC. This is actually a technology-related business vision, directing attention to the technological convergence and the long-run complementarities among computer and telecommunication technologies for sustaining existing businesses as well as creating future businesses.[26]

Another example was Toshiba's E&E (energy and electronics), also a technology-related business vision. In fact, these types of corporate specific concepts and visions flourish in Japanese business, often linked to some top managers as originators.[27] Within such a business vision, diversification may consciously proceed into intermediary product areas and from there to long-run target product areas. This intermediary diversification is used primarily for learning about technologies and markets, although cash may be generated as well for financing further diversification. A case in point is the multimedia area which is targeted by numerous companies, who attempt to enter this area at some entry point, building upon their specific resource strengths, and then penetrate the area through various diversification paths along which the resources could be further developed in stages. Moreover, the efforts in new technologies and product areas are often persevering, often formed with moderate resource levels, and occur in a corporate climate that permits repeated failures. This is in contrast to many Western companies, which often embark on grandiose programmes with too little tolerance for failure, resulting in premature stoppages of what must, after all, be considered exploratory efforts in new technologies. (see, for example, Hayes and Abernathy 1980).

Another important feature in this context is the continual small improvement of products and technologies in a step-by-step manner (*kaizen*).[28] However the product variant proliferation is perceived by some companies as going too far and therefore uneconomical. New technologies are also often created through a particular breakthrough, which cannot be achieved through a series of small steps, and then followed by several smaller improvements, which secure increasingly dependable and superior performance together with lower costs.

6.5.2   Economies of Speed

Characteristic of technology exploitation is the well-known speed-to-market behaviour in the Japanese commercialization of new technologies, as illustrated above by Hitachi and Canon and shown in Table 6.9. Exploratory efforts in new technologies may start very early in industry, and proceed for many years in parallel in many Japanese companies operating in various product areas, but once their commercial feasibility is established, the final pace of commercialization is very rapid, spurred on by domestic competitors. To have R&D resources for basic technology development and exploratory work is therefore a prerequisite for reducing time-to-market in product development. Concurrent management and concurrent engineering with strong integration of simultaneous or overlapping, rather than sequential, activities for product development, production and marketing are then used for reducing time-to-market, as is well known.[29] Japanese firms also appear to be quicker than US firms to reach the market with new products, at least in the case where the products are based largely on external technology rather than in-house R&D.[30]

Concurrent management may further be applied not only to different functions in developing a new product, but also to the development of different product generations, whose development phases may overlap. That is, R&D for the second (or even third) generation is started before the first product generation is launched on the market. Of course, trade-offs must then be made between time and costs, and also between lost and gained sales through internal 'cannibalization' among the different product generations of the company. Moreover, customers may be lost entirely to the company if two generations are spaced too far apart in time, thus creating a need for an intermediate generation (or version or model) that serves as a 'gap-filler', although it cannibalizes on the preceding generation.

As is also well known, Japan has in the past extensively acquired technology from abroad through various means, not least through licensing in, and has used this technology for commercialization on the domestic market in the first place but also increasingly on international markets. As Japan has reached, and in a number of cases surpassed, the technological levels of the West, the possibilities of sourcing suitable technology from abroad have decreased.

This is a tendency that has been reinforced by an increased control of technology transfer to Japan by Western companies. Japan has also built up an impressive indigenous R&D as she tries to access technology increasingly through other means, such as joint ventures, research cooperation and technology exchanges. In accessing new technologies in these ways, patenting plays an important role (see Chapter 7). Moreover, one source of technology that is increasingly utilized by Japanese industry is Western universities.[31] At the same time, Japanese R&D is becoming increasingly internationalized (see Chapter 5).

These patterns of behaviour also contribute to a kind of economies of speed, which arise from what can be called 'speed to technology'. This is actually a type of speed to input markets or factors, rather than speed to output markets, which is what is commonly meant by the phrase 'speed to market'. Speed to technology, then, contributes to speed to market.

In this context one can note that concurrent management may also be applied to the different phases of entering new business areas. However, the prevailing feature so far in Japanese companies is that technology-related product diversification has proceeded more stepwise in an evolutionary fashion, as described above (see, for example, Figure 6.1). Thus, in the commercialization of new technologies there are races in several directions – speed to technology (input market) and speed to (output) market. The outcomes of these races determine market lead time. Patent races, in which the winner gets all, are part of these races, making 'speed to patent' important. In general there are multiple patent races in connection with developing and sustaining a new product (see Chapter 7). Speed to patent and speed to market and technology should then be seen as complementary races, rather than as substitutes. Winning a strategic patent (see Chapter 7) is one very effective way to create substantial market lead time since such a patent not only slows down but blocks the competitors in their race to the market. Monitoring patenting activities of others is an important means for speed to technology. Sometimes in Western companies, patenting is seen as slowing down speed to market; in this case, insufficient patenting resources may be the actual impediment.

6.5.3   Dynamic Application Orientation and User Cooperation

It is almost a truism to say that application and user orientation are the crucial features of technology exploitation. Still there are some important points that are not self-evident, some of which are more specific to Japan.

Weak science and research culture
Japan has had a weak science and research culture during the catch-up process, which has mainly focused on technology – acquisition, adaption and deployment. Scarce resources for industrial R&D in the 1950s and 1960s led industry to economize on dearly acquired technologies from abroad.[32] In fact, in S&T and R&D work, a strong and prestige-focused science and research culture often fosters counterproductive attitudes towards the commercialization of new technologies, with its need for less glamorous development and application engineering work. To build up a science and research base avoiding such attitudes is a current and future challenge for Japan, especially since a science culture can easily become stronger than the national and corporate cultures. It may then be useful to recognize that honoured features of science, such as creativity and pioneering, are critical features in engineering as well. History of technology abounds with cases where creativity in applying existing technologies to new applications has made a big difference.

Application visions
The application orientation is often dynamic or sequential in the sense that a series of applications can be envisaged as feasible over time, in contrast to a single application. Such a stepwise application vision can be developed through curious and persistent exploratory work and experimentation with new technologies already at an early stage. The different applications may correspond to different business areas as part of a stepwise (rather than concurrent) technology-related diversification as described above. The applications may also correspond to different market segments in the same business area, segments that require increasingly high technical performance. Usually, Japanese companies have climbed up the quality ladder, while several Western companies, at least in the military–industrial complex, have climbed down or ignored mass-market applications altogether. Kodama (1995), referring to the Japanese approach of 'trickle-down', describes this circumstance very well.

Broad market orientation
Application orientation is different from a narrow market orientation that focuses only on existing customers and their needs. Applications are characterized by physical attributes of a product or a technology in a certain usage context. Identifying those technical performance variables that give extra value added

per R&D dollar to users in potentially large user groups gives guidance to R&D. A company that has maintained an innovative position for a long time thus has developed an R&D logic with preferences that have lost some of their economic relevance. For example, a company having developed centrifugal separators for years for applications in liquid food processing (for example, milk, juice), oil purification and so on, may have its R&D focused on the degree of separation as the primary technical performance variable, while for most users the reliability of separators in terms of its mean time between failures is the performance variable that primarily improves the user's economy. Users often do not have this kind of knowledge either, and it may not be readily available or perhaps even given much thought.

User cooperation
This leads to the fourth point, which is the conduciveness of user cooperation to innovation. Such cooperation has generally increased, not only in Japan, and much has been written about it. An excellent work on the importance of user cooperation is von Hippel (1988a).

6.5.4   IP Protection, Licensing and Monitoring

As is evident both in the questionnaire responses (see Table 6.5) and in the case studies, IP protection, licensing and monitoring is an important feature of technology exploitation in Japan. This will, however, be dealt with in detail in the subsequent Chapters 7, 8 and 9.

6.6   STANDARDIZATION AND IPR

In an increasing range of business areas, the setting of technical standards becomes highly important for commercializing new technologies, as technological interdependencies proliferate among products and services and compatibility among products and components imply significant benefits to consumers. Standardization and IP have both become recognized in recent decades as vital elements of business strategy. However, standard-setting and IPR tend to create conflicts of interest, and these conflicts increase, depending upon how standards are set, as the value of IP and the value of compatibility of technical solutions increase. This has been the case especially in information technologies related to computers, telecommunications, audio/video and so on. Licences (including patent pools) offer a natural way of conflict resolution but can be difficult to negotiate and offer other problems as well.

Standards may be set informally as de facto standards *ex post* as a result of market dominance (compare the saying 'volume begets standards') or they may be set by formal agreements *ex ante* (through consensus standards or planned standards) or by some combination of market forces and agreements at some stage of commercial development. In order for a company to get its proprietary technical solution accepted as a de facto standard, rapid buyer diffusion is important, which could be stimulated by low prices of products (penetration pricing). Imitation of the solution among other sellers is at least as important. Rapid seller diffusion could be stimulated by low prices of licences or by giving everyone the right to use the technical solution in their products (that is, to create an open standard). Alternatively, seller diffusion could be halted (for example, by strong IPR) so that the company's proprietary technical solution becomes dominant. Thus IPR could be used in several ways to advance de facto standard setting.

As the stakes in standard-setting are high and technology moves fast, there is a premium on early standard-setting (although premature standardization may jeopardize the further technical developments around the standard). Thus, standardization tends to be related to newer technologies as well as involving a deeper level of technical detail. Altogether these factors imply a growing volume of standards. This in turn leads to a closer interaction between standardization and the formation of IPRs and patents in particular. In general, IPR tend to complicate *ex ante* standard-setting. Standard-blocking patents, that is, patents that block a proposed or factual standard, become especially crucial. The value of such patents to patent holders could be tremendous, especially in the case of global standards. At the same time, a non-generous licensing policy by the patent holder could lead to the standard being abandoned. The classic case in point was the battle between the VHS and Betamax standards for VCRs, starting in 1975, where JVC's generous licensing policy contributed to the VHS victory in the mid- to late 1980s, inflicting the largest business and morale loss to Sony in its history (see Granstrand 1984 and Grindley 1995). Since then, the strategic role of standards in commercializing new technologies has been astutely recognized in Japan, as elsewhere. In that connection, the increasing importance of patents has also been recognized. A number of Japanese cases of standard-setting in connection with VCR, CD, DAT, ISDN, HDTV and DVD are described in Sigurdson (1996). See also reports from IIP, for example, IIP (1995).[33] Here the European GSM system for mobile communications is given as an illustration of the problems with patents in standard-setting. The case also illustrates how patent disputes could change the patent culture in a whole industry. In particular, the GSM case triggered a turnaround in Ericsson regarding IP (see also Chapter 5).

In the early 1990s, the GSM system involved more than 2000 patents, of which about 30 were standard-blocking patents. However, patenting had traditionally been considered a secondary issue in the telecommunications industry, especially among the traditionally monopolized national telecommunications service providers. This held true also in the early developments of GSM in the early to mid-1980s. Few, if any, really imagined that someone from the outside could step in and disturb the cooperative and consensus-seeking standardization process by patenting an invention and refusing to license it on generous terms. This lax IPR mentality also applied to Ericsson as an equipment supplier, as well as to some other European telecommunications companies, in addition to the national service providers in Europe. A kind of club mentality had developed in the telecommunications community in Europe with a gentleman's agreement to be generous to each other when it came to patents. The public-good orientation among the monopolized telecommunications service providers, thriving on administratively sustained high price levels as they were, had penetrated the whole sector. To let a patent block a standard, for example, was considered unfair, if not mutiny, among traditional telecommunications companies.

The situation changed drastically in the late 1980s when Motorola, as a newcomer on the European scene, started to use patents aggressively. It is easy to overly dramatize this, and it is difficult to find out what really happened amid all the accusations. European manufacturers said that they had had a licence agreement with each other for the new digital cellular GSM standard. Discussions in standardization bodies were also conducted in an open atmosphere and ideas about standards and specifications exchanged without much concern about patents. Suddenly a company such as Ericsson found itself in a position where it could possibly have been forced to pay royalties to someone else for inventions that Ericsson people thought they had originated. Moreover, Motorola could have blocked a GSM standard by its patents. Motorola could also have complied with the European claims to offer a licence but only for Europe. Thus it could have achieved a strong monopoly outside Europe when the GSM standard was adopted elsewhere.

In this process Motorola got the image as the 'bad guy,' for example, stealing ideas from the GSM work of others and patenting them and misusing its patent power in general. Motorola, on the other hand, claimed that it had a long track record of competing in the electronics industry, for which patenting was an integral part of doing business, and that the 'GSM group' recognized too late the serious nature of the pertinent IPR issues and specifically the Motorola patents.

All in all, the conduct of Motorola triggered a new era of heightened IPR awareness in telecommunications, leading to an irreversible track of new patenting and competitive behaviour in general, on which service providers have also embarked, pushed by privatization, liberalization, competition, internationalization and globalization in general. Motorola thereby illustrates the role of competition spurred through new entrants, so often observed in economic history.

In summary, the reasons behind the increasing importance of patents in standard-setting in the telecommunications industry since the 1980s are:

(i) volatile collective agreements regarding standard-blocking patents were challenged by aggressive patent holders, recognizing the tremendous commercial potential of patents in standard-setting; (ii) standards became increasingly linked to new technologies and sub-technologies with patent protection possibilities; (iii) the consumer electronics industry, with its competitive practices, became more involved in telecommunications, while competition intensified in general in the industry.

6.7 SUMMARY AND CONCLUSIONS

Since World War II, Japan has rapidly and successfully developed into a technology-based state. Capabilities in acquiring and exploiting technology have evolved during Japan's catch-up process in a way that has found traditional innovative leaders in the West with strong S&T capabilities and S&T cultures falling behind.

This chapter has made a brief review of the pros and cons of being an early or late mover on the market, a review that can help explain the dynamics of the often observed phenomena of catching up, forging ahead and falling back and then perhaps coming back again. In its transition from a catch-up stage to a more innovative stage, Japan has had to contemplate these dynamics, that is, whether or not success ultimately tends to breed failure that can again produce conditions for success. The general challenge ahead is to make the transition from a technology-based state to a more balanced and sustainable intellectual capital-based state.

The capabilities in managing technology and IP that have developed in Japan, especially in her large corporations, have some specific features, although they often build upon management concepts and techniques which have originated in the West. Based on survey data and interviews, the chapter has pointed out country differences as well as sector differences in various technology management strategies and IP management strategies. Access to technology as well as competition is a major limitation to profit from innovation as perceived by the Japanese corporations. Unlike European and US corporations, Japanese corporations considered patents as the most effective means of capturing the profits from innovation by restricting competition. The major limitation of patents as perceived was their inability to restrict competition from inventing around these patents. From society's point of view, patents should restrict competition but only up to a point where the dynamic efficiency from more innovations arising from strong patent protection balances against the static inefficiency from monopolistic pricing based on strong patents. Although difficult to assess, there seemed to be no sign of an unbalanced trade-off on average across industries. Patent laws could be tailored differently for different industries, taking into account that limitations to profit from innovation and limitations to patent differ across industries. However the general patent policy has always been to treat industries equally. Exceptions have occurred, such as in the pharmaceutical industry, where prolonged patent life times have been granted. Industry-specific rates of subsequent innovations also effectively limit actual length of patent protection. The delineation of a permissible patent scope is moreover to some extent dependent upon industry-specific practices.[34] Thus, there is already some room for tailoring patent protection for different industries. The policy issue of how to tailor industry-specific patent protection is very complex, however, not the least because of the many-to-many correspondence between technologies and industries as a result of generic technologies and multi-technology and multipatent products and processes. Although benefits of tailoring could be demonstrated, the costs of tailoring may very well be prohibitive.

A number of specific features in Japanese strategies for exploiting technology were elaborated. One such feature, differing sharply from the West, was the propensity to engage in technology-related product diversification in co-evolution with product-related technology diversification, thereby benefiting from economies of scale, scope and speed. The case of Canon was given as an illustration. Speed to market and speed to technology were other important features, as were application diversification based on application visions and user cooperation. Emphasis on intellectual property management was a further important feature.

Finally, this chapter described how issues concerning patents and standardization have become much more closely intertwined and altogether commercially important in recent decades.

NOTES

1. An attempt to understand Japan's techno-economic success (although punctuated by recessions) must take into account a broad range of factors pertaining to Japan as well as to the countries with which she competes and cooperates, especially the USA (see Chapter 5). All the efforts by scholars, policy analysts, politicians, consultants, managers, investors, journalists and others to explain Japan's industrial success and dominance in many sectors are almost an industry in itself (perhaps dominated by foreigners). That 'industry' will not be discussed here, except for a reminder about a few commonly voiced explanatory factors. Although the kind of macro success Japan has enjoyed in the current period of history probably can best be understood as a result of a dynamic process with a multitude of factors interacting in complex ways over time, longer lists of explanatory factors do not necessarily add progressively to an understanding. Classifying factors, for example, into categories such as macro- and micro-level factors as done here, is also difficult and is an approximation at best. Keeping all such reservations in mind, technology nevertheless appears to have been a decisive factor in Japan's successful post-war development.

2. Success may sometimes breed success but this seems to be less common among innovators and early movers in the long run (see, for example, Utterback 1994; Leonard-Barton 1995). However, cumulation of capabilities to sustain a lead is still a possibility.
3. At the same time, IBM accelerated its pace when observing Japanese initiatives and advances.
4. It should be remembered that Japan's economic growth and catch-up have been partial and unbalanced between sectors (although with considerable equity in society at large), sustaining a divided economy, with several still backward sectors. (For further readings about large corporations and their management, see, for example, Aoki 1988; Aoki and Dore 1994; Aoki and Rosenberg 1987; Fruin 1992; Miyazaki 1995.)
5. This, by the way, illustrates two things. First, how innovation and imitation processes occur in management just as in technology. Second, how the roles of innovators and imitators may shift back and forth over time among actors (countries, companies, individuals), thereby inducing them to play a mixture of innovator/imitator roles over time in intertwined processes of catching up, forging ahead, falling behind, recatching up and so on (to use the terminology in Abramovitz 1986).
6. The terms acquiring, building up and sourcing can be used interchangeably here. A common distinction is between internal and external sourcing, where internal refers to in-house and external refers to the various other sourcing strategies.
7. For studies of industry–university collaborations, although without the international dimension, see Lee and Mansfield (1996) and Rosenberg and Nelson (1994). For a study of how corporations view their collaborations with local R&D organizations, including universities, see Pearce (1994).
8. Technology selling is typically licensing out but also comprises selling contract R&D and engineering services.
9. See Granstrand and Sjölander (1990b) and Lindholm (1994) for details of this strategy.
10. It is in the nature of R&D that only a portion of the R&D work is successful in the sense that inventions are made or technical specifications are met, and only a portion of technical success leads to commercial success in terms of market acceptance, and even then economic success in terms of total returns on investments is not guaranteed. For example, Mansfield et al. (1977, pp. 22–32) found that 43 per cent of the projects were not technically successful, and 35 per cent of technically successful projects were not commercialized, and 26 per cent of commercialized projects were not economically successful.
11. There are several ways to express this function – capturing the returns from R&D, appropriating the benefits of innovation, protecting the competitive advantage of new or improved products and processes. No essential distinction between these expressions is made here.
12. See Appendix 2 for a discussion on the questionnaire design and methodological issues.
13. The US study used a scale from 1 to 7 so its data have been transformed to the scale 0 to 4 used here. The survey respondents in the US study were typically R&D managers, while the respondents in this study were typically IP managers, who were likely to put more emphasis on patents. Nevertheless, patents were not emphasized in the Swedish responses.
14. Probable reasons for this are discussed in Chapter 9.
15. Question F4 in Table 6.6 is similar to question F6 in Table 6.5 and was included also for checking sensitivity of results. As seen, variations in observations occur when some means are excluded, but the main conclusions remain much the same.
16. See, for example, Levin et al. (1987), Mansfield (1986), Taylor and Silberston (1973).
17. There are many significant differences between chemical, electrical and mechanical engineering corporations in Japan, a point that has been emphasized in the interviews.
18. Note that being first on the market means having a monopolistic position during market lead time.
19. Note that Appendix 4 gives numbers by which the statistical significance of observed differences in the perceptual data can be calculated approximately.
20. Compare 'related diversification'. 'Synergetic' is used here to emphasize that (positive) synergies are accomplished.
21. There are several studies of the relation between product diversification and growth in the West, but with disappointing results, for example, Montgomery (1994), Ravenscraft and Scherer (1987). See also Chapter 4.

22. The issue of diversification has been covered in several studies by the author and his colleagues. A quantitative study by Oskarsson (1993) corroborates the interview findings.

23. In the words of Dr Yamaji, CEO of Canon in 1992, diversification in the real meaning refers to this first type of diversification into technologies and markets completely new to the company, while 'derivative diversification' refers to related diversification.

24. In the economics literature, a recently coined term for such technologies is 'general purpose technologies' (see Bresnahan and Trajtenberg 1992).

25. Strictly speaking the terms 'technology fusion', 'technology convergence' and 'technology confluence' refer to a process by which two or more technologies merge into a new kind of technology (for example, mechanics and electronics merging into mechatronics), while technology diversification refers to the general process of broadening a technology base, thereby enabling economies of scope by combining technologies without necessarily considering a new combination of technologies as a new technology itself. Technological convergence may also refer to a process by which two technology bases increasingly overlap, that is, their technological distance decreases. See Rosenberg (1963).

26. Although a vision ought to be far-reaching into the future and have a long life, it cannot be a catch-all concept with an eternal life. Thus it can gradually become deceptive and direct attention away from complementarities with new technologies outside the originally envisaged ones.

27. For the use of visions as a management tool in Japanese business, see Fransman (1994).

28. There is by now quite an amount of literature on this. An early book in English is Imai (1986), although perhaps somewhat overplaying the role of *kaizen* according to Branscomb and Kodama (1993).

29. See, for example, Chandler (1990), Okimoto (1983), Nonaka (1990), Stalk and Hout (1990) and Cordero (1991).

30. As shown in a study of about 200 Japanese and US firms by Mansfield (1988a, b). Actually, both innovation times and innovation costs were shown to be lower for Japanese firms, but not in the case where the new products were based on internal technology.

31. The questionnaire data in this study show this, although not tabulated here (see Granstrand 1999).

32. The policy in Japan at the time to acquire technology through licensing in rather than through joint ventures with foreign partners for the domestic market (although such ventures occurred as well) also put pressure on indigenous companies and their R&D personnel to learn how to exploit the acquired technology in all respects, without being able to resort to a joint-venture partner.

33. There is also a growing literature on standards and IPR in general, see, for example, Farrell (1989).

34. Regarding aspects of the scope of patents, see the already classic article by Merges and Nelson (1990) and also David (1993). In new technologies it is difficult to delineate a balanced scope, see, for example, Brandi-Dohrn (1994) and Barton (1991, 1995).

7. Intellectual property policies and strategies

CHAPTER CONTENTS

7.1 CHAPTER OUTLINE

Chapter 6 highlighted the general importance of IP and patenting for the commercialization of new technologies. In this chapter we shall elaborate on the advantages and disadvantages of patents in general and then consider policies and strategies for patenting, as well as for trade secrets and trademarks.

Finally, total IP strategies including the concept of combining the various IPRs into a multiprotection system will be advocated.

7.2   ADVANTAGES AND DISADVANTAGES OF PATENTING

7.2.1   Advantages of Patenting

Traditionally, the primary motive for a company to apply for a patent is to increase the economic returns of its R&D efforts by ensuring restricted but enforceable monopoly rights, that is rights to exclude others from the protected technology. This is in concordance with the regulator's motive. However there are a number of other important motives for patenting, as described in Chapter 3. Table 7.1 provides a list of ten common patenting motives or advantages encountered in literature and in the companies interviewed, which were compiled for the questionnaire survey. The table also shows the relative importance of each motive, as perceived by each sector, from the sample of large Japanese corporations. *Protection* and *bargaining* advantages of patents constitute two broad categories of *external advantages*, corresponding to items 1 to 3 and 4 to 7 respectively in Table 7.1, with corporate image improvement as a third category of external advantages. A fourth category is *internal advantages* of patents, corresponding to items 9 and 10.

Technology protection
As seen from the table, the protection of product technology offered by patents is the single most important advantage regardless of industrial sector. This is as expected. For process technology, the protection advantage ranks third to highest, although the difference from second most important advantage is not significant.[1] The high ranking of patents as a source of retaliatory power is noteworthy. This defensive aspect of patents was also emphasized in the interviews.

Retaliatory power and patent arms race
As each process or product becomes increasingly linked to several patents and each patent to several processes or products (although the latter perhaps to a lesser extent, see Chapter 5), companies become increasingly interdependent on each other's patent portfolio, which in turn puts a premium on second-order deterrence and relative bargaining power in general. *Second-order deterrence* occurs as a result of an imitator or potential infringer holding patent rights relevant to some business area critical to the innovator or original patent right holder. Such a business area may not even be an area in which the alleged infringer has

Table 7.1 *Advantages and disadvantages of patenting in large Japanese corporations*

(Scale: No importance = 0, 1, 2, 3, 4 = Of major importance;
Tend. = Tendency 1987–92: Decreasing = –1, 0, + 1 = Increasing)

(Code) Question	Chemical (n = 9) Tend.	Electrical (n = 10) Tend.	Mechanical (n = 5) Tend.	Total (n = 24) Tend.
(F8) How important are the possible *advantages* that patenting may give your company?				
I. *External advantages*				
a) *For protection*				
1. Protecting proprietary product technology	3.89 (0.5)	3.60 (0.6)	4.00 (1.0)	3.79 (0.7)
2. Protecting proprietary process technology	3.00 (0.3)	3.30 (0.4)	3.40 (1.0)	3.21 (0.5)
3. Creating retaliatory power against competitors	3.11 (0.4)	3.40 (0.6)	3.20 (0.8)	3.25 (0.6)
b) *For bargaining*				
4. Giving better possibilities of selling licences	2.89 (0.5)	3.10 (0.6)	2.40 (0.6)	2.88 (0.6)
5. Giving better possibilities of accessing technology				
through cross-licensing	3.00 (0.5)	3.30 (0.6)	2.60 (0.8)	3.04 (0.6)
6. Facilitating R&D cooperation with others	2.44 (0.3)	2.40 (0.3)	2.00 (0.4)	2.33 (0.3)
7. Giving a better bargaining position in standard-setting	2.22 (0.1)	2.90 (0.5)	2.00 (0.4)	2.46 (0.4)
c) *For image*				
8. Improving the corporate image	2.11 (0.0)	2.70 (0.3)	2.20 (0.2)	2.38 (0.2)
II. *Internal advantages*				
9. Providing motivation for employees to invent	2.56 (0.3)	2.90 (0.5)	2.40 (0.2)	2.67 (0.4)
10. Providing a measure of R&D productivity	2.11 (0.1)	2.50 (0.5)	2.40 (0.6)	2.33 (0.4)
(F9) How important are the possible *disadvantages* that your patenting may give your company?				
Disclosing of technical information	2.25 (0.1)	1.70 (–0.1)	1.20 (0.0)	1.78 (0.0)
Incurring direct costs of patenting	2.38 (0.3)	1.80 (0.3)	1.40 (0.0)	1.91 (0.3)

Note: The highest and lowest values for each industry are overlined and underlined, respectively.

211

a business, but only has patent power for possible retaliation. Thus, retaliatory power through a broad patent portfolio held by a competitor may weaken the protective advantage of single patents held by an innovator. Similarly an innovator can strengthen deterrence with a broad patent portfolio. Thus the protective advantages of patenting become increasingly dependent upon large patent portfolios producing a kind of arms race situation. At the same time, the vulnerability of companies to infringement accusations increases with their diversity of businesses and technologies. This opens up possibilities for inventors and small firms, with perhaps just one patent and without any vulnerable manufacturing, to act as 'patent extortionists' by accusing large firms of infringement and escaping their retaliatory power.

Licensing out

The connections between patents, products and processes increase in general due to the emergence of generic technologies ('multiproduct' technologies) as well as 'mul-tech' products and processes (see Chapters 4, 5 and 6). As a consequence, companies tend to become technologically dependent upon each other, especially diversified firms operating in complex technologies.[2] This increasingly makes patents into bargaining chips.[3]

Licensing out is a bargaining situation where patents have always played a role. Although they are not necessary for selling licences, they are most helpful. This is a traditional and intended advantage of patents. What has happened, as indicated in interviews, is that companies have increasingly taken out patents outside their immediate product areas and used them for licensing business. Traditionally, companies have sold licences for their existing product and process technologies and for certain geographic markets or applications where the company has not found it possible or worthwhile to manufacture and/or sell products directly. However, with more exploratory R&D in more generic technologies and with more active patenting and technology intelligence, the opportunities for more 'stand-alone' licensing businesses has increased.

Cross-licensing

The advantage of patents in accessing technology through cross-licensing is also noteworthy (see further below). Here one should also note that the difficulties or high cost in accessing technology ranked high among perceived limitations to profit from innovation, as shown in Table 6.6.

Cooperative R&D

Cooperative R&D offers another type of bargaining situation in which patents are advantageous, both for identifying and attracting R&D partners and for negotiating with them. As cooperative R&D has increased in industry, as discussed in Chapter 6, the advantage of patents has become more pronounced in that context. Still, that advantage ranks at the bottom compared to other advantages, as seen from Table 7.1.

Standard-setting

Standard-setting provides yet another but fairly new type of bargaining situation in which patents are often important. The importance of patents in connection with standard-setting rapidly increased during the 1980s in the tele-communications, computer and consumer electronics industries among others. As described in Section 6.6, standard-setting became more economically important and more involved with new technologies, often earlier in the innovation processes and at a more detailed level. By and large this has only recently become a recognized strategic role for patents (see also Chapter 5 on trends). However, although more standard-setting involves patents, far from all patents involve standard-setting and thus the ranking in Table 7.1 is not as high.

Corporate image

Improving the corporate image was a low-ranked advantage of patents, but still clearly recognized, as indicated in the interviews and also by the attention paid to the ranking of companies based on their patenting activities, such as the ranking of the top ten patentors in the US (see Chapter 1). The public image of the company as being technologically progressive is generally cultivated among large Japanese companies, not least as a means for attracting graduate engineering students.

Internal advantages

As seen from Table 7.1, the internal advantages of patenting ranked low across industries. The advantage of patents as an indicator of R&D productivity was ranked especially low, which is interesting in the light of the frequent use by economists of patent statistics for productivity analysis, as described in Chapter 9. The use of patents for internal reward schemes and motivation in Japanese companies is frequently acknowledged in the literature (see Chapters 5 and 6). It was also acknowledged by the companies interviewed, but as Table 7.1 shows it is not of major importance relative to other advantages. Thus the internal advantages of patents as 'carrots' and 'yardsticks' are on the whole of less importance.

7.2.2   Disadvantages of Patenting

Turning to the perceived disadvantages of patents, it is first interesting to note that in total they are ranked significantly lower in Table 7.1 than any of the advantages, which is one way to explain the high levels of patenting in Japanese companies. This holds particularly true for the electrical and mechanical companies. Second, one may note that disclosure is less of a disadvantage in all three industries than the direct costs of patenting, although the difference is not significant. Whether this is an indication of the inordinately high direct costs associated with patenting is left as an open question here.

Another observation is that industry differences in the perceived advantages and disadvantages of patents are not strikingly large on the whole, although significant ones exist in the set of bargaining advantages. Chemical companies seem to be significantly more sensitive to the disadvantages than companies in other industries. The industry differences regarding perceptions of advantages of patents (as shown in Table 7.1) as well as regarding perceptions of limitations of patents (as shown in Table 6.7) are fairly small compared to the significant industry variations regarding perceptions of the role of patents relative to other means for appropriating benefits from innovation (as shown in Table 6.4). If nothing else, this should serve as a reminder of the limitations of perceptual data and the difficulties in interpreting various differences among them.

7.2.3   Defensive and Offensive Advantages

There are of course other ways to formulate and classify advantages of patents and rationales for their use.[4] One way is to look at defensive versus offensive motives behind patenting. It could be said that a most important motive behind patenting – from a company's point of view – is to block competitors in either or both of two senses, the first being offensive and the second more defensive (compare Chapter 3):

1. To block competitors from using a technology and in so doing increase their costs and time for imitation and/or for inventing around the patent, in order to increase their willingness to pay for a licence or to stay away from a market (thereby ensuring 'market freedom').
2. To block the competitors from blocking oneself, and thereby ensure 'design freedom'.

Among engineers in many companies in the West, the traditional motive for patenting has been to protect significant inventions for one's own business, while not engaging primarily in the patenting of minor inventions or patenting outside one's own business area. In this sense, patenting has traditionally been used primarily for directly protecting one's own businesses. However, there has been a gradual shift of emphasis from this more 'gentlemanly' behaviour towards other more offensive purposes and aggressive action, where patents are used more strategically as both a competitive weapon and an economic asset.[5] This is also reflected in the way patents are being used in various bargaining situations.

As a reminder that there have been Western companies that historically have practised modern, less 'gentlemanly', patenting strategies, the following deserves to be cited from a large US company in the 1930s:

> In taking out patents we have three main purposes – (a) to cover actual machines which we are putting out, to prevent duplication of them . . . (b) to block the development of machines which might be constructed by others for the same purpose as our machines, using alternative means . . . (c) to secure patents on possible improvements of competing machines, so as to 'fence in' those and prevent their reaching an improved stage. (Cited in Folk 1942, p. 39)

7.3   IP POLICIES

Since most of the Japanese corporations in the sample had a written, corporate-wide patent policy, in contrast to many Western firms, a general note about the rationale of policies is in order. A policy is a set of statements to be used as a general guideline for operations in an area. The common distinction among policies, objectives and strategies is that strategies refer to specific courses of action taken over time, perceived as instrumental in reaching certain objectives, while being constrained by policies. A policy therefore simplifies decision-making and action taken by narrowing down options and focusing attention and efforts in the organization. Such a policy is typically fairly long-lived and not specified in terms of time. A (business) policy can express basic business ideas, missions and philosophies for a company as well as being educational. There are many views on how policies should look ideally and how they should be conceived. For example, a policy should strike a balance between the very general and the very specific.

A policy pertains to a certain area of operations. With many interdependent policy areas, a need for policy coordination arises. Policies also evolve over time, mostly as a result of complex policy-making processes, especially in large organizations.

Regarding patenting and IP in general, policies have evolved in stages corresponding to the increasing importance and attention attached to IPRs in companies. Table 7.2 gives one illustration. These stages can be compared with the stages in the evolution of corporate patent organizations as shown in Table 8.5. As shown, both IP policies and IP organizations have evolved so as to become more comprehensive, strategic and integrated with business management and technology management (including licensing in/out).

As IP policies become increasingly elaborated in companies, more policy issues come to the forefront. For most policy areas in a large company, especially when uncertainty is high and options are many, the demand for policies exceeds the supply from policy-makers. It is, then, useful to have a 'living policy' in the sense that there is always one set of policy issues pending, awaiting a policy decision, and another set of policies already in place. As some written policies, as well as rules and guidelines in general, may outlive their usefulness over the course of time, it may also be beneficial to make clear which policies have become obsolete.

Table 7.2   Stages in the evolution of corporate IP policies

Stage	Characteristics of IP policies
1	• IP ignored
2	• Rewards for patents
	• Intellectual property issues left to the legal department
3	• Selective patenting based on the evaluation of pros and cons of disclosure
	• Licensing in if needed and licensing out if requested
	• Trade secrets defended in court
	• Review of patent positions
4	• Intellectual property opportunities are part of business strategy, project selection and project management criteria
	• In-licensing to maintain focus, speed, external point of comparison, and learning opportunities
	• Technical staff rotate through intellectual property department
	• Out-licensing based on business and technical assessments
	• Comprehensive trade secret policies

Source: Based on Adler et al. (1992, p. 27). Permission to use the table contents has been provided by *Sloan Management Review* for a fee paid to the journal.

There are many policy areas and policy issues pertaining to patenting and IP, such as:

- coordination of patenting across business divisions;
- coordination of patenting with R&D management;
- licensing policies;
- patent-related reward schemes for employees;
- when, where, and how to file patent applications (timing, countries, routes and so on);
- patent mapping, clearance and review procedures;
- education and training;
- outsourcing of patent operations;

- IP handling in external R&D cooperations, joint ventures, acquisitions and spin-offs, and so on;
- patent handling in standard-setting;
- infringement and litigation.

When a policy area such as patenting suddenly receives extra attention, there is a tendency to propose and formulate policies that are too numerous and too specific, thus failing to distinguish a policy from a mere manual with operative instructions.

Many Western companies have not yet reached a stage with clearly formulated IP policies, therefore a patent and licensing policy for the Anonymous Business Corporation (here ABC) is presented as follows, briefly presented for the sake of illustration:[6]

General Each ABC manager with a comprehensive business responsibility is accountable for the build-up and exploitation of ABC's intellectual capital, including its IPR. Patenting is to be considered a strategic issue, implying, for example, its presence in strategic plans and in strategy-meeting agendas. The business economic aspects of patents should be clearly expressed.

Specific ABC's current policies to be followed as a rule until further notice, allowing for exceptions and changes as decided by the Corporate IP Board, are as follows:

1. Multiple IP protection must be used for each business segment, that is, whenever possible combining patents, secrets, trademarks, designs, copyrights and utility models to strengthen overall protection.
2. A strategic patent position or the equivalent competitive advantage must be ensured in each core business.
3. Before entering a new technology and/or a new business, patent clearance must be undertaken.
4. If patent protection has been achieved for some parts of the business, vigorous follow-up patenting or patent acquisitions must be ensured.
5. As a main rule until further notice, allowing for exceptions, patents should be applied for whenever possible and at an early stage, starting in a suitable country with international applications covering major industrial countries and markets of current interest to ABC, as well as markets of importance to competitors and markets which can be expected to become of commercial interest to ABC within ten years.
6. 'Speed to patent' must be ensured so that speed to market is not jeopardized.
7. Technical and commercial collaborations with lead users, lead suppliers, competitors, other companies, universities, independent inventors and

other parties are important and should be encouraged. Hereby ABC should strive to become the lead patentor in all collaborations especially with users, universities, consultants and inventors. In collaborations with competitors and suppliers, ABC can accept shared patent right agreements, if they are compatible with business goals and licensing strategies.

8. Increase patenting activities in the USA in particular, and file more priority applications in the USA as well.
9. Prophylactic publishing[7] can be used in specially motivated cases, but never as a substitute for patents.
10. Offensive patenting for blocking others outside of ABC's own business on a systematic basis should currently be avoided.
11. ABC has an open licensing policy, subject to proper royalty determination reflecting the commercial and strategic value of its patents and intellectual capital.
12. ABC should actively search for licensing and cross-licensing agreements with other parties.
13. Ample caution must be exercised in dealing with intellectual property related to de facto standards.
14. Infringement detection and litigious action regarding all IPRs should be proactively pursued with a long-term economic view.
15. ABC respects the IPRs of other companies as legally recognized in their respective countries, and refrains from all kinds of wilful infringements.

It should be noted here that policy statements could as well be formulated regarding desirable emphasis or de-emphasis on any of the commercialization strategies in Table 6.4, or on any of the advantages or disadvantages of patents in Table 7.1 – linked to the company and business situation in question. Similarly, secrecy and intelligence policies could be formulated in terms related to Table 7.5.

7.4   PATENT STRATEGIES

7.4.1   Patent Strategies in General

The literature in economics and management on patent strategies is generally very thin, as was the case for technology strategies until that area grew popular in the 1980s. The popularity of the strategy concept has also started to grow in the IP community. Several works on IP strategy, mainly from a legal perspective, have appeared, see, for example, Anawalt and Enayati (1996) and Glazier (1995). A more management-oriented work is presented by Momberg and Ashton (1986). Manuals and textbooks (as well as licensing strategies) for patenting, often discuss patent strategies in terms of when (in the R&D process), where (choice of countries), why and how to patent. Patenting strategies described by statistical indicators of patenting and the patent portfolios of firms and related to their economic performance have been studied by Ernst (1995). Patent strategies in Japanese industry have been studied by Rahn (1994). Various business history studies also account for patent strategies used in the evolution of an industry or a company. A recent example from the electronics industry is given in Takahashi (1994).

In these types of works, various ways are used to characterize and classify patents and patenting strategies. Below, a somewhat novel way to represent these strategies, based on the concept of a technology space, the product life cycle and the technology life cycle, will be used. Patent strategies could also be defined at the level of individual patents or at the level of the patent portfolio for a business or a company as a whole. Here, patent strategies will be discussed at the portfolio level. Patent strategies are also put into the context of other strategies such as technology strategies as described in Chapters 4 and 6.

Patenting in technology space

In order to illustrate various patent strategies it is useful to think abstractly of a general technology space in terms of a technological terrain or technology landscape, which is gradually explored by R&D processes. Parts of the terrain with (roughly) similar R&D difficulties in terms of costs could be delineated by R&D isocost curves, in principle resembling altitude curves. Various maps of this technology landscape could be constructed, revised and improved as R&D proceeds. (See further Chapter 9.) A patent could be represented on such maps by a circle enclosing the technical solutions in the claims of the patent. The size of the circle could also be used to indicate schematically the scope of the patent. With this type of map a number of generic patent strategies could be illustrated as in Figure 7.1, based on the configuration of multiple patents. Of course, configurations in reality are not as 'neat' as in the figure, which aims at illustrating different cases in principle. Moreover, patent strategies can obviously not rely solely on configuration considerations, but must also take into account the actual qualities of individual patents and patent claims as well as the company situation in general (whether the company is leading or catching-up and so on). With this in mind a number of generic patent strategies could be described as follows:

Ad hoc blocking and 'inventing around'   Typically as a result of ad hoc efforts, small resources and/or disregard of small patents and portfolio effects, one or a few patents are used in this case to protect an innovation in a special application. The possibilities to invent around are many, and R&D costs and time for inventing around are low.

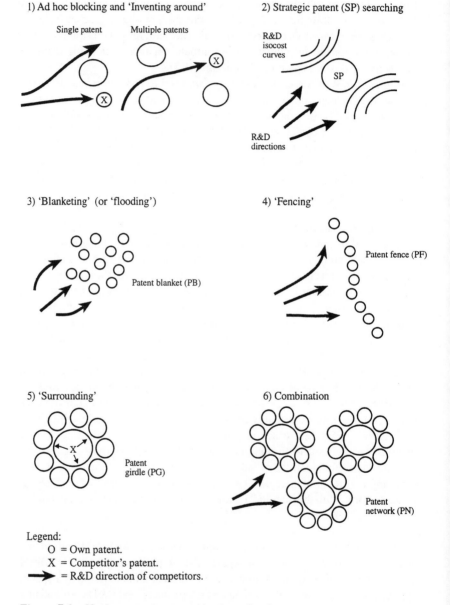

Figure 7.1   Various patent strategies in technology space

Strategic patent searching   A single patent with a large blocking power is (somewhat ambiguously) called a strategic patent. In other words, strategic patents have deterringly high or insurmountable invent-around costs and are therefore necessary for doing business within a specific product area.

'Blanketing' and 'flooding'   In the case of blanketing, efforts are made to turn an area into a jungle or a minefield of patents, for example, 'mining' or 'bombing' every step in a manufacturing process with patents, more or less systematically.[8] Flooding refers to a less structured way of taking out multiple patents, major as well as minor, in a field and may result from patenting-reward schemes as much as from a conscious strategy. Blanketing and flooding may be used as a strategy in emerging technologies when uncertainty is high regarding which R&D directions are fruitful or in situations with uncertainty about the economic importance of the scope of a patent.

Typically, blanketing and flooding make use of the possibilities to take out patents on minor inventions from a technical point of view. As mentioned in Chapter 5.8.1, such minor patents are often frowned on by engineers and inventors and sometimes referred to as 'petty patents', 'junk patents' or 'nuisance patents'. However, such judgements are based surprisingly often on the technical characteristics rather than on the possible economic importance of the patent. Minor patents can be used as nuisance patents to slow down competitors. Minor patents may also be useful in building the bargaining power of a patent portfolio. Nevertheless, it must be kept in mind that not all patents are economically motivated and that a blanketing or flooding strategy is only economical up to a point.

'Fencing'   This refers to the situation where a series of patents, ordered in some way, block certain lines or directions of R&D, for example, a range of variants of a chemical sub-process, molecular design, geometric shape, temperature conditions or pressure conditions. Fencing is typically used for a range of possibly quite different technical solutions for achieving a similar functional result. (See the citation in the end of Section 7.2 above, which also shows that 'fencing' is an old strategy, which was actually described by Alfred Marshall).[9]

'Surrounding'   Typically this is the case when an important central patent of some kind, especially a strategic patent, can be fenced in or surrounded by other patents, which are individually less important but collectively block the effective commercial use of the central patent, even after its expiration. Often, surrounding patents pertain to different applications of a basic invention. Surrounding could be used to get access to the surrounded technology, for example through cross-licensing. This is an important possibility if a competitor gets a strategic patent.

Other competitors can then hope to win a second patent race for application patents that could possibly block the exploitation of the strategic patent, which in turn would create possibilities for cross-licensing. (For an alleged example of this, see Spero 1990.)

Combination into patent networks This refers to the building of a patent portfolio in which patents of various kinds and configurations are consciously used to strengthen overall protection and bargaining power.

Patenting over time

The patenting patterns in Figure 7.1 are snapshots of the result from patenting activities over time, involving several races for patents of various types – product patents, process patents, application patents and so on. Different patenting strategies over time can be considered as well. Two principal types of diagrams could be used, one showing the development over time of some economic variable (for example, cash flow) and one showing some technology-related variable (typically of technical performance).[10] A simple illustration of a cash-flow diagram is shown in Figures 7.2 and 7.3. Here two alternative patent

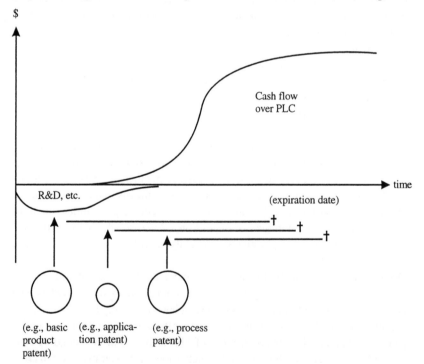

Figure 7.2   Sporadic patenting in the product business development process

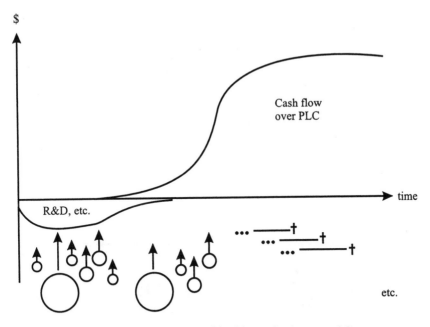

Figure 7.3   Continuous patenting and build-up of patent portfolio

strategies are illustrated in connection with the cash flow over the product life cycle (PLC) of one product generation. In the first case, called *sporadic patenting*, just a few patents at key steps in the R&D process are taken out. In the second case a conscious effort is made to build up a rich patent portfolio, and patents are applied for more or less continuously in the R&D process. This second strategy can be called *continuous or follow-up patenting* and results in the build-up of a patent portfolio for the product business in question. The portfolio is composed of a number of product patents, application patents, production process patents and so on, reflecting the shifts of emphasis in R&D work in the different PLC stages. This is more costly and discloses more information as well as requiring more astute management of patent maintenance and expiration, but gives a broader and more long-lasting protection while reducing the risk for the innovating company to be foreclosed by a fast competitor. It should also be noted that continuous patenting is somewhat along the same lines as continuous improvement or *kaizen*. However, continuous patenting is applicable not only to continuous improvements of a product. In developing a product of a systems nature, for example a power transmission system, many technologies are involved with patentable advances on many fronts as R&D proceeds, while the final product may represent a radical step in increased overall technical performance.

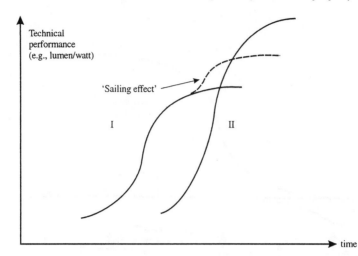

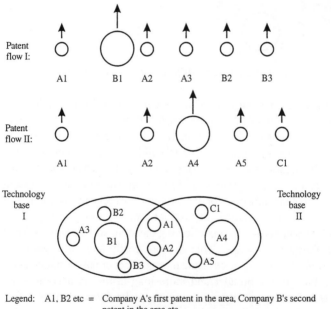

Legend: A1, B2 etc = Company A's first patent in the area, Company B's second
                      patent in the area etc.
         I, II   = Two technical performance curves, corresponding to technology
                      base I and II, represented by two overlapping sets of technologies,
                      being partly protected in technology space by two patent flows
                      over time. The 'sailing effect' refers to improvements in
                      technical performance in response to threats from new technologies.
         Circles   denote scope of patents
         Arrows   denote patent granting dates

Figure 7.4   Patenting strategies in the case of competing product generations

Figures 7.2 and 7.3 illustrate two patenting strategies of a firm in the context of one product generation. Figure 7.4 then illustrates the patenting behaviour of different competing companies A, B and C in two competing product types or two subsequent product generations. These are predicated on two technology bases (sets of technologies), denoted I and II, with partly competing (substituting), partly complementary technologies. The shift from one product generation to the other thus involves a transition to new technologies, perhaps involving a radical innovation. The technical performance of the two product generations or types often improves over time, as shown by the schematic S-curves in Figure 7.4. An example would be digital technology superseding analogue in mobile telephony. Company B holds a major patent for technology base I and concentrates its R&D on further improvements in that area,[11] while company A builds patent positions in both technology bases. Company C is a new entrant in the area and focuses only on technology base II. Thus the competing companies have different patent shares in the different technologies for the competing product generations or product types, just as they may have different market shares. Typically, established firms with high market and patent shares for an established product generation are slow to build up strategic patent positions in a new competing technology, thereby risking the loss of market share in the new product generation. At the same time, new innovative firms get an opportunity to enter the market, which has often been the case historically in connection with a radical innovation or technology transition (see, for example, Schon 1967 and Utterback 1994).

R&D investment strategies   Naturally, patenting behaviours or strategies are linked to the R&D strategies of the competing companies. For a single-product generation, R&D strategies typically shift along the PLC from emphasizing product R&D to process R&D and application developments. In connection with a product generation shift involving a technology transition, general R&D investment strategies and responses are:

1. Investing in improvements of the old technology in the existing product generation (yielding the 'sailing effect', see note 11).
2. Investing in a new product generation based on some version of the new technology.
3. Investing in a hybrid generation, based in parts on both the old and the new technology, as a 'gap filler'.
4. Introducing the new technology in an evolutionary manner in the existing generation (for example, piecemeal replacement of transistors with integrated circuits).

5. Abandoning the emerging technology and jumping to the next major new technology. (This is a risky strategy.)
6. Doing nothing (wait and see).

When and how to enter the new technology (if at all) and when and how to exit the old technology are thus crucial timing decisions for technology management. It is also easy to fall behind because of a failure to build up patent positions in the emerging technology, as mentioned. Thus there are not only races for product, process and application patents for a particular type or generation of a product, but for several competing products and technologies. The old saying that in patenting the winner takes all refers to a single patent race, while in a typical technology-based business there is a multitude of patent races. Finally it should be noted that since patenting is a reflection of R&D strategies, at least to some extent, patent information is useful to outsiders in tracking down these strategies. R&D strategies can then be somewhat disguised by patent flooding or decoy patenting (see further Chapter 9).

7.4.2　Patent Strategies in Japan

Several of the patenting behaviours and strategies described above were found in the Japanese corporations, mainly through interviews and case studies. In summary they were:

1. Patent blanketing (patent invasion of new technologies), flooding, fencing and surrounding.
2. Building of patent portfolios and patent networks.
3. Early-stage patenting, and continuous patenting, also of minor advances and variations ('patent everything as soon as possible').
4. Increased emphasis on the quality of patents (for example, search for 'strategic patents').
5. Patenting also for licensing out, including accessing new technologies through cross-licensing.
6. Building of patent power for deterrence, retaliation and bargaining.
7. Increased patenting in USA.
8. Use of patents for stimulation of R&D personnel.
9. Development and maintenance of a patent culture.

Several of these behaviours and strategies have also been acknowledged by patent offices, and some of them have occasionally been reported in the literature (see, for example, Rahn 1994). The rational aspects of these strategies should not be overplayed. Effective as many of them are, they have nevertheless evolved over time as historical products, rather than as a result of a few rational strategic decisions, as will be described below.

Evolution of strategy

For a long time, Japanese companies have emphasized the quantity of patents (see Chapter 5), although well aware that the technological and economic importance of individual patents differs widely. There is also a general feeling that many Japanese patents are of minor technical and economic importance,[12] while Western patents are often more significant on average. This may have been true in the past and is still true as far as Japanese patents in Japan are concerned. Although it may still be true as well in several technologies for Japanese patents in the USA and Europe, there are numerous studies indicating the relatively high quality of Japanese patents in many industrial sectors.[13] The strategy of extensive patenting of minor improvements in Japanese companies evolved in connection with the catch-up process in the post-war era (see Chapter 5). A careful study of patent information was necessary in order to trace useful technologies and suitable licensors as well as to control the risk of infringing on patents of others when imitating and modifying products and processes. However, improvements were gradually made on imported technologies, aided by quality circles and suggestion systems. The urge both to improve the technology of others and to invent around the patents of others spurred small inventions, which were then readily patented. A patent was perceived among R&D personnel as a precious sign of world technical leadership. Patenting thus gained a prestigious value, probably more so in Japan than in the West. Methods such as patent mapping and patent reviews or audits (see Chapter 9) were designed and developed over the years in order to cope with the patents of others and to build a patent position of one's own. Patent analysis in this way provided a 'navigational map' for both reaching and advancing the technological frontier.[14]

Historical conditions in connection with a long process of catching up and competing with the West, including strong domestic competition at the same time, have given rise to different patenting behaviours (that is, patent 'flooding' or patent 'blanketing' and patent 'fencing'). As these behaviours have become functional for businesses, they have been more consciously refined and used, thereby gaining the status of conscious strategies. These behaviours and strategies in turn have become more and more relevant for technologically leading and innovative companies as new products and processes involve an expanding range of expensive technologies, forcing even leading companies now and then to play catch-up in some technologies. No one can afford to take (much less sustain) the lead on a broad range of technological frontiers. The IP management capabilities that Japanese industry built up during its catch-up phase also paid off in the subsequent phase of industrial development, giving Japanese industry a competitive advantage over many Western companies.

Strategic patents

The recognition in Japanese industry of the importance of achieving a high quality of patents has increased in recent years. This is due in part to the fact that Japan reached and advanced many technological frontiers herself in the 1980s, which led to patenting in new fields. The lawsuits from the USA and concomitant legal challenging of patents have also contributed to this recognition. The direct costs of patenting have also grown considerably, and since they are the same for both major and minor patents, any cost-cutting effort naturally aims at screening out (economically) minor patents. Finally, the adoption of a multiclaim system in Japan broadened the possibilities to increase the quality of a patent application.

Efforts have been made in Japan to focus more on the quality of patents and to increasingly obtain what are called 'strategic patents'. Broadly speaking, a strategic patent is a patent of decisive importance for someone wanting to commercialize a technology in a product area.[15] In other words, a strategic patent creates inhibitive costs for anyone wanting to invent around it (see Section 7.4.1, above).

Hitachi is a case in point here, as shown in Table 7.3. The clear definition of 'strategic patent' and the clear, quantified objectives for acquiring such patents are noteworthy. Such patents can be acquired through one's own R&D or through external acquisition. If successful over a number of years, such a patent strategy can lead to the build-up of substantial patent power for Hitachi with the possibility of blocking hundreds of product areas and companies.

Canon has a policy that a strategic patent[16] should be acquired before commercialization starts in a new business area. The acquisition can occur either through Canon's own efforts or through licensing in. If this cannot be ensured, the area is not entered. In addition, Canon wants to be the sole innovator in at least one respect. This latter policy of Canon is not typical for Japanese companies. Many companies rely upon the possibility of obtaining a licence from a strategic patent holder. For example, Canon invested heavily in the commercialization of the ferroelectric liquid crystal (FLC) technology for flat panel displays, while many other companies were watching by and large, relying upon getting a licence from Canon should FLC prove viable in the end. Relying upon the possibility that a licence will be obtainable from someone who succeeds in a field is not an uncommon strategy among large companies. The current and possible future technological interdependencies among large companies account for this type of delicate and risky trust.

Table 7.3   Example from Hitachi of patent policy and objectives ('The third term campaign to increase strategic patents' as of 1992)

1. Contents	
Action policy	• Enhancing quality of patents (Integrating business and patent strategies)
Basic measures	• Specify rivals and acquire five cases of strategic patents for each major product item's technology. • Strengthen activities to acquire basic patents that capture in advance the future needs of society markets.
Specific examples of measures	1. To establish patents on a sales point that allows the company to defeat others 2. PAS[1] and special R&D project aimed at acquiring leading-edge patents

2.   *Level of strategic patent*[2] *and number of cases annually certified (summary)*

Level	Corporate target	Salient points of certification
Gold	25 cases	Basic invention top level in the world
Silver	75 cases	Basic invention top level in Japan
Copper	200 cases	Inventions that can be aggressively used as a sales point for Hitachi's mainstay products

Notes
1. PAS = patent strategy system.
2. Strategic patents mean basic and inevitable patents that must be used by our company and others in major products of the present and future.

Source: Documentation provided by Hitachi.

The process scheme for creating strategic patents at Toshiba is shown in Figure 7.5. Here one may observe how product planning and technology analysis feeds into R&D and strategic patenting.

A certain industrial and nationalistic codex also comes into play, especially regarding licensing on foreign markets, but its importance should not be overplayed. In the early 1990s, many leading-edge companies in Japan had an 'open licensing policy', meaning that every technology is in principle available for others to license if the terms are 'right'. Hitachi, for instance, declared in the early 1990s that it had an open policy making all patents available for licensing. NEC claimed they seldom refused to sell a licence and perceived no

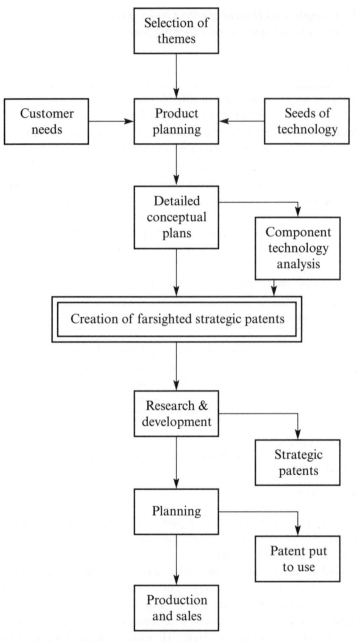

Source: Documentation provided by Toshiba.

Figure 7.5   Strategic patent searching at Toshiba

risk in creating a new competitor with a single licence. However, in the mid-1990s some of these companies questioned and modified this open licensing policy, thereby taking a step towards more selective licensing. Still, the technological interdependence between products and between companies force clusters of companies to license fairly openly among themselves to avoid retaliation.

Licensing policies may of course differ among companies. In general, since the Betamax–VHS systems battle between Sony and JVC Matsushita in the late 1970s and 1980s, there has emerged a recognition of the importance in some cases of building groups or families of companies through liberal licensing in order to support a new product or business system.[17] This may be part of a business strategy to combine the promotion of buyer diffusion (that is, market penetration) with the control of seller diffusion, that is, the spread of the technology among competing and/or cooperating producers.

Licensing policies may also be declared open on other grounds: for image-building, for cross-licensing, for royalties and so on. In general, the decision to license out or not is a matter of pricing. The cost of negotiating a single licence agreement is increasing, however, which induces companies to enter more broad-based licence agreements, perhaps also more multilaterally than bilaterally (see Table 5.12). This may stimulate new patterns of cooperation and competition, such as systems competition, that is, competition between families of cooperating companies, linked to different technical systems.

The search for strategic patents in a new technology creates a race among companies. There is also a second race for the surrounding patents taking place in order to fence in any conceivably strategic patent. These surrounding patents are often linked to production processes or to different applications and may be identified through a systematic application analysis.[18] The surrounding patents may then be used by competitors when bargaining about the original strategic patent. In the extreme case, the strategic patent may not be able to be used without infringing a surrounding patent. To avoid this situation, the strategic patent holder is also compelled to search for surrounding patents. However failure to pursue follow-up patenting in this and other situations has been common among Western firms, large as well as small. The traditional engineering attitude has been to apply for a patent only in the case of inventions with high technical qualities. Technically minor inventions, to which category many application patents and surrounding patents belong, have been down-played and patenting has often been ignored. There has also been a belief, not least among inventors and small firms, that a single good patent is sufficient to protect a new business. Firms may also lack resources and management attention concerning patenting. Circumstances like these have resulted in the ignoring of follow-up patenting and failure to build up patent portfolios over time.

The outcome of this second patent race determines, in principle, the distribution of bargaining power among the competing companies and their prospects for cross-licensing. To obtain surrounding patents is thus a case of fencing out or fencing in, depending upon whether the surrounding patent holder is the holder of the strategic patent or not. This is a stereotypical example but it illustrates the interdependence of patents. For instance, it should be noted that the two patent races do not necessarily follow upon each other neatly in time. An old patent may become one of the surrounding patents to a strategic patent over time. Since many companies start to explore a new field early and take out patents with parallel R&D approaches, the interdependencies among

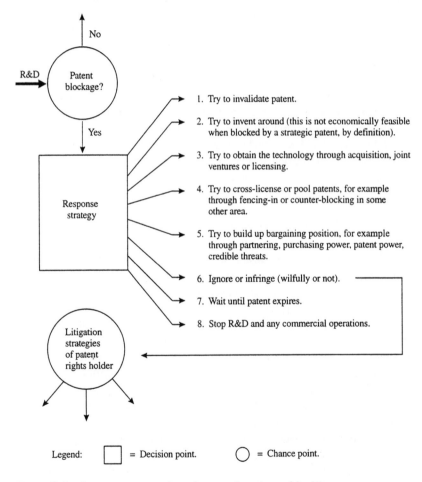

Figure 7.6   Response strategies when confronting a blocking patent

companies and patents might become quite complicated. Such interdependence is likely to become more important in the future as the number of technologies related to a product increases.

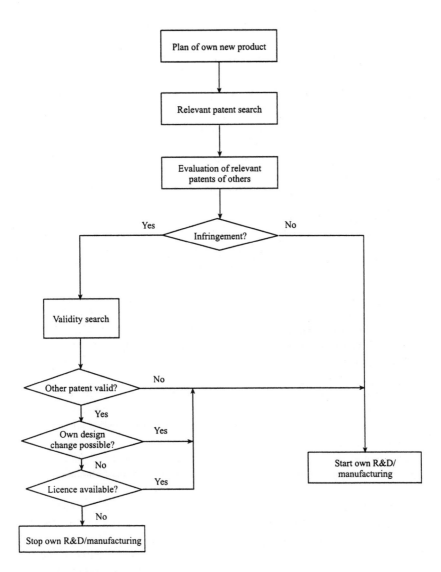

Source: Documentation provided by Toshiba.

Figure 7.7   Typical patent clearance procedure in Toshiba

7.4.3   General Response Strategies when Confronting a Blocking or Strategic Patent

When confronting a blocking patent, a number of strategic responses are possible, as shown in Figure 7.6.

Similar response strategies apply when confronting blockages by a patent blanket or a patent fence. For example, when entering a new business a patent map may show a jungle of patents, in which case a company like Toshiba has allowed its IP department the right to veto any further R&D in that area. Such patent clearance procedures become important as patents and technological interdependencies proliferate.[19] Needless to say, it is also important both to pursue them early in the R&D process,[20] and to make R&D management responsive to patent clearance. Figure 7.7 shows a typical patent clearance procedure in Toshiba. In relation to the validity search, one should note that such a search cannot be made conclusive in principle, unless a patent is litigated. Ultimately it is the courts who decide on validity, which introduces a chance element into patent clearance – as well as in patent enforcement, as is dealt with next.

7.4.4   Litigation Strategies

Figure 7.8 shows the patent enforcement procedure in Toshiba in response to detection of possible infringement. Infringement monitoring in a large international corporation such as Toshiba with a large, diversified product and patent portfolio may in fact be difficult, especially if products go into the production processes of customers. To pay off, infringement monitoring costs must not exceed expected benefits from patent enforcement, involving probabilities of deterrence, detection, favourable settlements by courts or otherwise, and damages or licensing payments. If this is not the case, patenting may not pay off either.

If infringement occurs or there are substantial grounds for suspicion, various strategies for legal enforcement of patent rights could be employed. Litigation strategies can be characterized in general terms, such as offensive/defensive, just like patent strategies, but it is difficult to make a structured list of legal strategies that preempts all available possibilities in various legal systems. Before choosing an offensive litigation strategy one should also assess the risks of retaliation, which in addition to risks of counter-litigation include risks of losing some business.

Litigation processes also contain many stages and contingencies, from the filing of complaints to the ultimate appeals. Formal decision analysis using decision trees with subjective probabilities may be a useful tool for analysing such decisions as well as patent strategy decisions in general. Parts of the full decision tree structure are indicated in Figures 7.6–9. However it must be kept in mind that often reality is not easily cast into structured frameworks such as these.

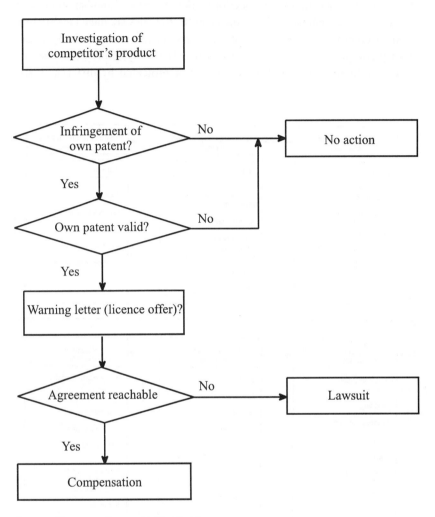

Source: Documentation provided by Toshiba.

Figure 7.8   Typical patent enforcement procedure in Toshiba

7.4.5   Summary of Technology and Patent Strategies

Figure 7.9 summarizes the various strategies outlined in Chapter 4 and dealt with in Chapters 6 and 7 regarding sourcing and exploitation of new technologies and patenting. The next section will give an additional summary of technology scanning and secrecy-related strategies. Trademark strategies will also be discussed in connection with 'superior marketing' as still another strategy in product commercialization. Thus, different IP strategies are linked to different product commercialization strategies. Moreover the various strategies are mostly complementary. A product business is also typically comprised of several elements that could be promoted or protected by different IPRs.

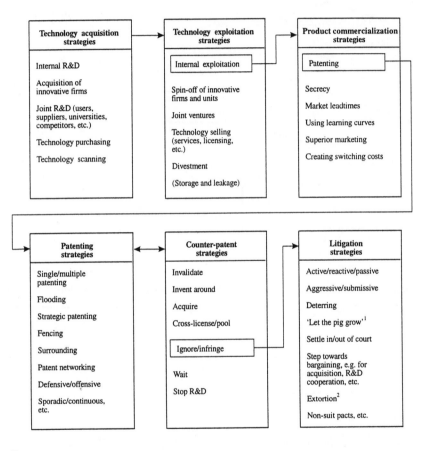

Notes
1. Refers to postponed filing of complaints in order to increase bargaining power. This strategy may backfire in court. (See Chapter 6.)
2. Litigation used as a primary business idea for collecting damages or royalties, exercised by some inventors or patent brokers or lawyers, possibly acting on behalf of inventors on a commission basis (for example, getting 30–50 per cent of any collectable damages). This strategy may also backfire in court.

Figure 7.9   Summary of technology and patent strategies

Altogether these conditions surrounding a business prompt the concept of multiprotection, that is, the use of not only a portfolio of patents but a portfolio of IPR as described in Section 7.7 below.

7.5   SECRECY STRATEGIES

7.5.1   General Secrecy Strategies

Part of a company's technology can at least temporarily be protected by secrecy rather than by patents. Company secrets are also protected by law, giving rise to unregistered rights. However the legal protection of secrets is generally weak.[21] Thus, if secrecy protection as an alternative to patent protection is to be effective, it is very much up to the company itself (which is in fact true regarding patent protection as well).

There are a number of general means or secrecy measures for preventing other companies from finding out about a company's technical developments. These means serve to counteract the available legal, semi-legal and illegal means for technology scanning open to the competition to find out about the company's technologies.[22] Table 7.4 summarizes the importance attached to these measures and countermeasures by the Japanese corporations. Figure 7.10 then summarizes these general secrecy and scanning or intelligence strategies. As seen, the implementation of an internal secrecy policy ranks highest in importance. Such a policy could address any of the other secrecy issues in the table. The control of publishing by researchers and employees is of special concern. Learning from patent disclosures or other publications ranks as the most important means for intelligence gathering, while the avoidance of patenting ranks significantly lower as a secrecy measure. This is again an indication that patenting provides net informational benefits to industrial society as a whole. This also suggests that publishing through patent documentation is one promising way of increasing control over publications. (An interesting approach or philosophy in this context was voiced by Dr Yamaji, former CEO of Canon; see Chapter 8.)

Employee loyalty to companies in Japan has traditionally been very high. The interfirm mobility of people has also traditionally been very low, with widespread lifetime (or rather long-time) employment among large companies (although things are changing). In contrast to the West, for example in Silicon Valley, hire-overs of key employees among Japanese companies are not a primary IP concern, at least not yet, although some hire-overs occur and create attention and irritation. The fragmentation of proprietary information in the company for secrecy purposes, thereby lowering the probability that somebody has 'the full picture' of an R&D project, makes defection less consequential.[23] This, of course, does not allow for open internal communication, which in turn is important for R&D productivity and innovativeness in the company. However,

Table 7.4 *Importance of secrecy and technology scanning strategies in large Japanese corporations*

(Scale: No importance = 0, 1, 2, 3, 4 = Of major importance; Tend. = Tendency 1987–92: Decreasing = –1, 0,+1 = Increasing)

(Code) Question	Chemical (n = 9) Tend.	Electrical (n = 10) Tend.	Mechanical (n = 5) Tend.	Total (n = 24) Tend.
(F10) How important on an average are the following means for preventing other companies from finding out about your company's technical developments?				
(a) Control of publishing by researchers and employees	3.11 (0.38)	2.50 (0.60)	3.20 (1.00)	2.88 (0.61)
(b) Controlled access to facilities	2.88 (0.29)	2.50 (0.50)	2.80 (0.80)	2.70 (0.50)
(c) Monitoring of visitors and temporary employees	2.44 (0.25)	2.10 (0.10)	1.60 (0.20)	2.13 (0.17)
(d) Avoidance of patenting	1.78 (–0.13)	1.60 (0.00)	1.20 (–0.20)	1.58 (–0.09)
(e) Implementation of an internal secrecy policy	3.00 (0.38)	3.00 (0.60)	3.20 (0.80)	3.04 (0.57)
(f) Efforts to increase employee loyalty to the company	2.11 (0.00)	2.40 (0.30)	2.60 (0.20)	2.33 (0.17)
(g) Efforts to prevent competitors from hiring over key R&D personnel	2.22 (0.25)	1.50 (0.20)	2.00 (0.20)	1.88 (0.22)
(h) Fragmentation of technological information among managers and other employees	1.78 (0.00)	0.90 (–0.10)	1.80 (0.00)	1.42 (–0.04)
(i) Counterintelligence	1.56 (0.25)	1.40 (0.10)	1.20 (–0.20)	1.42 (0.09)

238

(F11) How important on an average are the following means for finding out about your competitors' technical development?

(1) Licensing the technology	2.38 (0.13)	2.50 (0.30)	1.60 (0.20)	2.26 (0.22)
(2) Learning details from information provided in patent disclosures	3.56 (0.50)	2.90 (0.30)	3.00 (1.00)	3.17 (0.52)
(3) Learning details through publications or open technical meetings	3.33 (0.50)	3.00 (0.30)	2.80 (0.80)	3.08 (0.48)
(4) Learning details through informal conversations with employees of the innovating firm, competitors, buyers, suppliers, consultancy firms, universities etc.	2.78 (0.00)	2.40 (0.20)	1.60 (−0.20)	2.38 (0.04)
(5) Hiring R&D employees with experience from competing firms	1.78 (0.00)	1.10 (0.10)	1.00 (0.00)	1.33 (0.05)
(6) Acquiring the product and reverse-engineering it	2.67 (0.13)	2.00 (0.10)	2.60 (0.40)	2.38 (0.17)

Note: The highest and lowest values for each industry and question are overlined and underlined, respectively.

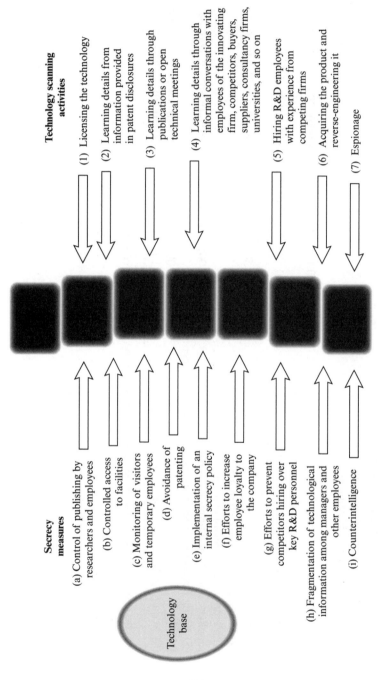

Technology scanning activities

(1) Licensing the technology

(2) Learning details from information provided in patent disclosures

(3) Learning details through publications or open technical meetings

(4) Learning details through informal conversations with employees of the innovating firm, competitors, buyers, suppliers, consultancy firms, universities, and so on

(5) Hiring R&D employees with experience from competing firms

(6) Acquiring the product and reverse-engineering it

(7) Espionage

Secrecy measures

(a) Control of publishing by researchers and employees

(b) Controlled access to facilities

(c) Monitoring of visitors and temporary employees

(d) Avoidance of patenting

(e) Implementation of an internal secrecy policy

(f) Efforts to increase employee loyalty to the company

(g) Efforts to prevent competitors hiring over key R&D personnel

(h) Fragmentation of technological information among managers and other employees

(i) Counterintelligence

Technology base

Figure 7.10   Technology scanning and secrecy strategies in general

fragmentation may not always be possible either. Sometimes, in large as well as in small companies, there are a few key individuals whose outstanding competence is critical to the company, which makes the company vulnerable to their loss through defection, hire-overs or even death.[24] In this situation, loyalty (and health!) is very valuable to the company.[25]

In this context one may also note that detrimental secrecy barriers are often erected by individuals or small groups for personal reasons such as striving for fame, prestige, power and/or rewards. Company reward schemes for inventions and patenting can strengthen this tendency and thus counteract their purpose to stimulate innovativeness, which typically requires rich internal communications and collaboration among several individuals and groups in the company.

Finally, the total costs and benefits of an extensive secrecy or information security system have to be considered. High R&D costs give high incentives for technology scanning. At the same time an extensive system of internal and external secrecy barriers or layers of 'firewalls' is also costly, both in terms of direct costs and in terms of the innate detrimental effects.[26]

7.5.2 Secrecy and Prophylaxis as Alternatives to Patents

In the companies studied, it was commonplace to file a patent application as early as possible in the R&D process and to build up 'patent power' in technologies of interest by systematically analysing patenting possibilities.[27] This patent power was then used in conjunction with speed to market. This was also important in fast-moving areas, which was in contrast with the expression 'technology moves so fast that it renders patents useless' that has sometimes been used in Western companies as an argument against patenting.[28] Only rarely did a company resort to secrecy as an alternative to patent protection. Typical cases where secrecy protection (or no patent protection) was considered (assuming a low risk of being blocked by patents of others) were:

1. One is convinced of having a substantial technological lead and that it will take a long time for competitors to catch up even if they overcome the secrecy barrier. This is seldom the case, however.
2. The competitor's cost and time for overcoming the secrecy barrier, for example, by reverse engineering, are substantial. This may be the case for production technologies which leave no traces in the marketed product that can be used by competitors for their reverse engineering.
3. Infringement monitoring is difficult (costly) and/or of little value because of low enforceability in courts, high legal costs or low damages. This may be country-specific, however.

4. The possibilities to invent around are numerous and cheap, while costly to block efficiently with patents. This may be the case in certain new technologies.

These cases do not exclude each other. Altogether they contain factors to consider when assessing whether to use patent protection or not.

Sometimes, but fairly seldom in Japan, prophylactic publishing is used, whereby technical information is disclosed to prevent competitors from fulfilling the novelty requirement for obtaining patent rights. This possibility may also be used in the following obscure way, at least in Japan. The company files a patent application and then withdraws it (well in advance to be sure of timely bureaucratic functioning) before 18 months have elapsed, at which time the patent application would be published. If a competitor files a similar patent application later on, the company may oppose it and point to the earlier withdrawn application as evidence for invalidating the competitor's patent. This opposition information is then disclosed publicly and the period of secrecy that the company has enjoyed ends. Obviously, the event of public disclosure must be taken into account when using this mode of protection. Thus this trick of filing an application for patent protection, only to have it withdrawn or pending, is a curious but legal possibility for obtaining a combination of secrecy and prophylactic protection.

7.6   TRADEMARK STRATEGIES

7.6.1   Trademarks in General

Trademarks have increased in general importance, as described in Chapters 1, 4 and 5. This is for various reasons. One simple reason is that trademark protection, in contrast to other registered IPR, can be perpetuated permanently and thereby accumulates value if managed properly through advertising and so on. Another reason is that information overflow makes buyers increasingly influenced by brands and trademarks in their purchasing behaviour.[29]

Trademark values, although very difficult to assess, can also become extremely high, as shown in Table 1.3. Many business situations ask for the valuation of trademarks, for example, mergers and acquisitions of companies, licensing in and out of trademarks, claiming damages in case of trademark infringement, or for accounting purposes. There are four general approaches to valuation: (i) cost-based (for example, based on accumulation of advertising costs and so on); (ii) income-based (based upon influences on purchasing behaviour or influences on sourcing costs on input markets, for example, costs for recruiting graduate engineers); (iii) based on market valuations and comparisons of similar trademarks; and (iv) indirect valuation methods, based on other indicators or indices assumed to be correlated with trademark values. Factors such as brand awareness, brand loyalty, reputation and brand coverage go into the calculation.

As with any reputation-based value, trademark values are vulnerable to bad publicity and customer dissatisfaction, but they are surprisingly resilient in the long run, once they have gained strength.[30] A special threat to a trademark is so-called dilution. This happens when a trademark becomes so successful that it is incorporated into everyday language and loses the distinctiveness that is required for legal protection.[31] Some companies go to great lengths in order to prevent this. A registered trademark can also lose its legal protection if it is not used at all.

As shown in Table 1.3, the list of the eight most highly valued trademarks or brands in the world did not contain any Japanese trademarks even as late as 1995. However the efforts that go into the building of trademark values in Japan are substantial and strategically managed. Just as several Japanese companies have been on the list of the top ten patentors in the USA for many years, several of them are likely to be on the list of the top ten valued trademarks in the years to come. The perpetuation of trademarks favours old ones in such listings, everything else being equal. (Coca-Cola started in the 1890s.) However, it is possible to build strong trademarks in a fairly short time. This is true for industrial as well as consumer products, as shown by Intel, starting in 1968.

Just as with bodies of knowledge, and technologies in particular, trademarks offer economies of scale, scope and speed. Economies of scale, static as well as dynamic, can be reaped both in expanding sales in an area for which trademark protection already exists and in extending the trademark to a new area, at least under some circumstances.[32] Economies of scope may arise when one trademark is combined with others. A common case is when a company's trademark or image is combined with the trademark or image of one of its products. Trademarks from different companies may also be combined (double branding or co-branding). More generally we can talk about building image value by several agents and at several levels – national image (NI) (for example, for product quality or for tourist industry), corporate image (CI), business image (BI) and personal image (PI) (for example, of a rock star or a Nobel Prize winner). Image values of course apply to other entities as well – cities, teams, professions, characters and so on. Some of these entities have protected names, some of which can be licensed. Certain subjects also have positive image values, such as ecology, medicine and technology (especially hi-tech), although it is usually not possible to protect them by exclusive rights.

These different images can be combined in many ways and create economies of scope. Diseconomies of scope can also arise if some images are negative in themselves (the 'rotten apple' effect). The possibilities for combining different trade names and images can obviously become numerous. A company can also build several trademarks over time. Economies of speed may finally accrue when a well-reputed trademark helps to speed up the market penetration for a new product. An unknown, perhaps new, company with a new product can then gain speed advantages by letting a well-known company market the new product on an original equipment manufacturing (OEM) basis.

One can note some similarities between trademark strategies and patent strategies in this context. First, a trademark can be given a broad coverage just as a patent can be given a broad coverage or scope.[33] Second, a trademark can be made strategic in the sense that it is unavoidable to customers and the public at large, not by forces of nature as with patents, but by corporate forces and ingenuity. Every person is exposed to many different sights and sounds every day, and we are influenced by all sorts of habits and compelling circumstances that could be used by cunning advertisers, much more in fact than we are currently used to or want. However, 'overadvertising' may occur in the sense that consumers start to react negatively to being bombarded with certain messages, in which case the value of a brand may decline. Reverse cases may also occur, that is, no advertising may make an already prestigious brand even more prestigious. Third, certain areas (like computers) are already crowded with trademarks. Flooding or blanketing attractive areas of terminology with trademarks is also possible to some extent, although, in contrast to patents, limited by the requirement that a trademark must be commercially used. Moreover, three- and four-letter words (like Sony) are being used up as trademarks. All in all, it is getting harder to get good trademarks, which further increases the value of established ones. Fourth, surrounding one's strategic patent with own application patents is somewhat similar to having a corporate brand (like Sony) being surrounded by business brands (like Walkman, Discman, Handycam). Finally, a 'network' of all sorts of brand names, packaging designs, logos, company uniforms, designs, informative marks and other symbols, can be built, which altogether constitute what is sometimes subsumed under the labels of corporate identity and corporate aesthetics.

7.6.2   Trademark Strategies in Japan

Some types of branding behaviour or strategies commonly found in Japan were:

1. General upgrading in the building and enforcing of trademarks (also for industrial products, not only for consumer products).
2. Long-term upgrading of the national image in contrast to the earlier downplaying of 'made in Japan' (which played badly in the West during the 1950s).
3. Conscious building of corporate image, broad branding and joint CI/BI (see Figure 7.11).

4. 'Strategic branding' (building brands inevitable to the customer and the public, who cannot avoid being exposed to them).
5. Mixing OEM with branded sales.
6. Use of technology for prestige (use of 'technology image').
7. Combining patents, trademarks, designs, copyrights and so on into 'multiprotection' (see below).

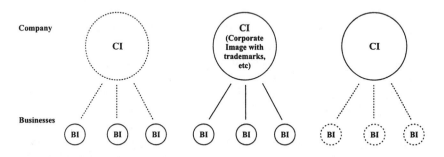

Note: BIs could correspond to different business or product areas, as well as to different market segments (for example, segmented along quality or price dimensions) in a business area.

Figure 7.11 Building separate corporate and business images (CIs, BIs) versus joint CI/BI-building

The building of joint CI/BI is noteworthy. This choice of strategy results partly from the diversified character of Japanese companies, which made it natural to distinguish both the company and its various businesses. The auto industry provides an illustration, simplified here. In Europe it has been more common to place emphasis on CI-building (that is, using only the company names, for example, Volvo, BMW, Mercedes-Benz) while in the USA it has been more common to emphasize BI-building (for example, GM's use of car brands like Pontiac and Cadillac). Concentration on CI/BI-building in Japan has thus produced the combinations Toyota–Corolla and Toyota–Camry. Broad branding is also used in Japan and this practice also emanates to some extent from the diversified character of Japanese companies. Compare, for example, the narrow Coca-Cola brand with the Yamaha brand, which covers musical instruments as well as various motor vehicles.

Trademark management at Sony
Sony provides a good illustration of trademark management, having been top-ranked in Japan as a best-practice company in this regard. The tradition in Sony of emphasizing and creatively deploying trademarks goes back to the founders,

especially Mr Morita (see, for example, Morita 1986). At an early point (and early for Japan) he wanted to build up a strong Sony corporate image, refusing even to supply on an OEM basis at times.[34] In 1995 Sony had about 10 000 trademarks registered in the world. The use of these is centrally controlled from the corporate IP department at headquarters in Tokyo. There is a special CI committee attached to top management. There is also a corporate enforcement group for trademark and design enforcement worldwide. There are many infringers on Sony's trademarks, partly because Sony has been shifting production to emerging countries with cheaper labour. Enforcement with the intention to wipe out counterfeit products on the market and locate their suppliers is considered very important. In 1995, about 700 infringement cases (about 500 in Asia) were handled by this group, costing about US$5 million annually to handle and yielding only 10–20 per cent back in damages.[35] Enforcement is difficult, especially in China. The pressure from the USA to enforce IPR is also considered helpful. Sony gets many proposals to license trademarks to third parties, but the basic policy is not to license out the corporate trademark. A product brand can be licensed out, however, for example, the product brand Walkman for shoes. (Cross-licensing is much less common for trademarks than for patents, but is becoming increasingly popular.)

The building of joint CI/BI (for example, Sony Walkman) is consciously managed and coordinated corporate-wide across the more than 150 subsidiaries. There are numerous possible combinations of Sony trademarks and logos and numerous external as well as internal proposals for using them. Therefore, a main role of the CI committee is to review and judge different combinations and to formulate criteria and policies for them.[36] Thus there is also a need to enforce trademarks internally.[37]

Enforcement of trademarks, logos, designs and copyrights on the Internet is also a rapidly increasing concern, as is the use of the Internet in general for CI/BI-building. This concern also involves trademark clearance, the same as for patents. The information supply to the Internet is growing rapidly and includes many protected informative marks. At the same time it is easy to electronically duplicate, quote or deform, for example, trademarks.

As Sony's businesses change and diversify, they will start to combine in new ways, which basically complicates the 'hierarchical' CI/BI-building process. The traditional grouping of businesses is also becoming increasingly obsolete through diversification and rapidly moving technologies (for example, for the Internet or in the convergence of communications, computers, publishing and entertainment). Moreover, acquisitions, joint ventures and other tie-ups link Sony trademarks to other brands and trademarks (for example, Columbia). A single CI such as Sony may then become insufficient, and traditional CI/BI combinations may become less effective or attractive. Further, parallel brands for similar products may be used. Entering a new business area as a late-comer may also make certain CI/CI combinations (and possibly also some BI/BI combinations) attractive, thereby using double branding in a tie-up with another company already established in the area. Partnering becomes increasingly common in industrial convergence, such as the one between computers, communications and media, and thus calls for the redesign of trademark strategies. All in all, these are some considerations for future trademark strategies, not only for Sony, due to the changing nature of businesses and technologies.

7.7   MULTIPROTECTION AND TOTAL IP STRATEGIES

During the 1980s a trend towards dealing with IP in a more comprehensive way emerged in Japanese 'best-practice' companies. This was reflected both in how policies and strategies were formulated and in how IP-related activities became organized in the company (see Chapter 8).

As discussed in Chapter 4, there are many types of intellectual property or assets in a company – patents, trade secrets, trademarks and so on. There are also many ways to create these assets jointly in connection with a particular business. These different ways are mostly complementary and raise the total asset value when used in combination. This is in line with the IC view of the firm, described in Chapter 4. Thus it is justified to talk about the importance of creating *multiprotection systems* and *total IP strategies.*[38] This idea seems quite natural and acceptable to people in industry. Nevertheless, patent matters dominate when dealing with IP. This is often reflected by work specialization, as well as by terminology, in a manner that is deceptive. The governmental organizations are called 'Patent Offices', consultancy firms are often called 'Patent Bureaux', experts are called 'Patent Attorneys', associations are called patent associations, company departments are called the 'Patent Department' with a 'Patent Manager' and company policies are called 'Patent Policies'. In such circumstances it is easy to pursue an unbalanced approach to IP matters, perhaps placing too much emphasis on patents and too little on trademarks, trade secrets, copyrights and designs, and above all to neglect complementarities among different IP elements.

If IP matters should be treated more comprehensively, how much more comprehensively? And if IP matters are important, what is the proper role of IP management in technology management, business management and corporate management? The question of how to 'size' and position IP management in the company is highly relevant. Intellectual resources, including general competence as well as technology, are pervasive throughout the whole corporation, but pervasiveness in itself is not an argument for putting IP management in the centre of the whole company organization. There are many pervasive activities in a company that should from time to time be placed at the centre of attention by means of organization, campaigns, culture building, management policies, management fads and so on. We shall return to these issues in Chapter 8.

Multiprotection is practised not only among leading Japanese companies. In fact, leading US companies have developed such practices long ago. Coca-Cola, for example, has skilfully built up and maintained multiprotection. The recipe for the Coca-Cola soft drink is a well-protected trade secret, as is well known.[39] A patent has a limited lifetime, while a secret can possibly last for ever, at least in theory. This is especially important for products with long lifetimes, which in turn may result from slow-moving customer preferences or slow-moving product technology. The machinery for the process technology, including the distribution process (for example, vending machines), has been systematically analysed and protected by patents. The unconventional Coca-Cola bottle has design protection and the Coca-Cola name and logo have trademark protection.[40] The IPRs are strongly and systematically developed and promoted by R&D and marketing activities and so on, and enforced by infringement monitoring and legal action. It is not an accident that Coca-Cola has maintained one of the most highly valued trademarks in the world (see Chapter 1), although its value was not initially clear to the company.[41]

Selecting and securing property rights for various elements constituting a business is not enough for multiprotection. The rights have to be enforced and infringers have to be deterred. IBM, for example, has pursued a very hard-nosed enforcement and litigation policy over the years through frequent litigation and the pursuit of the legal process to fruition, despite the legal costs and the prospect of losing (see Mody 1990). Thus IBM has apparently considered it more important to win a war than to win every battle.[42] In this way IBM has kept competitors and inventors wary about infringement. IBM has also sustained its IPR-consciousness, which has been combined with a licensing policy, sometimes a quite generous one (although partly due to anti-trust decrees).[43]

Japanese companies, on the other hand, have traditionally avoided litigation and court settlements.[44] This is well known, even to the extent that some inventors and companies accuse Japanese companies of infringement in order to have them settle for a licence rather than risk going to court. However, things are changing and many Japanese companies are becoming more litigious, at least when they are attacked. For example, when Motorola sued Hitachi in 1989 for infringing on a number of Motorola's patents, Hitachi counter-sued Motorola for infringing on Hitachi's patents. As a result, the court in effect stopped the sales of the corresponding products of both Motorola and Hitachi, a court decision that apparently hurt Motorola more than Hitachi (see Anawalt and Enayati 1996, p. 342). This also illustrates the retaliatory power of large patent portfolios as well as the vulnerability of being a large, diversified hi-tech litigator.

A business can be broken down into various constituent elements and product technologies that could be covered by various IPR, resulting in an IPR package or multiprotection system for the business. In principle, this corresponds to an analysis of the elements in Table 7.5.

Table 7.5   Analysing the business element – IP connections

Business element/component	IP type (example)
1 Business idea	Trade secret
2. Business plan, method	Trade secret, patent
3. Product technology (equipment, materials, ancillary products)	Patents, utility models
4. Production/process technology	Trade secret plus a know-how licence
5. Component technology	Maskwork protection
6. Systems configuration	Open information, prophylactic publishing
7. Software, orgware, data	Patents, copyright, trade secret
8. Auxiliary services	Trademark, trade secret
9. Distribution technology	Patents, utility models, trade secret
10. Marketing concepts	Copyright, open public relations information
11. Packaging design	Designs
12. Company and business names, logos, slogans and symbols ('company aesthetics')	Trademarks, copyright, designs

Different IP types sometimes substitute for each other at the business component level. The typical example being that patent protection and secrecy protection substitute for each other for a particular invention. In general, however, the different IP types can also be used to complement or reinforce one another. Altogether, the different business elements or components in Table 7.5 form a *business system* in a product area. A business system with its business components thus encompasses products and their components and technology bases, together with the other elements in Table 7.5. This concept thereby focuses on the total set of intellectual resources or intellectual capital needed to make a customer offering and conduct a business deal.

At the level of a business system the various IPRs should be complementary as a rule, forming effective multiprotection as a means for commercialization and enhancement of the business. Figure 7.12 illustrates how the value of a total

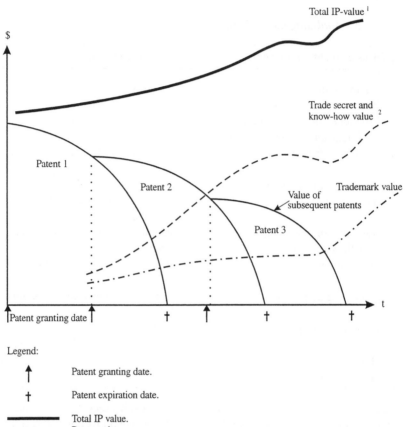

Legend:

↑   Patent granting date.

†   Patent expiration date.

━━━━   Total IP value.
─────   Patent value.
─ ─ ─ ─ ·   Trade secret and know-how value.
─ · ─ · ─ · ─   Trademark value.

Notes
1. The total IP value is not necessarily the sum of the values of various individual IPR since the latter may not meaningfully be added.
2. Cumulating through R&D, external technology and know-how acquisition, plus training and learning (experience) in personnel in general. While the stock of know-how may cumulate (although not necessarily so, due to, for example, hire-overs of personnel and spin-offs) the value of the stock may fluctuate, for example, due to obsolescence and new substituting technologies, and also due to new valuation methods.

Figure 7.12   Total value of an IP portfolio

IPR portfolio is built up in principle (although not all possible IPRs are illustrated), disregarding the difficulties to assign meaningful values to individual IPR, values which moreover may not be additive as a rule.

For a multibusiness corporation there is a need to coordinate IP protection across businesses (that is, regarding company logos, trademarks and so on and licensing). Multiprotection in a multibusiness corporation, then, necessitates the formulation of company-wide IP policies. Such policies become more necessary if the IP organization is decentralized.

7.8   SUMMARY AND CONCLUSIONS

This chapter started by describing a classification of various advantages and disadvantages of patents from a company point of view and the importance attached to them by the corporations surveyed. There are many types of perceived advantages of patents. Four main categories of advantages can be distinguished, which in order of perceived importance were (i) *provision of protection*, (ii) *bargaining power*, (iii) *internal advantages* and (iv) *image improvement*. Several of the advantages of patents increasingly accrue as they become part of a patent portfolio and a patent arms race in the company, something that was emphasized repeatedly in interviews. There was also a certain shift from defensive to more offensive motives behind patenting, although it is difficult to draw a sharp line in between. The perceived advantages of patenting by far exceeded the perceived main disadvantages concerning disclosure of information and direct costs for filing.

Since most Japanese corporations had a corporate-wide patent policy in contrast to many Western corporations, the chapter thus elaborated on the rationale and content of an IP policy in general. As IP has gained increasing strategic importance and top management attention, patent and IP policies evolve, often in stages similar to how the IP organization evolves, and become more comprehensive, strategic and integrated with business and technology management.

Continuing the elaboration of various generic technology strategies and commercialization strategies in Chapter 6, Chapter 7 described various generic patent strategies, counter-patent strategies and litigation strategies as well as other IP strategies in general, such as secrecy and scanning (counter-secrecy) strategies and trademark strategies. Figures 7.9–11 summarized these typologies of generic strategies or strategic options.

Patent strategies can be classified in various ways, such as pertaining to legal aspects of individual patents, pertaining to when, where, why and how to patent, or pertaining to patent portfolio composition in statistical terms. The chapter presented in particular a classification pertaining to the patenting pattern in technology space and in 'life-cycle time', that is, over time in relation to the stages in the product life cycle and the technology life cycle.

Concerning IP strategies in Japan, a number of commonly used strategies were described, such as flooding, fencing and continuous patenting as well as CI/BI-building of trademarks. Such strategies have been developed in the past by leading companies in the West, and in the USA in particular, but have been adopted, refined and applied more systematically by Japanese corporations in a manner not unlike what has happened with several other management techniques originating in the West. In the Japanese corporations surveyed, there was an increased emphasis on quality rather than quantity of patents and on strategic patenting in particular. The chapter presented illustrations from the electrical corporations Canon, Hitachi and Toshiba regarding patents and from Sony regarding trademarks.

Finally, the use of what was called multiprotection and total IP strategies for a business system with all its product and service components rather than for an individual product was described and advocated. In this way, the value of the IPR portfolio is enhanced and the company's intellectual capital leveraged.

NOTES

1. Appendix 4 gives the approximate size for a difference to be significant.
2. In the extreme the technological interdependencies between products and between companies may result in 'hold-up' situations in which individual companies have bargaining power to hold up further developments for some time. Thus the IPR system may counter its purpose when such interdependencies result in bargaining breakdown. Instances of this have always occurred, but they seem to increase, for example, in multimedia.
3. For some readings on this, see von Hippel (1982, p. 102), Winter (1989, p. 54) and Grindley and Teece (1997).
4. Compare Rahn (1983, p. 489) who cites the following 'secondary' functions of patents: (i) attack; (ii) hedge; (iii) motivation; (iv) reputation; (v) credit. Compare also with Table 3.1, which also gives motives for having a patent system as a whole in society, in contrast to a company's motives behind using it in various specific situations.
5. The shift towards more aggressive action at business level is not necessarily beneficial for technical and economic development on the whole. On the contrary, it tends to produce hold-up situations and raise transaction costs (see further Chapter 10). The notion of excessive competition has also increasingly gained ground in this context.
6. For an example of IP policy in a Western company (Union Carbide), see O'Brien (1986).
7. The term 'prophylactic publishing' is commonly used to refer to disclosing technical information about an invention with the purpose of preventing prospective patentors from fulfilling the novelty requirement.
8. Various military terms and analogies are used among patent practitioners.
9. See Marshall ([1890] 1994, p. 520). See also Scherer (1980, p. 451) which describes how DuPont fenced in their invention of nylon by patenting a range of molecular variations of polymers with potentially similar properties to nylon. In this way, fencing in several dimensions may come close to systematic blanketing.
10. Several technical performance variables could of course be considered, as well as several economic variables. Some technical performance parameters directly affect customer utilities or customer value, while others pertain only to the 'inner' working of the product or process.

The latter type of technical parameters may be called design variables (or internal performance variables or configuration characteristics). (See also Chapter 9).

11. Compare the so-called 'sailing effect', which refers to improvements in late stages of a maturing technology. These improvements are made mainly in response to a perceived threat of a new technology. The expression was derived from the performance of sailing ships, which was boosted in response to the arrival of ships powered by steam engines (see Graham 1956).

12. It is important to distinguish between technical and economic aspects when talking about the level, importance, quality or 'size' of an invention, technical advance or innovation. Although there may be a positive correlation between a high level of invention (that is, technical quality) and its economic importance, the correlation may be weak and there may be many economically important but technically minor inventions, as well as many economically unimportant but technically major inventions.

13. A commonly used indicator of patent quality is citation rate, despite its many flaws (see, for example, Mogee 1991; Trajtenberg 1990; Narin 1993; Narin et al. 1984; and Carpenter et al. 1981 for a seminal work). As shown in Chapter 5, the quality of Japanese patents is indeed high in many industrial sectors, using this indicator. Similar results are presented in Frame and Narin (1990). See also Section 5.8.1 for the distinction between technical, economic and legal qualities of a patent.

14. Information gathered through personal communication with Mr S. Saba.

15. Some also use the terms 'essential patent', 'basic patent', 'generic patent' or 'inevitable patent'. However, certain such terms are also used in other senses (see the Glossary).

16. Naturally it is often not clear at once whether a patent is strategic or not, and the perception of a patent being strategic may have to be revised in the light of later technological developments.

17. The Betamax–VHS battle has been widely reported; see, for example, Rosenbloom and Cusumano (1987), Grindley (1995) and Granstrand (1984). It now qualifies as a classic case of the importance of strategic licensing. Oddly enough and far less well known is that the technological interdependence was such that had Sony won the battle, JVC would still have been rather well-off through collection of royalties from Sony.

18. An alleged case of this is described in Spero (1990), in which Mitsubishi was accused of having fenced in a strategic patent held by a small US firm, with the purpose of acquiring it through cross-licensing. (The article represents the small firm's view of the case.)

19. For a good illustration of the legal complexities involved, see Merges (1994).

20. Patent clearance was unfortunately performed too late in the standardization work of the GSM system for mobile communications, as described in Chapter 6.

21. The protection of trade secrets also varies between countries. In Japan, trade secret protection by law has traditionally been weak, while secrecy protection in practice has been relatively effective in industry, due to, for example, low interfirm mobility of personnel and high employee loyalty.

22. Note that in order for a piece of information to be protected by trade secret law, at least in the USA, it is necessary (but not sufficient) that the information holder can show that secrecy efforts have been made. A case in point is when Motorola was denied trade secret protection when a number of key people left to go to the competitor Fairchild in 1968 on the grounds that Motorola had not done enough to protect its trade secrets (see Adler et al. 1992, p. 27).

23. The various legal, economic and managerial issues involved in balancing the IP interests of employers and employees have, of course, been subjected to much debate. A practical overview of the issues from a managerial and legal perspective is given in Spanner (1984) and Swais (1996). Trade secrets may also be traded by employees among firms. For interesting works, see von Hippel (1988a,b).

24. Companies may be vulnerable in another sense as well. Key inventors in a company may be tracked down by outsiders, using patent information. The monitoring of their subsequent work as reflected in patent applications may then give useful hints of promising R&D directions and strategies (see further Chapter 9).

25. An interesting scheme for the fragmentation of information for the purpose of preserving a trade secret is the one allegedly used by the Benedictine monks for protecting the recipe for their liqueur. Only the abbot knew the whole secret, while two monks knew different halves

of it. When the abbot died, one of these two monks was promoted to abbot, thus being informed by the other monk, while informing a new monk replacing him in turn. One can note that such a scheme for preserving a trade secret with minimal risk of leakage is probably optimal in some sense, although there is a risk that the two monks would defect together and start up their own business. (This last point was made by Professor F.M. Scherer.) One can also question whether such long-lived secrets benefit consumers in the long run.

26. Charles Kettering, the legendary R&D manager of General Motors, is quoted as having once said: 'When you lock the doors of the laboratory you lock out more than you lock in'.

27. Note that in patent races 'the winner gets all' in the sense that all patent rights for a specific invention are given to at most one applicant. However, the need for many patents to support a business and the possibilities to license patents among companies means that there are multiple patent races and a market is not necessarily lost if some patent race is lost.

28. This argument was used, for example, in the computer industry (for example, by Digital Equipment) in its early stage. As an industry matures in some sense and technology slows down, the argument becomes less valid.

29. In common terminology, a trademark is the legally protected part of a brand. A brand name refers to the vocal characteristic of a brand, while a brand mark refers to the visual characteristic. Here the term 'trademark' will be used in a broad sense.

30. Examples of the temporary dipping of trademark values and company goodwill can be found in connection with disasters, scandals, or occasionally deficient products (like Intel's early Pentium processor). Note in this context Intel's innovative use of trademark protection for industrial components, not visible to consumers, by the phrase 'Intel inside' linked to a logo.

31. An example is the risk of diluting the Xerox name, by using it in everyday phrases like 'to xerox' something or to take a 'xerox copy'. Initially, 'Xerox' as a term carried no meaning to customers.

32. Successful trademark extension is not guaranteed, and there is a body of literature on how to go about it; see, for example, Aaker (1991).

33. The dimensions of coverage or scope of a trademark pertain to geographical coverage, product area coverage and 'psychological coverage', where the latter refers to the type of values with which the trademark is associated (security, quality, health, low price and so on). The psychological coverage is built up, for example, through advertising trying to 'load' the trademark with various values.

34. The name Sony is derived from a combination of the Latin word for sound (*sonus*) and the word 'sunny', and began to be used in 1958. The company, which started after World War II, was earlier called Tokyo–Tsushin–Koio.

35. Thus the share of detected trademark infringements was about 7 per cent, which can be compared to about 9 per cent for patents, although with large industry variations (see Table 5.10).

36. For example, a proposal from Sony America to use 'Sony University' for training services of non-Sony people (for example, dealers) was turned down because the CI committee thought it would be deceptive, leading the general public to think Sony would go into the university business and leading students to think they would get jobs at Sony.

37. As an example there are eight different internal manuals for advertising, language guidelines, communications and so on.

38. This does not necessarily imply that IP activities should be centralized. However, in a decentralized IP organization, the need for comprehensive IP policies and strategies is even more emphatic. The term 'multiprotection system' has been suggested by Dr A. Mifune.

39. Note that conventional food recipes are not protectable by patents, although early patent-like protection in Venice during the 15th-century Renaissance, as well as in Sybaris in ancient Greece, originally gave protection to recipes of famous chefs. This is not to say that the Coca-Cola recipe is not patentable (at least as a medicine, in principle), or that Coca-Cola's preference for keeping it a trade secret is due to uncertainty about patentability.

40. The bottle has received US trademark protection as well, which was the first example of a three-dimensional trademark.

41. According to Professor F.M. Scherer the early development of the Coca-Cola image was quite accidental, and only after some time did the company realize what a valuable asset they had and took aggressive steps to protect it.
42. Note that although 'hot' patent wars may break out now and then, the common patent war is 'cold', with ongoing deterrence and negotiations.
43. For further readings about IBM in these respects, see Mody (1990) and Grindley and Teece (1997).
44. This has also been true for many US companies.

8. Intellectual property organization and management

CHAPTER CONTENTS

8.1 CHAPTER OUTLINE

This chapter will describe developments in the organization and management of IP resources and activities in large Japanese corporations. Special attention will be paid to what can be called a patent culture in those corporations. Such corporate patent cultures have developed over a long period, as described in Chapter 5, but have been strengthened considerably from the 1980s onwards through developments in IP organization and management, spurred by the outbreak of 'patent wars', notably with large US corporations. Accordingly, IP resources have increased substantially, and the IP organization has become upgraded, more centralized, more comprehensive, and has received more attention by top management, technology management and business management. It appears as if Japan, partly as a result of the pro-patent era, has developed still another area of management in which Western companies have much to learn. The chapter also addresses the possible future role of IP management and the further evolution of corporate management and organization. With the increasing role of intellectual capital and the further emergence of what we can call intellectual capitalism (see Chapter 10), it is conceivable that IC management will develop, engulfing IP management. Which countries and companies will take the lead in this development is an open question.

8.2   IP RESOURCES

The level of IP resources in Japanese corporations is considerably higher than in most Western corporations, as is the output in terms of patent applications (see Chapter 5). As mentioned, the IP resource levels have also increased during the 1980s, as have the numbers of patent applications. Table 8.1 gives some examples of top IP spenders among large Japanese corporations in different sectors.

As seen from Table 8.1, the electrical corporations top the list regarding the total number of patent employees. The electrical industry was also the first and hardest hit by the patent wars and therefore reacted early by building up in-house resources. In terms of the ratio of patent employees to total employees, Canon is leading. However, it must be kept in mind that the degree of outsourcing and centralization of IP resources and R&D varies among the corporations. The degree of consolidation also varies. The figures for the total number of employees, total sales and total R&D are self-reported in the questionnaires complemented with officially reported figures.

Table 8.2 then shows the general picture of patent and R&D resources in the sample. A few observations in relation to Table 8.2 are noteworthy. First, total patenting costs have grown considerably between 1987 and 1991, more than sales and R&D. However, the growth of in-house patenting staff is much less, except for the electrical industry which has been a forerunner in building up IP resources in the 1980s. The lower overall growth of in-house patent employees compared to the growth of patenting expenditures is probably due primarily to growth in foreign applications, but it could also be due to a growth lag that reflects both a temporary peak in work load and bottlenecks in the more long-term build-up of IP resources that lead in turn to the growth in outsourcing. It could also be due to circumstances specific to the mechanical corporations, which show the largest difference in growth ratios for patent engineers and in-house patent costs.

Patent employees in large Japanese corporations are predominantly engineers, few are economists and lawyers. The main strategy in building up in-house competence has been to 'convert' engineers to patent specialists, as is also indicated by the growth in the percentage of engineers in patenting. There are, moreover, significant differences across industries in the degree of centralization of patent employees.

Table 8.1 Japanese corporations with most patent employees, 1991

Corporation	Patent employees[1]	Total employees[3]	Patent employees/ total employees (%)[4]	Total R&D (US$ million)[2]	Total sales (US$ million)[2]	R&D/ sales (%)
Electrical						
Toshiba Corp.	370	162 000	0.23	2 390	35 507	6.7
Canon Group	350	62 700	0.56	830	14 053	5.9
Matsushita Electric Co. Ltd	340	210 848	0.16	2 887	49 619	5.8
Hitachi Ltd	330	324 292	0.10	3 690	58 173	6.3
Fujitsu Ltd	210	155 779	0.13	2 947	25 880	11.4
Sony Corp.	200	110 000	0.18	1 504	27 068	5.6
Mechanical						
Honda Motor Co., Ltd	150	85 500	0.18	1 459	32 342	4.5
Toyota Motor Corp.	130	102 423	0.13	3 233	74 099	4.4
Chemical						
Asahi Chemical Ind.	70	27 018	0.26	300	9 785	3.4
Mitsubishi Kasei Corp.	70	17 000	0.41	379	9 479	4.0

Notes
1. Number of persons working more than half time with patenting activities according to questionnaire. See note 4.
2. Consolidated data, including majority owned subsidiaries worldwide. Conversion rate used is US$1 = 133 Japanese yen.
3. Consolidated employee data.
4. Hitachi, Honda, Toyota and Asahi reported non-consolidated data. It is therefore possible that the number of patent employees may be greater than shown due to additional staff in majority owned subsidiaries not reported. This would produce higher patent employee ratios for these companies.

Sources: Questionnaire survey by the author and colleagues. Corporate annual reports.

Table 8.2   Patent and R&D resources in large Japanese corporations

(Code) Question	Chemical (*n* = 9)	Electrical (*n* = 10)	Mechanical (*n* = 5)	Total (*n* = 24)
(A1a) Total sales globally in 1991				
(US$ million)	6 341	33 096	30 791	22 582
Growth ratio 1991/1987	1.31	1.43	1.45	1.42
(A2a) Total number of employees				
in 1991[1]	13 906	153 056	60 771	81 649
Growth ratio 1991/1987[2]	1.23	1.15	1.03	1.14
(B1) Total R&D expenditures				
worldwide in 1991 (US$ million)	255	1 984	1 285	1 190
Growth ratio 1991/1987	1.38	1.56	1.50	1.53
(E7) Cost of in-house patenting				
department activities and purchased				
services in 1991 (US$ million)	8.0	51.5	22.4	27.0
Growth ratio 1991/1987	1.63	1.35	1.17	1.43
(E6a) Number of persons working				
more than half-time with patenting				
activities in the company in 1991	40.80	217.20	94.80	121.60
Growth ratio 1991/1987	1.04	1.35	1.01	1.23
thereof:				
(E6b) Percentage engineers 1991	83.80	62.60	76.80	74.00
Growth ratio 1991/1987	1.01	0.96	1.05	1.00
(E6c) Percentage lawyers 1991	4.90	6.30	2.20	4.90
Growth ratio 1991/1987	0.86	1.58	0.73	1.11
(E6d) Percentage working in				
central/corporate headquarters 1991	75.00	37.60	46.20	54.10
Growth ratio 1991/1987	1.00	1.10	0.95	1.02
Key resource ratios				
(E6a/A2a) Percentage patent workers				
in the company 1991[2]	0.32	0.17	0.22	0.18
(E7/B1) Patent cost/R&D cost 1991 (%)	3.10	2.60	1.70	2.30
(B1/A1a) R&D/sales 1991 (%)	4.00	6.00	4.20	5.30

Notes
1. The figures for the chemical and mechanical sectors are underestimated due to the inclusion of non-consolidated company employee data.
2. Ratios are based solely on reported employee data from company questionnaires.

The chemical corporations were found to be most centralized and the electrical corporations least centralized, although with a trend towards centralization among the latter. On average, patenting is also more centralized than R&D and engineering.[1] For example, about 20 per cent of IP personnel are located at corporate headquarters in Toshiba, while the other 80 per cent work in various operations departments in the corporation. For engineers in general at Toshiba, about 19 000 have at least a Bachelor's degree or the equivalent, and of these only 10 per cent work in corporate laboratories, while 10 per cent work in development laboratories and the remaining 80 per cent in various other operations departments.

A final observation is that on average 'patent intensity' in terms of the ratio of patent costs to R&D costs is still fairly low, that is, about 2.3 per cent, which by the way is less than half the average R&D intensity, that is, the ratio of R&D costs to sales. However, some companies such as Toshiba have a patent/R&D cost ratio of about 10 per cent.[2]

8.3   IP ORGANIZATION

8.3.1   Organizational Options for IP in General

There are various options concerning the organization of IP activities. They could be combined in different ways, for example, in a three-tier organization with IP activities at corporate, business area and business unit levels plus parallel IP activities in an independent foreign subsidiary or newly acquired company, all supplemented with outside patent firms, and law firms. Thus, IP activities could be:

1. centralized at corporate headquarters (mostly as a staff function);
2. decentralized to business areas, business units and subsidiaries, domestic and foreign;
3. decentralized to one business division as a 'lead-house' with corporate-wide IP responsibility;
4. organized as an independent IP business unit in the corporation;
5. externalized to a supplier organization, with one, two or more patent bureaus, agents, attorneys and law firms (more than one is definitely advisable for a large company), or to collective IP resources shared with others.

At the functional level IP may be organized:

1. as organizationally separate functions for various IPR (patents, trademarks, copyrights and so on);

2. as a comprehensive IP department, integrating various IP activities;
3. integrated with R&D, a special innovation company, a legal department, a licensing department, a department for intelligence, information and documentation, or with marketing.

Rarely is an IP department organized as a profit centre or business unit. Often it is a cost centre with a cost-sharing arrangement, possibly with some services sold internally as well. As a typical staff service function, the IP organization works in a matrix arrangement with the line organization. Coordination is also achieved through committees, liaison people and the like.

Traditionally in Western companies, IP matters have not attracted a great deal of resources and attention concerning their organization. Usually, IP activities have been split into patenting and other activities and attached in a subsidiary manner as staff or service functions to other functions in the corporation. A traditional large Western corporation has typically had some kind of patent department attached to R&D or a legal department at corporate level with some liaison engineers decentralized. Trademark-related activities have been attached mostly to marketing. Sometimes, there has also been a separate licensing department. While there has naturally been a certain amount of writings about the work operations of IP-related departments and their staff, especially patent departments, there have been few systematic studies across companies, industries and countries. A classic study is Taylor and Silberston (1973), which contains a sub-study of patent and licensing departments in approximately 30 UK companies in the chemical and engineering industries. Some of the findings in the Taylor–Silberston study may well represent the traditional situation in many other Western companies and will therefore be described here.[3]

Taylor and Silberston distinguish between four types of patent organizations.[4] The types (1–4) differ primarily in terms of size (from small to large), degree of internationalization of specialist operations (from low to high), and degree of formal organization and management (from low to high). The four types refer only to patenting, and thus do not differ in terms of an expanding set of functional responsibilities outside the patenting area. The first type of patent organization has no specific arrangements other than having a chief engineer or a technical manager assuming responsibility for patenting. There is no special staff and therefore the engineer or manager must rely fully on outside patent agents. The second type of patent organization has an in-house patent specialist with a very small staff but still relies greatly on outside patent agents. The third type, considered a typical industrial patent department in the study, has a central patent department at corporate headquarters, headed by a specialist middle manager as patent manager, who is qualified as both a patent agent and an engineer. This department has a central staff, supplemented by liaison individuals or small units of patent specialists in the R&D and production units as well as some outside patent agents, especially for work on foreign applications. The fourth and final type is termed the 'super patent department' in the study. The total staff of this type of patent organization ranged from about 35 to 50 patent employees, including secretarial and clerical staff, performing all professional patent work except that which needed foreign agents. The largest of such patent departments, of which there were only a few in British industry at the time (late 1960s), were able to handle several hundred UK priority applications. There were perhaps five or more foreign applications for each of these. Licensing was likely to be a separate department. The traditional functions of the patent department as identified in the study included: obtaining and maintaining patents (including identifying patentable inventions in the organization and deciding whether to patent or not); opposing patent applications of others; handling infringements; linking up with licensing and litigation when needed; dealing with foreign patent work; and performing as a clearing-house for technical information in the firm, including the monitoring of patenting by others.

8.3.2   Patent and IP Organization and Management in Large Japanese Corporations

The patent organizations in large Japanese corporations in the 1990s have a number of common features that clearly distinguish them from the traditional patent organization in large Western corporations.

IP resources
The resources devoted to IP activities are not just slightly larger, they are often larger by a magnitude.

Centralized IP department
Responsibilities for patenting and other IP matters have been integrated and centralized into a comprehensive IP department at corporate level. In fact, all 24 corporations in the sample had a centralized patent department with corporate-wide responsibilities for patent coordination, headed by one central corporate patent manager. Usually, this department had similar responsibilities for other IP matters as well; there was an organizational trend showing evolution from a patent department to an IP department and from a patent manager to an IP manager.

Status of the IP department
The status and power of the patent and IP department has risen. Questions about patents and related matters were discussed regularly at company board meetings

in most of the corporations, and often the IP manager reported directly to the CEO. The career paths to top management positions have often resided substantially in R&D with involvement in IP matters, and several Japanese CEOs were strongly IP-oriented. The IP department was thus of strategic concern under proactive management, not just a reactive service department. Consequently, there was a need for sustainable in-house competence on a substantial level and scale. Still, much patent work was outsourced.

Clearing-house

Substantial emphasis and resources were devoted to having the patent department serve as an active clearing-house for technical information, with activities for technology scanning internally and externally, patent mapping, patent clearance, dissemination and so on. Sometimes, technology intelligence was conducted in special subsidiaries as well. Such information-related activities are clearly important but in Western companies they have been difficult to maintain, coordinate and link to decision-making. Often the Western patent department has scanned and disseminated patent information without adding much value for the user, and without much follow-up and feedback (compare Chapter 9). Japanese firms also experience difficulties like these, but they tackle them in more determined and systematic ways.

Integration of IP and R&D

Good working relations between the patent department and R&D were emphasized. This is a natural concern in Western companies as well, however the Japanese patent department was usually more powerful than a reactive service department purely under the aegis of R&D. Patenting people were involved regularly in the early stages of R&D, not casually called in at too late a stage as has often been the case in Western companies. Patent management operated pro-actively rather than reactively responding to requests from business and R&D operations and was expected to take sufficient initiative in order to secure viable patent positions in various business and technology areas. Needless to say, that is not an easy task as business divisions become increasingly independent. In general, corporate patent management in Japan had more power than their Western counterparts.

To illustrate, in one corporation a review of patent positions was undertaken regularly at an early stage of entering a business and/or technology area. If the review showed an unfavourable 'jungle' of patents, the IP manager had the clout to hold up the project until some kind of patent clearance (for example, through licensing) had been undertaken. However, more common than vetoing, an IP manager had the responsibility of bringing such a situation to the attention of higher management.

Patent (IP) culture

The Japanese patent organization was immersed in what can be called a patent culture in the corporation. This is an important feature that will be dealt with in the next section.

8.4   PATENT MANAGEMENT AND PATENT CULTURE

Chapters 5 and 6 have described how Japanese industry, and large corporations in particular, have developed a general orientation concerning patenting. This orientation could best be described as a patent culture residing within and between companies.[5] The patent culture did not develop as a result of a grand design but was instead part and parcel of a catch-up process that started after World War II and was further strengthened after the emergence of the pro-patent era in the 1980s. That is not to say that managerial action cannot influence the formation of a culture in business, such as a patent culture. The early efforts of Mr Takahashi, at the national level, are one example of such action (see Chapter 5). The efforts of Mr Saba, former CEO and Chairman of Toshiba, and Mr Yamaji, former CEO and Vice-Chairman of Canon, provide other examples.

The question is to what extent can a patent culture be fostered by managerial action in a corporation. A more general question is how a corporate culture in general could be formed. Japanese corporations are renowned for having built strong corporate cultures by various means. Needless to say, a well-functioning culture of some sort could be an effective vehicle for coordinated, purposeful action, and as such, could work as an efficiency-enhancing control mechanism. At the same time a culture could become a barrier to change. Moreover, in society as well as in large corporations, there is a fair amount of cultural diversity with several sub-cultures that may clash with one another.[6]

Thus there is a need for management to consider how to influence cultural formation and change. General managerial instruments that are mentioned in the management literature as useful in bringing about cultural formation and change are strategy and policy formation, recruitment, promotion, restructuring of communications through organization and location, and campaigns of various sorts. There are also less tangible managerial actions representing elements at a fundamental level within a culture, such as actions that influence language and values, create symbols and rituals, integrate company life with social life and leisure activities, take on social responsibilities, strengthen ideologies, nurture common myths, and create implicit incentive and penalty structures. The importance of company leaders as role models who live as they preach is also extremely important.

These are all general elements in fostering a culture in a corporation, and it is in the nature of things that an exhaustive listing of elements cannot be made and that many elements are intangible, requiring much managerial sophistication. When it comes to building a corporate patent culture similar to those found in the large Japanese corporations studied, the elements become more specific. Some of these elements, as observed, are dealt with below, in no particular order.

1. *Top management involvement in patenting and IP*   Top management involvement is indeed a necessary but insufficient condition. It is typical for most Japanese corporations to have top management involved in technology and R&D. Many corporations, too, have had a preference for technologists as CEOs, although there are corporations such as Hitachi and Toshiba that prefer a succession of technologists and commercialists as CEOs. In either case they are almost always members of top management with an appreciation of patenting matters, often having direct personal experience. Some top managers make it a habit to ask questions about the patent situation during business presentations, and some also make it a habit to visit labs and discuss, among other things, patenting in more casual ways. It is important to show concern and at the same time refrain from letting obsolete or otherwise insufficient technical knowledge or one's own pet ideas misguide R&D.

2. *Patenting and IP as a common concern for all engineers*   Although specialists are always needed for patent work, it is considered important not to consider patenting primarily as a specialist function but to make patenting a common concern for all engineers. Training courses, job rotation and career paths with at least an early stint in a patent department are important, together with the other measures described below.

3. *Patent policies and strategies integrated in business plans*   Without a requirement that makes patenting and IP a regular and specified item on the agenda of business plans, business managers will easily neglect the IP situation or let IP strategies become too generalized and watered down. Integration of business and IP aspects is not only a matter of thinking hard and coming up with cunning ideas but is also a matter of two-way communication with some integration of business language and IP language. 'What is our unique competence in this business?' is a common question in business analysis. The equally important, but less commonly used IP-related question is 'How can we protect our unique competence in this business?'.

4. *Clear patent objectives*   Clear, quantified objectives for patenting were common among the Japanese corporations in the study. An example is given by Hitachi, which had the objective of increasing the number of strategic patents by 25 per year, as described in Chapter 7. There are many arguments against quantifying objectives, and often patenting people produce such

arguments. One argument is that quantified objectives are said to stimulate quantity rather than quality of patents and foster unfruitful competition. On the other hand, quantification focuses attention and provides clear yardsticks for rewards and penalties, as well as for improvements. The arguments for quantifying objectives appear to be stronger when building a patent culture. Such objectives then function as symbols and provide a basis for habitual behaviour, even rituals, such as 'kamikaze research', which describes the patenting frenzy in Japanese companies at the end of the budget year in order to meet quotas. Such behaviour could be seen as going too far, but nevertheless is part of the patent culture.

5. *Clear patenting incentives for R&D personnel and organizational units*
The issue of how to reward inventive work by individuals, teams and units is a very important and fundamental question in both Japanese and Western firms. This is a complex issue that could be elaborated at great length. Without doing so here, one can just point to the clear and fairly strong reward schemes employed by Japanese firms, often developed without the adversarial relationship between the firm and the inventor that easily develops in Western firms. The following citation is in contrast with the top management view, not uncommon in Western firms, that R&D people basically are salaried for doing inventive work.

> We try to encourage the view that the company's value to society lies in developing new technology. We also try to provide a corporate environment where thought and originality are rewarded.
> We give annual cash awards to the employee who has applied for the most patents that year and to those who have developed patents or software of an outstanding nature. (Keizo Yamaji, former CEO, Canon Group)

6. *Fostering of behavioural attitudes and norms*   Fostering of behavioural attitudes, norms, habits and standards conducive both to technology protection by patents and secrecy and to technology intelligence can be done in various ways. For example, certain reading and writing habits of engineers can be encouraged, as in Canon. A citation by Dr Yamaji may again illustrate:

> I encourage our researchers to read patent specifications rather than academic theses and to write patent applications rather than technical reports. I also tell them to make virtual experiments (*Gedanken* experiments) in order to have them apply for more and more patents, so that we can be prepared for the era to come when only some companies, strong in patents, will cooperate with each other and survive. (Keizo Yamaji, former CEO, Canon Group)

Canon, as well as other companies, also tries to encourage writing habits by aligning the reporting on R&D work to the norms and standards used in patent documents. In this way, patent application work is facilitated while thinking in patent terms is encouraged.

Speaking, listening and observation habits of engineers, sales people, managers and so on could also be influenced for protection and intelligence purposes, although extreme behaviour in this regard may be counter-productive in other respects.

7. *Visible organizational means* Tangible and intangible means for building a patent culture have to complement each other. Examples of visible organizational means besides the ordinary patent organization are patent promotion centres, patent liaison officers distributed in the organization, corporate-wide patent campaigns, patenting prizes and patent strategy seminars.

8. *Language, methodology and philosophy* A common language is central to any culture. One way to foster a professional language for a patent culture is to develop concepts and tools and employ them in a methodology for analysis and in communication, which could be further turned into a philosophy. The patent-mapping methodology described in Chapter 9 was developed in Japan by JPO initially and then improved over time by large corporations. It has been a useful methodology for several purposes in itself, but at the same time it has contributed to building a patent culture through its influences on language, analytical perspective, conceptualization and communication.

Finally, it must be emphasized that corporate patent cultures are embedded in and reinforced by an overarching industrial and national culture, conducive to patenting, inventions, intelligence and so on. There is a wide range of institutional arrangements for this with government agencies and initiatives, legislation, associations, institutes and so on. The historical dimension is important and Chapter 5 gives some features of it for Japan. The large Japanese corporations as a whole play an increasingly important role. The corporate IP managers know each other well and are part of various 'old boy networks' (to use a Western term). The Japan Patent Association is a good example of a longstanding organization catering primarily to the interests of large corporations.[7]

8.5   IP ORGANIZATION AT TOSHIBA AND HITACHI

Toshiba is one of the leading Japanese corporations in the IP field, with top rankings in terms of, for example, number of patent applications and patent employees. Thus, it is natural to look at the history, organization and management of IP in Toshiba in greater detail, as shown in Tables 8.3 and 8.4 and Figures 8.1 and 8.2.

Table 8.3 Key historic events in Toshiba's corporate, technology and IP organization

Some key events in corporate organization		Some key events in R&D organization		Some key events in IP organization	
1870	Shibaura Electric established				
1890	Tokyo Electric established (first producing light bulbs)				
		1906	R&D laboratory established in Shibaura Electric		
				1912	Patent Section established
		1918	Matsuda R&D laboratory established in Tokyo Electric		
		1931	Tsurumi R&D laboratory established in Shibaura Electric		
1939	Toshiba established as merger of Tokyo Electric and Shibaura Electric				
				1944	Patent Division established
1960s	Cooperation with NEC and GE in computers				
		1961	Corporate research laboratory established		
		1968	Heavy industry research laboratory established	1968	A decentralized system adopted
		1970	Production engineering laboratory established		
				1972	Start of trainee education for foreign countries

Year	Event	Year	Event
1976	Adopts GE type of organization (with business portfolio analysis, business units, etc.) Decides to focus on electronics and information technology		
1978	Exit from mainframe computers	1978	Laboratories in business units established in a three-level organization under business sector laboratories and corporate laboratories
		1979	Washington Intellectual Property Office ('WIPO') established
1980s	Promotion of globalization, and E&E (energy and electronics) strategy. Later extended to 3E – energy, electronics and environment	1980s	Various new laboratories established, e.g. a VLSI laboratory in 1984 The 'Tokken' system for R&D management established together with the three-level R&D organization
1989	Information and communication technologies account for more than 50 per cent of sales	1989	Intellectual Property Division established

Sources: Material from Mr Saba, Mr Takayanagi and Mr Norichika; Miyazaki (1995); and interviews.

269

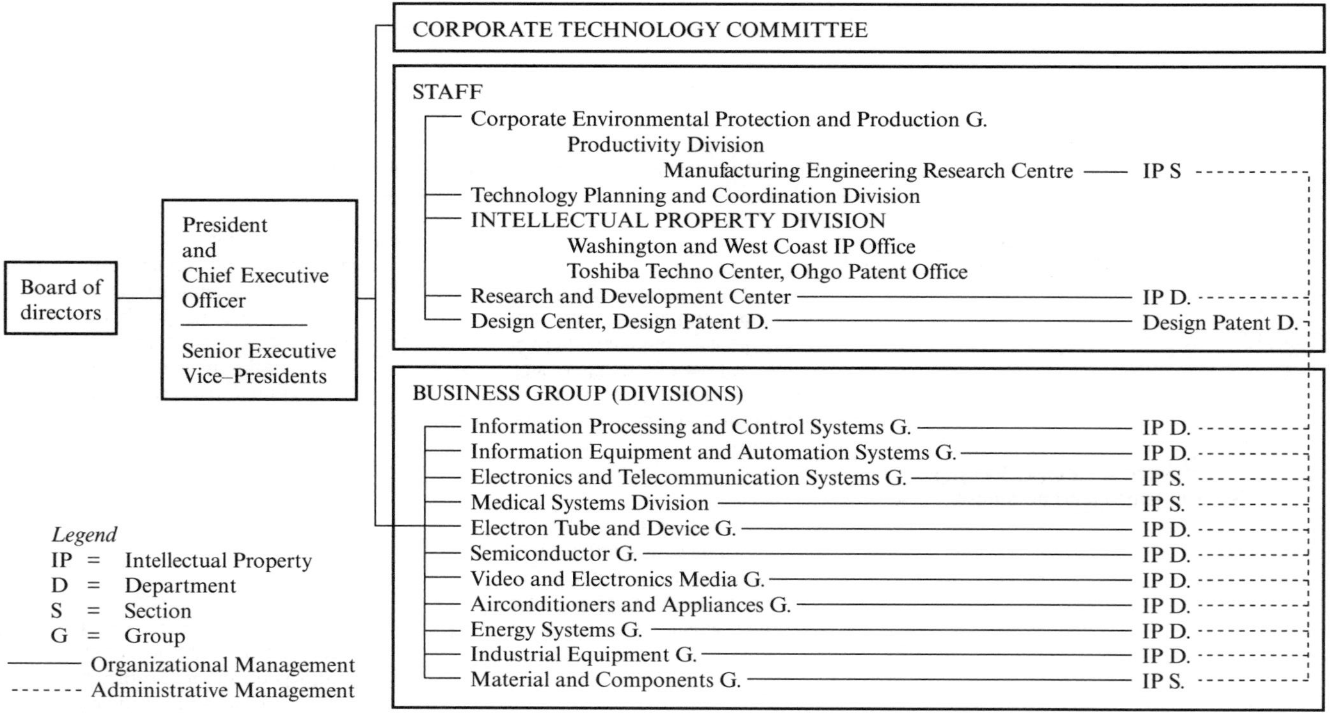

CORPORATE TECHNOLOGY COMMITTEE

Board of directors

President and Chief Executive Officer

Senior Executive Vice–Presidents

STAFF

- Corporate Environmental Protection and Production G.
  - Productivity Division
  - Manufacturing Engineering Research Centre —— IP S
- Technology Planning and Coordination Division
- INTELLECTUAL PROPERTY DIVISION
  - Washington and West Coast IP Office
  - Toshiba Techno Center, Ohgo Patent Office
- Research and Development Center ———— IP D.
- Design Center, Design Patent D. ———— Design Patent D.

BUSINESS GROUP (DIVISIONS)

- Information Processing and Control Systems G. —— IP D.
- Information Equipment and Automation Systems G. —— IP D.
- Electronics and Telecommunication Systems G. —— IP S.
- Medical Systems Division —— IP S.
- Electron Tube and Device G. —— IP D.
- Semiconductor G. —— IP D.
- Video and Electronics Media G. —— IP D.
- Airconditioners and Appliances G. —— IP D.
- Energy Systems G. —— IP D.
- Industrial Equipment G. —— IP D.
- Material and Components G. —— IP S.

Legend
IP = Intellectual Property
D. = Department
S. = Section
G. = Group
——— Organizational Management
------ Administrative Management

Figure 8.1 Toshiba IP organization (as of 1995)

270

Table 8.3 indicates that the organizational history of Toshiba and its R&D and IP resembles, at a very general level, the organizational development in a large Western corporation. The corporation grew, diversified, refocused and internationalized. At the same time, R&D, established early as a separate laboratory grew, diversified, differentiated into product and process development and research and organized into a mix of centralized/decentralized laboratories under a technology management structure. At a later stage, R&D became internationalized, a process that began fairly late in Toshiba. The IP organization became established as a patent department at an early stage, even by Western standards (comparable to stage 2 in Taylor and Silberston's study, described

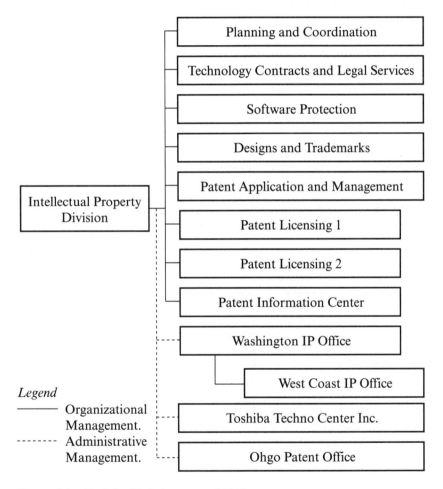

Figure 8.2   Toshiba IP division (as of 1995)

above). The IP organization has historically been oriented around patenting, which grew and was upgraded in the organization, adopted a centralized/decentralized mix, internationalized, and finally consolidated into one large department with various IP activities that grew up in a diversified way over the years. Thus developments in the corporate organization shaped, often with some time lag, the developments of the R&D organization, which further shaped the IP organization.

Figure 8.1 shows the overall Toshiba corporate IP organization in the mid-1990s. One can note that each business group has an integrated IP department or section under the business group management but also a functional administrative management arrangement with the corporate IP division. The latter in turn is at the same staff level as R&D and the design centres.

Table 8.4   Toshiba's patent education system (as of 1995)

Career stage	IP-related personnel	Engineers
When entering the company	IP generally	IP generally
Introductory education	Basic education First-term collective education Second-term collective education	Freshman course on business and patent/IP rights
1–3 years	Advanced course Research of precedent cases	Basic knowledge about the patent system Patent surveys Ways to summarize proposals
Mid-level personnel	Selection Drafting specifications in English Patent application management Patent specialty courses System of overseas patent study	Patent review/patent maps Improving the quality of proposals
Deputy managers	Family training[*] Patent supervision	Family training* Patent supervision
Managers	Family training Patent strategy	Family training Patent management

Note: * Training and socializing in off-the-job settings (signs of titles and positions removed, night-time sessions and so on)

Source: Mr K. Norichika, Toshiba.

Management Function of Intellectual Property

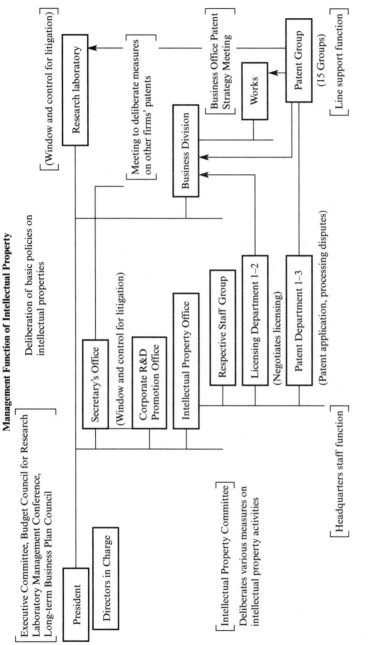

Source: Hitachi.

Figure 8.3   IP management in Hitachi

273

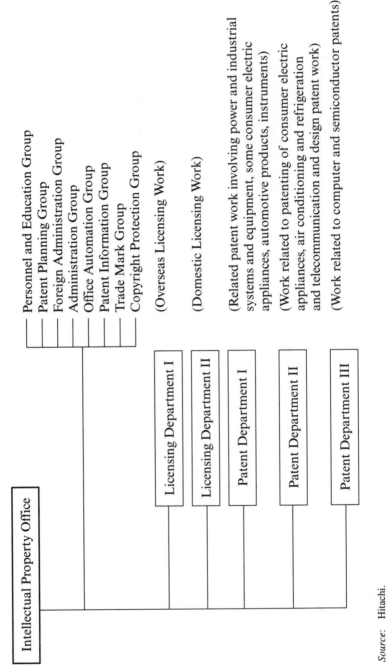

Intellectual Property Office

- Personnel and Education Group
- Patent Planning Group
- Foreign Administration Group
- Administration Group
- Office Automation Group
- Patent Information Group
- Trade Mark Group
- Copyright Protection Group

Licensing Department I (Overseas Licensing Work)

Licensing Department II (Domestic Licensing Work)

Patent Department I (Related patent work involving power and industrial systems and equipment, some consumer electric appliances, automotive products, instruments)

Patent Department II (Work related to patenting of consumer electric appliances, air conditioning and refrigeration and telecommunication and design patent work)

Patent Department III (Work related to computer and semiconductor patents)

Source: Hitachi.

Figure 8.4   Organization of Hitachi's corporate IP department

Figure 8.2 further shows the inner organization of the IP division, with departments for each major type of IPR, except trade secrets, plus departments for licensing and patent information. Toshiba Techno Center also performs patent analysis but for various reasons is organized separately. Finally, there is a relatively large department for planning and coordination of IP departments in

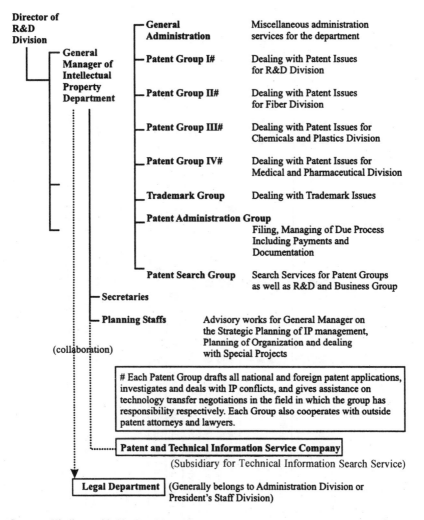

Source: Kindly provided by Dr Akira Mifune.

Figure 8.5   Representative organization of a corporate IP department in a large Japanese chemical corporation

IP tasks

IP tasks	Invention group	Business group	Relevant department	IP department	Committee or conference
1 Strategic planning of intellectual property management					Steering committee for R&D activities
2 Obtaining of patent rights					
Drafting and request for application	○	▽		☆ ◉	
Final drafting and application procedure	●	●		☆ ◉	
Request for examination	○	●		☆ ◉	
Registration and payments	▽	●			
3 Obtaining of Foreign Patent Rights					Patent evaluation and foreign patent application committee
Request for application	●	○	▽	●	
Drafting and application	●	▽ ●		☆ ◉	
Registration and payments	▽	●		☆ ◉	
4 Patent assessment and maintenance	●	◉	● ▽	○ ◉	Patent evaluation and maintenance committee
Watching for possible conflicts	●	○	▽	●	
Opposition and actions for infringements	●	○	▽	☆	
5 Agreement on technology transfer	▽	◉ ○	● (Legal dept)	◉	Steering committee for project
6 Patent approval or patent clearance	○ or ●	● or ○	● or ▽	◉	Patent committee for project
7 Patent information management	☆	● or ★	▽ or ●	☆ or ★	
8 General affairs					
System management		◉	●	◉ &	
Award management	○	●	▽	○ &	
IP education	▽	●		☆	
Follow-up of new laws and regulations	▽	▽		☆	

Legend:
◉ = Decision;   ○ = Requesting or planning;   ● = With discussion;   ▽ = Information;   ☆ = Execution;   ★ = Collaboration.

Source: Kindly provided by Dr Akira Mifune.

Figure 8.6   An IP organization model representative of a large Japanese chemical corporation

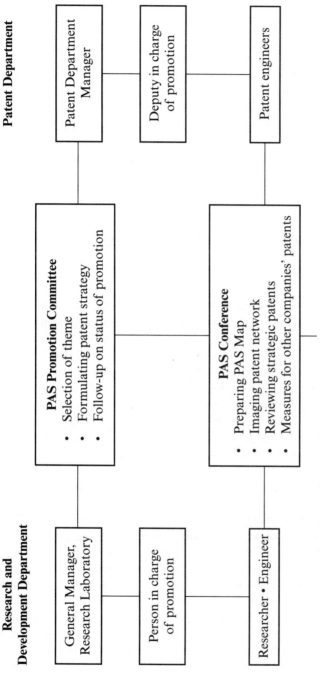

Patent Department

**Research and
Development Department**

Patent Department Manager

Deputy in charge of promotion

Patent engineers

PAS Promotion Committee

- Selection of theme
- Formulating patent strategy
- Follow-up on status of promotion

PAS Conference

- Preparing PAS Map
- Imaging patent network
- Reviewing strategic patents
- Measures for other companies' patents

General Manager, Research Laboratory

Person in charge of promotion

Researcher • Engineer

Pivotal research and development • Acquiring strategic patents and use of rights • Eliminating patents posing as obstacles

Source: Hitachi.

Figure 8.7 Hitachi's 'PAS System' (patent strategy system)

business groups. Thus, the IP division is by and large comprehensive, and represents another stage beyond the 'super patent department' in the study by Taylor and Silberston (1973).

Education in IP, both for IP personnel and engineers corporate-wide, is important in Toshiba, as in any company seriously responding to the pro-patent movement. Table 8.4 shows Toshiba's patent education system.

Similar, although not identical, IP organizations can be found in other large Japanese corporations, as illustrated in Figures 8.3 and 8.4 in the case of Hitachi, and in Figures 8.5 and 8.6 in the case of a representative chemical corporation (as a contrast to the focus so far on electrical corporations). Figure 8.7 also gives a bird's-eye view of how R&D and patent departments cooperate in the Hitachi case.

8.6   FURTHER STAGES OF THE IP ORGANIZATION

8.6.1   Introduction

As we have described in this chapter, the leading-edge Japanese patent department of the 1990s is clearly another stage beyond the 'super patent department' found in a few leading UK firms during the late 1960s as studied by Taylor and Silberston (1973). The patent departments in some of the largest US firms have also evolved substantially since the 1980s. In the wake of the patent wars and the pro-patent era, many Western firms have in fact initiated processes for overhauling their patent organizations.

A natural question, then, is how the patent and IP organization in large firms will evolve into still further stages. First, one can note that temporary variations occur which may not be significant for long-term trends or shifts. A certain cooling has affected the US–Japan patent wars since the early 1990s, and some reductions of IP staff have been made in several Japanese corporations during the Japanese recession in the mid- and late 1990s.

The long-run trend showing an increasing role for intellectual capital in firms, as described in Chapter 4, is most likely to have profound effects on their future IP organization and management, especially in an increasingly competitive environment. Already, many industrial firms have major portions of their assets as well as their investments geared towards IC, and new types of firms are emerging in which IC clearly dominates (see Chapters 1, 4 and 10). Compared to the large share of IC in the total resources of large technology-based corporations, the share of resources devoted to the IP department appears minor and mis-matched indeed. Patent departments have always been minor entities in firms, even in Japan, and still are viewed as functional departments despite the growth of their resources and their transformation into IP departments with more comprehensive IP management responsibilities.

However, the formal organization of IP-related activities is not the most important concern. For the foreseeable future, few people in a traditional manufacturing firm would dream of formally reorganizing R&D, advertising, human resource departments and so on into one large department, division or business area for intellectual capital with some kind of executive corporate IC manager.[8] Nevertheless, an organizational arrangement of that sort could be feasible. In fact, a 'pure' IC firm or a firm in which IC resources dominate could in itself be viewed as such an arrangement, in which case the CEO is the corporate IC manager. Having an IC unit accountable on a normal balance sheet and profit/loss account is thus feasible. This is certainly not to say that accounting and organizational principles would make a large IC unit an attractive solution in a more traditional manufacturing firm. A few US companies have tried to let the patent department operate as an internal profit centre. Internal and external licensing agreements then provide a suitable institutional mechanism. The experiences are mixed, however, and there are risks of short-termism, high transaction costs and transactions detrimental to the core business divisions. There have also existed pure technology licence brokers in traditional industries, but without manufacturing and the possibilities of bundling proprietary technology with physical products they are vulnerable in the long run. In service industries, like insurance, more creative attempts have been made to account for IC on the balance sheet, but so far without separate profit/loss accounting.[9] Appointments of IC managers or Intellectual Capital Directors have also occurred in this context. What is far more important than the formal organization, though, is how the informal organization, the culture and the organization as a whole will change in response to the increasing role of IC.

At a general level, there is a shift in management thinking towards knowledge management, the knowledge-based corporation, the learning organization and so on. However, it could be argued that knowledge *per se* is not the primary concern for a firm. It is when knowledge is turned into an exploitable resource in a competitive environment that it becomes of value to a firm, that is, when knowledge becomes an asset or a piece of intellectual capital. The same could be said about interpersonal relations when viewed as corporate resources. The ways (or strategies) to turn knowledge and relations into IC are many, some of which are objectionable in society. Ownership is one way in principle, but it is difficult to exercise for institutional and social reasons. Having intellectual workers as 'slaves' owned by the firm is indeed infeasible, and exploitation of personal relations is limited by social conventions. Many limitations of ownership of intellectual resources relate to very strong and fundamental cultural elements in societies in general, such as concern over personal integrity, individual freedom, democracy and so on. Some limitations also derive directly from the institutional framework, in particular, the legal framework.

More important to a firm than the ownership aspect of IC *per se* is the control or managerial aspect. That is, the key issue from a firm's point of view is how to obtain and maintain sufficient control of the possible rents from IC for appropriation purposes. It does not necessarily have to be total control, only control that in some sense enables satisfactory appropriation of rent streams for the firm as an IC possessor (or IC controller). For this purpose, there are no ready-made managerial philosophies or tools. What we can call IC management and IC organization are most likely to develop as a professional area in the future at various levels – corporate, individual, national and so on. Two kinds of scenarios for organizational and management development will be elaborated here. The first will be called an extended patent department, and the second will be called a distributed IC management with IC resources and responsibilities distributed in the organization.

8.6.2   An Extended IP Department

Can the patent and IP department in large technology-based corporations be extended beyond the type of IP departments emerging in Japanese industry? Without elaborating in detail, a few arguments for such extensions will be offered.

Communication node
IP-related aspects penetrate a wide range of activities in a firm. The more IC-based the firm is, the greater the penetration. This penetration often requires two-way communications, which give IP staff large contact networks in the organization and the IP department the potential to become a communication node in the firm.

Attention to detail
IP-related activities have to be focused, especially because of their legal aspects. Dealing with IP requires focusing on concrete inventions, trademarks and so on, and attention to order and detail. Trade secrets are less concrete but may still require attention to detail.

Emergence of IC
As has been repeatedly emphasized, the value of IPR as assets and competitive means has increased substantially since the 1980s and will probably continue to increase. Firms in general will become increasingly IC-based. In addition, the range of 'pure' IC firms will evolve further in various industries and service businesses, and new types of IC firms are likely to emerge.

Short- and long-term management

IP-related activities have a wide span in the time dimension. They interact with technical and commercial activities in both the short and long run. There are immediate patent races where the winner takes all, as well as patents that may be kept valid for 20 years. Licensing contracts are typically long term, which necessitates long-term planning. Thus, IP-related activities instil both urgency and long-termism, and thereby have the potential to induce people to try to integrate the often conflicting short-term and long-term views of a business firm.

Technical information centre

IP-related activities are, and must be, closely connected to many sources of detailed information of various kinds – technical, commercial and so on. Thus, the IP department may also function as an information centre or clearing-house for technical and commercial information in the organization. This is especially the case for technical information, which will be dealt with more fully in Chapter 9. The time value of patent-related information also gives an incentive to deploy new information and communication technologies. This in turn may further be used to extend the role of the patent department as a technical information centre, as well as to extend its role in information security, which also relates to trade secret protection.

Integration of licensing and patenting

Licensing in and out is one area that sometimes has been integrated with patenting and IP. Although company situations and licensing strategies differ, the need to centralize licensing and integrate it more with patenting has increased in general, everything else being equal. This is mainly due to the increasing amount of cross-linkages between patents, technologies, products, companies and markets arising from diversification and internationalization. New generic technologies emerge, products and companies become increasingly 'mul-tech', that is, multitechnology based, and companies increasingly become globalized (see Granstrand and Sjölander 1990a; Granstrand and Oskarsson 1994). These cross-linkages or interdependencies in turn require increased coordination, especially since licensing contracts are long term in nature. Too often companies, small as well as large, regret having sold a licence on an ad hoc basis by a too independent and opportunistic business unit.

Integration of IP and R&D

R&D and technical cooperation agreements of various types also increasingly involve IP matters that, just like licensing, may require central coordination and cooperation with the IP department.

Integration of patenting and technology scanning

Another area that to some extent has been integrated with patenting is technology scanning, using patent information. This is an area in which capabilities of various sorts (methods, data bases, communication networks, software tools and so on) develop fast, and Japanese companies are in the forefront together with some US companies. (This will be the main topic of Chapter 9.) At one extreme, these activities could be limited to a rudimentary form of 'patent watching' and the standard distribution of the front pages of patent documents in the company, something that is not uncommon in Western firms. At the other extreme, activities could extend into fully-fledged technology intelligence integrated with business intelligence and perhaps further integrated with technology planning.

Technology planning

Technology planning in itself is an activity that is quite strongly emphasized in Japanese large corporations – again in contrast to many Western companies, in which strategic planning, long-range planning, technology planning and so on, on the whole became demoted after the oil crises. It could be argued that an activity like technology planning is more justified in companies trying to catch up. However, that argument does not fully explain the emphasis put on technology planning in some leading Japanese corporations, where technology planning departments are headed by highly qualified, mid-career technologists supported by a staff of considerable size.

Trade secret and information security management

One further area, which naturally relates to IP but has not yet been managed in a systematic way, is the trade secret area. Trade secret legislation is weak in many countries, but strengthening measures are being taken and companies seem more willing to take trade secret-related disputes to court.[10] However, it is in the nature of secrecy itself that measures must be strengthened primarily by the companies themselves. This could be done in various ways, but an extended IP department is a natural locus for a central lead-house responsibility for corporate-wide trade secret management, an area that probably will develop in the future and possibly under other names such as information security. Such an arrangement is also aligned with the role of the IP department in technology intelligence, as well as with the need to complement patent protection with a more comprehensive view on protecting rent streams, rather than protecting pieces of property.

Generation of inventions

One possible, although controversial, role for an extended IP department is to generate inventions, that is, to perform some inventive work, a role that is traditionally assigned to R&D. The IP department should, of course, not take over that responsibility from R&D but have it as a supplementary task. With competent patent engineers, cross-training of engineers in the IP department, and technology intelligence and IP activities vested, the IP department would be well positioned to contribute to inventive work.[11]

Competence development

Certainly more roles and responsibilities could conceivably be relevant for an extended IP department, and some are likely to evolve in the future that are as yet inconceivable. One role deserving special consideration is the role of the IP department as a platform for competence development, in other words as a training ground or a section in a corporate university. IP-related activities need to link technological, commercial, economic and legal competencies. These correspond to distinct bodies of professional knowledge, education and careers, which gives an IP department the potential for being a platform for extended competence development. This competence development is not intended primarily for the IP department itself, but for the company as a whole. Clearly, many companies have not been particularly patent-oriented in the past and have consequently staffed their patent department with too few qualified people.[12] If the IP department takes on additional new roles and responsibilities, its need for internal competence development further increases. However, what is suggested here is that IP-related activities are suitable elements in learning processes for many other company activities as well. IP is a nexus of technological, commercial and legal aspects that requires order and attention to detail, focused both on the short term and the long term. Thus IP can provide a vehicle for competence development in several professional disciplines, as well as for linking those disciplinary competencies together in concrete ways. Moreover, general IP-oriented training may be needed in management and employee development in general in order to make the company more IP-conscious. For example, engineers get training in systematic functional design and technology analysis through analysing patents, as well as getting a feel for market analysis and business operations through preparing licence agreements and negotiations. These perspectives and skills are then useful to build upon in technology management training. Similar examples could be given for other non-engineering professional categories. An extended IP department can provide such an interdisciplinary training ground in many of the usual ways – courses, seminars, case work, projects, on-the-job training, job rotation and so on.

8.6.3   Distributed IC Management

As IC becomes increasingly important to firms and countries, it is natural to ask what the proper managerial responses should be, which of course is the billion dollar question. In the second scenario of distributed IC management the following are a few response strategies that could be employed.

Extensions of the IP organization

What has been said so far points to the need to consider an extended IP organization as one response. However, a formal organization with departments, committees, managers, specialists and so forth is insufficient. The arguments in the quality-management movement of the 1980s against sole reliance on such an organizational response apply in this context as well.

Transformations of corporate culture

The transformation of corporate culture is likely to be a complementary response to an extended IP organization. Just as the patent organization could be extended to an IP organization, which could further be extended to an IC organization (perhaps ultimately encompassing the whole firm if it became sufficiently IC-based), the patent culture could be transformed into an IP culture and perhaps further into an IC culture. Needless to say, cultural change is far from something that can be managed at will. However, as described in the previous section, cultural change can be influenced to various degrees by managerial action. Having some kind of patent culture already in place is thus a good starting point.

Extending a patent culture to be a more comprehensively IP-oriented culture means extending the property dimension. A further extension from IP to IC means adding a value dimension and broadening the concern from mere legal property protection to rent control or rent protection and the acquisition, development and exploitation of IC on the whole. In principle, then, the managerial actions mentioned in the preceding section have relevance for building an IC culture as well, although there will be additional difficulties (for example, in clashes between the company and a wider range of groups of people with strong concern about their individual IC or their group's IC).

Distributed management

Cultural formation and change take time, often too much time in the fast pace of contemporary business. Thus a third type of managerial response may be necessary. This is what could be called distributed management, which refers to a corporate-wide focused reorientation with responsibilities distributed at management levels with no central responsibility except to top management. For the most part, such an organization is implemented swiftly on a broad front in order to create momentum in mobilizing and motivating the organization, as well as to save time. Only a few (at the most) corporate-wide re-orientations can be implemented at the same time. Often a similar reorientation is implemented in many companies across industries at about the same time. Its form could be labelled a 'corporate campaign', a 'crash programme' and the like, and its content a 'managerial or organizational innovation', a 'management revolution' and the like. It could also be a short-lived management fad, especially if it fails. Attempts to make too many corporate reorientations at the same time also considerably weaken their prospects of success.

In the recent past, there have been several such reorientations in the corporate world based on various rationales, reorientations which on the average have been quite successful at least on the surface. Thus, there have been reorientations focusing on inventory levels, total quality, lead times and core competencies. The foci of these reorientations or movements share certain features, which then can be seen as likely requirements for success. Thus the focus for a successful corporate-wide reorientation can be characterized as:

- being concrete in character;
- being able to penetrate a wide range of activities;
- having a potential for visible improvements;
- attracting realistic expectations in a situation susceptible to organizational change;
- having a direct and credible (and positive) influence on the basic and acceptable objectives and visions of the organization.

These requirements could very well be fulfilled by IC-related activities. Thus, IC could be the focus of a reorientation through distributed management. As with any form of distributed management, there are then two sorts of rationale. One is that the activities or operations in focus become improved. The other is that many other types of related activities also become improved in the process. This might seem to be a superficial side-effect, but it may in fact be the most important effect. By focusing on lowering inventory costs at all stages (through *kanban* and so on) the whole production and distribution organization can be improved, since its slacks and deficiencies are more likely to surface. By securing and increasing quality in a broad sense, innovativeness in the organization can be improved. By lowering lead times, both improved efficiency and innovativeness across R&D, production and marketing functions can be attained. By focusing on core competencies, which by common definition are deemed more valuable, widely applicable and difficult to imitate, these competencies could be improved and exploited more efficiently, while at the same time increasing the awareness of the strategic value of IC. By focusing further on IC and its dynamics, IC management could be improved at all levels in the corporation, while at the same time improvements in overall efficiency and innovativeness are likely. Anyone with experience in intellectual work knows that it has a tremendous potential for productivity improvements, although it takes hard work to achieve.

8.7   SUMMARY AND CONCLUSIONS

Partly as a result of a long process of catching up with the West and partly as a response to the pro-patent era emerging in the 1980s and the 'patent wars' – hot as well as cold – with US corporations, large Japanese corporations have developed leading patent management practices and resourceful, comprehensive IP organizations. Apparently patent management is still another example of a management area in which Western corporations have much to learn from Japan.

Taylor and Silberston (1973), being one of the very few systematic studies of patent organizations in industry, identified four types or stages. In relation to these, the patent organization in large Japanese corporations represents a quite different fifth type, as summarized in Table 8.5. A hypothetical sixth type is also described. Needless to say the different types do not have to follow upon each other, and the table certainly does not suggest that the future IC firm will be or should be organized around the patent department.

Table 8.5   The evolution of the corporate patent organization

Type	Characteristics
1	Headed by part-time technology manager plus outside patent agents[1]
2	Full-time patent manager with small staff plus outside patent agents
3	Specialized patent manager with a corporate patent department and liaison people in business divisions
4	'Super patent departments' (35–50 persons). Separate licensing department[2]
5	Comprehensive IP department (50–500 persons) of Japanese type. Patent culture[3]
6?	Extended IP organization? (For example, for technology acquisition and exploitation, technology intelligence, technology planning, information management, idea generation, competence development)
(Future scenario)	Merging with distributed intellectual capital management

Notes
1. Outside patent agents are used in all types but their relative importance is largest in types 1 and 2.
2. This is the fourth and most advanced type identified in the study of UK firms by Taylor and Silberston (1973).
3. Comprehensive IP departments of this size can also be found in some leading Western firms. For example, IBM reportedly in 1989 had 240 professional employees linked to its Intellectual Property Law Department. However, in contrast to large Japanese IP departments, IBM's was much more internationalized (with about 30 locations globally and about 10 per cent of the patent professionals located in Japan), decentralized (with only about 5 per cent working in corporate headquarters) and lawyer intensive (with about 60 per cent being US lawyers). See also Table 8.2, above.

Many large Japanese corporations could also be said to possess a patent culture, which can be characterized as having: top management involvement in patenting and IP; patenting and IP as a common concern for all engineers; patent policies and strategies integrated in business plans; clear patent objectives; clear patenting incentives for R&D personnel and organizational units; behavioural attitudes and norms conducive to technology protection and technology intelligence; visible organizational means to promote attention to patenting; and special language, methodology and philosophy.

Patent organizations have also developed in many companies in the West during the pro-patent era, although to a lesser extent on average than in Japan. In general, the patent department has moved from being a small, reactive service department, often with low status and narrow operative tasks decoupled from the business and top management, towards a larger proactive organization with more comprehensive IP responsibilities, more status and power, more commercial orientation, more strategic concern and more interaction with technology management, business management and top management. In addition to having grown, diversified and become more integrated in the corporation, the IP organization has also become internationalized as the R&D organization has internationalized.

Further developments in IP management and organization are conceivable. As the role of intellectual capital, comprising IPR, human capital and other intangibles, becomes more important in firms, intellectual capital management, encompassing IP management, might develop in various ways. The IP organization may be further extended in terms of resources, tasks and responsibilities, and there are a number of arguments for different types of extensions. The IP organization may also become subordinate to a type of distributed management of intellectual capital, signifying a reorientation of the whole company organization towards its intellectual capital, somewhat analogous to the total quality management movement.

NOTES

1. A similar result was found in Etemad and Dulude (1987) for a sample of large European, Japanese and US MNCs.
2. A study by the author of ten large US corporations (GE, ITT, Xerox, Pfizer, Motorola, 3M, Honeywell, Control Data, RCA and Zenith) in 1985 showed a patent-to-R&D cost ratio in the range 1–3 per cent. However, the ratio of number of patent applications per R&D dollar has been more than ten times higher in Japan relative to the USA in leading chemical, electrical and mechanical corporations.
3. Another of the rare studies of size and organization of patent departments is Bertin and Wyatt (1988), who made a questionnaire survey in 1983–84 of 118 large firms (corresponding to a response rate of 22 per cent) in 15 countries and six sectors. The average number of full-time employees involved in patenting services in nine responding Japanese firms was 118.

4. The authors call them successive stages of patent organization, but present no historical evidence that the types constitute stages in some sort of evolution of the patent organization. Nevertheless, given that patent resources grow overall, the types are likely to follow roughly upon each other, possibly with some leaps.
5. The concept of culture has come into popular use – and misuse – in management in the last few decades. Despite a certain vagueness and tendency to use culture as a catch-all concept, it will be used here since it captures some important, if yet evasive, features of organizations. A standard textbook in social psychology has the following definition: 'Culture includes all institutionalized ways and the implicit cultural beliefs, norms, values and premises which underline and govern conduct' (Krech et al. 1962, p. 380).
6. A subculture is simply 'a culture within a culture'.
7. JPA was formed in 1938 by patent attorneys employed in some large corporations including Toshiba and Hitachi. It was originally called Chrysanthemum Feast Club (Chōyō Kai) and was renamed Japan Patent Association (Nihon Tokkyo Kyōkai) in 1959 (Rahn 1983, p. 473).
8. Labels such as Chief Information Officer (CIO), Chief Knowledge Officer (CKO), IC Director, Intellectual Asset Manager and the like do crop up, however, as fads within information businesses proliferate.
9. See *Fortune* (1994) for the case of the European insurance company Skandia. The article also illustrates how US companies like Dow Chemical run their patent departments as profit centres.
10. An example of a large-scale secrecy legal case is the one regarding Volkswagen's hire-over of Mr Lopez from GM, where GM allegedly lost many trade secrets. Other examples come from biotech firms in Silicon Valley, where movement of key personnel between firms is accompanied by secrecy suits.
11. Note also, as described in Chapter 9, that patent mapping, as developed in Japan, could be and is used as a creative tool as well.
12. In all fairness it must be said that some of these have a high level of professional competence and insight into the company's technologies, but they are bogged down in various tasks, leaving their real competence underutilized.

9. Analysis of patent information

CHAPTER CONTENTS

9.1 CHAPTER OUTLINE

As part of the 'patent deal' between inventors and society, inventors have to disclose information about their inventions in exchange for patent rights, as described in Chapter 3. This information should be sufficient to allow a skilled person or team to reproduce the particular invention (although that is not always the case in practice since patentees often try to minimize what they disclose in their patent applications). A patent document thus represents value to prospective imitators, at least when the patent expires. In addition, patent information is also of value, and even more so, to inventors and firms performing related R&D, because it assists in their technical decision-making. Patent information also adds value to economic decision-making among a variety of other agents, for example, policy-makers. Thus, patent information may be helpful, for example, in avoiding some overinvestment of R&D in a particular field, pointing out technological trends, assisting in division and coordination of inventive labour, finding collaborators and so on. But some patent information may also have detrimental effects *per se*, besides the inherent distortive effects (such as monopolistic abuses, see Chapter 3) of patent rights themselves.

This chapter will describe how patent information is used and can be used. Since this topic is rich and rapidly expanding, this presentation cannot be comprehensive. Therefore, this chapter is intended to serve as a textbook introduction in much the same way as Chapter 3 did on patent rights.

9.2   PATENT ANALYSIS IN GENERAL

9.2.1   Sources of Technical Information

Research methodology in economics and management has come a long way since Adam Smith and Frederick Taylor, and there is no reason to believe that this evolution will cease. New methods for collecting, analysing and presenting data and information are being developed. Computers and telecommunications will expand the availability of empirical information and its amenability to analysis. Large amounts of information are already collected or are collectable about patents, publications, personnel (human capital), products and pecuniary flows, pertaining to companies, R&D, products, production, trade and so on. Some of these data sources have only recently begun to be exploited on a significant scale in economics and management aided by computers and statistical methods.[1] For a sample of studies using patent and/or publication data, see Archibugi and Pianta (1992), Boitani and Cicotti (1990), Brockhoff (1992), Cantwell (1995), Carpenter and Narin (1993), Chakrabarti (1989), Chakrabarti and Halperin (1990), Comanor and Scherer (1969), Eaton and Kortum (1996), Ehrnberg (1996), Faust (1990), Glismann and Horn (1988), Granstrand et al. (1997), Griliches (1984), Grupp (1994), Jaffe (1989), Jaffe et al. (1993), Malerba and Orsenigo (1995, 1996), Miyazaki (1995), Mogee (1991), Narin and Noma (1985), Narin et al. (1987, 1992), Pavitt (1985), Soete and Wyatt (1983) and Trajtenberg (1990).[2] For the use of detailed product line statistics see Scherer and Ross (1990, Ch. 17), and for the use of detailed educational statistics see Jacobsson and Oskarsson (1995) and Jacobsson et al. (1996). Some data sources have been underexploited, for example, the technical data about products and processes available in patents and publications as mentioned earlier. Some data sources are clearly deficient but they have been improving over time and are increasingly becoming internationally harmonized, for example, the data about R&D and technology trade (licensing in/out) as collected according to OECD standards. At the same time, several data types commonly used in economics, such as traditional industry and trade statistics, are increasingly losing their validity due to rapid technological changes and the diversification and internationalization of companies across industrial and national borders.

Turning specifically to direct sources of technical information and knowledge, one may distinguish between four types of what can be called *technical information carriers*:[3]

1. Patents.
2. Publications (that is, S&T publications).
3. People (that is, S&T professionals).
4. Products/processes (S&T artefacts).

These technical information carriers could be used as indicators of technology-related resources and activities. However, the four types of technical information carriers have some similarities and dissimilarities, as well as relative advantages and disadvantages as indicators or detectors for different purposes (see Table 9.1). Needless to say, there are complementary sources of information, such as R&D, innovation, market and firm statistics.

In this context patent information, despite its many and well-recognized inadequacies, stands out as a unique source of technical information. More than any other source, it is collected, screened and published according to internationally agreed standards. It continually provides an assessment of the state of the art together with at least a rudimentary measure or metric of technological change. It thereby enables a transparent accumulation of knowledge on a global scale.

The inadequacies of patent information emanate from variations in companies' propensity to patent, classification errors, international differences in patent systems, patent office behaviour and so on. In addition, reading as well as writing patent documents may be tedious and boring for the non-specialist. The latter point may be tackled by management through efforts in building a patent culture. (See Chapter 8 and the way top management in Canon has encouraged the reading of patent documents. See also Yamaji 1997.) Education and training in this respect is important. Moreover, company guidelines for reporting R&D results in internal publication series could facilitate the adaptation of R&D reports to patent applications.[4] In addition, presentational techniques could often improve.

Patent information also serves many purposes and user groups, which calls for the need to customize it for the appropriate audience. Patent-oriented indicators for benchmarking raise the interest among business managers. Patent maps (see below) produced according to some internal standards are useful for various R&D decision-makers and business managers, while drawings and other details in patent applications are useful for R&D and design people.

However valuable in itself patent information may be, it could, and mostly should as well, be fruitfully combined with information from other data sources including publications, seminars, informal contacts and so on. There are various

Table 9.1 Comparison of technical information carriers

Type of carrier	General nature	Universal classifications of technology areas	Metric of technology[1]	Citation information[2] available	Pros[3]	Cons[3]
1. Patents	Disembodied[4] Public	IPC USPC[5]	Simple accept/ reject standard[6]	Yes	Length (time span), breadth (range of technology areas), depth (amount of detail) of coverage Quality control Easy access Standardized Codified	Biased coverage Delayed Misclassifications (e.g. in new areas) Variability
2. Publications[7]	Disembodied Partly public	LC UDK INSPEC etc.	No common standard	Yes, as a rule	Length, breadth, depth of coverage Partial quality control Partly accessible Codified	Biased coverage and content Delayed
3. Professionals	Embodied Private	Educational categories	Several levels and grades, partly standardized	No[8]	Depth Timeliness Accessible Creative	Subjective bias Proprietary Partly tacit
4. Products	Embodied Partly public	No common one[9]	Physical performance metric but not directly for information[10]	No[8]	Enables reverse engineering Objective Partly codified Precise measures of performance	Costly to access before market introduction

Notes

1. That is, measure of the size of an advancement in technical knowledge.
2. Or genealogical or longitudinal information, that is, information about relations to previously appearing technology carriers in the category. Latitudinal information in the classification system (that is, information about related classes in the form of multiple classifications) is sometimes available (for example, for patents).
3. The assessments of pros and cons are indicated only briefly here. For more details see, for example, Archibugi (1992), Griliches (1990) and Pavitt (1985).
4. 'Disembodied' means that the physical nature of the carrier is not relevant (for example, paper, electronic storage) and that the information is completely codified and retrievable. Part of a professional's knowledge is tacit and products may not be fully possible to reverse-engineer.
5. Many users consider the US patent classification system more technology-oriented than the IPC system.
6. It should be noted that variations in practice in this standard might be substantial as the minimum level of invention required is difficult to specify in advance once and for all. In addition, different patent offices apply different standards. The standards may also vary over time, across technologies and also among patent examiners. The final validity of a patent is moreover decided in court if challenged. Finally, a patent granted to an invention only indicates that the invention meets the patenting criteria but is not a measure of how well these criteria have been met.
7. Including all storage forms on physical substrates (papers, CD-ROM and so on). Patent publications are excluded since they are treated separately.
8. Genealogies could be constructed but are not readily available.
9. Industry classifications (for example, ISIC) could be used as proxies. Note that the concordance between product classes and patent classes is far from one to one (see, for example, Scherer 1982, who also suggests patent offices should provide industry codes as well).
10. Indicators of hi-tech versus lo-tech (or hi/med/lo-tech) products exist, loosely referring to the amount of technical information in a product. The term 'technometrics' refers to the measuring of technical performance in physical terms.

293

complementary benefits to be reaped when combining patent information with other types of information, depending in turn on the purpose of the analysis, of course. This must be kept in mind when reading the following sections, which primarily deal with patent information.

9.2.2   Application Areas of Patent Analysis

It is important to delineate what patent information actually comprises. There are several primary sources of patent information.

1. *Patent documents*   The main component of patent information is that provided in written form in the publicly available documents that have formed the basis for the decision to grant a patent to the patent holder. The patent document contains various items, such as application and issue date, name and location of inventors and assignee, title, abstract, claims, description, patent classification, references to other patents, and priority information.[5]
2. *Auxiliary documents*   There are various auxiliary documents and information items produced during the patent application processing procedures, most of which are publicly accessible.[6] The content and nature of these information items vary a great deal from case to case, since they derive from varying, less standardized procedures such as state-of-the-art search reports, opposition and invalidation claims, appeals and so on.
3. *Proprietary information*   There is proprietary information related to a patent application both on the patent applicant side (that is, the related R&D information) and among third parties, for example, companies opposing a patent application or attempting to invalidate a patent.
4. *Licensing information*   There is information about licensing of patent rights; information that is usually proprietary and seldom disclosed by the parties involved.
5. *Maintenance information*   There is information about the maintenance of patent rights including when these rights were dropped by patentees due to non-payment of the maintenance fees to the patent office.

All these different types and sources of patent information then provide selected inputs to various public and private patent data bases, mostly computerized and mostly obtainable at a cost (which can be substantial).[7]

Thus patent information is a multifaceted concept. Below, we shall use it in the narrow sense of the standard patent information basically provided by the patent application documents. Such aggregated patent information can in general be used as both technological and economic indicators. More specifically, patent information can be used to indicate:

1. Company's and competitor's technological profile, strength and positions in various technologies and markets as indicated by patent profile, volume, shares, breadth, maturity, patent portfolio composition, citations and so on.[8] This is useful for company benchmarking as well as for identifying strategic groups of companies with similar patent strategies or new entrants or technological actors in general.

2. Technological conditions and changes in general such as technological trends, fluctuations, distances, convergence, genericness, interdependencies, family (cluster, system, bloc) formation, entries, exits, transitions, concentration, maturity, ageing of technology base, diminishing returns, spill-overs, linkages to other technologies and sciences and so on, as well as more specific technological conditions such as fertile R&D directions, likely strategic patent positions, infringement risks, shifts from product to process R&D, and revival of old technical ideas.

3. R&D growth, productivity, fluctuations, and concentration of inventive activities as indicated by patent counts, patents per R&D dollar or per employee, citations and so on.

4. Suitable targets for technology acquisition through company acquisitions, mergers, joint ventures, R&D cooperation, licensing, hire-overs of key inventors and so on.

5. R&D and technology investment strategies.

6. International marketing strategies.

7. Valuation of a company's technology assets.

8. Opportunities for cross-licensing.

9. Technological strength, positions and actors of countries or regions, for aiding, for example, actor identification or locational decisions regarding R&D and/or production.[9]

10. Fluctuations related to business cycles, investments, economic growth and aggregate S&T growth as well as patent office resources.[10]

11. History of technology and economic history.

Table 9.2 gives a more detailed overview of the useful patent information items for some of the more important applications above. The use in regular R&D work of the technical information given in the patent claims and the invention description in general should finally be recognized as the major application of patent information (item 6 in Table 9.2).[11] Some (fairly simple) illustrations of benchmarking using patent information are also presented in Appendix 2.

9.2.3 Some Caveats when Using Patent Statistics

It is tempting to use patent statistics for a number of purposes. Especially since patent statistics have been made available electronically, the propensity to use

Table 9.2   Patent information for technology and competitor analysis

Analysis application	Useful patent information items
1. Analysis of competitors' technology (benchmarking)	Patent class codes (main and side class code) and year of application for competitors give their patenting profile, patent positions (patent application shares), R&D directions and entry/exit pattern in different technologies
2. Technology breakthroughs, shifts, trends and forecasting	Patent counts over time in different patent classes for absolute and relative growth trends. Multiple classifications for, e.g., technology fusion and technology diversification. Patent citation data for weighing technological importance and age of technology base
3. International market analysis	Patent country codes and country coverage of patent families of competitors
4. Valuation of technology assets[1]	Patent volume and patent shares, patent citations, patent renewal fees, patent vintage structure
5. Tracking and monitoring of key inventors/actors	Inventor/actor name, assignees, invention history, patent class codes, citations
6. Navigation, monitoring possibilities for inventions and infringements in regular R&D work, including creation of new ideas and inventions or invention principles[2]	Patent claims and invention description

Notes
1. The highly skewed distribution of patent values presents a large difficulty in valuing a patent portfolio. Various other indicators and approaches must complement patent information, such as data on stock market responses to patent related news, panel data or questionnaire data. For surveys of this application, see Pakes and Simpson (1989), Schankerman (1989), Griliches et al. (1988), Griliches (1990), Trajtenberg (1990) and Scherer (1998).
2. This is the traditional application of patent information. For illuminating historical accounts of how skilful inventors have traditionally used patent information, see Hughes (1971) and Cooper (1991).

them for indicative purposes has increased. It is likely that this use of patenting information will grow and new indicators, methods, data bases and services will come into use, based on patent statistics combined with other types of statistics, as mentioned above. It is, then, important to recognize general caveats, sources of errors and factors to consider, both when using and producing patent statistics. A list of such factors to consider would include:

1. Purpose of analysis (for example, benchmarking).
2. Company consolidation (so that, for example, patent counts and R&D statistics refer to the same company entity).
3. Quality of patents (type of patent in terms of level of invention, blocking power, profitability and other technical, economic and legal qualities and so on).[12]
4. Technological coverage (number and scope of claims).
5. Market coverage (applications and countries covered by patents for an invention).
6. Multiple classifications, reclassifications and creation of new patent classes in the patent classification systems.
7. Reassignments of patents (for example, among patent classes or company assignees).
8. Varying classification and citation behaviour and errors at the patent examination side.
9. Whether patent counts refer to patent applications, patents granted, patents in force, priority patents or patent families.
10. Whether patent counts refer to national patents, PCT patents and/or EPO patents.
11. Grounds for nationality assignments of inventors and assignees.
12. Fluctuations of patent counts over time, company, country and classes.
13. Competitor and inventor IPR strategies (for example, decoy patenting, flooding or avoidance of certain types of patenting).
14. Links between R&D activities and patenting (for example, time lags).
15. Links of patent classes with publication areas, product areas and industrial sectors (such matches are difficult and so-called concordance lists are often unreliable).
16. Differing patent systems and legal environments among countries.

This listing is long but not exhaustive. Thus caution must be exercised when using and producing patent statistics, and any conclusive results must be fairly robust, and hopefully corroborated in other ways as well.

9.3 GENERAL TECHNO-ECONOMIC ANALYSIS

Mappings for managerial use are dominated by simple two- or three-dimensional graphs and matrices.[13] A general class of such mappings is what can be called techno-economic mappings over time, or *T/E/t*-mappings. These mappings relate the behaviour of some technology-related variable *T* to the behaviour of

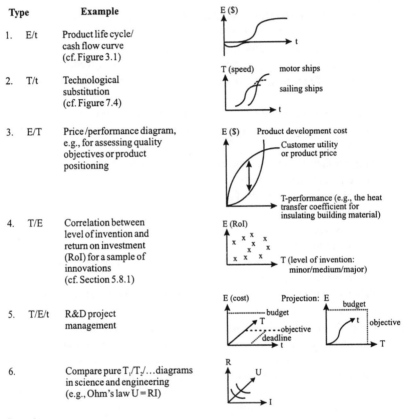

Type		Example
1.	E/t	Product life cycle/ cash flow curve (cf. Figure 3.1)
2.	T/t	Technological substitution (cf. Figure 7.4)
3.	E/T	Price/performance diagram, e.g., for assessing quality objectives or product positioning
4.	T/E	Correlation between level of invention and return on investment (RoI) for a sample of innovations (cf. Section 5.8.1)
5.	T/E/t	R&D project management
6.		Compare pure $T_1/T_2/\ldots$ diagrams in science and engineering (e.g., Ohm's law $U = RI$)

Legend:
T = technology-related variable, usually related to physically measurable variables, describing design characteristics or technical performance of some sort (real or expected).

E = economic variable, usually related to values or monetary flows (real or expected).

t = time.

Note: Several *E*- and especially *T*-variables may be needed. It may be difficult to quantify the variables on higher-order scales (that is, to use metric and normed scales rather than only nominal and ordered scales). However, a conceptual analysis is always possible.

Figure 9.1 Examples of techno-economic mappings

some economic variable E over time t. Typically T is a physically measurable attribute or technical variable (or vector), while E typically is a monetary or value-related variable (or vector). Sometimes a compound T–E variable, for example a productivity measure, is used as well. Figure 9.1 shows some examples of common $T/E/t$-mappings.

There is often a need to go beyond such common $T/E/t$-mappings and try to map out technologies, seen as the 'soft' competence parts, and link them to 'hard' (that is, physically measurable) technical dimensions and then ultimately link them to economically-oriented dimensions. Various sources of technical information as described above, can be used for this additional category of technology mappings.

Figure 9.2 shows a general framework for doing such an extended techno-economic analysis at business and company levels. Briefly, the framework at business level consists of constructing a series or family of mappings (which may be partial and qualitative) among the following sets of elements:

Mapping elements

- Technologies in the technology base of the business (see Chapter 4).
- Technical design and performance variables of the product, services and production processes.
- Customer (or user) utilities and producer costs.
- Applications (that is, usage systems with different physical interaction with the product; see Chapter 6).
- Market segments (that is, clusters of buyers with similar purchasing behaviour).
- Strategic groups (that is, clusters of sellers with similar strategic behaviour).
- Market penetration or diffusion processes among buyers and sellers of the product (being influenced, for example, by commercialization strategies; see Chapters 3 and 6).
- Economic outcomes (growth, profits, market shares and so on).
- Investments in R&D and new technologies, production equipment, marketing and so on.

Technology base   For a company with several business areas, their technology bases may overlap (as may their entire resource bases). The linkages across business areas and between the technology bases and the business characteristics must then also be mapped out (for example, for reaping economies of scale and scope in diversification; see also Chapter 4). One central feature of this approach to techno-economic analysis is the notion of a technology base (or technical competence base) of a product and of a company. The technology base of a

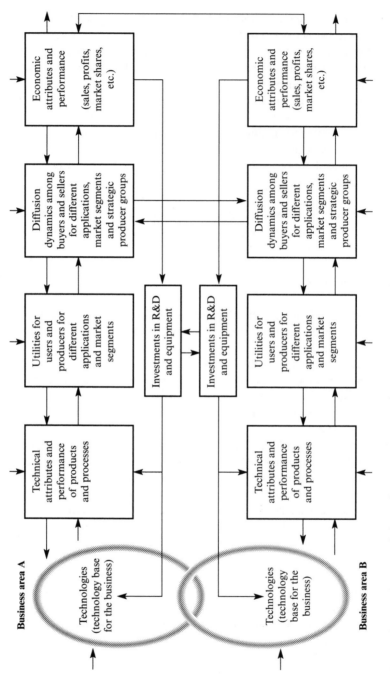

Business area A

Business area B

Figure 9.2   A framework for techno-economic analysis at company level (with two business areas)

product and of a company consists of those technologies and sub-technologies that are related to the product and the company respectively. The technology base can be built up in various ways through investments in R&D and new technologies (see Chapters 4 and 7). The technology base can also be exploited in various ways through investments in complementary assets, joint ventures, licensing out and so on (see Chapter 6). If relations between the technologies in the technology base are considered as well, we can also talk about the technology system of a business or a company. Patent information, then, is useful for mapping out a technology base or a technology system.

Technology versus technical performance Another central feature of this framework is the mapping between 'soft' technology and 'hard' technical performance and functionality.[14] Different sets of technologies typically allow for different attainable levels of performance. Technology is defined, as elsewhere in this book, as a body of knowledge about industrial techniques, which are patentable in principle.[15] However, the term 'technology' is sometimes used to denote an *area* of possible knowledge as well, in contrast to the body or content of knowledge *per se* that can be classified as belonging to the area. This can give rise to misunderstandings, for example, a patent class constitutes a technological area (at the corresponding level of classification) while a patent that falls into the patent class is part of the technology or body of knowledge in that area.[16] Thus, we have to distinguish between *technology* and *technological area*, just as bodies versus areas of competencies in general have to be distinguished in many cases. The matter is further complicated by the fact that knowledge is not easily classified and the definition of different classes depends on the knowledge at hand. Thus, it may be necessary to use multiple classifications as well as to redefine existing classes and add new classes as new knowledge emerges.

Techno-economic links A third feature of the framework is the mapping that explicitly links (technology-related) technical variables with economic variables. There are two such mappings at the product business level: one that links technical performance to customer utilities and producer costs, and one that links economic variables to technical ones through investments in new technologies and equipment.

Technology diffusion A fourth feature is the analysis of diffusion of new products among buyers and the diffusion of their production technologies among sellers (see Chapter 3). To trace technology diffusion among sellers, patent information can be used to indicate entries and exits of different firms in different technological areas. Also, the diffusion of a generic technology into various application areas can be mapped using patent information.

We shall confine ourselves for now to those mappings that especially deal with technologies, that is, technology mappings for which patent mappings are useful. These will be illustrated in the next section.

9.4   PATENT MAPPING IN JAPAN[17]

9.4.1   General Description

As mentioned in Chapters 5 and 8, special methods, subsumed under the label 'patent mapping', have been developed in Japan in the post-war period. Various methods of analysing patent information have been developed in the West as well. To some extent the methods are similar, as they draw on the same type of information and use similar approaches. However, the degree to which such methods are systematically developed and employed on a broad scale appears to be much higher in Japan. In many Western firms the activities geared towards analysing patent information are fairly straightforward and often consist simply of watching new patents in some narrowly defined set of patent classes that are traditionally thought to be of persistent relevance to the firm. Copies of the front pages of relevant patents are then regularly distributed among R&D personnel, who are encouraged to seek further information from the central patent department when the need arises.

Activities of this sort might sometimes be sufficient in small firms with a narrow product range and keen patent engineers and patent attorneys. More often, though, a rudimentary level of patent analysis results from inadequate resources – perhaps only a part-time engineer and a secretary are employed. Sufficient or not, this type of patent analysis could rather be called 'patent watching' in contrast to 'patent mapping'. Below, patent mapping will be briefly described together with some examples. However, the exposition is introductory and is not intended to be anything like a handbook or manual.

Patent maps are produced for different purposes (see below), using different pieces of patent information which are refined, analysed, interpreted and represented in various ways. Usually patent maps take the form of two- or three-dimensional diagrams, graphs (for example, networks), tables or matrices. The common dimensions (or variables) in patent maps are as follows:

1. Time.
2. Patent class, sub-class and so on (equated with technology, sub-technology and so on).
3. Function and sub-function.
4. Application and sub-application.
5. Product and sub-products.
6. Actors (for example, inventors, firms, nations).
7. Industry class or characteristic.
8. R&D resources.

Categories such as patents, technologies, functions, applications and products are all possible to distinguish at various levels in a larger classification system, which could be universal or tailored for a specific situation. For categories such as these, scales are constructed, showing, for example:

1. Number of patents granted or patent applications.
2. Number of products.
3. Number of patent applicants (assignees, firms, inventors).

Numbers like these may be calculated as annual or cumulative (over some time period) and are in general used as a measure of relevance or weight of some sort, pertaining to levels or changes in levels of the scale. Based on numbers like these, patent profiles may be constructed for products, technologies, inventors, companies, nations, industries, regions and so on.

The graphs, networks and matrices are then obtained by combining the dimensions, for example, into:

1. Patent class by patent class network, with relations based on side classifications or citations or linkage to a common product, function, application, inventor, firm or other patent (see example below).
2. Technology-by-product matrix with patent linkages.
3. Technology-by-industry matrix with patent-based relevance measure.
4. Product-by-product matrix with patent linkages.
5. Split drawings with sets of relevant patent classes, indicating the technology bases of the components (sub-products).

9.4.2   History of Patent Mapping in Japan

Patent mapping was originally developed at the JPO in the 1960s for the purpose of facilitating the patent examination process. The first patent map in Japan was published by the JPO in 1968 (see Figure 9.3).

The first patent map showed the extension of an air micrometer measuring technology into various product functions, features and design principles and into various application areas. The map also showed how the extensions into functions on the one hand, and applications on the other, are linked through the flow of patents over time.

Gradually, the main locus of developments as well as applications of the patent-mapping methodology shifted over to industry, especially to the large technology-based corporations. At the same time the range of purposes and specialized methods broadened. Altogether, patent mapping has developed into a useful tool not only for IP management and technology management at large but also for R&D work. Thus patent mapping could be considered an innovation, and as such

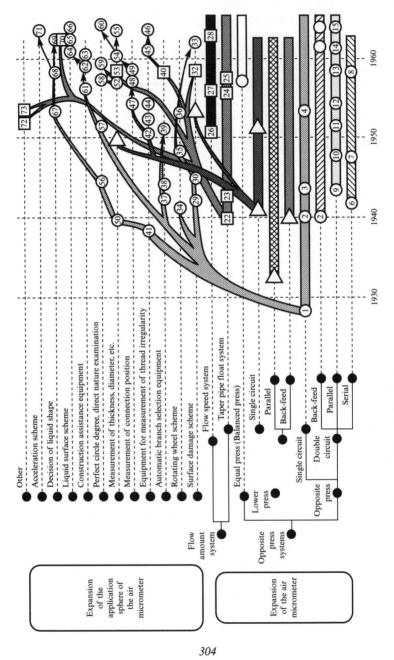

Figure 9.3   First patent map (published by JPO)

comparable to innovations like project-planning methodology (PERT, CPM (critical path method) and so on) and technological forecasting methods. In addition, patent-mapping methodology has a large potential for being developed further, for example, together with other methods and indicators for technology analysis and technology management. It should also be kept in mind that benefits from the use of patent information is in line with the intentions of the patent system from society's point of view (see Chapter 3). However, since the costs and benefits of developing special methods for analysing patent information may be great, developers may be induced to keep them partly secret in turn. It is also becoming increasingly difficult to make effective use of patent information because of the large and growing amount of such information, the ever-changing focus of R&D throughout a broad range of technologies and a shortage of adequately trained experts, a shortage that is felt also in Japan.[18]

9.4.3 Purposes

There may be many purposes and applications for patent mapping. Seven purposes will be outlined below. It should also be kept in mind that patent mapping is but one tool for techno-economic analysis as described earlier. Complementary information, for example about business directions, is generally needed, particularly when combining patent maps with market analysis.

Creative tool
An important purpose of patent mapping is to assist in the creation of new ideas. In fact, through regular patent-mapping activities, the IP department and patent mappers, wherever they are located in the organization, may become an essential source of inventive contributions. Thus through patent mapping the IP department may adopt a much wider role in the R&D organization than is usually recognized, at least in the West (see also Chapter 8).

Intelligence tool
A second purpose is to aid in technology analysis and business intelligence activities. This is comprised of identifying technology trends, company (competition) trends and market trends. New patentors (firms) with new technologies may be discovered and possibly targeted for surveillance concerning licensing, acquisition or cooperation, as well as concerning highly productive outside inventors for possible hire-overs.

Patent maps may also be used to identify the structure of technology systems and relations among different technologies. The maps also show how much information is revealed to competitors by one's own patenting activities. This may in turn guide those companies who engage in decoy patenting, that is, patenting with an intention to misguide the technology intelligence activities directed towards the firm by its competitors. The actual extent of decoy patenting in practice is difficult to assess, of course, but appears to be very marginal. However, 'blanketing' and 'continuous' patenting strategies (see Chapter 7) may in effect decrease the possibilities for competitors to detect patterns in patent maps.

Management tool

A third purpose of patent mapping is to aid technology and R&D management in assessing the productivity and quality of the in-house R&D function, as well as of other technology-related functions, for example, production and decentralized engineering, such as application engineering in subsidiaries.

Bargaining tool

A fourth purpose of patent mapping is to assist in negotiations. A good patent map is a useful indicator of the technological and legal strengths and weaknesses of one's own firm and of its competitor or partner, and as such becomes a useful bargaining tool, especially if the competitor does not have similar information. Each party most likely has a patent map, possibly confidential and possibly differing in quality but nevertheless a map, which may be valuable in negotiating a licence, settling disputes, avoiding court, lowering royalties and so on. But patent maps may also be helpful in finding and negotiating with partners for R&D cooperation, cross-licensing or for any type of technology acquisition and exploitation (see Chapter 6).

Litigation tool

A fifth use of patent mapping is in litigation and court situations, where it can be used to facilitate the process and influence all persons involved – outside lawyers, the defendant, judges, consultants and so on. Thus a patent map may become a tool for litigation.

Communication tool

Certain patent maps are useful as a general communication tool, not least in explaining technology, product and competition matters to business and corporate management. Simple benchmarking, as presented in Appendix 1, is also very effective in getting management attention.

Educational tool

Patent mapping is useful in educating not only patent staff but engineers and technology managers in general, as well as the company's intelligence people and legal personnel. Patent mapping is a concrete method that operates with fairly precise information in order to illustrate various issues critical to technology analysis. Moreover, patent mapping illustrates technological developments, linking them to competition and commercial aspects as well as various issues in techno-economic analysis.

9.4.4 Examples

Some illustrative patent maps are shown below.[19] A patent network map is shown in Figure 9.4, a patent-by-country map in Figure 9.5, a patent-by-technology map in Figure 9.6, a patent-to-product map in Figure 9.7 and finally a patent-to-product matrix in Table 9.3. Note that Table 9.3 links inventions or technologies to different technical characteristics of the product, some of which are directly affecting customer utilities and manufacturing cost. However, it is outside the scope here to draw any inferences from the examples. Needless to say, there are numerous other types and variants of patent maps, depending upon the purpose. Finally, Figure 9.8 shows how Toshiba performs patent reviews in every step of the innovation process, and how patent mapping feeds into this review process, and Figure 9.9 shows the patent information system at Hitachi.

9.5 SUMMARY AND CONCLUSIONS

The stock of publicly available patent information in the world is in fact a tremendous and unique source of technical knowledge. For various reasons (such as lack of time, costs, varying information quality, ignorance), this source of information has traditionally been underutilized, but the ongoing computerization of the patent system rapidly offers increasing possibilities to tap this valuable resource. The costly and tedious act of digging into patent archives and the subsequent distribution of patent documents are gradually being replaced by computerized patent databases, data mining and information processing, thereby drastically improving both the costs and benefits for companies using patent information. At the same time, patenting propensities have increased and become more consistent, increasing both the quantity and quality of patent information. However, the set of basic information items for a given patent has changed very little.

The present study as well as other studies show how companies have increased their use of patent information and consider such information to be one of the most important means for technology and competitive intelligence. It is significant that most companies have not considered the avoidance of patenting worthwhile in preventing other companies from finding out about their own technical developments. This is an indication that patenting may provide net benefits to industry as a whole (that is, patenting could be considered a positive sum game in this respect).

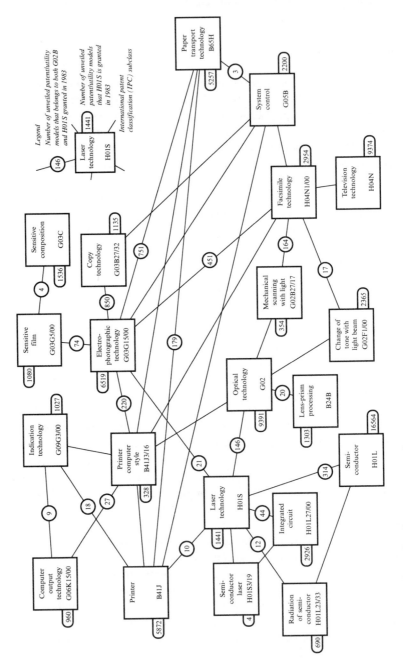

Figure 9.4 Example of patent network map

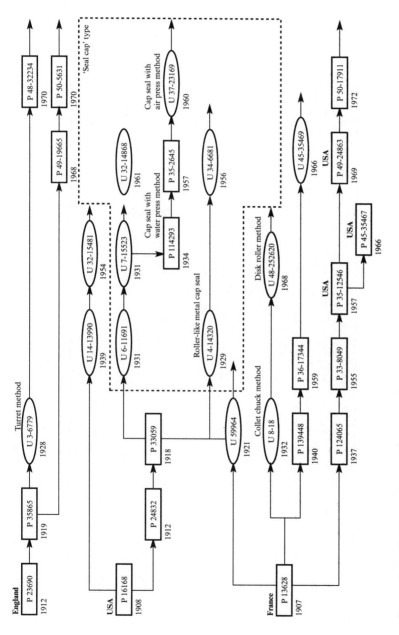

Figure 9.5   Example of patent-by-country map

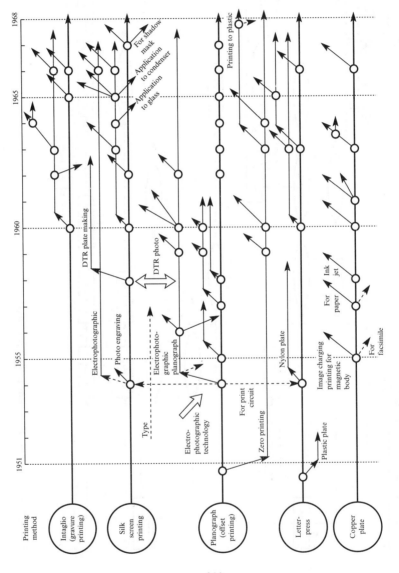

Figure 9.6 *Example of patent-by-technology map*

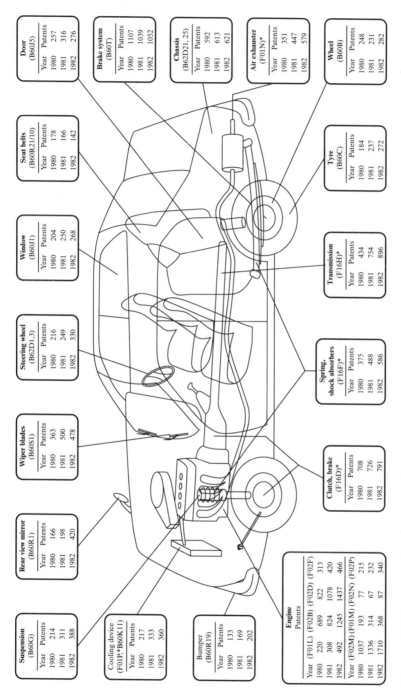

Figure 9.7 Example of patent-to-product map

Table 9.3   Example of invention-to-product matrix

Date of application / No. of notification	Name of invention / Applicant	Core: Quartz and double quartz glass	Core: Glass with other ingredients	Core: Others	Clad: Quartz and double quartz glass	Clad: Glass with other ingredients	Clad: Others	Flame oxidation method	Method with two melting pots	Layer fusion method	with indication powder	Ion exchange method	Pull-out method	Fibre bundle formation roll method	Dope material and dope method	Flood pattern	Distribution pattern	Multiple layer pattern	Others
62.5.25 48-30125	Glass formation technique *Owens-Corning (?) Fibre Glass Corporation*	•							•										
38.6.22 48-30126									•								•		
63.2.14 48-31734	??									•									
44.5.7 48-37696	??																	•	
44.9.25 48-37731	??		•									•						•	
44.3.22 48-37852	Method for manufacturing plastic fibre optics plate *Fuji Photo Film*																		•
44.7.28 48-37854	*Matsushita*																		
44.9.25 48-28267	??		•													•		•	
44.12.23 48-38268	??																		
69.3.28 48-38269	??																		
69.6.9 48-33291	??														•		•		
41.4.14 49-212	??													•					
69.1.24 49-904	*Western Electric*																		
42.1.19 49-4344	Optical thin film *Olympus Optical Co. Ltd*	•			•													•	

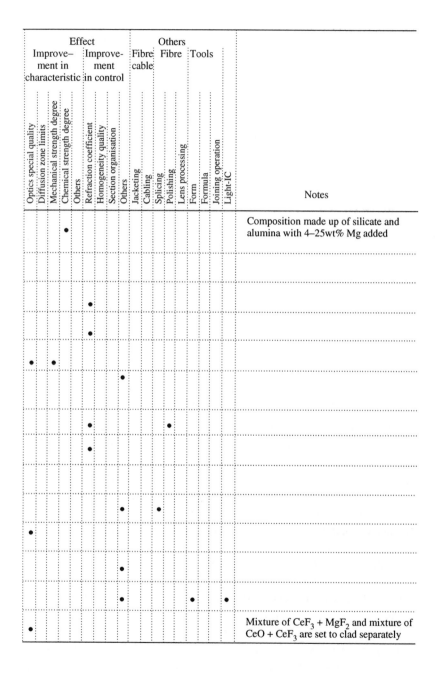

Optics special quality	Diffusion zone limits	Mechanical strength degree	Chemical strength degree	Others	Refraction coefficient	Homogeneity quality	Section organisation	Others	Jacketing	Cabling	Splicing	Polishing	Lens processing	Form	Formula	Joining operation	Light-IC	Notes
			•															Composition made up of silicate and alumina with 4–25wt% Mg added
					•													
					•													
•		•																
							•											
					•							•						
					•													
							•					•						
•																		
							•											
							•							•			•	
•																		Mixture of $CeF_3 + MgF_2$ and mixture of $CeO + CeF_3$ are set to clad separately

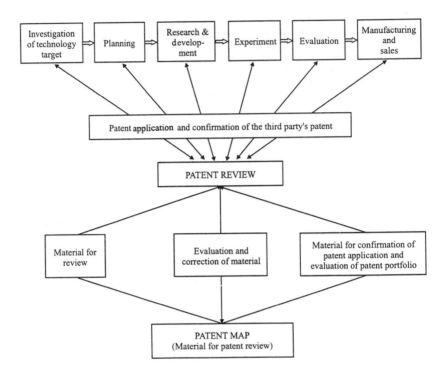

Source: Document provided by Toshiba.

Figure 9.8   Patent review structure in Toshiba

The literature on the use of patent information as technology indicators and/or economic indicators has grown rapidly as well, and this chapter gives a number of references. Patents were also compared with other technical information carriers, such as publications. Several application areas of patent analysis were described, such as competitor benchmarking, technology analysis, international patenting analysis, valuation of technology assets and tracking of key inventors, together with a number of caveats. Patent analysis was then put into the general context of a framework for techno-economic analysis, which could be used to integrate various applications of patent analysis.

From this general description, the chapter then described the nature and origin of the so-called patent mapping methodology developed in Japan. Broadly speaking, patent mapping mainly uses patent information as technology indicators. This methodology originated in the Japan Patent Office in the 1960s and has since been adopted and developed further in industry and in the leading large corporations in particular. Patent maps have a variety of applications, for

PATENT INFORMATION CONTROL SYSTEM

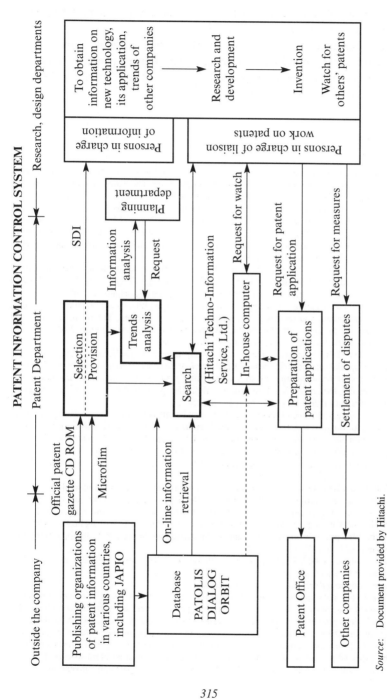

Source: Document provided by Hitachi.

Figure 9.9 Hitachi's patent information control system

example as a tool for creativity, intelligence, technology management, bargaining, litigation, communication and education.

The chapter finally gave a number of fairly simple illustrations of patent maps, including a patent network map, a patent-by-country map, a patent-by-technology map and a patent-to-product map, and illustrations of how Toshiba and Hitachi have organized patent information analysis.

NOTES

1. Consultancy firms (such as Derwent and CHI) as well as patent offices have long since offered various patent information services and databases. There are numerous (hundreds or thousands) of databases with World Patent Index and Inpadoc being two traditionally important examples. *World Patent Information* is a central journal in this area.
2. For significant early works using patent statistics, see Tisell (1907, 1910) – regarded as pioneering by Merton (1938, p. 469) and Schmookler (1950, p. 123) – Griliches (1964), Schmookler (1966) and Scherer (1959). For good surveys of such studies, see Archibugi (1992), Basberg (1987) and Griliches (1990).
3. A *technical information carrier* (or a technology carrier) is meant as an entity that carries technical information or knowledge, that is, technology. Technology in products and professionals is sometimes called embodied technology, while patents and publications carry disembodied technology. Some people, moreover, distinguish between technical knowledge, being embodied, and technical information, being disembodied. The distinction between tacit knowledge and codified knowledge has also become common. Disembodied knowledge is then codified, but the converse is not necessarily true.
4. The patent claims in a patent application are usually difficult to write because of the legal aspects and the special language often required, and therefore also not easy to read, but the specifications in the patent documentation are similar in writing to any other technical documentation.
5. For details, the reader is referred to actual patent application forms (which vary across countries, although with many common elements).
6. Getting access to some of these documents may be difficult, however, for example, getting access to so-called interference case records in the USA for assessing who has priority to an invention under the 'first-to-invent' rule in the USA. (See, for example, Kingston 1995, who proposes using interference procedures as a model for resolving IPR disputes.)
7. There are several public and commercial database services, provided by Derwent, JAPIO, Inpadoc, Lexis, Westlaw and so on.
8. These concepts are made precise and operationalized in various ways in applications. For examples, see Narin et al. (1984) and Battelle (1985) for early works and various other works. See, for example, Narin at al. (1992), Brockhoff (1992) and Mogee (1993) for applications at company level, which is of primary importance here. For applications primarily at the S&T policy level, see, for example, Archibugi and Pianta (1992), Grupp (1991), Van Raan (1988) and Sigurdson (1990).
9. For example, in the USA, the Bay Area with Silicon Valley ranked highest in the mid-1990s in terms of patents per capita.
10. See Griliches (1990) for an excellent overview.
11. This traditional application can witness new developments as patent information becomes computerized and can be subjected to various types of content analysis. The potential in this area is illustrated by the scheme developed by the Russian patent engineer G. Altschuller who claims that there are a number of principles of invention that could be detected by analysing patent information. Certainly expert systems based on computerized patent information could be expected to become widespread, valuable tools in technical problem-solving. It is even conceivable that a computer would be able to generate a new patentable invention.

12. The technical and economic qualities of patents are typically very skewly distributed. See, for example, Scherer (1998) on the skew distribution of profits from different patents.
13. This is partly due to presentational reasons, partly due to need for simplicity. The latter is often overplayed by various consultants, who appear to assume that modern professional managers suffer cognitive limits (rather than time limits). A severe shortcoming of the low dimensionality of mappings for managerial use is that the time dimension is often neglected, thereby inviting only a static analysis.
14. Function, functionality and set of dimensions of a technical performance variable or parameter are taken as roughly synonymous concepts here.
15. Technology, technical knowledge and technical competence are also taken as synonymous here, although one may, when needed, distinguish between knowledge and skills and let the concept of competence encompass both knowledge and skills.
16. Similarly, a publication class in some library classification has to be distinguished from a specific publication belonging to that class.
17. Helpful discussion with and comments from A. Mifune, K. Norichika and Y. Tanaka on this topic are gratefully acknowledged, as is the material from the JPO and translation work by M. Magnusson and T. Ide.
18. Hence, it could be argued that patent offices or some other public agencies should take part in developing and disseminating such methods.
19. By courtesy of the JPO.

10. Intellectual capitalism and beyond

CHAPTER CONTENTS

10.1 CHAPTER OUTLINE

This chapter will attempt to synthesize and discuss the findings in the preceding chapters as well as to elaborate further on the theme of intellectual capitalism as introduced in Chapter 1. After a brief summary of the preceding chapters, their implications will be pursued in the context of intellectual capital and intellectual capitalism, which is a phenomenon that has become even more established and pervasive in economic and technical life as of late. The chapter will in particular argue that the co-evolution of technology, TBFs, markets and legal systems will shape the economic system into what can be called intellectual capitalism.

10.2 SUMMARY OF PRECEDING CHAPTERS

Chapter 1 gave a background with some trends of general relevance: (i) growth and accumulation of S&T knowledge becoming increasingly complex, diversified and expensive and controlled by private firms, especially large ones; (ii) relative shifting from material to immaterial sources of economic growth; (iii) strengthening of capitalism as an ideology and deployed economic order; (iv) internationalization and globalization; (v) emergence of a multi-polar world that is politically, economically and managerially increasingly complex; and (vi) emergence on a large scale of new information and communication technologies, that is, infocom technologies or ICTs.

Chapter 1 also described the emergence of a pro-patent era in the USA in the 1980s, and the rising value of IPR and intellectual capital. Japanese large corporations had notably developed patent resources on a broad front.

Chapter 2 showed how various basic IP notions among humans, such as ownership of secrets, fruits of intellectual labour and identity symbols, can be found in primitive societies as well as in ancient cultures and in various religions. These basic IP notions have largely persisted over time. For several centuries, certain countries have designed IPR systems with the prime motive of fostering economic progress in society, thereby creating a new economic institution for IP. These systems have had similar basic features, which have also been surprisingly resilient over time, despite profound changes in industry and R&D over the centuries. Chapter 2 also conveyed the fact that in economic history and the history of technology there are no clear signs that IPR have had a major impact on the whole. Neither have IPR received much attention historically among economists and legal scholars in general. However, absence of the signs of effects need not be a sign of the absence of effects. The long-run trend is that investments grow, technology cumulates and the links between technological changes and economic changes gradually become stronger. The impact of IPR is thus likely to become more apparent sooner or later. The recent emergence of a pro-patent era may be interpreted as one such signal.

Chapter 3 gave an overview of innovation and diffusion processes and the role of patents in these processes. The pros and cons of patents were described from the points of view of inventors, companies and society. Finally, some economic literature and theory of patents and other IPR were surveyed briefly. It was shown how patents, copyrights and trade secrets can be analysed in essentially the same framework, where possibilities to recover R&D investments for a new product are offered through possibilities to raise the operating profit margin and the market share during an initial time period on the market. Trademarks also give opportunities to raise operating profit margin and/or market share, but do not give any time-limited monopolistic powers on factor input markets as do patents.

Chapter 4 puts IPR, as a part of immaterial or intellectual resources, in the context of the firm as a viable capitalistic institution, operating in a nexus of markets: factor markets, product markets, super-markets for corporate control, and sub-markets for internal decentralized control. The nature of the IC-based firm, with the technology-based firm as a particularly important case, was described, especially noting its resource structure and processes for resource acquisition, growth and diversification. The management factor (including the entrepreneurial function) and the business idea, matching resources to market needs, were seen as key intellectual capital elements in any firm.

In Chapter 5, the rise of Japan to an industrial power and her deployment of an IPR system were described. Japan's lack of natural resources has prompted her to make a virtue of necessity by focusing on the build-up of intellectual capital resources, making Japan the first candidate for being an IC-based state. The build-up process has until recently chiefly been a catch-up process, which has given Japan some special problems as well as skills of value for the next stage of innovative development. Skills in managing technology and IPR are important examples of such skills. Chapter 5 also revealed some trends regarding IPR, as assessed by the large Japanese corporations in the sample studied.

The quantity and quality of Japanese patents were then analysed. Various explanations behind the large flow of Japanese patents were discussed. In particular, factors with a long standing in Japanese history were emphasized as explanatory. Such factors include the early recognition of the patent system after the Meiji Restoration and the long catch-up process, which was accompanied by special incentive systems and legislation and an emerging patent culture, especially in recent times. The emergence of a pro-patent era in the USA in the 1980s reinforced the factors contributing to the large volume of Japanese patents. The quality of Japanese patents has also increased and is currently equal or even in several cases superior to Western patents. Thus, there is a parallel between the quality movement in Japanese patenting and the quality movement in Japanese products.

Chapter 6 elaborated upon how new technologies were acquired and commercialized in Japanese corporations through various strategies.

Chapter 7 continued to describe and analyse corporate strategies, but now with a focus on IP strategies, that is, strategies for patenting, secrecy and trademarks. Finally, the concept of multiprotection through the use of IPR in combination was put forward.

Chapter 8 focused upon resources, organization and management of IP activities in the large Japanese corporations. The emergence of IP cultures and comprehensive IP management skills in leading Japanese corporations was described in particular.

Throughout the empirical Chapters 6, 7 and 8, some corporate cases such as Canon, Hitachi and Toshiba were described in more detail. These companies operate in the information and communication technologies (infocom) sector, which is of particular importance to the formation of intellectual capital, as will be discussed below.

Chapter 9 reviewed the use of the other side of the patent coin, that is, the use of patent information in technology and competitive intelligence. Again, large Japanese corporations have developed special skills and methods, and the methodology labelled 'patent mapping' was described and illustrated. Such methods, and other methods for technology analysis, can be expected to develop further as different types of technology-related information are being produced and distributed electronically and become of increasing value as R&D costs and technology investment costs in general become more and more substantial. Appendix 1 further illustrates the use of patent information for corporate benchmarking.

10.3   TOWARDS INTELLECTUAL CAPITALISM

10.3.1   Introduction

Since the downfall of the Soviet type of socialism, there is no doubt that capitalism in one form or another is as strong and globally active as ever. Needless to say, capitalism comes in many varieties and is evolving in various ways. Much has already been written on the diverse types of capitalism seen as emerging in contemporary society, such as 'alliance capitalism', 'corporate capitalism', 'Japanese capitalism', 'shareholder capitalism', 'informational capitalism' and so on (see Castells 1998; Dunning 1988; Gerlach 1992; Johnson 1993; Rosenberg and Birdzell 1986; Thurow 1996; Williamson 1985). In this chapter, we shall elaborate on the notion of intellectual capitalism as a synthesizing theme, linked to the preceding chapters. We shall also argue that intellectual capitalism is evolving in society due to various factors and with more or less unknown consequences, thus requiring intellectual preparation and institutional developments.

The arguments will be presented as follows. After a note on the concept of intellectual capitalism, indicators of the emergence of intellectual capitalism will be presented. The possibilities of a reversal will be discussed and dismissed. Then analysis and reflections will focus on ten levels: the individual, the profession, the company, the industry and the market, as well as on technological, managerial, institutional and international levels. At the international level, harmonization of different national IP regimes will be discussed, albeit briefly. The prospects for a unifying intellectual property paradigm for science, technology and culture – if needed at all – will then be raised, albeit much more briefly than the topic requires for policy analysis. Some needs for future institutional developments will also be identified. However, it is not the purpose of this chapter to formulate specific policy recommendations. Finally, an outlook on the future is given.

10.3.2   What is Intellectual Capitalism?

The concept of intellectual capital was introduced in Chapter 1 and further specified in Chapter 4 in the context of a firm. Intellectual capital essentially comprises all immaterial resources that could be considered as assets, being possible to acquire, combine, transform and exploit, and to which it is possible to assign, in principle, a capitalized value. 'Intellectual' is thus used as roughly synonymous with 'immaterial'. 'Human capital' is commonly used to refer to intellectual capital specifically embodied in humans, excluding IPR.

What, then, is intellectual capitalism? Standard dictionary and textbook definitions of capitalism refer to an economic system characterized by private ownership of the means of production and by operation of a market with enterprises competing for profit and so on.[1]

Hence a condition for intellectual capitalism to be present is to have private ownership of intellectual capital. This is what the IPR system as an institution allows. However, most intellectual property rights are temporary. When patents and secrets expire, the information content becomes public property.[2] In this sense, there is a feature of 'intellectual socialism' as well. Still, if the share of industrially useful knowledge generated in the private domain compared to the public domain is large and if its growth rate is also large, then at some point privately-held knowledge will dominate. For example, if technical knowledge is doubled every seventh year and all new knowledge is privatized through patents for 20 years before it enters the public domain, then close to seven-eighths (= 87.5 per cent) of the knowledge is under private ownership at any one point.[3] The exact figures are not important here, of course, but the fact is that if privately-held knowledge grows faster than that which is publicly held, it will dominate in the not so distant future.[4]

In order to justify talking about the emergence of intellectual capitalism, it is also reasonable to require that intellectual capital in some sense dominates as a means of production, compared to physical means, and that it dominates capital values, investments and profit sources, although these are difficult to determine and relate to intellectual capital. Several indicators can then be used, for example Solow-type residuals,[5] Tobin's q, Becker-type accounting of human capital, and the ratio of R&D investments to physical investments, a ratio that in many technology-based firms exceeded unity in the 1980s (see Chapter 1).

The practical accounting problems are large, however, and efforts are being made to develop new accounting concepts and methods.[6]

Other indicators of an emerging intellectual capitalism include the growth of IC-based firms, professions and personal wealth, the emergence of technology markets and other IC markets, and the growth of IC products. In summary, one can observe not only a growing share of intellectual capital in traditional firms, products and professions but also a growth of 'pure' IC firms, products and professions, and above all, a growing concern in many quarters about intellectual capital.[7] An overview of indicators is presented in Table 10.1.

10.3.3 Reversal of the Pro-patent Era?

As described in Chapters 1 and 2, a pro-patent era arose during the 1980s, originating in the USA. The developments that led to the establishment of a pro-patent era were initially separate and had underestimated consequences, but gradually merged together with other developments, and gained momentum. Later, concern over various abuses of IPRs surfaced, signalling that the pro-patent movement might pave the way for, if not an anti-patent movement, at least some reformist movements. Concern over whether the US initiatives might backfire has also been raised. The question, then, is whether the pro-patent movement has gone too far, and whether it should be reversed or modified if possible.

Technically speaking, it is not difficult in principle to make legal changes that would downplay the role of patents, just as a number of legal changes put the pro-patent era in motion. However, there are a number of counteracting forces.

Manageable growing pains
First, it is not clear that the pro-patent movement has gone 'too far' in a broad sense. Many would argue that there are certainly abuses, but that they could be handled, as a first try by improvements (small adjustments) in the legal framework, rather than downplaying the system entirely. One should also keep in mind that the pro-patent movement is in a young stage and the associated legal framework still reflects the thinking of a previous era. Misfits and abuses could therefore be expected and accepted in a transitory stage for some time before they could be used as arguments for a reversal. The type of transaction costs incurred by the patent system in its totality can, moreover, hardly be persuasively shown to have risen too much compared to the viable alternatives. It may also be recalled that the strengthening of an IP regime is an attractive policy measure in IP-rich countries, since it does not incur large costs to government.

Large immaterial investments
Second, the patent portfolios and patent management skills built up within a number of large, leading corporations in the United States and Japan, as well

Table 10.1 Indicators of the growing importance of intellectual capital

Indicator	Indication	Reference
1. Ratio of intangible to tangible investments	Increase in both magnitude and recognition of intangible assets[1]	European Commission (1998) TNO (1995)
2. Ratio of R&D expenditures/capital investments	Ratio surpassed 1.0 for large Japanese corporations in 1986. Conveys the emergence of a 'Knowledge Industry'	Kodama (1995)
3. Solow-type residual	Aggregate growth is accounted for by factors other than labor and physical capital, primarily technology	Pioneering works by Abramowitz (1956) and Solow (1957), followed up by many others (e.g., Denison 1985, see Griliches 1996)
4. Tobin's q-value	Emergence of IC-based companies (pure as well as hybrid)[2]	Tobin (1968, 1969) Hall (1993)
5. IPR values (patents, trademarks, trade secrets, copyrights, designs)	Growing registration,[3] value, litigation and damage claims.	Sirilla et al. (1992) Tri-lateral Report (i.e., JPO, USPTO, EPO 1996)

6. IP-related crime and misconduct	Growth of intellectual theft, piracy, counterfeiting and infringement, and organizations dealing with these issues[4]	Counterfeiting Intelligence Bureau (ICC 1997)
7. Trade in intellectual products	Emergence of technology markets[5]	Bureau of Economic Analysis (1994)
8. Wages related to human capital (including personal image value of 'stars')	Growth of salary levels in intellectual professions[6]	Becker (1964) Frank and Cook (1995)
9. Sources of personal wealth	Emergence of intellectual capitalists[7]	Forbes (1997)

Notes

1. An increase of 62 per cent in intangible assets for the European Union 1985–92. Intangible assets rose 48 per cent worldwide from 1989 to 1993 while total assets rose only 28 per cent. Due to the non-conformity in company accounting for intangible assets, these numbers represent the increasing recognition of intangible assets as well as conveying an increase in sheer magnitude.
2. In Lewellen and Badrinath (1997), Tobin's q-values were calculated from a sample of 678 non-financial US corporations from 1975–91. An upward trend ranging from a value of 1.082 in 1975 to 1.781 in 1991 is evident.
3. A 74 per cent increase in worldwide patenting occurred between 1991 and 1995. Although first filings are on the rise, most of this increase was due to a large increase in subsequent filings. For statistics and an explanatory attempt, see Kortum and Lerner (1997). The number of IPR-related lawsuits are also increasing, and in Japan faster than average (Arai 1997).
4. Worldwide counterfeiting was estimated at between 5–7 per cent of total world trade in 1995, approximately US$250 billion. This constitutes an increase of about 150 per cent from 1990 to 1995. Software piracy is estimated at about 46 per cent of sales worldwide, costing manufacturers approximately US$13.2 billion in 1995. The figures are uncertain however.
5. US royalties received and paid between 1987 and 1993 rose 106 and 162 per cent, respectively.
6. The wage dispersion is larger than the IQ-dispersion in society for various reasons. The value of individual intellectual capital, as indicated by wages, derives not only from the value of competence but also from 'relational capital' (see Chapter 4), increasing returns and bargaining position.
7. A few examples of intellectual capitalists are Gates (Microsoft), Moore (Intel), Ellison (Oracle), Knight (Nike) and Clark (Netscape).

as in other countries, represent considerable investments and competitive advantages to the individual corporations. These corporations will not easily accept a devaluation of their immaterial assets. Rather they will lobby for a continued strong patent regime.

Value of technical knowledge
Finally, it must be kept in mind that technical knowledge, like knowledge in general, is of steadily increasing economic importance and will therefore attract private efforts. Even if the patent system was abolished altogether or a moratorium on patents was created, another type of IP regime would most likely evolve to take its place, at least partially.[8] After all, a secrecy-based IP regime is always a possibility.

Along this line of thought, it could even be argued that some kind of strengthening of IPR would come sooner or later. This strengthening would not come about primarily because an advanced intellectual capital-rich nation wanted to correct tendencies to underinvest in R&D, but because it wanted to protect and exploit more fully the R&D investments of its industry.[9]

10.3.4   Rise of Intellectual Capitalists

The emergence of capitalism in connection with industrialization is commonly associated with the emergence of individual capitalists such as John Rockefeller, Andrew Carnegie, Cornelius Vanderbilt, Knut Wallenberg, Alfred Krupp and so on. They typically amassed and commanded large resources as means for industrial production. These resources had been acquired through various activities (discovery of raw materials, technical inventions, financial inventions, speculation, manipulation and so on), cumulated (through heritage, business expansion and so on) and exploited. Intellectual capital in the form of business ideas, trade secrets and so on, naturally played an important role in this process, as did business skills and mere luck (see Chapter 4). However, on the whole, the ownership of physical and financial capital dominated wealth generation and distribution. Key features of the emergence of this type of capitalism included the resulting skew distribution of ownership and control of production means and the opposing roles of capital interest and labour interest.

As information, knowledge and competence cumulate and gain importance in industrial production, as well as in the economy in general, their role as a source of personal wealth is likely to increase. This can be checked by scanning the list of the world's wealthiest people and looking at the sources of their wealth and how it has changed over time.[10]

Such lists reveal a certain upward mobility of people basing their wealth more conspicuously on intellectual capital. However, this is not sufficient evidence for claiming that there is an increasing number of intellectual capitalists, only an indication.

The emergence of a few extremely wealthy intellectual capitalists is worth noting. More important, however, is the relevance of intellectual capital generally at the individual level. Knowledge and experience are essentially gained, held and used by individuals, directly or indirectly. Individual secrecy offers perfect excludability. As jobs and professions become more intellectual than manual, many of them become more dependent upon intellectual skills (for example, creativity, competence and reputation) specific to certain individuals, such as top researchers, artists, managers, surgeons and other specialists.[11] Such individuals with distinctive and not easily replicated competencies and personal images (see Chapter 7), then, could exercise rent control over their intellectual assets or capital. In principle, strategies available to companies to appropriate rents from new technologies, as described in Chapter 6, are available also for individuals who want to appropriate rents from their skills and knowledge. Secrecy is often a particularly effective method for individuals. Since individuals know more than they can tell, that is, they also have tacit knowledge (in the words of Polanyi 1962), some secrecy is even a necessity at the individual level. Individuals can build up and exploit their competence in a manner similar to how companies build up and exploit their resources, as described in Chapter 4, in particular with regard to technical competence.

There are many strong complementarities among intellectual resources across individuals, who thus have incentives to combine them. There are also complementarities between material and immaterial resources. These complementarities are difficult if not impossible to capitalize directly through markets. Individuals often join various organizational forms, such as teams, guilds, small or large firms, associations and universities. These organizational forms constitute the essential repositories of intellectual capital, complementary to intellectual capital held by individuals.[12] For example, one way to capitalize upon a business idea and complementary intellectual resources is to bundle resources by starting a small firm and, after some time, offer it for sale. The US wave of initial public offerings of small firms, whose valuable resources are mostly intellectual, illustrates this point. It is also illustrative that many of these initial public offerings pertain to firms based on information and communication technologies at large. New billionaires are created very fast in this way, much faster than billionaires were created among traditional industrial capitalists.

There are many individuals and small firms who prosper as well in more traditional areas of professional competence, for example, lawyers, physicians and accountants. There is also a growing number of new professional specialities based mostly on intellectual skills, such as consultants of various sorts. Thus, intellectual professions (IC-based professions or IC services) are growing and diversifying.

Individuals usually exploit their intellectual capital through salaries from employer firms, which could be seen as the firm renting their embodied intellectual capital. At the same time employees learn and gain experience on the job and thus build up (appreciate) their individual intellectual capital further, which they can then capitalize on by salary raises, promotion, or changing jobs and/or employers. A sign of evolving intellectual capitalism at the individual level is the rising salary level in many IC professions. Large technology-based MNCs compete worldwide for the best talents, for example, in R&D. This is particularly felt in R&D-intensive industries such as pharmaceuticals, computers and communications. These industries are, in this regard, probably precursors rather than exceptions. Of course, demand and supply conditions vary within the S&T field, between countries and over time. Some areas in this labour market become overheated for some time, some specialities are substituted for others and so on. New discoveries may rapidly change the need for new competencies in an industry, while the educational system is slow to respond. Moreover, competence building is a slow process at the individual level, as we all know. Thus, imbalances between supply and demand on markets for S&T labour are likely to occur, especially shortages.

Higher education has been shown to pay off for individuals, at least in the USA, despite increasing costs (see Becker 1993). Moreover, there are increasing wage differences in the USA and other Western countries, especially between jobs requiring specific intellectual skills and other jobs.[13]

Similar wage differences are emerging in Japan.[14] Otherwise intellectual capitalism at the individual level is not characteristic of Japanese society, at least not yet. Also, the formation of new, technology-based firms is not (yet) a well-developed form of entrepreneurship in Japan; nor is a venture-capital market, as is well known. Japan can be viewed as an emerging (albeit slowly perhaps) intellectual capitalist state, but the intellectual capitalism in Japan is more collectively oriented. It will be interesting to see if this state of affairs will persist, or if intellectual capitalism at the individual level will evolve in Japan as well.

10.3.5   Rise of IC Firms and IC-intensive Industries

As knowledge in general, and technology in particular, increasingly cumulate and penetrate every economic activity, the resource bases of individuals, professions, firms, regions, nations and so on become penetrated to varying degrees. The rise of knowledge firms, knowledge industries and the like is thus commonly recognized and widely discussed. Here we talk about IC firms rather than knowledge firms, although the two concepts are closely connected. An important characteristic of an IC firm is its concern with the build-up and exploitation of immaterial resources – of which knowledge is one prominent part, but not the only part – and its concern with turning these resources into capital, subjected to some form of rent control for economic purposes.

The extent to which immaterial resources are transformed into intellectual capital differs, however, as does the concern over capitalizing and rent control. The share of intellectual capital in the firm's resources also differs, and firms could be roughly classified as having a minor, major, or dominant (more than 50 per cent) share of intellectual capital. It is possible to conceive almost 'pure' IC firms. Most, if not all, firms in a reasonable sense have some intellectual capital, as discussed in Chapter 4. This is not a new phenomenon. Yet, as mentioned above, there is a growing number of firms and industries in which intellectual capital dominates in some economic sense over other types of capital or resources as productive factors. Such firms, which we can refer to as typical IC firms, are found in R&D-intensive industries such as the pharmaceutical and infocom industries.[15] But they are also found increasingly in more traditional manufacturing industries as well as in service industries.[16] Then there are 'pure' IC firms, in which intellectual capital is more or less the only productive factor.[17] These firms are growing in number and types. Examples are consultancy firms (for example in engineering and management) law firms, investment banking, software firms and organizations such as universities, research institutes, music bands, art companies and libraries, although such organizations are usually not thought of as firms.[18] Consequently, more 'pure' IC industries arise, such as the management industry, the legal industry, the software industry and the music industry, although not so commonly recognized as industries, at least not in their early stage of formation.

The formation of firms is also becoming more IC-oriented. In other words, entrepreneurship is getting more IC-based, both in 'autonomous' entrepreneurship (in the form of independent inventors, new start-up firms and so on) and corporate entrepreneurship (in the form of start-up of new businesses within an existing large firm). New technologies (in infocom, biotech, materials and so on) provide plentiful opportunities, and more are likely to come in the following decades in view of growing R&D investments and technology combinations.[19]

The nature of managing IC firms differs in many respects from firms based on physical resources (for example, regarding human resource management, accounting, marketing). Other managerial skills, different business logic and other business models are needed. The pure IC firms such as R&D firms, software firms, consultancy firms and insurance companies will probably lead the way in pushing the managerial frontiers (for example, in accounting) in intellectual capitalism.

The emerging intellectual capitalism goes hand in hand with the rise of intellectual capital in firms and industries in general. In fact, it may be argued that large and small firms, especially technology-based firms, are leading the way into intellectual capitalism. The large firms currently control the lion's share of the world's technology as indicated in studies of R&D investments, patents and the like (see Patel and Pavitt 1995), and the concentration of technology to large firms is increasing. Large firms also team up with each other as well as with small firms for various reasons, not least for pooling and joint exploitation of their intellectual capital.[20] Thus, large firm complexes or quasi-integrated structures or networks emerge as an important feature of intellectual capitalism. This is not to say that small and new firms play a declining role in intellectual capitalism. On the contrary, new IC firms are a fundamentally important feature of intellectual capitalism, but small and large firms often develop in symbiosis.

As described in Chapter 4, the firm is a very viable economic institution, co-evolving with technology. There are, moreover, no signs of decline of this institution with some other kind of competing economic institution taking over. For example, with regard to IC formation, firms control most of the world's technology as mentioned above. Firms, large and small, are also increasing their role in science as well as in higher education, as both users and producers, not to mention as suppliers of educational material and equipment for science as well as education. Many universities, especially private ones, are also becoming more firm-like, with university management becoming increasingly influenced by business management, concepts and methods. At the same time, older institutions, which traditionally have played an important role in formal education, historically the church and, in present days, government, are in relative decline.

The limited liability joint-stock firm and the large firm in particular are thus primary economic institutions for intellectual capitalism, just as they were for traditional capitalism (see, for example, Rosenberg and Birdzell 1986). The nation-state, on the other hand, is becoming relatively weaker, as discussed by many authors. Its place and role in intellectual capitalism will be examined in Section 10.3.6.

10.3.6   Rise of IC States

In the course of history, the rise and fall of nations has been linked to changing resource conditions and systems for acquiring and exploiting resources. Thus, it may be argued, as done by Abramovitz, Rosenberg, Wright and others,[21] that the rise of the USA was in no small measure dependent upon her abundant exploitable resources of certain kinds and the capitalist system, as it evolved with, for example, the limited liability, joint-stock company. The development of the US economy thereby came to be technologically congruent with its resources, to borrow a term from Professor Abramovitz.[22]

As technology advanced, in particular in the latter half of the 20th century, it opened vast possibilities to become less dependent on scarce natural resources. Examples are the invention of optical fibres, silicon chips and cellular telephony.

At the same time, some countries poor in natural resources, Japan in particular but also South Korea, have chosen to make a virtue of their situation by investing in immaterial resources. Japan has thereby become a prime candidate for becoming, sooner or later, an intellectual capital-based state (or IC state), in the sense that intellectual capital occupies a dominating rank in the national resource base.[23] Japan would then present a new case of technological congruence. It can also be expected that Japan will push the frontiers of intellectual capitalism back in the future (beyond the recession of the 1990s), although not alone. Important parts of US industry and regions such as Silicon Valley are similarly IC-intensive and will foster the further development of intellectual capitalism as, most likely, will countries like South Korea sooner or later.

These examples will lead to emulation in other parts of the world, while new technologies will continue to lower the dependence upon natural resources. The role of nation-states and their governments in this development can be of great importance in facilitating necessary transitions. But the economic powers will rather be concentrated among the collective intellectual capitalists, be they individuals or firms, and especially large firm complexes and their managers and prime governors. Many nations have poor economies, as far as the state is concerned, but the situation may be different in regard to their citizens and corporations.

Being an IC state requires constant innovativeness. Many people have argued that Japan will for various reasons not become innovative on a large scale. However, the arguments are often weak and there is evidence to the contrary. This is an issue that can be elaborated at length. Suffice it to say that reality has already proved the innovative capability of Japan to a considerable extent in some areas. In addition, it is possible for Japan's industry to internationalize further and source and foster innovative talent abroad.[24] Nevertheless, moving to a more innovative stage definitely seems to require substantial changes in large parts of Japanese society, for example, in the educational system and in the legal system, and failure to become innovative on a large scale might be fatal. Being innovative is simply a fundamental issue for the economic security of an IC state.

Various types of intellectual capitalism will emerge, including a particular Japanese variety. It is only natural to assume that hybridization of intellectual capitalism and traditional resource-based capitalism will take on various forms in various countries.

10.3.7 Rise of IC Markets

Markets, as well as firms, are primary capitalistic institutions. Just as traditional firms become increasingly IC-based at the same time as more pure IC firms emerge, traditional product and factor markets become increasingly IC-oriented at the same time as more pure IC markets emerge. The arguments behind these statements for markets will not be spelled out here in the same detail as for firms. It should suffice to note that as products, services and firms become increasingly technology-based, or more generally IC-based, their corresponding markets become more IC-based as well. One example is pure information products like books, software, airline tickets and music sold over the Internet. Another example is the growing 'super-market' for innovative firms (see Chapter 4). As the role of human capital is upgraded and professions become increasingly IC-oriented, so do the corresponding labour and service markets.

IC markets may pertain to each of the IC elements described in Chapter 4, alone or in combination, that is, bundled together into a 'transactionable object'. Of particular interest in this context is the emergence of technology markets of various kinds. Some of them have existed for a long time, for example, markets for licences (patent and know-how licences, often in combination)[25], and engineering services. For these markets, the IPR system has traditionally been of decisive importance as it defines tradeable objects (see Chapter 3). Some new markets have emerged in recent decades, for example, markets for trading small, technology-based firms and projects, and various venture capital markets and over the counter (OTC) stock markets. As technology can be embedded in products, services, labour and firms, markets for these may also be looked upon as embedded technology markets.

The difficulties involved in designing and operating IC markets should be noted. Inherent properties of information, as dealt with in Chapter 2, give rise to a number of problems leading to market deficiencies or market failures and economic crime in information markets.[26] Nevertheless, many information markets do function and actors learn how to operate in them. As for technology markets, the codifiability of various technologies, which is limited in emerging technologies but is improved through further R&D, does offer possibilities for overcoming some of the problems with information markets. That is, it may become possible to specify technologies sufficiently for trade to occur without revealing so much that the risk of mere theft or fraud frustrates the technology trade. In other words a kind of *second order codifiability* exists and could be further developed. In addition, technological interdependencies imply interdependencies among market actors over time, which offer some possibilities for self-policing among actors. Still, it is likely that a kind of IC-related economic crime will continue or even develop further, and that this will threaten the performance of IC markets.

Internal IC markets have also emerged and continue to emerge in large corporations (that is, sub-markets as dealt with in Chapter 4). Quite normally, companies sell various professional services internally, including R&D. Some companies even use licensing internally as well as trade projects internally. Diverse schemes are employed, some of which are rather pseudo-market in nature.

Finally, it should be noted that some types of exchange in society could take on characteristics of an IC market. Mutual building of trust, relations and obligations among humans could be seen as formation of relational capital that could generate benefits and could be transferred to some extent. Another example, as pointed out by Schumpeter, is political voting which might be viewed as a market-like exchange oriented around trust and power. Political ventures are also acquiring more business-like characteristics. This is not necessarily for the better, but nevertheless, it can be taken as support for the increased concern to manage relational capital as part of intellectual capital.

An important example relates to communication or the mere exchange of information. This can be seen as a bartered exchange of intellectual capital. When clear utilitarian concerns enter into such exchanges, it is justified to regard them as constituting IC markets to some extent, even though these markets may be very differentiated or specific to the parties in the exchange. However, if information is exchanged for money, it is a clear-cut market transaction. New information and communication technologies open up vast possibilities to codify, store and transact information and thereby possibilities to convert the traditional bartering in communication into regular markets for information. This is dealt with in Section 10.4.

10.4 TECHNOLOGY AND INTELLECTUAL CAPITALISM

10.4.1 Role of the IPR System

Let us first discuss how the intellectual property system affects technology and then move on to how new technologies affect the evolution of intellectual capitalism. Society's main rationale for having a patent system is to stimulate technological innovation and diffusion (Chapter 3). Thus, by design, there is an impact of the IPR system upon technology. The size of the impact is debatable (Chapter 2). The impact on R&D investments could be substantial in some industries, particularly in drugs and chemicals (Chapter 5). Technology-based corporations increasingly emphasize the role of patents and employ elaborate patenting behaviours and strategies (Chapters 6 and 7). In addition, patents are complemented by other intellectual property rights into a multiprotection scheme in order to exploit the company's R&D and new technologies (Chapter 7). Given rising R&D costs, abundant technology-based business opportunities, strong IP regimes and improved technology and IP management skills (Chapter 8), there is little reason to believe that this trend of strengthened IPR will be reversed, at least not in the short and medium term.

However, at the same time, there are increasing signs of, and concern over, IPR counteracting their purpose and hampering technological progress and entrepreneurship, especially among small firms. Such signs and concerns are of great age, but are increasingly justified for several reasons.

Evolution of technology

The changing character of technology creates misfits between technology and the legal framework designed to foster it. It is an inherent tendency that changes in legislation lag behind changes in technology, legislation being by tradition and design more reactive than proactive or anticipatory when facing uncertainty. Today, technology advances fast, perhaps faster than ever in absolute terms. Some of these new technologies challenge fundamental concepts in the IP system, and it is not clear at the outset whether and how they could be given protection under the current IP regime. Well-known examples are software and biotechnology. Less well-known examples are new surgical methods, new teaching methods or even new athletic techniques, depending upon how broadly the concept of technology is interpreted. As the cost and prospective value of new technologies and inventions increase, the push for IP protection will increase. To some extent the IP system will evolve to accommodate such new technologies and inventions, although cases and periods of underprotection as well as overprotection will most likely occur. Yet, a more challenging problem for the IP system remains. New technologies are interacting with each other and with old technologies in complex and interdependent ways. As a result, products and services become increasingly based not only on new technologies but also on many different technologies. That is, products and services become more multitechnological, or 'mul-tech', which is different from becoming 'hi-tech' in the sense of using some advanced, new technology. At the same time more generic (or 'general purpose') technologies appear, so in this sense, technologies also become more multiproduct. All in all, the cross-links between new products and technologies proliferate. This means that patents and businesses become more cross-linked and interdependent with each new business becoming reliant on an increasing number of patents and each new patent having an impact on an increasing range of businesses on average.

Sources of technology

The sources of new technologies also proliferate as more firms and nations invest in R&D. In addition, firms increasingly internationalize their sourcing and exploitation of new technologies (that is, both factor input and product output markets become more global). Thus, in a new technology as well as in a product market, there will be not only more players on average, but increasingly interdependent players in a mixture of cooperation and competition ('coopetition' or 'competeration'). Technology trade, for example through licensing and cross-licensing, then becomes increasingly necessary. This is because the IPR necessary to sustain a business become increasingly fragmented among players, who are ready to enforce or otherwise exploit their rights, thereby creating a web of problems (for example, hold-ups).

Abuse of the IP system
The two factors mentioned so far put increasing demands on the well-functioning of technology markets. Strategic firm behaviour in using and abusing the IP system is yet another factor that further complicates the functioning of technology markets. Some inventors and small non-manufacturing firms act as 'patent extortionists'. Large corporations, on the other hand, aggressively build up patent portfolios and employ various patent strategies. They, moreover, combine them with various other IPR into a kind of multiprotection, and thereby build up bargaining and retaliatory power. As IP-based bargaining power increases in industry, asymmetries in bargaining power become more likely to appear – between new and old firms, between small and large firms, and between companies adapted to strong and weak IP regimes in different sectors and countries. These asymmetries put innovation and entrepreneurship at risk, which especially endangers small manufacturing firms. (New types of insurance are being tried but with expensive premiums.) Thus, due to several factors, the IP system may slow down, misdirect or hold up innovation and diffusion, although not necessarily discouraging all R&D investments. Consequently, there is, as always, a mixed verdict over whether the IP system promotes technological innovation and diffusion, but perhaps the doubts in the mix are increasing. The pendulum continues to swing between trust in and suspicion of the IP system.

10.4.2 Role of New Technologies in General

Now, what about the question: how will new technologies affect the evolution of intellectual capitalism? At a general level the creation of new business opportunities based on new technologies is crucial. Is there any reason, though, to expect that the technology wells will dry up? Although some limits to new technological discoveries are definitely conceivable in the long run, there are certainly no signs of limits for the foreseeable future, at least for a few generations ahead.[27] Mother Nature has strange ways of exhibiting herself, but she will not stop doing so, although she will never totally expose herself to mankind. On the contrary, progress of all sorts in various S&T fields is being made at a high, perhaps accelerating pace.[28] New advances in different fields of S&T combine to produce still more new advances. Thus, there is cross-fertilization with a combinatorial mechanism, and as long as technological opportunities multiply through some combinatorial mechanism, their growth will be self-sustained. In addition, fundamental breakthroughs, for example in physics or medicine, and the emergence of new generic technologies (for example, new materials with design of material properties at atomic level), continue to fuel the opportunity-generating process.[29] At the same time the 'life cycles' of such S&T advances are long, encompassing several human generations.[30]

But is there a need for new technologies? Again with appeal to conspicuous realities (poverty, disease and so on), one can dismiss most claims that the needs of the world to which technology may cater will cease to exist in the foreseeable future. Yet, what about effective demand (that is, the demand for real products by solvent customers) being less than a general need? In the advanced, industrialized parts of the world, the demand for new technologies shows no signs of decline, for several reasons.

1. *Old technology creates demand*   This demand is derived to some extent from the need to deal with various side-effects or consequences of earlier deployed technologies, for example the need for environmental protection. In this sense, new technologies generate new demand, although usually with a time lag. One can argue about the balance on the whole and claim (as Ellul 1990 does) that technology continues to create more problems than it can solve. However, even if new technologies on balance create more problems than they solve (which is hardly provable), it does not follow that effective demand for them will decline. As long as the costs and benefits of new technologies are unevenly distributed in society, which is likely to be the case, politically strong groups will evolve as beneficiaries, supporting effective demand.

2. *New technology creates demand*   To some extent, new types of demand are created by new technologies, for example, demand for new types of information or audio-visual entertainment created by information and communication (infocom) technologies. More generally, as uncertainty grows with increasing complexity in society, the demand for information grows, especially when production and distribution of information create information asymmetries, which is the case under intellectual capitalism. Thus intellectual capitalism will reinforce itself with respect to production and distribution of information.[31]

3. *Persistence of old demand*   Old types of demand persist, some of which are insatiable, for example, in health care and life prolongation (and vanity as well for that matter). In these areas, new technologies are continually presenting new prospects. One might argue that some types of old demand are declining. For example, it can be said that the demand for new military technologies, derived from the demand for security, will decline in the apparent aftermath of the Cold War. Unfortunately, that seems far from true, at least to any radical extent in the long run. On the contrary, needs for security as well as justice will live on and, as wealth accumulation and inequalities

proceed together with uncertainty, the demand for technologies to enhance security and property protection at all levels in the global society will persist and probably increase.[32] Again, we see here an element of self-reinforcement, not only in intellectual capitalism, but in capitalism on the whole, which is derived from the excludability characteristics of private property and unequal access.

4. *Conspicuous demand*   The need for 'conspicuous consumption', to use Veblen's concept,[33] will persist and probably grow, for example, in Japan and other *nouveaux riches* Asian countries. Much of this need is technology-related, and some demand new technologies, largely because they are new.

5. *Insatiable demand*   Various demands, old and new, technology-derived or not, tend to be insatiable by any particular set of new technologies. Improvements are attained, but they are seldom, if ever, ultimate solutions. It is true that some technologies come into dominance for long periods of time, yet not because they offer perfect solutions, but because it happens to take time to find and sufficiently implement better ones.[34] Sooner or later technological substitution sets in.

6. *Technological substitution*   On balance, the rate of technological substitution seems to increase rather than decrease, as life cycles of new products and technologies tend to become shorter. Despite cases of technology persistence (Graham 1956), technology conservatism (Bohlin 1995), technology monopolies (Arthur 1988), dominant designs (Utterback 1994), technological interdependencies and lock-ins (Rosenberg 1994) and so on, technology competition and technology substitution rule in the long run.

7. *Population effects*   Demand is of course affected further by changes in population. The possibility that such changes set in to the extent that demand for new technologies would vanish is slim indeed, however.[35]

Profits from innovation

In summary, there is a persistent, effective demand for new technologies and there will be further technological opportunities, but will there be possibilities to make private profits from investment in them? More specifically, how will these opportunities to profit from innovation be affected by the new technologies themselves? This is our question at hand. That is, will new technologies improve the possibilities for innovators to appropriate the rents from innovations for which there is both a potential demand and supply?

First of all, innovations may become very profitable, even extremely profitable, as witnessed by various studies (for example, Scherer 1998), but innovations are often associated with many failures, false starts and high costs. The dispersion of profits from innovation may even deter entrepreneurs from proper investments. The question is not so much whether imitators will 'free-ride' innovations and reap large profits as well, but whether prospective innovators can trust their capabilities of making sufficient profits to justify their investments, compared to their alternative investment opportunities. These alternatives include the opportunity to engage in a waiting game, that is to wait and see if someone else innovates and then imitate. There are also (currently growing) opportunities to sell the innovation 'packaged' as an innovation company on markets for corporate control.

The capability to control the rent streams from the immaterial resources or intellectual capital deployed in the innovation process becomes a crucial consideration, especially as innovations become increasingly based on intellectual capital. One may argue that information cannot be owned.[36] Nor can humans be owned, and outright slavery in intellectual and creative work, for example, in R&D, is practically infeasible, at least under democratic forms.[37] Therefore intellectual capitalism would have a weak basis in the form of private ownership in firms, according to this line of argument. However, and this is important, ownership *per se* is not the primary issue. Rather, it is how private parties (firms, individuals) can control (manage) the rent streams derivable from immaterial resources and turn these streams into intellectual capital. The separation of ownership and control issues is thus important to consider.

In order to control resource rents, *excludability* is critical, that is, possibilities to lock in customers and lock out competitors. This is true regardless of the material or immaterial character of the resources. However, excludability varies among resource types and business situations. In general, excludability is more difficult to accomplish for immaterial resources, which is precisely why IPR has been instituted. Thus, one way to raise excludability, and thereby the possibilities for appropriating resource rents, is to bundle resources having low excludability with resources having high excludability. This is typified by embedding immaterial resources in material ones, which in business jargon is sometimes referred to as 'productification' or 'commodification'. Immaterial resources can also be embedded in individuals and in small companies, which could be put up for sale. Thus, product markets, labour markets and stock markets offer ways to appropriate benefits from immaterial resources and products in addition to 'pure' markets for such resources and products. For the latter type of markets, it has always been a problem to enforce excludability and prevent free-riding as well as theft. However, excludability is not a given, but can be changed by new technologies. Infocom technologies, especially, offer new possibilities to raise excludability while also lowering transaction costs.

10.4.3   The Role of ICTs

The natural way to exclude others is by means of secrecy, which is effected by the balance between *secrecy-enhancing* and *secrecy-destroying* (intelligence gathering, scanning) technologies. This balance shifts over time. Code-making and code-breaking have always had their problems, but currently (1998) it seems as if encryption technology has reached a point of very high efficiency in ensuring cheap, high-quality secrecy, which can be made widely available.[38] Such secrecy-enhancing technologies in a broad sense will have extremely important consequences, as they can radically improve excludability for business purposes as well as for military purposes.[39] On the other hand, various instruments, chemical analysis, surveillance and sensor technologies facilitate reverse engineering, which in turn facilitates both imitation and infringement detection, thereby having a mixed impact on excludability.

In fact, who benefits from what, how, where and when is largely an informational problem, as are billing and money-handling. Thus, as ICTs advance, it might be expected that various transaction costs could be lowered and that investors can be remunerated more easily through higher excludability. This applies to goods in general, which therefore would narrow the range of public goods, everything else being equal.[40] For example, signalling and sensor devices at gates to toll roads that automatically identify cars and credit their registered owners or drivers would facilitate private road investments on profitable routes. Similarly a range of traditional public goods and services will be – and already is – affected by new infocom technologies aimed at raising excludability. Broadcasting is a classic example of public goods that are affected as well, where scrambling, coders and decoders, standards and two-way communications enable producers to charge their users through pay-TV and pay-radio.[41] The extent of traditional broadcasting will, moreover, be diminished by new technologies offering interactivity and selectivity to consumers. This also holds for the traditional broadcasting method of teaching. Broadcasting, once referred to as a 'democratic technology', is being replaced, at least in relative terms, by interactive and selective communication. Thus, ICTs enable investors and producers to build electronic locks and fences around their properties in order to generate and control their rent streams. These possibilities may not be welcomed by society at large, and various forces may counter them.

The possibilities and tendencies to raise excludability through new technologies favour capitalism, including state capitalism, but do they favour intellectual capitalism in particular? It is argued here that in fact they do, although we have barely seen the beginning as yet. Moreover, they do so not in isolation, but in combination with other factors. In any case, they open up possibilities for privatization of immaterial resources and the appropriation of rents. This is partly due to their bundling with material resources and improved excludability in relation to the resulting products and services. In addition, many informational products or services are likely to be made proprietary and subjected to private rent control more easily through different ICTs. These technologies not only produce and distribute more information faster, but they produce and distribute more differentiated information at more differentiated rates. New information of relevance to intellectual capitalism is far from solely produced through traditional R&D, although new technical information (that is, new technologies) constitutes perhaps the most important part of immaterial resources and is a main driver of intellectual capitalism. For example, new sensor technologies (in a broad sense, including technologies for detection, registration, measurement, identification, surveillance and so on) enable the collection of vast amounts of data of all sorts.

These data have value in themselves, although often only in isolated instances. However, when they are cumulated and combined with other data, their value may be considerably raised, thus giving an incentive to build databases, expert systems and the like. (Think, for example, about all the transactional information that can be gathered from 'electronic traces' through credit cards, cash cards, bar codes, phones, TV-shopping, the Internet and so on, and used not only for marketing but also for extending and creating markets that link together consumers with similar tastes and spending and moving habits.) Moreover, new information (text, data, sound, images) is increasingly produced in electronic form (for example, in publishing), further enabling the build-up of computerized databases that can be equipped with access control and customized search, filtering and linking techniques.

These databases can be and are being made proprietary and have become great sources of controllable rent streams by various means. Examples of such means are exclusive access to data sources and data suppliers, speed in updating information with a time value, subscriber and feedback arrangements with users and so on. These kinds of information production thus enable the accumulation of intellectual capital.[42]

Altogether, information asymmetries proliferate through new ICTs. These asymmetries may be temporary, and sometimes they may be reduced, for example, through interventionist rules and regulations. In any event, the information asymmetries essentially create lead times in some market operation. Secrecy-enhancing technologies or other access-restricting technologies may, moreover, prolong the market lead times.

In addition to faster communications with more differentiated rates, other trends in communications and information distribution are of relevance to intellectual capitalism. Human communications are becoming increasingly electronic and embedded in telecommunication systems. Electronic communications need equipment with access possibilities. They also require a certain level of resources and competence to operate, as well as absorptive capabilities at the receiving end. Second, telecommunication networks proliferate into 'networks of networks' with increasing demand for dedicated, private networks complementing open, public ones, further increasing connectivity. Third, telecommunications in turn are becoming increasingly interactive and selective, multimedial and asynchronous at the same time, in order to save time by using asynchronous time slots and comparative advantages of audio and video messaging in everyday life. This also requires routeing, switching, storage and retrieval, in turn requiring technical machinery. Audio–video conversion technologies like speech to text conversion are likely to revolutionize communications. Fourth, human-to-human communications are increasingly complemented and/or replaced by human/machine communications, with machines both as intermediaries (for example, answering machines) or as end communicators (for example, computerized databases, possibly with voice control and intelligent dialogue systems). Also, machine-to-machine communications is growing (with terminals communicating with each other or with control systems with computers, switches, routers, servers and so on, and with new types of intelligent antennas).

As a result of such communication trends (that is, trends in the distribution of information) possibilities open up for control of access to information and information flows by private interests, which are difficult if not impossible to efficiently regulate by public bodies.

There are also trends in information production towards more information in total, more codified (especially digitalized) and electronically processed information, more produced, altered and stored information, more differentiated and tailor-made information, and more information overflow. (The latter requires costly capabilities for information search and filtering – possibly aided by devices such as search engines and information agents, for example, 'Internet assistants'.) The trends in information production combined with the trends in communication result in increasing informational asymmetries and proprietorship, which in turn creates market lead times and possibilities for extracting rents from information. The market lead times deriving from information asymmetries are typically temporary, and they may even be quite short, depending upon the rate of diffusion of new information. Still, at any given point in time, a substantial amount of information is likely to be in the hands of just a few actors.[43]

Still more important, perhaps, is that the time needed to exploit any asymmetry may be quite short. The profit margin can also be kept higher if other actors are unaware of their information lags (that is, a kind of second-order secrecy applies). If any proprietary investments for creating the asymmetry can be kept sufficiently small, total profitability is ensured.

Thus, an important feature of intellectual capitalism is the control of rents from temporarily-held immaterial resources such as information. Infocom technologies are important in creating these temporarily-held resources as well as in facilitating the control of rents from them.

Other technologies may also be thought of as facilitating the creation of market lead times, such as technologies for laboratory automation, manufacturing automation (lab and fab automation), marketing (for example, through the Internet) and distribution. However, these are not technologies that could typically be directly used to create market lead times through slowing down seller diffusion or building entry barriers with a temporary duration. Technologies may be used to speed up the time to market but they create market lead times only to the extent that they are unevenly distributed among actors.

Communication networks, such as the Internet and related private network designs (intranets, extranets), are highly important for the emergence of intellectual capitalism. They provide various kinds of IC products and IC markets as well as the means for exclusive access, especially with new kinds of protocols and digital payment systems. The Internet has also given rise to a number of intellectual capitalists, as have ICTs and other technologies in general, for example, Bill Gates, Steve Jobs, Rupert Murdoch, Hans Rausing and Ralph Landau. (Compare these with traditional capitalists like Rockefeller, Carnegie and Vanderbilt.).

How do technologies that lower copying and imitation costs, specifically reproduction costs for informational products – that is, technologies that help overcome or destroy rather than enhance excludability – affect the market? The moving print type, which appeared in the 15th century, greatly reduced the cost for the reproduction of books, and thereby enlarged the market for those kinds of intellectual products. Xeroxing similarly lowered the cost of copying. In neither case was there a complementary technology (in contrast to legal means) that could help the information-originator to appropriate or control the rents from the original information. Software copying is also cheap, technically speaking. Legal protection against software piracy has also been strengthened. However, more efficient methods to control software copying or access, based on new technologies as well as on new business methods, are available. The high stakes involved on global markets promote progress in this field. Again, new ICTs offer possibilities for rent control, for instance, the bundling of services and products; market leveraging; the lack of interoperability, standards or gateway technologies; biometric user identification and registration; codes and so on.

However, users do not want to become locked in by high switching costs. Many users (including corporate users) also count on having the opportunity to do some extra copying for free, which some producers may tolerate. Thus, there is an element, considerable at present, of a black market. In some cases, producers also encourage copying and diffusion of certain software with the intention to hook (lock in) users on future products and services. But this is another attempt at rent control. Regarding large-scale software piracy, producers, especially in the USA, will probably find a mix of technological, managerial and political solutions that reasonably fulfil their purposes, at least in the parts of the world which are open for policing and enforcement in some way.[44]

Thus we may conclude that, by and large, new technologies are fostering the emergence of intellectual capitalism, while intellectual capitalism fosters the emergence of new technologies in a positive feedback loop (that is, in a virtuous or vicious circle depending on political taste). New ICTs are especially important to this positive feedback in the techno-economic system in society. Such a link between new technology systems (families of interrelated technologies) and the emergence of new ways of organizing an economy (new economic systems) was also present in the rise of early capitalism in connection with industrialization. The new technologies of particular relevance to the first industrial revolution were new energy technologies, epitomized by the steam engine, and new material-processing technologies, characterized by the loom and the mill (saw mill, steel mill and so on).[45] However, new technologies by themselves do not change anything in isolation from management, policies and institutions. This is the subject to which we now turn.

10.5   MANAGEMENT AND INTELLECTUAL CAPITALISM

It has earlier been argued that there is an emergence of IC firms of various types, of which the technology-based firm, focused on in the preceding empirical chapters, is a particularly important example. One can speak of a still broader category of knowledge-based organizations, which further includes universities, libraries, consultancy firms and so on.[46] While certainly not a new phenomenon, knowledge-based organizations grow in numbers and types as knowledge accumulates and becomes more differentiated in general.

Knowledge-based development is accompanied by a corresponding development of management resources, in themselves knowledge-related.[47] To the extent that management can be viewed as a resource, one could speak of supply and demand of management as well as of a management market, a management industry and similar concepts (see Chapter 4). What is important in this context is to recognize that there is an evolution of management, just as there is an evolution of technology. There are many examples of how new managerial specialities and innovations have evolved (for example, international marketing management, industrial R&D management, database management).

Thus, capabilities for managing knowledge-based organizations will develop as the organizations themselves evolve and place new demands on their management. In particular, IC management will develop, implying accumulation and differentiation of managerial knowledge and skills in how to acquire, develop and exploit IC resources, subject to various forms of competition and utilitarian considerations. Traditional industrial management practices and theory have co-developed together with the traditional industrial firm and its traditional resource structure. As IC firms evolve and the role of intellectual capital in traditional firms evolves, IC management will develop gradually in some directions, and radically in others.

This does not necessarily mean that IC management will develop into a special new sub-discipline of management or that there will be a special new breed of IC managers. What it means is that the management of intellectual capital will become more skilful ('professional'), sophisticated and resourceful in terms of experience, concepts, tools, methods and so on. Improvements will stem both from gradual learning by doing and through discrete managerial innovations.

Several lines of managerial developments are likely to become closely interconnected into a web of management skills constituting IC management. One line runs from *technology management*, which since the 1970s has broadened the traditional R&D management.[48] A second line runs from *patent management*, which in the 1980s started to become broadened into *IP management*. A third line runs from personnel management, broadened into *human resource management*, concerned with competencies, creativity, relations, motivation of intellectually talented people and so on. A fourth line runs from *sales management*, broadened into *marketing management*, including not only concerns with trademarks and image (reputation) building, but broader concerns of how to market, distribute and sell knowledge, embodied as well as disembodied, on consumer as well as industrial markets. Closely related is *purchasing management*, which will develop correspondingly to attend to the purchasing of knowledge, embodied as well as disembodied. However, such purchasing, for example licensing in or recruitment, is mostly subsumed under technology management and human resource management. Nevertheless, improved skills in both marketing and purchasing management contribute to the well-functioning of IC markets, for example, technology markets, given a suitable institutional framework (legislation and so on).

A fifth line runs from *management accounting and control*, which actually is a crucial line for the furthering of IC management, due to the need for new measurements and the inherent problems involved. There are other conceivable lines from traditional management to IC management as well, but the purpose here is to illustrate rather than survey them in order to highlight some contours of the more comprehensive IC management, which is long on future but short on history.

Given that we can see not only some emerging components of IC management, but also improvements of its functioning over time, it is evident that IC management will foster intellectual capitalism, just as it has been fostered already. In that respect, intellectual capitalism as a phase of capitalism becomes congruent with IC management just as intellectual capitalism becomes congruent with ICTs. The difference is that IC management is developing more directly in response to intellectual capitalism than are ICTs. The point here is that some of the currently recognized limitations of IC management, in its current state as a cluster of fragmented management skills and responsibilities, are likely to recede in years to come. This is both because new IC management skills will develop, and because technologies supporting IC management will develop, not least ICTs.

Thus there are a number of positive feedbacks among intellectual capitalism, IC management and ICTs. What then are the consequences of these developments? Where will this troika lead us? What about the institutional developments that are crucial to intellectual capitalism and to capitalism in general? This will be dealt with next.

10.6   THE FUTURE OF THE IPR SYSTEM

What is likely to happen with the IPR systems in the world ahead? This is of course discussed widely in many forums. Here, only an overview will be given.

10.6.1   Pro-patent Movement

As discussed above, a major reversal of the pro-patent or pro-intellectual property movement is not likely. On the contrary, this movement is likely to continue, with the USA as the leading activist, at least for the foreseeable future. However, certain features of the IPR systems will be tempered, altered and added.

10.6.2   International Harmonization

Is the international harmonization of the IPR systems likely? Is it desirable? These questions are extensively discussed in NRC (1993). Practitioners often advocate international harmonization (perhaps less so among lawyers and patent attorneys). One argument is that diversity in national innovation systems promotes innovativeness, and therefore diversity in national IPR systems is a positive factor (see Foray 1994). However, the IPR system diversity comes at a cost, and any necessary diversity could be maintained in other ways. International harmonization of IPR systems is highly desirable regarding their key aspects, such as grounds for priority (first to file versus first to invent), because of the costs that are otherwise incurred in and around innovative work.[49] International harmonization is also increasing and is likely to continue. Regional harmonization has advanced in Europe through the EPO. Every year new countries are joining the PCT system, and a community patent might not be far away. Harmonization among the regions of Europe, Japan and the USA is also progressing. The MNCs, through their lobbying organizations, are an important factor behind this drive. Internationalization of corporate and national economies is also important. Internationalization of the national legal systems in general is much slower, implying that the internationalization of IPR (and contract) legislation could be pushing legal harmonization at the international level. Some MNCs are also internationalizing their litigations (suing in different national jurisdictions). North–South harmonization is more of an open issue.

It might further be argued that the current system with national patent offices could be substantially consolidated on a global basis.[50] This may not currently be such a 'hot' political issue, but the potential for rationalization is there, reinforced by the potential of new ICTs.[51] Competition among national patent offices is likely to emerge and is already under way in Europe. Economic integration together with price/performance-conscious MNCs, in conjunction with an increasing need for both broad and deep competence in the patent office, will be driving forces; political and cultural factors (for example, language factors) will hamper progress, but to a weaker degree in the longer run.[52] Political forces behind 'strong' patent offices are also likely to aid competition, once set in motion. Nevertheless, the national systems of patents have developed over centuries, from time to time considerably influenced by national protectionism, which still is and will continue to be a significant hampering force.

10.6.3   Abuses of the Patent System

A third issue is how to deal with abuses of the patent system. Many examples surfaced in the pro-patent era. In general, one may expect that various 'fixes' will be initiated, especially by the US, rather than major overhauls (see Merges 1995b; Warshofsky 1994).

One proposal is that the level of inventiveness (non-obviousness) required for patentability should be raised. Narrowing the scope of a patent, especially in emerging technologies, might also benefit developments. These measures are necessary to decrease the hold-up problems and blocking power of many minor patents, as well as the blocking power of major patents in applications remote from their original area of application. The costs of patent processing and patent litigation, too, could be lowered in this way.[53] Future patent flooding may also increase considerably when (rather than if) countries like China start patenting on a broad scale. Moreover, it is probable that 'computer-aided patenting' will come into play. That is, computers and expert systems will generate certain types of inventions (for example, based on combinatorial alterations of inventive elements) or inventive inputs that form the basis for patent applications.[54] Such computer-generated inventions are likely to be minor, and non-obviousness requirements must reasonably filter away most of such inventions.[55] The impact on R&D and innovation efforts, as well as on diffusion of technical information, would probably not be significantly weakened in total by raising required levels of invention and limiting patent scope, but this must be analysed further.

10.6.4   Harmonization of IP Regimes

A fourth issue is whether intellectual property regimes will and should be harmonized. Different co-existing intellectual property regimes have evolved over time, linked to various sectors of society and their institutions, organizations, norms and so on. Science and universities constitute one, industry and technology another, military and government still another, and culture and artists a fourth. These IP regimes are partly overlapping and interdependent, and this trend increases as technology and economic concerns continue to penetrate modern societies. Clashes between IP regimes occur more frequently, for example, in industry/university collaborations. Table 10.2 shows the differences between the IP regimes in science and technology. Pressure is thereby arising to align different IP regimes with each other and to find complementary solutions at least.[56]

Table 10.2   Comparison of IP regimes in science and in technology

Regime feature	Science	Technology
Priority	First to publish (First to discover/write)	First to file (First to invent)
Criteria	Newness to the field Non-obviousness	Newness to the world Non-obviousness Industrial applicability
Examination system	Publishers Journal editors and referees	Patent offices Patent examiners
Opposition system	Informal	Formal
Sanction system	Informal	Formal
Legal basis	Copyright matters codified in law, otherwise weak Professional norms	Codified in patent law
International coordination	Strong in some disciplines. No unifying framework or treaties	International treaties and cooperation
Licensing provision	General permission to use 'publication pool'	Usually subject to patent holders' discretion
Remuneration system	Citations Reputation Community prizes and job offers Research grants Promotion Non-contract-based	Royalty or lump-sum payments or barter Product or licence sales Contract-based

10.7   THE FUTURE OF INTELLECTUAL CAPITALISM

It might be considered far-fetched to look at the possible future of intellectual capitalism, as it has not had much of a history and presence yet. Still, some early thinking about its future may be a worthwhile undertaking. What about any self-destructive or stagnating tendencies in intellectual capitalism? What about issues of past concern in capitalism – capital concentration, obsolescence of the entrepreneurial function and so on. These are all pending questions for the future.

To be sure, the future of capitalism attracted great attention at each stage in its past. Among scholars, Marx and Schumpeter stand out. Several works of current scholars have already been mentioned. Table 10.3 gives an overview of the works of some widely recognized scholars on the future of capitalism.[57]

While there is substantial consensus among current scholars that we are approaching a so-called information (knowledge, service and so on) society (age, era and so on), there is not (yet) much emphasis on aspects like private ownership and control of information and its rent streams.

In summary, it has been argued here that we are witnessing a gradual transition or evolution to intellectual capitalism, from and still co-existing with traditional capitalism. New technologies in general, and ICTs in particular, constitute a major factor out of several interdependent factors behind the transition. Other important factors would include intensified international competition; rise of large MNCs; managerial developments; rise of countries like Japan (being poor in natural resources); US activism; and institutional developments.

Certainly, many past concerns over the effects of capitalism apply to intellectual capitalism as well, such as concern over capital concentration, inequalities and unemployment, all of which may be aggravated in intellectual capitalism. Unemployment in certain types of more IC-oriented professions may also gradually become substantial. If so, there may not be a growing government or public sector to absorb intellectuals who might otherwise instigate social unrest.[58]

New concerns over intellectual capitalism are also likely to appear. A most probable example is economic crime, or IC theft and fraud in and among developed and developing countries. Infocom technologies may actually offer attractive crime opportunities because of the expense of policing and law enforcement. In fact, there will be substantial difficulties in providing proper legislation in a timely manner.

Overall, various types of transaction costs could become exceedingly high in intellectual capitalism. On the other hand, ICTs might also offer new opportunities to lower them, but probably at the cost of increased societal control and perceived losses of personal integrity and freedom. Thus, intellectual capitalism may clash with one set of fundamental human values.

One conceivable scenario for the future, admittedly in a technocentric spirit, is that new technology systems will again change the economic system. Such a future change would be away from intellectual capitalism, perhaps to new or hybrid forms of economic systems which are not readily classifiable as capitalistic. A new family of technologies is emerging in and around biotechnology and medical health care – let us call them biohealth technologies.

Table 10.3 *Characterization of some authors on the future of capitalism*[1]

Author	Future of capitalism	Main characteristics of future stage	Type of transitory mechanism	Main driving factors in transition
Marx	Socialism/ communism	State-owned means of production	Self-destruction	• Growing social pain and inequalities • Wasteful business cycles, instability, duplication and differentiation • Concentration of capital and political power • Exploitation of workers and public resources • Growing hostility among workers against capital owners • Worker-led revolution
Schumpeter	Socialism	State-owned means of production	Self-destruction	• Increasing obsolescence of the entrepreneurial function • Destruction of protecting stratum • Destruction of capitalist institutional framework • Growing hostility towards capitalism
Drucker	Post-capitalism	Knowledge as primary resource Capitalist institutions survive New 'classes' – managers, service workers, intellectuals	Gradual evolution[2]	• Knowledge and knowledge workers • Management • ?[2]
Rosenberg	Evolution	Continued experimentation and modification of capitalist institutions	Self-construction	• Inherent experimental feedback structure
Thurow	Stagnation	Capitalism with stronger dependence upon human capital and 'brainpower' industries	Lack of competing economic system	• Technology • Ideology

Notes
1. These characterizations are gross simplifications by necessity.
2. A specific transitory mechanism is not explicated, nor is a set of main driving factors.

Today, such technologies emerge under quite capitalistic forms in corporations and also to a varying extent in hospitals and related institutions, at least in the USA. The patent system itself has traditionally worked best from a company point of view in the chemical and pharmaceutical industry, and now the system is being extended into genetic engineering. However, the generation and exploitation of biohealth technologies clash with fundamental humanistic values. At a global level, with less homogeneous capitalistic traditions, such clashes may increase to such proportions that intellectual capitalism has to change. Possibly pressures for change will also come from the greying baby-boom generation of World War II, if the health-care sector does not perform satisfactorily under capitalistic forms that are put in place.

Another scenario is that national struggles over intellectual capital will become destructive on a large scale. Military escalation may of course arise from such struggles or fear of them, just as from traditional struggles over land and other physical resources (like fresh water). In addition, military power will be IC-intensive in itself.

10.8   SUMMARY AND CONCLUSIONS

Despite various prophecies to the contrary – wishful or not – capitalist economic systems are as strong as ever after the rise of competitive Asian economies, the downfall of the Soviet Union and the current resurgence of the US economy. Capitalism may come in many varieties, however. This chapter has argued that capitalism is now being transformed into a most important new form, that can be called *intellectual capitalism*. In broad terms intellectual capitalism can be interpreted as a confluence of a capitalist economy and a knowledge or information economy. More specifically, intellectual capitalism refers to an economic system with basic capitalist institutions (private property rights, private profit, competitive markets and free enterprise) in which productive assets and processes, as well as commercial transactions and products, are predominantly intellectual or immaterial rather than physical in nature. Despite palpable problems in accounting for intellectual capital and products (an exciting research area in itself) an unfolding shift towards intellectual capitalism is indicated by various indicators (Solow-type residuals, Tobin's q, Becker-type human capital accounting, intangible investment ratios, emergence of a pro-patent era, share of corporate R&D to total R&D in the world, growth of technology markets and markets for corporate control and so on).

This chapter further argued that the main driving force behind this shift is technological change and the accumulation of new technologies in general. More specifically, the family of information and communication technologies, *infocom technologies*, plays a pivotal role in the emergence of intellectual capitalism, not unlike the role played by the family of material and energy technologies in the emergence of original capitalism. ICTs not only enable fast, cheap and differentiated production and distribution of various old and new types of information, but they also enable recording, codifying, packaging and mass marketing of information, making it commercially available at a low transaction cost. The traditional malfunctioning of pure information markets thereby becomes mitigated. Consequently, human communication and information barter, be it on a habitual, altruistic or profit basis, becomes more easily commercialized. Vast opportunities to profit from innovation and increasing competitive pressures at all levels in society will ensure that, in fact, information and communication will become far more subjected to commercial transactions than we have as yet expected, let alone hoped.

A number of key functionalities are offered by ICTs to support intellectual capitalism. Increased *collectability, codifiability, connectivity, processability, interactivity, selectivity, and controllability* in communications deserve special mentioning. These functionalities enable economic agents to profit from information, for example, by raising *excludability* through building electronic locks and fences around information assets. Although we have an almost global IPR system in place, ownership of information *per se* (including knowledge, competence and data) is not eventually the decisive issue for intellectual capitalism. Rather, it is the ability of economic agents to control the rent stream from information that is crucial. Such control has traditionally been accomplished by embedding information with physical products or with individuals and more recently by embedding it in small companies as well. Appropriation of benefits, then, has been accomplished by using product markets, labour markets and stock markets. ICTs now significantly enhance the possibilities to control rent streams from intellectual capital and products and raise excludability and lower transaction cost without necessarily relying on IPRs, although the latter are increasingly important as well. Thereby, IC management with technology management as an important part becomes a key managerial issue in most companies, large and small. Old companies and organizations in general, such as libraries and universities, will have to transform and adapt, and new ones, such as data mining companies, information brokers and content providers, will appear. Similarly, IC-oriented policies (for education, R&D and so on) become of key governmental concern, especially in nations like Japan and South Korea which are poor in natural resources. However, by and large, it is yet too early to fully identify all managerial and policy implications of the emerging intellectual capitalism.

New technologies, then, play two main roles for intellectual capitalism. First, they constitute a lion's share in the generation of intellectual capital and products and second, and more specifically for ICTs, they serve to privatize the benefits from intellectual capital and products by raising excludability and lowering transaction costs. The Internet with its web sites is a most important illustration of how ICTs play both these roles and thereby foster intellectual capitalism on two accounts. The Internet provides a marketplace in the true, original sense of the word – a meeting place for prospective buyers and sellers, displaying merchandise and quoting prices with the possibility of communicating about prospective transactions. The marketplace provided by the Internet and related networks is growing rapidly into an efficient, fast, global mass market with numerous information products and linked databases and with a concomitant rapid growth of electronic commerce in general. However, the fastest growth will probably be in information and multimedia-related commerce, especially with new generations of Internet protocols and digital payment systems enabling 'click and pay' functions for 'microtransactions' of information on a large scale.

This chapter concluded with two scenarios. One regards the future of the *intellectual property rights system*, originally designed to foster innovation but perhaps increasingly counteracting its own purpose. However, amid the rhetoric of sceptics, a reversal to a weak IP regime is not likely. Rather, fixes will be attempted, as well as further international harmonization and rationalization. A certain convergence of the IP regimes, linked to science and technology, respectively, is also likely.

The second scenario regarded the future of intellectual capitalism altogether. Various authors (for example, Marx, Schumpeter, Drucker, Thurow and Rosenberg) have emphasized different self-destructive, evolutionary or stagnating tendencies inherent in capitalism. As for intellectual capitalism it is probably not overly technocentric to assume that new families of technologies will appear that will again fundamentally change the economic system, gradually or not. For example, a new technology family or technology system is emerging in and around biotechnology and health care, what we perhaps can call *biohealth technologies*. It is not inconceivable that intellectual capitalism will increasingly be perceived in society to clash with fundamental humanistic values, especially in connection with biohealth technologies. Such clashes may very well spur the emergence of new types of economic systems, be they capitalist, quasi-capitalist or something else, yet to be identified.

Just as Schumpeter described the process of 'creative destruction' within the capitalist system, capitalism itself may undergo a similar process. Although intellectual capitalism may represent an advancement in the development of capitalism and create greater opportunities for those firms that exploit its potential, this does not imply that society as a whole is better off.

In religious belief systems Adam and Eve were punished for eating from the tree of knowledge, and Zeus punished Prometheus for giving fire to mankind. The message here is that knowledge, and technology in particular, is power, and power is dangerous. Although knowledge can be used to enlighten, it has too often been used to suppress and dominate. Ultimately the fruits of knowledge, growing higher and higher up the tree, may not be so sweet to mankind as we compete for a taste without learning how to control our appetite.

NOTES

1. According to Gardner (1988, p.4) an *economic system* is defined as 'a set of institutions involved in making and implementing economic decisions'. An *institution* in turn is defined as 'an organization, practice, convention, or custom that is material and persistent in the life and culture of a society' (ibid.). Examples of capitalist institutions are business corporations, banks, competitive markets, property rights and profit motives.
2. The circumstance that patented knowledge is publicly disclosed is equivalent to viewing it as privately owned knowledge being leased or licensed out for free under certain limiting conditions on its commercial use by the licensee.
3. Since 20 years allows for close to three doublings, the stock of knowledge at the end of the 20th year is close to eight times as large as the initial stock. This simple calculation assumes that all new knowledge is both patentable and patented. Similar calculations could of course be done for technical know-how held as secrets, taking into account the rate by which they leak out (that is, 'expire').
4. De Solla Price has calculated that doubling times for scientific knowledge have been about 10 to 15 years for centuries (see Jantsch 1967). Scientific knowledge is not patentable in principle. However, assume for the sake of the argument that scientific knowledge with a doubling time of 10 years takes about a generation, say 20 years, to diffuse to a broader public, then only a quarter, or 25 per cent, will be publicly held at any point in time.
5. Solow-type residual refers to the statistical residual factor when output growth is accounted for by input of production factors such as labour, land and physical capital. Solow-type residuals have been interpreted as a measure of the technological progress of an economy, but they incorporate more factors than technology taken in an engineering sense, for example, organizational factors. See Solow (1957) and Griliches (1996).
6. The Scandinavian insurance company Skandia is one good example, see Edvinsson and Malone (1997). See also Stewart (1997), and Kaplan and Norton (1996).
7. For the rise of IC-based firms, see Granstrand (1998). For the increasing importance and functioning of technology markets, see, for example, Caves et al. (1983), Adelstein and Peretz (1985), Granstrand et al. (1992a), Geroski (1995), Arora (1995, 1996) and Athreye (1998). For the rise of markets for innovative, small firms, see Granstrand and Sjölander (1990b) and Lindholm (1994). For a classic work on the inherent problems in information markets, see Arrow (1962) and also Arrow (1974).
8. A moratorium on patents, that is, a temporary and possibly selective stoppage of patent granting, has not been much discussed but is none the less a possibility in principle. A moratorium could, for example, be argued to serve the purpose of mitigating abuses and slowing down the privatization of certain new, generic technologies and stimulate their diffusion, thereby allowing for lagging countries and firms to catch up. The use of shorter maximal patent lifetimes in some LDCs has been motivated on similar grounds. The threat of a moratorium might also discipline user and abusers of IPR.
9. One could ask why the US pro-patent developments in the 1980s did not occur earlier (see Chapters 2 and 5). Misplaced monopoly and tariff notions about patents among free trade and competition advocates were probably one delaying factor.
10. Such lists are provided, for example, by the journal *Forbes*. At the top of the *Forbes* 1994 list of the most highly valued personal fortunes are William H. Gates III (with US$36.4 billion related to Microsoft), Warren Buffett (with US$23.2 billion related to holdings, for example, in Coca-Cola), Hans Rausing (with US$9.0 billion related to the Swedish packaging MNC Tetra Laval), and Yoshiaki Tsutsumi (with US$8.0 billion related to Japanese real estate).
11. Of course, there are mixed cases of manual and intellectual skills, like those of surgeons and musicians, as described in Chapter 4.

12. Thus note that the relation between intellectual labour and intellectual capitalists is different from the relation between manual labour and traditional capitalists.
13. It is interesting to note that salaries (as well as individual fortunes) seem to have a more skewed distribution in a capitalist society than intelligence, although there are problems in measuring the latter.
14. Professor Higuchi, personal communication.
15. The concept of the infocom industry refers to the information industry and the telecommunications industry and includes especially data, media and telecommunications industries.
16. The distinction between manufacturing and service industries is fuzzy and easily obscures the role of technology and intellectual capital in both. Therefore a discussion of a transition from manufacturing to service industries becomes difficult and even misleading, and will be omitted here.
17. Note the possible distinction between the role of intellectual capital in the total capital structure and the role of intellectual capital as productive input. In principle, an IC firm can own lots of idle land, idle mines and so on, just as people, say on a farm, can have a lot of unexploited knowledge (idle minds).
18. Many organizations in this latter category lack motivation to capitalize their knowledge and extract rents from it in a narrow economic sense, and thus could be considered potential or dormant IC-based firms.
19. One could also refer here to possible long waves of innovations to come (that is, so called Kondratieff waves; see, for example, Freeman et al. 1982). The baby boom from World War II also contributes to a boom of innovations. The following oversimplified but illustrative calculation may illustrate a likely link between demographics and innovativeness. If a substantial share of baby boomers are peaking in technological creativity when 35 years old and it takes, say, about 5–10 years to innovation and another 5–10 years to substantial diffusion, the 1990s would witness much innovativeness.
20. For example, the transition to more team-work among individuals in R&D has progressed further into team-work among firms in R&D. See Dunning (1988), who refers to this as a form of alliance capitalism. This is an example of how the economic pursuit of new, complex technologies calls forth new managerial forms.
21. It is impossible to do justice to the works of these scholars in this limited space. The reader is therefore referred to their works, for example, Abramovitz (1986, 1991), Rosenberg and Birdzell (1986) and Wright (1990).
22. The concept could be seen as referring to a mutually reinforcing match between a technology system and a national economic system in a co-evolutionary process. (See Abramovitz, 1990, p. 3.)
23. This clearly does not imply that material resources are unimportant for Japan's development, nor does it mean that Japan has put her R&D efforts primarily into material resource-saving technologies.
24. Immigration of non-Japanese innovators and entrepreneurs into Japan is not very likely for the foreseeable future, however. Note the importance of similar immigration to the US economy.
25. For some interesting studies, see Arora (1996) and Caves et al. (1983).
26. For a classic work on this, see Arrow (1962).
27. Compare limits to observation posed by Heisenberg's uncertainty relation. Notions of limits to invention, exhaustion of discoveries and so on are old and persistent, as are their refutations. As an example, the US Patent Commissioner, Charles H. Duell, around 1899 voiced the opinion that all major inventions had already been made. A recent work expressing a similar opinion for science is Horgan (1996). Schumpeter refuted 'the widely accepted view that the great stride in technological advance has been made and that but minor achievements remain' (Schumpeter 1976, p. 117) by referring to the promises held out (in the 1940s) by chemical, electrical and construction engineering and the fact that future technologies are uncertain and therefore one cannot reason that there are diminishing returns to new technological discoveries.

28. Any observed slowdowns have been temporary so far, for example, the decline in patenting in the USA in the 1970s. Needless to say, the yield to R&D and inventive efforts in terms of potentially patentable advances is difficult to observe.
29. More examples are superconductivity and gene splicing.
30. Just think of semiconductivity, discovered in the late 1930s.
31. Note that in both Marx's and Schumpeter's analyses of capitalism in their days, they emphasized the auto-destructive character of capitalism on the whole in the long run, that is they argued that capitalism will destroy itself (but for different reasons).
32. These are projections made also by the growing firms in the security provision business (for example, Securitas), having developed far away from padlocks and guards.
33. See Veblen (1965).
34. An often quoted example is the QWERTY design of alphabetical keyboards; see David (1985) and Arthur (1988). The claimed superiority of the so-called Dvorak keyboard, that challenged the dominance of the QWERTY design, is highly disputable (see Liebowitz and Margolis 1990).
35. In his discussion of the possibility of vanishing investment opportunities on the whole, Schumpeter also dismissed this factor (1976, pp. 113–14).
36. Many authors have made such arguments; see, for example, Thurow (1996). Also note the expression 'information wants to be free'. See also Branscomb (1994).
37. Examples of a kind of intellectual slavery can be found in the dictatorial transfer and use of scientists in Nazi Germany and the post-war Soviet Union. Needless to say, productivity suffered as did the scientists.
38. Encryption codes have been considered munitions in the USA and subjected to export controls. Thus companies like Netscape, who use some encryption in their software, have had to comply with these controls, being classified as munition companies.
39. Criminal businesses are also greatly aided by encryption.
40. Recall that public goods are characterized by low excludability, non-rivalry in use and a high ratio of fixed costs to variable costs. Note that egalitarian or human rights aspects do not enter the definition of public goods.
41. Technology-based excludability can also be used for political purposes, of course, as when North Korea blocked its TV viewers from South Korean programmes by using another standard. Actually, creating incompatible standards is a way to enforce a certain kind of excludability.
42. New information businesses grow under various labels currently in vogue, labels such as 'data warehousing' and 'data mining'. A new breed of knowledge entrepreneurs or information exploiters is also growing.
43. As an analogue to illustrate the amount of information asymmetries in an economy, note that spontaneous (or epidemic) diffusion of information often follows a logistic process. If new information flows into the economy at a certain rate, and diffusion takes time to penetrate a population, at each point in time in a stationary state only a limited share of the population will have access to all new information.
44. Since society does not (yet) provide police forces for enforcement of IPR, IPR holders have to organize their own policing. Examples of private enforcement initiatives, probably a sign of a growing trend, are the formation of BSA (Business Software Alliance) and Counterfeiting Intelligence Bureau, see ICC (1997).
45. See Freeman et al. (1982) for a good overview of attempts to link 'Kondratieff waves' of new technology systems to fundamental changes in the economic system or changes in the 'techno-economic paradigm' in the words of Freeman and Perez (1988). See also Rosenberg and Frischtak (1984).
46. The concept of a knowledge-based organization, for which there are many terms, is not easy to define precisely, and the concept obviously runs the risk of becoming a catch-all. Nevertheless it will be used here to refer primarily to organizations with knowledge-related resources as a predominant part. Needless to say, many authors have dealt with such organizations in one way or another.
47. A fairly recently coined term for the management of knowledge-related resources is 'knowledge management'. For an overview see, for example, Shariq (1997). Strictly speaking, knowledge

management is embraced by IC management but is a broader term than technology management, with technology taken to mean a body of knowledge about techniques.

48. Technology management, then, is concerned with various forms of technology sourcing, not just in-house R&D.

49. The prognosis that 'first to file' will sooner or later be the predominant ground in the world, including the USA, has already been mentioned, in Chapter 2.

50. The *Changes for Breakthrough* report by the Commission on Intellectual Property Rights in the 21st Century recommends a worldwide patent network linking the tri-lateral patent offices (that is, JPO, USPTO, EPO).

51. The JPO says it will develop Cyber Patent Services by 2005.

52. The language factor in general as a national 'glue' is weakening fairly rapidly since English is gaining ground as a global language in S&T and business, as well as among younger generations. ICTs enabling, for example, broadcasting and the Internet, together with provision of contents in English further boosts English as a global language. Gradually English is also becoming a global language in education.

53. The substantial costs, times and uncertainties of patent litigation have always raised concern, see for example, Babbage (1832), Vaughan (1925) and Kingston (1995). For a recent overview, see Lanjouw and Lerner (1997).

54. This may appear as a preposterous scenario to some, but it is in fact quite feasible. Computer-generated musical compositions, art pieces, poems, visual patterns, logos, trade marks and so on are improving, as is the understanding of creative processes. In fact, a company called Invention Machine Corporation is moving in the direction of computer-aided patenting (or computer-aided innovation – CAI). The company originates from the idea of the Russian patent examiner Genrich Altschuller who postulates that there are general principles of invention (in fact an old idea elaborated by many scholars and inventors) that he and his collaborators have discovered in examining millions of patents. (See also Chapter 9.)

55. Compare the difficulty of applying the non-obviousness test to computers instead of to professionals.

56. For a discussion of the traditional IP regime in science, see, for example, Nelkin (1984), Merton (1988) and Long (1991), and Stephan (1996) and Eisenberg (1987) for how it may clash with the IP regime in technology and industry. The distinction between science and technology is becoming blurred, however (see, for example, Narin and Noma 1985). The division of intellectual labour between universities and companies is also less clear, with companies doing basic research (see, for example, Rosenberg 1989) and universities taking out patents (see for example, Henderson et al. 1995 and Bertha 1996).

57. Other and more works could have been selected, of course. Drucker (1993), Rosenberg and Birdzell (1986), Rosenberg (1992) and Thurow (1996) have been chosen as recent works by prolific and well-known writers, together representing both economics and management perspectives.

58. This was pointed out by Schumpeter as a feature of the welfare state in Sweden in the past.

Appendix 1 Japanese and Swedish corporate patenting – a comparative analysis

A1.1 RESEARCH QUESTIONS FOR CORPORATE 'BENCHMARKING'

As described in Chapter 1, the core empirical study for this book consisted of a number of sub-studies. One sub-study compared publicly available patent statistics for a number of large Japanese and Swedish corporations, some results of which will be presented below.

A broad picture of the patenting profiles of the largest Japanese and Swedish corporations is given here together with a comparison of the profiles for the important pairs of actual or potential Japanese and Swedish competitors. This comparison provides an illustration of a simple 'benchmarking' with respect to patenting activities without going into a detailed comparative analysis of separate business areas in the large corporations studied. Several tables of data are provided simply for the interest of readers in the corporations studied. However, more extensive elaborations on patenting statistics for benchmarking and other information purposes are possible. At the same time a great deal of care must be exercised when drawing conclusions based on patenting statistics, as described in Chapter 9. Thus, fairly elaborate descriptions of the methodology used and the caveats involved are given here for instructive purposes. This hopefully serves as a starting point for further exercises in utilizing patenting statistics *per se* and especially in combination with other sorts of statistics. More specifically this section highlights the following questions:

1. What is the total level and trend of patenting over time in the largest technology-based Japanese and Swedish corporations?
2. What is the width of the corporate technology base (or the extent of technology diversification) as indicated by patenting activities?

If used for benchmarking Japanese and Swedish patenting, the findings of this appendix should be viewed in relation to the findings in the other sub-studies of the overall project described in Chapter 1.[1]

A1.2   METHOD

A1.2.1   Sample Design

The large Japanese and Swedish corporations in the sample were selected according to the following criteria.[2]

1. The largest corporations with respect to R&D investments in 1990 in both countries should be included.
2. Together they should constitute a significant share of the total industrial R&D in the two countries.
3. The largest R&D spenders in each of the major industrial sectors should be included.
4. A number of actually or potentially competing Japanese and Swedish corporations should be ensured.

A 'corporation' is identified as a non-majority-owned entity together with its majority-owned subsidiaries. The Japanese conglomerate structure (the *keiretsu*) is not considered a corporation. Thus, for example, NEC and Sumitomo Chemical, which both belong to the Sumitomo *keiretsu*, are treated as separate corporations. The corporations have been viewed as they were consolidated at the end of 1990.[3]

Strictly speaking, 'large corporation' in the sample refers to large corporations with large R&D budgets. However, corporations with large budgets usually have large sales, so most of the major industrial corporations by sales in the two countries are included in the sample.

Large corporations, although mostly multinational, usually have an undisputed nationality, and in a few cases they may have two. The only example of the latter in the sample is the Swedish–Swiss ABB, which, however, has been referred to as Swedish. The final sample consisted of 2×22 corporations.

A1.2.2   Patent Data Collection

The level of patenting is indicated by a simple count of the number of patents granted each year. The USPTO data is counted according to the year the patent was published in the USA, and for the EPO according to the year in which the priority year for a patent began in Europe.[4] The EPO grants 'EPO patents', which give patent protection in a large number of European countries, including Sweden.

European patents are not the only possible means of obtaining patent protection in European countries. The propensity to use the EPO varies among companies as well as over time. The other possibilities are to apply for national patents in various countries separately via an international application or to apply for a PCT patent. The latter gives patent protection through specially authorized national patent offices in those PCT-associated countries that the applicant chooses to designate. The possibilities may also be combined. Thus, it is difficult to get an overview of patent protection in Europe through simple patent counts. However, it appears from the survey study that companies increasingly use the EPO. This notwithstanding, time-series data for EPO patents before the mid-1980s are suffering from a start-up bias, because in 1978 the EPO started creating a time lag between the patent application filing and registration date and the patent publishing and granting date, apart from other transient lapses.

The number of patent applications over time could have been used instead of the number of patents granted. However, some applications do not result in patents, and therefore, by looking at granted patents, poor applications are filtered out.[5] Additionally, application data for US patents are more difficult to collect.

The observation period from 1978–91 was chosen, which provides useful US statistics. As mentioned European patent data is not reliable before approximately 1985, since the EPO started its work only in 1978.[6]

The patenting systems and offices worldwide are supposed to use only one level of invention when assessing patentability. This level may vary among countries, however, although international harmonization is gradually taking place. It may also vary over time. Ideally, one would have wanted a finer scale of inventiveness, or technical quality of a patent (as definitely distinct from the economic quality of a patent), for measuring purposes. Patents vary widely with regard to their technical qualities (as they certainly do in their economic qualities). A simple patent count does not reflect these variations. To some extent, so-called citation data, that is, data on the number of times a certain patent has been cited in other patent applications, could be used as a quality indicator. This was done at the industry level, as described in Chapter 5, but was not broken down to the company level.

A1.2.3   Indicator Design

The limitations of patent statistics and the limitations of each single indicator based on such statistics should again be noted. Therefore several indicators are generally needed, even for the specific purpose of an analysis, in order to enable a sensitivity analysis.

The sheer volume of patenting by a company indicates its propensity to patent and its patent power. In order to *measure the volume of patenting*, one would ideally have wanted data on the portfolio of active patents or patents in force (that is, patents granted for which annual maintenance fees are paid by the patent holder in order to keep the patent in force) for each corporation over time. But such data are very costly to collect. Corporations vary considerably in their propensity and policies for maintaining patents over time in various countries. To some extent, long periods of observation of annually granted patents may give a clue to the rough size of the total volume of a corporation's patent portfolio.

Patents may be granted in various countries in which the applicant chooses to apply, based on the same invention. Thus, patent counts are not the same as invention counts. There are various ways to distil invention counts from patent counts but they have not been pursued here.

Several studies have shown the strong impact of technology diversification upon both corporate growth of sales and corporate growth of R&D.[7] Technology diversification is defined as the broadening of a corporation's technology base into new technologies, that is, increasing its width. Both the width and the increase in the width have an impact on sales and R&D. To *indicate the level and width of a corporation's technology base*, several indicators have been calculated. Thus, for each Japanese and Swedish corporation respectively, and for US and EPO patents respectively, the following indicators have been calculated:

n_{kt} = number of patents granted in year t by the USPTO and by the EPO, respectively, with main classification in class k in the US patent classification system and in the International Patent Classification (IPC) system as used by the EPO.[8] In contrast to the US classification system, the IPC system is hierarchical with, in falling order, levels for sections, sub-sections, classes, sub-classes and so on. Here n_{kt} is a count at IPC level three.

m_t = average number of patents granted per class in year t (classes with zero patents not excluded; inactive classes in the US system are excluded, that is, the number of classes in total that are actively used by the USPTO among the available classes in the system appears in the denominator of m_t).

D_t = diversity (or diversification) index in year t for the corporate patent distribution over classes, which equals $1 - H_t$, where

H_t = Herfindahl's concentration ratio = $\Sigma_k p_{kt}^2$, where p_{kt} is the share of a corporation's total number of patents in year t that fall in patent class k.

N_t = number of patent classes containing one or more patents granted to the corporation in year t.

G_{st} = $(n_{.t}/n_{.s} - 1)/(t - s)$, that is, relative change in number of patents granted from year s to year t, divided by number of years lapsed, thus simply indicating annual average (non-compounded) relative change in patenting between year s and t ($n_{.s}$ denotes $\Sigma_k n_{ks}$).

The index D_t indicates the width (breadth, diversity) of corporate patenting.[9] N_t also indicates the width of patenting but in a simpler and less robust way. However, N_t cannot be compared between the USA and Europe. The width of patenting in turn is an indicator of the width of the corporation's technology base or the technological diversity (or diversification) of a corporation. (Strictly speaking, technological diversification refers to the process of increasing technological diversity, that is, increasing the width of a technology base rather than the width itself.) Finally, G_{st} is a simple relative growth indicator, subjected to yearly fluctuations, however.

A1.3 DATA

Tables A1.1–2 and Figure A1.1 give the corporate patent profiles in terms of number of patents granted in Europe (represented by EPO patents) and the USA.[10] Indicators of level (or volume), width of the patent base and growth of patenting have been constructed as described in the preceding section.

Table A1.1 Patenting activities by Japanese corporations in Europe and the USA

Company	n^1	m^1	D^2	N^2	G^3
Europe[4]					
Canon	141	1.195	0.852	17	7.40
Fujitsu	1 468	12.441	0.819	42	−8.20
Hitachi	2 265	19.195	0.933	75	20.80
Honda	240	2.034	0.836	22	9.40
Kirin Brewery	25	0.212	0.746	8	0.80
Kyocera	5	0.042	0.640	3	0.40
Matsushita	996	8.441	0.913	53	−3.00
Mitsubishi Heavy Ind.	1 629	13.805	0.949	81	28.00
NEC	909	7.703	0.905	61	12.40
Nippon Denso	4	0.034	0.625	3	0.00
Nippon Seiko	5	0.042	0.560	3	0.00
Nippon Steel	222	1.881	0.873	27	3.20
Nissan	676	5.729	0.860	47	−11.40
OJI Paper	58	0.492	0.716	10	0.60
Sanyo	117	0.992	0.840	21	−1.00
Sharp	264	2.237	0.892	31	10.40

continued

Table A1.1   continued

Company	n^1	m^1	D^2	N^2	G^3
Shimizu	69	0.585	0.878	21	2.80
Sony	785	6.653	0.717	31	24.00
Takeda	323	2.737	0.573	15	1.00
Tokyo Electric Power	103	0.873	0.632	10	2.60
Toshiba	2 096	17.763	0.877	62	6.20
Toyota	580	4.9153	0.838	38	20.4
USA[5]					
Canon	7 009	18.300	0.927	140	70.00
Fujitsu	2 634	6.877	0.953	123	20.80
Hitachi	10 505	27.428	0.982	241	60.30
Honda	2 949	7.700	0.897	138	28.70
Kirin Brewery	70	0.183	0.939	30	1.20
Kyocera	135	0.352	0.952	48	1.20
Matsushita	4 000	10.444	0.978	211	22.50
Mitsubishi Heavy Ind.	2	0.005	0.500	2	0.00
NEC	3 286	8.580	0.964	114	37.10
Nippon Denso	18	0.047	0.877	13	0.20
Nippon Seiko	291	0.760	0.852	44	5.90
Nippon Steel	739	1.930	0.903	82	3.90
Nissan	3 948	10.308	0.926	156	21.10
OJI Paper	53	0.138	0.840	16	0.50
Sanyo	944	2.4648	0.973	145	8.5
Sharp	2 468	6.444	0.960	141	26.50
Shimizu	81	0.211	0.894	32	1.20
Sony	3 003	7.841	0.900	123	7.50
Takeda	753	1.966	0.879	61	4.70
Tokyo Electric Power	322	0.841	0.899	52	3.30
Toshiba	8 356	21.817	0.978	207	68.90
Toyota	3 403	8.885	0.917	156	–4.00

Notes
1. n and m are level indicators.
2. D and N are diversity indicators (indicating directly the width of corporate patenting and indirectly the width or diversity of the corporate technology base).
3. G is a growth indicator, equal to the annual average relative change in number of patents granted in 1980 and 1985 for Europe, and in 1980 and 1990 for the USA.
4. Granted EPO patents filed 1977–89.
5. Granted USPTO patents published 1979–91.

Table A1.2   Patenting activities by Swedish corporations in Europe and the USA

Company	n^1	m^1	D^2	N^2	G^3
Europe[4]					
ABB	1014	8.593	0.900	60	8.20
AGA	14	0.119	0.857	9	0.60
Alfa-Laval	100	0.847	0.815	19	1.80
Astra	115	0.975	0.629	11	1.20
Atlas Copco	70	0.593	0.800	15	−1.40
Electrolux	180	1.525	0.895	35	2.80
Ericsson	177	1.500	0.810	23	1.80
Gambro	70	0.593	0.800	15	−1.40
Nobel	147	1.246	0.899	31	6.20
Procordia	79	0.669	0.774	7	2.60
SAAB	48	0.407	0.891	17	1.00
Sandvik	50	0.424	0.854	20	−0.60
SCA	7	0.059	0.612	4	0.40
Skanska	4	0.034	0.375	2	−0.60
SKF	150	1.271	0.522	17	1.40
SSAB	15	0.127	0.844	8	−0.20
STORA	2	0.017	0.500	2	0.20
Swedish Ordnance	30	0.254	0.609	5	1.20
Televerket (now Telia)	7	0.059	0.735	5	0.00
Tetra Pak	181	1.534	10.456	18	0.40
Vattenfall	0				
Volvo	74	0.627	0.847	18	1.00
USA[5]					
ABB	2010	5.248	0.979	167	0.50
AGA	66	0.172	0.959	35	−0.70
Alfa-Laval	263	0.687	0.914	57	−0.80
Astra	191	0.499	0.813	35	0.00
Atlas Copco	173	0.452	0.917	46	−1.60
Electrolux	285	0.744	0.959	78	1.20
Ericsson	362	0.945	0.955	69	1.10
Gambro	96	0.251	0.835	25	−1.00
Nobel	770	2.010	0.959	104	−2.40
Procordia	155	0.405	0.898	31	0.20
SAAB	138	0.360	0.949	52	0.40
Sandvik	180	0.470	0.950	51	1.10

continued

Table A1.2   continued

Company	n^1	m^1	D^2	N^2	G^3
SCA	14	0.037	0.806	8	−0.40
Skanska	3	0.008	0.667	3	0.00
SKF	667	1.742	0.838	82	−1.00
SSAB	16	0.042	0.875	11	0.10
STORA	17	0.044	0.734	8	−0.10
Swedish Ordnance	21	0.055	0.834	11	0.10
Televerket (now Telia)	3	0.008	0.667	3	0.10
Tetra Pak	262	0.684	0.921	48	0.80
Vattenfall	0				
Volvo	234	0.611	0.948	58	−0.70

Notes
1. n and m are level indicators.
2. D and N are diversity indicators (indicating directly the width of corporate patenting and indirectly the width or diversity of the corporate technology base).
3. G is a growth indicator, equal to the annual average relative change in number of patents granted in 1980 and 1985 for Europe, and in 1980 and 1990 for the USA.
4. Granted EPO patents filed 1977–89.
5. Granted patents published 1979–91.

A few observations may be made right away. First, there are large variations between companies. Patents show a skewed distribution among the corporations, especially for Sweden, with ABB as an outstanding patentor, even if only half of its patents are considered. The top patentors are in electronics, especially in Japan.

Second, the Japanese corporations appear to focus more on the USA than on Europe in terms of volume, width and growth of US and EPO patents granted. Swedish corporations have larger patent volume and width in the USA than in Europe, but more patent growth in Europe. It is notable that Swedish corporate patenting in the USA has declined during the 1980s and the growth in Europe is modest if ABB is excluded.

Third, the patenting volume and width of Japanese corporations are much larger in general than for Swedish corporations. The question is to what extent the corporations are comparable. This will be dealt with in the next section.

A1.4   COMPARATIVE ANALYSIS

In this section, pairs of actually or potentially competing Japanese and Swedish corporations will be compared. The sole criterion for pairing the corporations is that they have at least one major product area in common, regardless of size of the corporations in terms of sales or R&D budgets. Since the corporations are already large by any standard, and mostly multinational, a common product area is the major factor determining the likelihood that they have met or will meet in the marketplace in Europe and/or the USA. Table A1.3 gives a comparison of the patent volume and patent width indicators for the pairs of competitors and Figure A1.1 gives some more detailed illustrations. It is immediately apparent that there is, with a few exceptions, a consistent pattern of larger absolute volume and width of Japanese corporate patenting activities in both Europe and the USA. However, apart from the general caveats and possible sources of statistical errors mentioned above, there are a number of additional considerations with regard to possible objections to this type of comparison.

Table A1.3   Comparison of corporate patenting activities in Europe and the USA

Corporate pair[1]	Sector	Sales ratio (1991)	Patent volume ratio (*n*–ratio) EP[2]	US[3]	Patent width ratio (*N*–ratio) EP[4]	US[5]
Hitachi/ABB	Electrical	5.5	2.2	5.2	1.3	1.4
Toshiba/ABB	Electrical	6.7	2.1	4.2	1.0	1.2
Takeda/Astra	Chemical	2.4	2.8	3.9	1.4	1.7
Sanyo/Electrolux	Mechanical	0.9	0.7	3.3	0.6	1.8
NEC/Ericsson	Electrical	3.7	5.1	9.0	2.6	1.6
Shimizu/Skanska	Construction	2.7	17.2	27.0	10.5	10.7
Nippon Steel/SSAB	Mechanical	11.8	14.8	46.2	3.4	7.5
Nissan/Volvo	Mechanical	3.4	9.1	16.6	2.6	2.6
Toyota/Volvo	Mechanical	4.5	7.8	14.3	2.1	2.6

Notes
1. The corporations paired have at least one major product area in common.
2. Ratio of number of EPO patents with priority 1977–89 for the two corporations in the pair.
3. Ratio of number of US patents published 1979–91.
4. Ratio of number of EPO patent classes with more than one patent with priority 1977–89.
5. Ratio of number of US patent classes with more than one patent published 1979–91.

When using EPO patents or European patenting statistics in general for comparing Japanese and Swedish companies, one should keep in mind that Sweden belongs to Europe while Japan does not. To the extent that a company's propensity to patent on its home market and its neighbouring markets might be expected to be higher than on other markets, European patenting statistics give

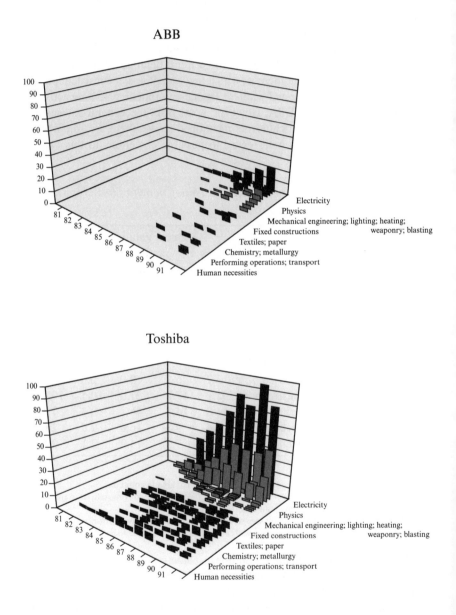

1

1

Ericsson

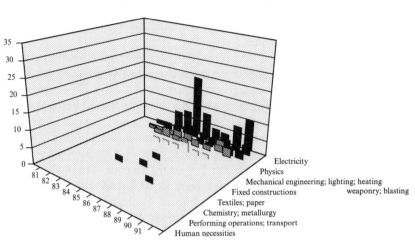

NEC

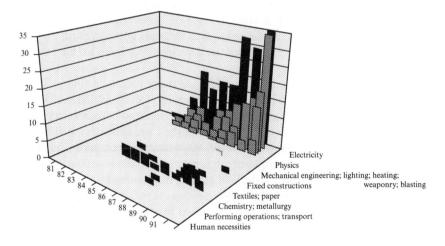

*Figure A1.1 The growth of patent portfolios (number of granted patents) in
Swedish and Japanese companies (EPO), 1981–1991*

a positive bias to Swedish companies compared to their Japanese counterparts, everything else being equal. From this point of view, US patenting statistics should give a more unbiased comparison between Japanese and Swedish companies. Moreover, the US patent statistics cover all patents in the USA with no specific transient effects as those arising from the start-up of EPO. Moreover, the various ways or routes to receive patents in Europe are not fully covered by EPO statistics. However, the general patterns found in EPO statistics are confirmed by the US statistics.

Second, a general caveat when comparing Japanese and Swedish patenting statistics concerns differences in the respective patent systems. As mentioned earlier, until 1987 the Japanese patent system did not really allow more than a single claim in a patent application while the European, including the Swedish, patent system allowed multiple claims. In the latter system, companies have had the possibility of filing a broad patent application with many claims while a corresponding application in the Japanese system would have to be split into many applications, one for each claim. Despite the adoption of the multiple-claim system in Japanese patent law, it might be expected that it would take time until the companies adopt the new system in practice. Furthermore, nothing prevents companies from filing single-claim applications, either in Japan or in Europe although such a practice could jeopardize individual applications.[11] Companies could, moreover, lower their patent filing and maintenance cost through using multiple claims. This is what many Japanese companies have often done when patenting in Europe and the USA. Thus, as a first step the Japanese and Swedish companies can by and large be compared using this methodology regarding their number of patents in Europe and the USA and increasingly so after 1987. In addition, it must be kept in mind that only a minor share of the Japanese corporations' patents filed in Japan are used for applications in Europe and the USA, and this share is smaller than the corresponding share for the Swedish corporations.

Still, it may be objected that Japanese company patents in Europe have a narrower scope on average than Swedish company patents and, indeed, Western company patents as a whole. Interviews with Japanese and Swedish companies indicate that this has been and still is in fact the case, although the difference might decrease in the future. However, this matter pertains to the quality of patents, apart from the mere quantity. It is naturally desirable to take the quality into account as well by using some kind of weighting procedure in the quantitative analysis of patent statistics. To some extent this is possible through the use of the number of times a patent has been cited in other patent applications, as mentioned earlier. Another possibility is to look at the age of cited patents in the patent applications, as done by Narin (1993) and others.

The breadth of patenting activities is much higher for Japanese companies, in both Europe and the USA. This pattern is consistently indicated by the breadth indicators D and N (as well as by standard deviations and entropy measures, although not shown here). Thus, there is no need at this level of analysis to correlate the indicators internally and qualify the interpretations based on differences in indicator design.

Regarding the higher volumes of patents granted for Japanese corporations, these do not directly indicate a larger patent power, as would a larger portfolio of patents in force. As mentioned earlier, the comparisons are based only on data for granted patents, which do not give the size of the portfolio of active patents of the companies. Companies do differ in their propensity for keeping patents in force by paying maintenance fees. The vintage structure of patent portfolios differs over companies and industries. The table data here give only the inflow to the company patent portfolios over a period of time, which is actually shorter than the patent lifetime of 20 years. There is no indication that Swedish companies tend to keep their granted patents in force longer than Japanese companies, on average.[12] Nor is there any indication whatsoever that Swedish companies in general had larger patent portfolios than their Japanese counterparts at the beginning of the period under observation, quite the contrary. If the patenting propensity of a company is persistently higher than for another company over a long period of time, its resulting patent portfolio will grow relatively larger if the companies keep their patents in force for similar times.

A natural objection is that the companies are not comparable since they might differ very much in terms of size of sales and/or size of R&D. Two points may be made in relation to this objection. First, the Japanese and Swedish companies in the sample are all large by any standard and the comparison of competitors does not differ by factors of ten or more, regarding either sales or R&D (with some exceptions). Second, when comparing two companies operating in a similar product area, their size in various respects matters for their competitive strength. Thus, the size of their sales and R&D as well as the size of their patent portfolios should, in fact, be compared together with other indicators (regarding product quality and so on) when judging the competitive strength of the corporations (as they are consolidated, indicating the level at which they are internally coordinated).[13]

When the purpose of benchmarking a competitor is to judge the market power derived from patents (for example, the probability of being able to block a competitor), a comparison of the relevant patent portfolios is justified as one indicator. A common difficulty in such comparisons, however, is that product areas and patent classes do not match very well. It is moreover difficult to sort out those patents which relate to a specific product area.[14] Some comparisons at a finer level of detail in the patent classifications were made in the study, but did not reveal any major deviations from the general pattern above. It is seldom the case that one corporation in the pair has a strong patent profile in one patent area while the other has a strong patent profile in another patent area.

Rather, the Japanese corporations commonly are strong in areas where their Swedish counterparts have most of their patents and are also strong in other patent areas. It could then be argued that patents in these other areas are less relevant in the comparison. For example, one could argue that many Japanese corporations are operating in electronics, thereby making them less comparable to Swedish mechanical engineering corporations. However, electronics is a technology of major relevance to competitiveness in the engineering industry in general, as has been described by Kodama (1986). Of course, not all technologies have synergistic relations and to some extent the argument is valid. For example, when Nippon Steel entered biotechnology (as was somewhat the vogue in the Japanese steel industry for a period in the 1980s), the competitive strength of Nippon Steel relative to the Swedish steel company SSAB in the steel industry did not actually increase.

In order to take this into account, one could adjust for the larger width of patenting in the Japanese corporations by simply comparing the *n*-ratios (patent volume ratios) and *N*-ratios (patent width ratios) in Table A1.3, which is a simple way of normalizing the data with respect to width of patenting. This kind of normalizing would disregard technological synergies and thus in fact favour the hypothesis that Swedish corporations have stronger profiles but concentrated in fewer areas. However, the *n*-ratio is generally significantly larger than the *N*-ratio, which does not support this hypothesis.

A1.5   POSSIBLE CAUSES AND EFFECTS OF DIFFERENCES IN PATENTING

What is behind the consistent differences in patent volume, width and growth between Japanese and Swedish corporations, as observed in the preceding sections? A full answer cannot be given here, but a few clues are offered. (A more comprehensive treatment is given in Chapter 5.) Some, though far from all, differences may be explained by the larger size of R&D budgets and IP departments and the wider range of product areas in the Japanese corporations. However, there are a multitude of factors behind the statistical differences that relate to historical differences in what can be called the *patent cultures* in Japan and Sweden, as described in Chapters 5 and 8. To repeat a bit here, Japan has consciously built up a patent culture, both at the national level and in industry, through the long process of catching up technologically with the West. In this process the Japanese had to learn several skills (for example, how to avoid Western patents). At the same time, taking out patents in 'holes' not covered by Western patents became prestigious for individuals, companies and the nation, and was a sign of gradually coming on par with the West. The fact that Japan is poor in natural resources has turned her eyes, hopes and energies on developing intellectual resources and securing intellectual property rights, not least in the long-run preparation for securing foreign input and output markets. The pursuit of IPR has traditionally not been particularly aggressive, however, especially not against the West, as this could have jeopardized the generally favourable conditions for transferring technology from the West to Japan, which prevailed for many decades after World War II (see Chapter 5).

Patents as legal instruments are designed to legally convey the right to exclude others. This makes them work like weapons in a legal war, which to some extent justifies the use of military analogies. When the US 'Japan-bashing' sentiments grew during the 1980s, induced by Japan's increasing economic success on US markets, IPR issues came to the forefront in US national and corporate policy-making. At the same time, a new court for patent appeals in the USA was created in 1982, and IPR were upgraded relative to anti-trust concerns (see Chapter 2). This resulted in a wave in the late 1980s of aggressive moves by US corporations and authorities in the IPR area against Japan and Asian NICs, for example, claiming infringement penalties and increased royalties for US patents. Since, by design, there are few good alternatives to fighting patents with patents,[15] this resulted in a patent war with, for example, escalating patent applications. This 'war' spread to Sweden but not to the same extent, and the Swedish corporations have often been slow to respond although, in all fairness, a number of Swedish corporations have in the 1990s reassessed their patent strategies and upgraded their patenting activities. The effects of the patent war should not be exaggerated, however. The most important explanation behind Japanese–Swedish patenting differences is still that the patent culture in large Swedish companies is weak compared with their Japanese counterparts for historical and managerial reasons. (See Chapter 8 for more details about patent culture.)

NOTES

1. This section is based on the report from one sub-study (no.2a) out of eight in the project. See Deiaco (1993), Granstrand and Sigurdson (1992, 1993a, b) and IVA (1993).
2. There are many methodological hazards involved in comparing corporations from nations of widely varying size, see, for example, Scherer et al. (1975).
3. Whether, when and how to consolidate companies in a study like this is a major problem, in fact. First, it is not clear, at least not without a sufficiently specific purpose, whether time serial data should refer to the company as it was consolidated at the year the data refer to (what from a methodological point of view we can call 'floating consolidation') or a fixed year ('fixed consolidation') and, if the latter, which year. Second, it is not an easy task to find all subsidiaries which may have patenting activities in a large corporation. Third, the names under which the patents have been assigned to a company may vary, even in spelling. Fourth,

reassignments of patents occur in the US patent statistics as acquisitions, mergers and divestments of companies occur but not without time lags and errors.

4. The so-called priority year is the 12-month period beginning at the date the first patent application for a specific invention was filed (see Glossary).

5. It is an interesting topic in itself to see why some patent applications do not result in patents granted and how the distribution of unfulfilled requirements varies over nations, sectors, companies, technologies and periods.

6. The US statistics in this period are not fully reliable either, since there were fluctuations in the annual number of patents issued due to budget and workload constraints at the USPTO, see Griliches (1989, 1990).

7. See, for example, Granstrand and Sjölander (1990a) and Oskarsson (1993).

8. Note that multiple classifications of a patent are common in both systems nowadays, but there is always a single main classification. Moreover, both systems allow for multiple claims in a single patent, thus allowing to some extent the applicant in principle to lump claims together into a single patent application. Before 1987, the Japanese patent system basically allowed only for single claims, which to some extent explains a larger number of Japanese patents in Japan. However, when Japanese companies patent in Europe and the USA, they may lump claims together in a single patent application, which they have often done, especially after 1987.

9. Other diversity indicators like standard deviation and entropy were used originally but are not reported here.

10. The assistance of M.Sc. Peter de Bellmond at the Swedish Patent Office in collecting and checking the data is gratefully acknowledged.

11. Earlier applications could be cited against later ones as prior art. Also the level of invention of individual claims could be insufficient.

12. The survey data showed similar average length of time patents were kept in force; see Table 5.14, which shows that average number of years a patent is kept in force is 10.5 for the Japanese and 11.4 for the Swedish corporations. The vintage profiles (distributions of patent ages at expiration) differed, however.

13. Note that if there is a patent dispute, the relative sizes in some sense of the patent holders are legally irrelevant. Nevertheless, small companies usually attract more sympathy than large companies in a dispute.

14. These difficulties are illustrated, for example, in Scherer (1982). To make a general matching of patent classes to product areas is particularly difficult and will almost always involve sources of error, even at fine levels of classification. It is possible to relate specific patents to specific products, but this involves considerable work as a rule. Besides, a patent may relate to many products and a product may be based on many patents (products are multitechnology-based and increasingly so, see Chapters 4 and 5). Thus, there is a many-to-many correspondence not only between patent classes and product classes but also between individual patents and products.

15. Compare the response strategies in case of patent blockage, described in Chapter 7. Several of these response strategies are in fact dependent upon bargaining power based on patents (patent power).

Appendix 2   The conduct of the questionnaire survey

A2.1   PURPOSE OF THE QUESTIONNAIRE SURVEY

The questionnaire survey had two direct purposes – first, to provide in itself a more general picture of IPR-related facts and perceptions in large corporations, and second, to complement other sub-studies in the overall study, particularly the interview studies of best-practice corporations in Japan and Sweden. There was also an intention to develop and test a questionnaire that could be used as an instrument for diagnostic and benchmarking purposes in other settings as well.

A2.2   METHOD

A2.2.1   Sample Design

The first and dominant sampling criterion was to include a major segment of the industrial R&D in Japan and Sweden, and thereby a major share of the IPR resources and activities.[1] The final sample came to consist of large R&D expenditure corporations, altogether covering over 50 per cent of the industrial R&D in Japan and more than 90 per cent in Sweden. This first sampling criterion determined the sample size for Sweden and, consequently, the same magnitude was used for Japan. Second, a coverage of primarily chemical, electrical and mechanical engineering industries was desired, with some additional corporations representing civil engineering (construction) and the pulp and paper industry. Third, a certain number of matching competitors (actual or potential with at least one major business area in common) were sought, which led to the addition of a few corporations. Table A2.1 lists the corporations that finally participated in the study. (Note the overlap between the sample for the survey and the sample dealt with in Appendix 1. This naturally arises from the similarity in sampling criteria, an overlap which was intended.) The questionnaire was sent out to 32 Japanese corporations and 23 Swedish ones, of which 25 and 20 answered, respectively, thus giving a response rate of 78 per cent and 83 per cent, respectively. No evidence of bias in the set of non-respondents was detected. Lastly, note that the tables in Chapters 5–8 refer only to the corporations in the chemical, electrical and mechanical engineering industries.

Table A2.1   List of Japanese and Swedish corporations participating in the survey study

Japanese corporations[1]	Main sector[2]	Swedish corporations[1]	Main sector[2]
Asahi Chemical Ind.	C	AGA	C
Canon Inc.	E	Asea Brown Boveri (ABB)	E
Fujitsu Ltd.	E	Astra	C
Hitachi Ltd.	E	Atlas Copco	M
Honda Motor Co., Ltd.	M	Bofors	M
Matsushita Electric Ind.	E	Ericsson	E
Mitsubishi Heavy Ind.	M	Gambro	M
Mitsubishi Kasei Corp.	C	Kabi Pharmacia	C
NEC Corp.	E	Mölnlycke	C
Nippondenso Co., Ltd.	E	Nobel	C
NSK Ltd	M	SAAB	M
Nippon Steel Corp.	M	Sandvik	M
Nippon Telegraph & Telephone	E	Scania	M
OJI Paper Co., Ltd.	C	Skanska	B
Shimizu Corp.	B	SKF	M
Showa Denko K.K.	C	SSAB	M
Sumitomo Chemical Co., Ltd.	C	STORA	C
SONY Corp.	E	Telia	E
Takeda Chemical Ind.	C	Vattenfall	B
Teijin Ltd.	C	Volvo	M
The Tokyo Electric Power Corp.	E		
Toray Ind.	C		
Toshiba Corp.	E		
Toyota Motor Corp.	M		
Yamanouchi Pharmaceutical	C		

Notes
1. In total, 25 Japanese and 20 Swedish corporations participated. An independent, non-consolidated subsidiary to a *keiretsu* in Japan and an independent, non-consolidated subsidiary to a corporate conglomerate in Sweden was treated as a separate corporation.
2. Sector classification was made on the basis of the main or largest sector in the corporation, using broad sector categories, corresponding to engineering industry categories. The categories were chemical (C) including pulp, paper and pharmaceuticals, electric/electronic (E), mechanical (M) and construction (B) (buildings, bridges and so on). Among the respondents there were 9C, 10E, 5M and 1B Japanese corporations and 6C, 3E, 9M and 2B Swedish corporations. Typically the corporations were active in several sectors and the main sector classification is just a first approximation.

A2.2.2 Questionnaire Design

The questionnaire was comprehensively designed to cover all major issues related to patenting and its role in corporate commercialization of new technologies. The questionnaire comprised 27 pages with more than 400 questions, corresponding to separate variables with factual as well as perceptual questions and including mostly closed questions but also a few open ones for qualitative answers. The complete questionnaire is annexed below. Tendency questions for 1987–91 were often added to the perceptual questions, which referred to the situation in 1992. Factual questions were asked for the two years, 1987 and 1991, in order to allow a rough time analysis and were designed in the most parsimonious way in order to limit the number of questions. The questionnaire was divided into the following sections or blocks of questions:

A. General company information (factual questions).[2]
B. General information about company R&D (mainly factual questions).
C. Technology sourcing (acquisition) and commercialization.
D. Information about the company's IPR and patenting activities (factual questions plus perceptual questions on IP-related trends).
E. Organization and management of IPR and patenting in 1992 (factual questions).
F. Role of IPR and patenting in technology commercialization (almost all perceptual questions).

A large part of the questions were generated from previous studies of multitechnology corporations and technology strategies (see, for example, Granstrand et al. 1989) and from an earlier study of patenting (Granstrand 1988). Some questions were inspired by Taylor and Silberston (1973). A few questions were selected from the so-called Yale study (reported in Levin 1987), and some questions regarding university research from a successor study designed by S. Ostry in collaboration with Professor Richard Nelson and others. However, most questions were newly generated in line with issues in the overall study, several of them in connection with the interviews. No specific hypotheses for testing were pre-formulated. The questionnaire was thoroughly discussed and commented upon in a pilot test with IPR representatives from a handful of the Japanese and Swedish companies, who made language suggestions and also suggested new questions. The questionnaire language was English, as suggested by the companies. The primary currency to be used was US dollars. The questions pertained to the corporation as a whole as it was consolidated at the end of 1991. Although everyone was convinced about the principle of keeping the questionnaire short, there were almost no deletions suggested by the practitioners.[3] Finally, it should be observed that the resulting questionnaire could also be used as a diagnostic and benchmarking instrument for a corporation in general.

A2.2.3   Survey Administration

The questionnaire was sent to the corporate patent or IP manager in the Japanese corporations, all of which had such a person. For the Swedish corporations, the questionnaire was sent to the CEOs, but was filled in by an IP manager or R&D manager corresponding as close as possible to the respondents in the Japanese sample. Ordinary reminders and follow-ups were made, as well as checks of the returned questionnaires.[4] The overall questionnaire response rate was high (around 80 per cent), and so were most of the various question response rates, particularly for the Japanese corporations, many of which completed the questionnaire in almost every detail. Several Swedish corporations were not able to provide a completed questionnaire, as the information sought was not readily available in consolidated form and was costly for them to collect.[5] In a few cases, answers were withheld in both Japan and Sweden for confidentiality reasons. The response rates for the perceptual questions were generally high, however.

A2.2.4   Data Analysis and General Caveats

The questionnaire responses were coded and univariate analyses performed. Low question response rates were analysed. No evidence of bias among non-responses could be detected.[6] Several variables were deleted from further multivariate analysis because of lack of data. Various fairly standard multivariate analyses were then performed. A few of the results of these are presented in Chapter 5.[7]

Some general caveats must be pointed out. First, the number of variables by far exceeds the number of corporations. This was by design in order to explore a wide range of issues among corporations with substantial R&D and IP operations, rather than to test pre-formulated hypotheses for a narrow range of variables. The small sample size in relation to the large number of variables naturally limits the possibilities for multivariate analysis. Also possibilities for generalizing within industries (main sectors) are highly limited, because of the small sample. Second, the subjective nature of perceptual questions necessitates caution in interpretation and generalization, especially over time. Third, the lower response for factual questions also necessitates caution. Fourth, country-comparative survey studies always involve methodological problems with results being possibly influenced by differences in country background and differences pertaining to history, language interpretation, perceptions, cultural attitudes and so on. Here, the corroboration of the results by the interview studies was important. Finally, this is an early study of its kind and many of the results must be considered exploratory.[8]

The complete questionnaire is appended (with original page numbers in square brackets at the foot of each page).

NOTES

1. R&D concentration in large corporations is high in both countries, and particularly in such a small country as Sweden. The concentration of IPR resources may be even higher than the concentration of R&D.
2. The distinction between factual and perceptual questions is important, although not always clear. Factual questions refer to facts that are possible to ascertain on higher-order measurement scales, apart from straight classifications, with little subjectivity of individual respondents involved. Perceptual questions (for example regarding relative weight of motives or causes behind a decision, policy, behaviour or trend) typically extract subjective assessments mostly on ordinal scales and only occasionally on higher metric and quotient scales (for example, percentage estimates). In the latter case, reliability may be improved by multiple assessments.
3. The advice on questionnaire design and administration by representatives of patent offices in Japan and Sweden and of Canon, Toshiba, ABB, Ericsson, IVA and AIPPI–Japan is gratefully acknowledged.
4. The assistance of Mr K. Iwanaga, Mr P. Reddy and Ms M. Franzén at the Research Policy Institute, University of Lund, and M. Sc. Bo Heiden at Chalmers University of Technology, is gratefully acknowledged.
5. This is partly a reflection of the generally lower degree of central coordination in Swedish corporations, partly a reflection of their lower levels of IP resources and management attention to IP matters.
6. Such evidence is difficult to find, of course.
7. The assistance of B. Areskough, Department of Mathematics, Chalmers University of Technology, is gratefully acknowledged.
8. The results of the survey, especially pertaining to the stark differences between Japanese and Swedish large corporations, are also presented in Granstrand and Sigurdson (1993a).

ANNEX TO APPENDIX 2: QUESTIONNAIRE FORM

The Role of Intellectual Property Rights (IPR) and Patenting in the Commercialization of New Technologies

A Study of IPR and Patent Management in Japanese and Swedish Corporations

MAIL QUESTIONNAIRE

Company name:

....

ISIC (International Standard Industrial Classification) code(s) of company activities (please give all the relevant 4-digit codes):

....

....

Contact name within the company:

....

Mail address:

....

Tel:

....

Fax:

....

Instructions: Please give facts and estimates pertaining to your corporation as a whole as it was consolidated at the end of 1991, including majority-owned subsidiaries worldwide. (If it is not possible to give consolidated data, please give data on separate questionnaires for the parent company as well as for important and majority-owned subsidiaries and mark what part of the corporate group the different questionnaires apply to.) If possible, use US dollars and indicate currency conversion rates, otherwise use Japanese yen and Swedish crowns, respectively.

[1]

The questionnaire is divided into the following sections: *Page*

A. General company information

A1a. Total sales globally in   1987: ....

1991: ....

A1b. Sales on foreign markets in percent (%) of total sales in

1987: ....%

1991: ....%

A1c. The five most important country markets in 1987 and 1991 by sales
(give %)

	1987 Name		1991 Name	
Country 1	....	%	....	%
Country 2	....	%	....	%
Country 3	....	%	....	%
Country 4	....	%	....	%
Country 5	....	%	....	%
Others		%		%
	Total	100 %	Total	100 %

A2a. Total number of employees in   1987: ....

1991: ....

A2b. Number of employees abroad
in % of the total number in   1987: ....%

1991: ....%

B. General information about company R&D

B1. Total R&D expenditures worldwide in your company
1987: ....
1991: ....

B2. Percentage of R&D conducted in foreign countries in
1987: .... %
1991: .... %

B3. In what five countries (including the home country – or home countries
in case your company is binational) did your company conduct most
of its R&D in 1987 and 1991? Please name and rank, and give the
approximate percentage shares (e.g. based on number of R&D personnel)
of the total R&D:

	1987 Name		1991 Name	
Country 1	....	%	....	%
Country 2	....	%	....	%
Country 3	....	%	....	%
Country 4	....	%	....	%
Country 5	....	%	....	%
Others		%		%
	Total	100 %	Total	100 %

B4. What was the percentage (e.g. based on number of R&D personnel) of your total R&D performed in the countries listed below ?

	1987	1991
Japan	...................%	...............%
USA	...................%	...............%
Sweden	...................%	...............%
UK	...................%	...............%
Germany	...................%	...............%
France	...................%	...............%
Other European countries	...................%	...............%
Asian NIC Countries (Korea, Taiwan, Singapore, Hong Kong)	...................%	...............%
Other countries	...................%	...............%
	Total 100 %	Total 100 %

B5a. In case your company's R&D has been internationalized, please indicate roughly the relative importance of the following motives and driving forces behind your company's internationalization of R&D during the last decade:

	Of no importance (= 0)	Of major importance (= 4)	Future tendency
Supporting local production	0 1 2 3 4		− 0 +
Supporting local customers and markets	0 1 2 3 4		− 0 +
Creating better access to foreign science and technology	0 1 2 3 4		− 0 +
Creating better access to cost-effective supply of R&D personnel	0 1 2 3 4		− 0 +
Local ambitions among subsidiaries	0 1 2 3 4		− 0 +
Local government regulations	0 1 2 3 4		− 0 +
Foreign acquisitions	0 1 2 3 4		− 0 +

B5b. Please indicate roughly the relative importance to your company during the last decade of the following inhibiting factors to internationalization of R&D:

	Of no importance (= 0)	Of major importance (= 4)	Future tendency
Need for close supervision and control of R&D	0 1 2 3 4		− 0 +
Risk of leakage of information	0 1 2 3 4		− 0 +
Need to have R&D close to domestic market	0 1 2 3 4		− 0 +
Economies of scale in R&D	0 1 2 3 4		− 0 +
Costs of coordination and communication	0 1 2 3 4		− 0 +
Government policies	0 1 2 3 4		− 0 +

B6. What was the approximate percentage of your company's total R&D expenditures that were:

	1987	1991
related to development of new products	..............%	..............%
related to development of existing products	..............%	..............%
related to development of new production processes	..............%	..............%
related to development of existing production processes	..............%	..............%
unrelated to specific products or processes, i.e. research	..............%	..............%

Total 100 % Total 100 %

[6]

B7. What was the approximate percentage of your company's total R&D
     expenditures that were :

	1987	1991
R&D centralized at corporate level	.... %	.... %
R&D decentralized in divisions and subsidiaries	.... %	.... %
	Total 100 %	Total 100 %

B8a. Total licensing receipts (as approx. % of total R&D)	1987	...................%
	1991	...................%
B8b. Total licensing expenditures (as approx. % of total R&D)	1987	...................%
	1991	...................%
B8c. Percentage of total licensing receipts coming from outside foreign license buyers	1987	...................%
	1991	...................%
B8d. Percentage of total licensing expenditures paid to outside foreign license sellers	1987	...................%
	1991	...................%

[7]

C. Technology sourcing and commercialization

C1. For your corporation as a whole, please indicate roughly the relative importance of the following *strategies for building up your technological capabilities* in 1987 and 1992 by circling the appropriate number :

	1987		1992	
	Of no importance (= 0)	Of major importance (= 4)	Of no importance (= 0)	Of major importance (= 4)

Strategies for technology sourcing

	1987	1992
In-house R&D	0 1 2 3 4	0 1 2 3 4
Acquisition of innovative companies (or business units)	0 1 2 3 4	0 1 2 3 4
Joint venture and other forms of cooperative R&D, e.g. with subcontractors	0 1 2 3 4	0 1 2 3 4
Purchasing of licenses	0 1 2 3 4	0 1 2 3 4
Other forms of technology purchasing, e.g. contract R&D	0 1 2 3 4	0 1 2 3 4
University collaboration with universities in:	0 1 2 3 4	0 1 2 3 4
– Japan	0 1 2 3 4	0 1 2 3 4
– USA	0 1 2 3 4	0 1 2 3 4
– Sweden	0 1 2 3 4	0 1 2 3 4
– UK	0 1 2 3 4	0 1 2 3 4
– Germany	0 1 2 3 4	0 1 2 3 4
– France	0 1 2 3 4	0 1 2 3 4
– Other European countries	0 1 2 3 4	0 1 2 3 4
– Asian NIC countries (Korea, Taiwan, Singapore, Hong Kong etc.)	0 1 2 3 4	0 1 2 3 4
Technology scanning (incl. monitoring and intelligence)	0 1 2 3 4	0 1 2 3 4

[8]

C2. For your corporation as a whole, please indicate roughly the relative importance of the following *strategies for commercializing (exploiting) your technological capabilities* in 1987 and 1992 by circling the appropriate number:

	1987		1992	
	Of no importance (= 0)	Of major importance (= 4)	Of no importance (= 0)	Of major importance (= 4)

Strategies for technology exploitation

	1987	1992
Internal exploitation (direct investment in production and/or marketing of technology-based products)	0 1 2 3 4	0 1 2 3 4
Creation of innovative firms (units, spin-offs)	0 1 2 3 4	0 1 2 3 4
Joint ventures	0 1 2 3 4	0 1 2 3 4
Technology selling (performing contract R&D, licensing out etc.)	0 1 2 3 4	0 1 2 3 4
Divestment	0 1 2 3 4	0 1 2 3 4

	1987		1992	
	Of no importance	Of major importance	Of no importance	Of major importance

C3. What is the magnitude of:

		1987	1992
a)	Uncommercialized technology	0 1 2 3 4	0 1 2 3 4
b)	Loss and leakage of proprietary technology	0 1 2 3 4	0 1 2 3 4

[9]

Please circle the appropriate number pertaining to the following propositions:

	False			True	
	−2	−1	0	+1	+2

C4. It has become increasingly difficult to acquire new technologies from outside the company

$-2 \quad -1 \quad 0 \quad +1 \quad +2$

C5. The possibilities of acquiring new technologies at lower cost from outside the company than through in-house R&D have increased

$-2 \quad -1 \quad 0 \quad +1 \quad +2$

C6a. In general, companies are overinvesting in R&D in certain areas

$-2 \quad -1 \quad 0 \quad +1 \quad +2$

C6b. If so, which R&D areas (give 1–3 examples)?

....

....

....

C7. Rate the contribution of research by universities in the following countries to the technological advance in your company's areas of technology.

	Of no importance				Of major importance	Tendency 1987–1992
(1) USA	0	1	2	3	4	− 0 +
(2) UK	0	1	2	3	4	− 0 +
(3) Germany	0	1	2	3	4	− 0 +
(4) France	0	1	2	3	4	− 0 +
(5) Japan	0	1	2	3	4	− 0 +
(6) Sweden	0	1	2	3	4	− 0 +
(7) Asian NIC countries (Korea, Taiwan, Singapore, Hong Kong)	0	1	2	3	4	− 0 +
(8) Others (Please name)	0	1	2	3	4	− 0 +

[10]

	Strongly disagree	Strongly agree	Tendency 1987–1992

C8. Rate your agreement with the following propositions about how industry in your company's areas of interest draws from university research:

(1) Learning is mostly through publications, technical reports, and open scientific or technical meetings. 0 1 2 3 4   – 0 +

(2) It is important to have personal contacts with those who are doing the research. 0 1 2 3 4   – 0 +

(3) Geographic proximity to universities is important. 0 1 2 3 4   – 0 +

(4) Industry funding of academic research is a useful vehicle for making that research more relevant to business and for gaining access. 0 1 2 3 4   – 0 +

(5) Hiring advanced-degree graduates of universities who are strong in a field of science or technology is an important way of learning about industrially relevant developments in that field. 0 1 2 3 4   – 0 +

(6) Universities in one's own country are more accessible than foreign universities. 0 1 2 3 4   – 0 +

(7) Having an R&D operation in a foreign country makes universities there more accessible. 0 1 2 3 4   – 0 +

[11]

		False	**True**

C9. a) R&D costs for new products have increased
during the last decade   –2 –1 0 +1 +2

  b) R&D times for new products have increased
during the last decade   –2 –1 0 +1 +2

  c) A broadening of the technology base for new
products is an important factor behind
increasing R&D costs   –2 –1 0 +1 +2

C10. a) Imitation costs for new products have
increased during the last decade   –2 –1 0 +1 +2

  b) Imitation times for new products have
decreased during the last decade   –2 –1 0 +1 +2

C11. When an outside new technology emerges as
relevant, your company will try to source it
externally in the first place (e.g. by licensing in)
rather than starting in-house R&D   –2 –1 0 +1 +2

C12. a) External sourcing of new technologies is
primarily used in order to save money   –2 –1 0 +1 +2

  b) External sourcing of new technologies is
primarily used in order to save time   –2 –1 0 +1 +2

C13. Your company's diversification into new product
areas is increasingly economizing upon
technological synergies with existing products –2 –1 0 +1 +2

C14. What is the approx. number (on an average)
of potential imitators to your company

  a) already operating in your product area?   –2 –1 0 +1 +2

  b) diversifying into your product area?   –2 –1 0 +1 +2

[12]

D.   Information about your company's IPR and patenting activities

D1.   Under which company names do you file applications for patents as applicant or assignee in:
(provide answer on separate sheet if necessary)

Europe

....

Japan

....

USA

....

Elsewhere

....

D2a.   Total number (suitably rounded off) of priority applications filed in

	1987	....
	1991	....

D2b.   Total number of priority applications granted and in force in your company's patent portfolio

	1987	....
	1991	....

D2c.   Total number of patents in force in your company's patent portfolio

	1987	....
	1991	....

D2d.   Total number of patents granted to your company in the USA in

	1987	....
	1991	....

D3a. In which five countries did your company have most of its patent applications filed in 1987 and 1991?

	1987 Name		1991 Name	
Country 1	....	%	....	%
Country 2	....	%	....	%
Country 3	....	%	....	%
Country 4	....	%	....	%
Country 5	....	%	....	%
Others	....	%	....	%

Total 100 %   Total 100 %

D3b. Name the five most important countries (or regions) in order of importance to your company when patenting an original invention.

	1987 Name	1991 Name
Country 1	....	....
Country 2	....	....
Country 3	....	....
Country 4	....	....
Country 5	....	....

D4. Share of patent applications for which patents are granted (approx. %):
Europe .... %
Japan .... %
USA .... %

[14]

D5a. Percentage of patents granted that are exploited commercially through own production (approx. %):

.... %

D5b. Percentage of patents granted that through own production have led to economically successful new products or processes (approx. %):

.... %

D5c. Percentage of patents granted that are licensed commercially (approx. %):

.... %

D6a. Your company's average number of years for keeping a patent in force:

.... years

D6b. Percentage of patents that are kept in force (approx. %) The maximum patent protection time:

.... %

11–15 years:

.... %

5–10 years:

.... %

0–4 years:

.... %

D7. Percentage of patents with domestic priority for which a foreign application was filed in

1987 .... %

1991 .... %

D8. Percentage of all priority applications for which priority was sought domestically in

1987 .... %

1991 .... %

D9. Percentage of own patents for which infringements were detected (rough estimate) in

1987 .... %

1991 .... %

D10. Number of patent litigations filed from your side against other firms or parties in

1987 ....

1991 ....

D11. Number of patent litigations directed against your firm in

1987 ....

1991 ....

D12. How many years on average before market introduction of a new product is a key patent sought in the R&D process?

.... years

[16]

D13.   How many years before or after market introduction is a patent usually granted?

.... years

D14a. For your first foreign filing of a patent application in Europe, do you currently use a:

PCT application   Yes / No

EPO application   Yes / No

National application   Yes / No

D14b. What changes have occurred in this respect in the period 1987–1991 (please specify):

....

....

....

D15.   (Trend assessment) In your opinion have any essential changes on an average occurred in your company during the period 1987–1992 with regard to the following? (please circle)

Specific trends:	**False** **True**
(1) Patents are sought earlier in the R&D and innovation process	–2 –1 0 +1 +2
(2) The use of patent literature as an information source has increased	–2 –1 0 +1 +2
(3) The resources for the firm's patent activities have increased	–2 –1 0 +1 +2
(4) Hiring patent agencies or similar outside assistance has increased	–2 –1 0 +1 +2
(5) The status of patent activities within the firm has increased	–2 –1 0 +1 +2

[17]

		False				True
(6)	The cost of license negotiation has increased	−2	−1	0	+1	+2
(7)	Licensing is becoming increasingly broad-based (block licensing etc.)	−2	−1	0	+1	+2
(8)	Patent pooling has increased in importance	−2	−1	0	+1	+2
(9)	The average number of years for keeping a patent in force has increased	−2	−1	0	+1	+2
(10)	The number of countries in which patents are sought has increased	−2	−1	0	+1	+2
(11a)	The frequency of patent infringements has increased	−2	−1	0	+1	+2
(11b)	The frequency of competitors' patents blocking your activities has increased	−2	−1	0	+1	+2
(11c)	The frequency of your patents blocking the activities of your competitors has increased	−2	−1	0	+1	+2
(11d)	The frequency of patent litigations has increased	−2	−1	0	+1	+2
(12a)	The possibility of finding generic patents (patents which open up an entire new technological area) has increased	−2	−1	0	+1	+2
(12b)	Your company's propensity to patent has increased	−2	−1	0	+1	+2
(13a)	Your company's propensity to license out has increased	−2	−1	0	+1	+2
(13b)	Your company's propensity to license in has increased	−2	−1	0	+1	+2
(13c)	The role of patents in joint ventures and cooperative R&D has increased	−2	−1	0	+1	+2
(13d)	Patents are increasingly sought in order to generate license incomes	−2	−1	0	+1	+2
(13e)	Increasing R&D costs have increased your propensity to license out	−2	−1	0	+1	+2
(13f)	Royalty rates have increased when licensing out	−2	−1	0	+1	+2
(13g)	Royalty rates have increased when licensing in	−2	−1	0	+1	+2
(14)	The strategic role of patents in your company has increased	−2	−1	0	+1	+2

		False				True

(15) The strategic role of licenses in your company
      has increased   −2 −1 0 +1 +2
(16) The role of patents in standard-setting
      has increased   −2 −1 0 +1 +2
(17) The role of cross–licensing has increased   −2 −1 0 +1 +2
(18) Top management attention to IPR and patenting
      matters has increased   −2 −1 0 +1 +2
(19) The importance of trademarks has increased   −2 −1 0 +1 +2
(20) The importance of prophylactic publishing
      (publishing of results in order to prevent others
      taking out patents) has increased   −2 −1 0 +1 +2
(21a) New products are related to an increasing number
      of patent classes   −2 −1 0 +1 +2
(21b) New production processes are related to an
      increasing number of patent classes   −2 −1 0 +1 +2
(22) New patents are related to an increasing number of
      product areas (i.e. patents are becoming more
      generic on an average)   −2 −1 0 +1 +2

Other trends:

(23) Trends in the way patents are sought by your company (please specify)
      (Sample answer: 'Patents are formulated with more and broader claims')

(24) Trends in your company's organization of patent activities (please
      specify) (Sample answer: 'Corporate centralization has increased')

(25) Trends regarding personnel in the patent departments of your company
      (please specify) (Sample answer: 'We have given engineers more legal
      training')

(26) Trends regarding where patents are sought (please specify country or
      region)

E.   Organization and management of IPR and patenting in 1992

E1.   Does your company have a written corporate-wide
patenting policy? (please circle)   Yes   No

E2.   Are questions about patents and related matters regularly
discussed at company board meetings?   Yes   No

E3a. Does your company have a centralized patent department
with corporate-wide responsibilities for patent coordination?   Yes   No

E3b. If yes, to which part of your company's organization does
it belong? (E.g. central R&D unit, corporate headquarters staff)

....

E4a. Does your company have one central corporate patent
manager?   Yes   No

E4b. If yes, to whom does he/she report? (please specify)

....

E4c. If yes, which is his/her educational background
(e.g. engineering, economics, law, other)? (please specify)

....

E4d. What was his/her previous position? (please specify)

....

E5.   Patenting and IPR matters are discussed by top management
every (please circle)
day / week / month / year / never

E6a. Approximately how many persons worked more than half–time
with patenting activities in total in your company in

1987   ....

1991   ....

[20]

E6b. What percentage of these persons were engineers (approx. %)?

1987 ....%

1991 ....%

E6c. What percentage of these persons were lawyers (approx. %)?

1987 ....%

1991 ....%

E6d. What percentage of these persons were working in central/corporate headquarters?

1987 ....%

1991 ....%

E7. Cost of in-house patenting department activities and purchased services (including patent filing costs and maintenance fees) in

1987 ....

1991 ....

F. Role of IPR and patenting in technology commercialization in 1992

F1. How large a percentage of your company's sales was based upon inventions with patents in force in (rough percentage estimate)

1987 ....%

1991 ....%

F2a. What rough percentage of the new products your company has introduced over the last 10 years would not have been developed had you anticipated that you could not patent the product?

......................%

F2b. Before introducing a new product on the market, your company requires as a matter of policy that at least one important patent is secured

Yes/No

F3. To what extent does each of the following limit the ability of your company to profit from innovation? (please circle)

		Of no importance			Of major importance		Tendency 1987–1992
(1)	Inability to prevent other firms from copying the technology	0	1	2	3	4	– 0 +
(2a)	High cost or limited access to capital	0	1	2	3	4	– 0 +
(2b)	High cost or limited access to technology needed	0	1	2	3	4	– 0 +
(3)	Lack of access to competent suppliers of needed equipment, or of specialized inputs	0	1	2	3	4	– 0 +
(4)	Problems of getting a product into production in a timely way	0	1	2	3	4	– 0 +
(5)	High costs or other difficulties in marketing	0	1	2	3	4	– 0 +
(6)	Difficulties in gaining access to foreign markets	0	1	2	3	4	– 0 +

F4. For your company on an average, how effective is each of the following means in preventing or deterring competitors from copying your new product technologies? (please circle)

		Not effective (= 0)		Very effective (= 4)			Tendency 1987–1992
1.	Patents	0	1	2	3	4	– 0 +
2.	Secrecy	0	1	2	3	4	– 0 +
3.	Complexity of process design makes copying very costly	0	1	2	3	4	– 0 +
4.	Lead-time advantages of the innovator make attempts at copying unprofitable	0	1	2	3	4	– 0 +

[22]

F5. To what extent does each of the following statements apply in describing the limitations of patents as protection of your firm's technology? (please circle the most suitable number)

	Not true	Very true	Tendency 1987–1991
(1) New products are not patentable	0 1 2 3 4		– 0 +
(2) New processes are not patentable	0 1 2 3 4		– 0 +
(3) Patents are probably not valid if contested	0 1 2 3 4		– 0 +
(4) Firms do not try to enforce their patent rights	0 1 2 3 4		– 0 +
(5) Competitors can legally circumvent patent rights or invent ways around them	0 1 2 3 4		– 0 +
(6) Technological development is so rapid that patents become irrelevant	0 1 2 3 4		– 0 +
(7) Patent proceedings require a firm to disclose too much of its information	0 1 2 3 4		– 0 +
(8) Compulsory licensing can be imposed by court decisions or regulations	0 1 2 3 4		– 0 +
(9) Firms engage in cross-licensing with competitors	0 1 2 3 4		– 0 +

F6a. How important to your company are on an average the following means for commercializing new *product* technologies?

	Of no importance (= 0)	Of major importance (= 4)	Tendency 1987–1992
(a) Taking out patents to deter imitators (or to collect royalties)	0 1 2 3 4		– 0 +
(b) Exercising secrecy	0 1 2 3 4		– 0 +
(c) Creating market lead times	0 1 2 3 4		– 0 +
(d) Creating production cost reductions	0 1 2 3 4		– 0 +
(e) Creating superior marketing and after-sales service	0 1 2 3 4		– 0 +
(f) Creating switching costs	0 1 2 3 4		– 0 +

[23]

F6b. In case the importance of patenting for commercialization of new technologies in general has increased, which are the three most important factors behind this increase in your opinion (please specify briefly):

....

....

....

F7. How important to your company are on an average the following means for commercializing new *production process* technologies?

	Of no importance				Of major importance	Tendency 1987–1992
(a) Taking out patents to deter imitators (or to collect royalties)	0	1	2	3	4	– 0 +
(b) Exercising secrecy	0	1	2	3	4	– 0 +
(c) Making implementation rapid	0	1	2	3	4	– 0 +

F8. How important are the possible *advantages* that patenting may give your company?

	Of no importance				Of major importance	Tendency 1987–1991
Protecting proprietary product technology	0	1	2	3	4	– 0 +
Protecting proprietary process technology	0	1	2	3	4	– 0 +
Creating retaliatory power against competitors	0	1	2	3	4	– 0 +
Giving better possibilities of selling licenses	0	1	2	3	4	– 0 +
Giving better possibilities of accessing technology through cross-licensing	0	1	2	3	4	– 0 +
Facilitating R&D cooperation with others	0	1	2	3	4	– 0 +
Giving a better bargaining position in standard-setting	0	1	2	3	4	– 0 +

[24]

Providing motivation for employees to invent	0	1	2	3	4		– 0 +
Providing a measure of R&D productivity		0	1	2	3	4	– 0 +
Improving the corporate image		0	1	2	3	4	– 0 +

Other (please specify) ....

....

F9. How important are the possible *disadvantages* that patenting may give your company?

	Of no importance		Of major importance			Tendency 1987–1991
Disclosing of technical information	0	1	2	3	4	– 0 +
Incurring direct costs of patenting	0	1	2	3	4	– 0 +

Other (please specify)..

....

F10. How important on an average are the following means for preventing other companies from finding out about your company's technical developments?

	Of no importance		Of major importance			Tendency 1987–1991
Control of publishing by researchers and employees	0	1	2	3	4	– 0 +
Controlled access to facilities	0	1	2	3	4	– 0 +
Monitoring of visitors and temporary employees	0	1	2	3	4	– 0 +
Avoidance of patenting	0	1	2	3	4	– 0 +
Implementation of an internal secrecy policy	0	1	2	3	4	– 0 +
Efforts to increase employee loyalty to the company	0	1	2	3	4	– 0 +

Efforts to prevent competitors hiring
over key R&D personnel

0 1 2 3 4   – 0 +

Fragmentation of technological
information among managers and
other employees

0 1 2 3 4   – 0 +

Counterintelligence

0 1 2 3 4   – 0 +

F11. How important on an average are the following means for finding out about
your competitors' technical development?

	Of no importance		Of major importance		Tendency 1987–1991
Licensing the technology	0	1	2	3	4	– 0 +
Learning details from information provided in patent disclosures	0	1	2	3	4	– 0 +
Learning details through publications or open technical meetings	0	1	2	3	4	– 0 +
Learning details through informal conversations with employees of the innovating firm, competitors, buyers, suppliers, consultancy firms, universities etc.	0	1	2	3	4	– 0 +
Hiring R&D employees with experience from competing firms	0	1	2	3	4	– 0 +
Acquiring the product and reverse-engineering it	0	1	2	3	4	– 0 +

Other (please specify)   ....

F12a. The patent laws in Europe, Japan and the USA provide adequate protection through

	Europe		Japan		USA	
	False	True	False	True	False	True
Legislation	−2 −1 0 +1 +2		−2 −1 0 +1 +2		−2 −1 0 +1 +2	
Law adherence	−2 −1 0 +1 +2		−2 −1 0 +1 +2		−2 −1 0 +1 +2	
Law enforcement	−2 −1 0 +1 +2		−2 −1 0 +1 +2		−2 −1 0 +1 +2	
Court practices	−2 −1 0 +1 +2		−2 −1 0 +1 +2		−2 −1 0 +1 +2	
Infringement penalties	−2 −1 0 +1 +2		−2 −1 0 +1 +2		−2 −1 0 +1 +2	

F12b. In your opinion, has patent protection grown stronger over the last decade as a means of protecting new technology on (please circle):

	False			True	
a. the US market	−2	−1	0	+1	+2
b. the European market	−2	−1	0	+1	+2
c. the Japanese market	−2	−1	0	+1	+2

F13. *Assume* hypothetically that the maximum patent protection time was changed in all of the important markets where your company operates. What would the effect be on your company's total R&D budget if the maximum patent protection time was changed as suggested below? (Give a rough percentage increase or decrease.) (It is of course difficult to forecast this impact objectively but try to give at least a rough estimate of the range of the impact.)

(a) increased by 3 years   + ... %

(b) decreased to 10 years   − .... %

(c) decreased to 0 years   − .... %
    (that is, patenting protection ceases entirely)

Appendix 3   Interview questionnaires

GENERAL QUESTIONS – CORPORATE LEVEL

Below is a summary of general interview questions addressed to best-practice companies regarding Intellectual Property Management, in order to set the stage for the interview series.

Q1. What strategies and methods in general are now used by your company for the economically successful development and commercialization of new technologies?

Q2. What are your managerial experience and philosophy regarding successful versus failing attempts to commercialize new technologies in your company?

Q3. In your company, what is the role of patenting and intellectual property rights in the development and commercialization of new technologies?

Q4. Which patenting and licensing strategies and tactics have been commercially successful in your company and why?

Q5. How are patenting activities organized and managed throughout your company?

Q6. How is technology scanning organized and managed throughout your company and what is the role of patent information in that connection?

Q7. In your opinion, how could the commercialization of new technologies be further improved in the future?

GENERAL QUESTIONS IN JAPAN – NATIONAL LEVEL

Q1. Which are the broad features of the historic developments of Intellectual Property Rights (IPR) protection by law in Japan?

Q2. Which are the current important issues regarding IPR protection in Japan?

Q3. Which are the main differences between Japan, on the one hand, and Europe and USA, on the other, regarding IPR legislation, especially patent laws, and prospects of harmonization?

Q4. What are the causes and consequences of the current US–Japan relations, termed 'patent war' by the press?

Q5. What are the likely future developments regarding broad cross-licensing, patent pooling etc. among large companies?

Q6. What are the likely future developments regarding IPR protection of basic research and science, and university research?

Q7. What is the role of IPR protection for small firms and independent inventors in Japan?

Q8. What are the present legal situation and future development of trade secret protection in Japan?

Appendix 4   Approximate confidence limits

Table A4.1   Approximate 95 per cent confidence limits based on t-test of group comparisons with unit variance and sample sizes n_1 and n_2

(Differences exceeding the threshold value in the table are approximately significant at the 5% level.)

$n_1 \backslash n_2$	5	10	15	20	25	30	35	40	45	50
5	1.46									
10	1.18	0.94								
15	1.08	0.84	0.75							
20	1.03	0.79	0.69	0.64						
25	1.00	0.76	0.66	0.61	0.57					
30	0.98	0.74	0.64	0.58	0.54	0.52				
35	0.97	0.72	0.62	0.56	0.52	0.50	0.48			
40	0.96	0.71	0.61	0.55	0.51	0.48	0.46	0.45		
45	0.95	0.70	0.60	0.54	0.50	0.47	0.45	0.43	0.42	
50	0.94	0.69	0.59	0.53	0.49	0.46	0.44	0.42	0.41	0.40

Table A4.2   Approximate 95 per cent confidence limits based on t-test of mean estimates from n observations with unit variance

(Estimates exceeding the threshold value in the table are approximately significant at the 5% level)

n	5	10	15	20	25	30	35	40	45	50
threshold	1.24	0.72	0.55	0.47	0.41	0.37	0.34	0.32	0.30	0.28

Glossary*

The purpose of this glossary is to explain the meaning of legal, technical, economic and managerial terms related to intellectual property and technology management.

Affidavit: A written declaration or statement of facts confirmed by an oath or affirmation of the party making it.

Appeal: A review of the decision of an inferior court by a higher court. In European civil law tradition, the reviewing court may review all matters, both matters of fact and matters of law. In the Anglo-American common law tradition, a court of review is generally limited to reviewing only matters of law.

Application: (Legal notion) A patent application consists of a description (specification), drawings (optional), claims and an abstract. The claims define the scope of the legal protection of the invention.

Assignee: A private or legal person to whom an assignment is made; grantee.

Base technologies: Technologies that a business draws on that are common to all competitors and do not in themselves allow for differentiation and premium pricing.

Basic patent: A key patent for a given technological area. A patent that forms the basis of a new technology or a new market.

Claims: The 'metes and bounds' of a patent are set forth by its claim(s). Each claim is required to be a one-sentence description of the invention. Claims may be directed to an apparatus, a chemical compound, a method of manufacture, the use of a device or a compound and so on.

---

* Prepared by the author and Dr G. Miksche and for legal terms by patent attorney T. Ewing, using Paul Goldstein, *Copyright, Patent, Trademark, and Related State Doctrines* (1993), *Black's Law Dictionary*, 6th edn (1990) and miscellaneous other sources.

Compulsory licence: A licence granted by a court or other public authority to a party having applied for it, allowing the party to use a copyright or patent without the explicit permission of the owner. Compulsory licences usually require the payment of a specified fee to the intellectual property right holder. Provisions for the grant of compulsory licences are found in most national IP laws, the USA being the most notable exception. Conditions of their grant are, however, very much restricted in the IP laws of the major trading nations.

Contributory infringement: Assistance in the unlawful making, selling, or using of a patented invention.

Copyright: An intangible, incorporeal right granted by statute to the author or originator of certain literary or artistic materials, such as plays, movies and books. The copyright generally lasts for a specified period, with the sole and exclusive privilege of publishing and selling the work to lie with the right holder during this specified period. Most of the major trading nations specify a term constituting the life of the author plus either 50 or 75 years. Thus, the exact date of the expiration of many copyrights cannot be precisely determined. Works produced for hire are generally limited to a term of 100 years.

Counterfeit: To forge, copy or imitate without authority or right.

Counter-patent: A patent used, or to be used, for retaliation or for exchange of patents of others.

Defendant: A person or party against whom relief or recovery is sought.

Design: A design patent protects the appearance of articles of manufacture. The present term of a design patent is 14 years in the USA.

Diffusion: The spread of an innovation through a population of potential users or producers, with or without modification. Usual distinctions are national/international, interfirm/intrafirm.

Discovery: (Legal notion) A pre-trial procedure which allows litigants to obtain information from each other prior to trial. Discovery is limited in most civil law jurisdictions. Discovery practice in the USA is generally considered the broadest in the industrial world.

Diversification: The process by which the diversity of activity areas of an agent (for example, a company) is increased. The activity areas may relate to businesses, markets, products, resources, technologies and so on.

Economies of scale: Benefits gained from doing the same thing in larger quantities or repeatedly. In production cost terms, economies of scale are present when the average cost per unit produced is decreased when quantities are increased.

Economies of scope: Benefits gained from doing different things at the same time. In production cost terms, economies of scope are present when the cost of producing several products jointly is less than the aggregate cost of producing them separately (for example, in separate plants or firms).

Economies of space: Benefits gained from doing something in particular locations.

Economies of speed: Benefits gained from doing something faster or earlier in time.

Emerging technologies: New technologies that may come to influence the competitive positions of a group of competitors.

Entrepreneurship: The realization of innovations by agents. Usual distinctions are autonomous/corporate/state/university.

EPO: The European Patent Office, based in Munich. As of 1998, the EPO has not been an agency of the European Union. The EPO was created by the European Patent Convention and began operations in 1978. The EPO can grant a valid patent for all EPC signatory states.

Equivalents, doctrine of: Interpretation of the scope of an invention which is broader than the literal wording of a patent claim. The doctrine of equivalents is a concept applied in determining infringement.

Espionage: An adversary attempt to obtain information without the knowledge and consent of its possessor or party concerned.

Essential patent: Roughly synonymous with 'strategic patent' (although the term is usually employed in a somewhat weaker meaning of high invent-around costs).

Expiration: All intellectual property rights except trademarks (trade names) and indications of origin exist only for some limited term. Thereafter the goods or service and so on may be freely used by anyone without permission of the former holder of the right.

File early, file often: A patenting strategy in which a company files patents continually on minor improvements, even while research and development of the whole invention continues. The strategy is often adopted in highly competitive industries.

File wrapper estoppel: Admissions of various sorts by the applicant during prosecution of a patent application that may be used for a restrictive interpretation of claims in infringement procedures.

First to file/First to invent: An inventor can be defined as either the first person to conceive of an invention or the first person to file a patent application on the invention. All major nations except the USA follow a first-to-file patent system (as of 1998). The maintenance of this type of patent system requires the patent office to review and rule on information not required by first-to-file patent systems; see 'interference'.

Function in patent claims: Patent claims may be of the 'means plus function' type. In this approach, an element of a claim may simply state that a capability be provided for performing a particular function.

Generic technologies: Broad scientific and technological areas from which a cascade of applications emerges (for example, microelectronics, based on solid state physics and containing applications in various hardware).

Grace period: Some countries (for example, the USA) allow patentees a grace period between disclosure of a patentable invention by the inventor and the filing of a patent application. In most other jurisdictions public disclosure prior to filing destroys patentability.

Idea: (Legal notion) In the Anglo-American legal system, the law of undeveloped ideas is an accumulation of common-law opinions addressing a claimed right to compensation for a defendant's unauthorized use of the plaintiff's idea. All of these opinions require that the plaintiff's idea be novel and concrete.

Infringement: The unauthorized making, using, offering and so on of an invention covered by a valid claim of a patent during the life of the patent.

Injunction: A court order prohibiting someone from continuing to proceed with some specified act or commanding someone to undo some wrong or injury. In patent litigation, the patentee may be granted an injunction against further unauthorized use and so on of the patented product or process by the defendant. To lift (annul) an injunction is termed injunctive relief.

Injunctive relief: See 'injunction'.

Innovation (technical or technological): An invention that has found a useful and commercially viable application. (Many definitions exist.) Usual distinctions are radical (or major)/incremental (or minor); product/process; technical/managerial (or organizational)/financial/social and so on.

Intellectual property: Certain creations of the human mind are given the legal aspects of a property right. Intellectual property is an all-encompassing term, which includes patents, copyrights, trademarks, trade secrets, right to fair competition and moral rights.

Intelligence: Collection and analysis of information through legal and illegal means, for example through espionage.

Interference: In the first-to-invent patent system in the US, an interference is a proceeding at the US Patent Office to determine the priority of invention between competing claimants, and thus entitlement to the patent.

Invalidation: Only a valid patent may be enforced. Thus, defendants in patent infringement litigation normally attempt to have the patent invalidated, thus making the suit moot. Defendants may attempt to show that the patent holder committed some type of fraud towards the patent office or that a patent should not have been granted due to prior art not having been interpreted properly or not having been kept confidential during prosecution.

Invent around (design around): Competitors will often attempt to avoid literal infringement of a patent by designing their invention in such a way as to avoid the patent claims. However, the laws of most of the major trading nations recognize that the scope of an invention may be larger than the literal wording of its claims; see 'equivalents, doctrine of'.

Invention: Most patent systems require patentable inventions to be those works of the mind which are novel, non-obvious, and industrially applicable. An invention must be novel, that is distinguished from what came before it, and must not be obvious to a person skilled in the relevant field (technological area) of the invention.

Invention (that is, technical): The first idea, sketch or contrivance of a new-to-the-world product, process or system, which may or may not be patented (Freeman et al. 1982, p. 201). (Many other definitions exist.)

Key patent(s): The most technically and economically important patent(s) for a specific product or process.

Key technologies: Technologies which directly influence those product performance and quality parameters that target customers are willing or prepared to pay a premium price for. Key technologies are also those (process) technologies that allow for major cost reduction if they are applied in the production process.

Laid-open publication: A patent application is kept confidential until either the granting of a patent, or in most countries, until the passage of a certain period of time, usually 18 months. If the patent application is still pending at the end of the time period, the application will be laid open for public inspection or published.

Level of invention ('non-obviousness'; 'technical progress'; 'technical step'): In order to be patentable, an invention must be novel and non-obvious beyond what would be readily apparent to a person skilled in the relevant field. The novelty requirement for copyrighted works is very low. In some cases, the mere selection and arrangement of information is protectable by copyright.

Licence: A permission granted by an IPR holder, the licensor, to another legal entity (person or company), the licensee, to make use of, sell or otherwise benefit from the underlying intellectual property under certain restrictive conditions. To license (as a verb) means granting such permissions, more precisely referred to as licensing out. Licensing in then refers to acquiring licences. Licensing is distinct from directly selling or transferring the property rights themselves.

Licences could be granted for any type of IPR, that is, for patents, trade secrets, trademarks, copyrights, designs and so on. There are many possible contractual variations of licence agreements. Common types of licences include exclusive licence (for only one user), sole licence (for only one user besides the licensor), sub-licence (the licensee permit to another licensee in turn), compulsory licence (a licence which has to be offered), grant-back licence (the licensee has granted the licensor licences on improvements made by the licensee), cross-licence (licences are swapped between licensor and licensee) and block-licence (licence for a bundle of IPR, for example, a package of patents).

Litigant: Party involved in litigation, either defendant or plaintiff.

Litigation: A contest in a court of law for the purpose of enforcing a right or seeking a remedy; a judicial contest.

Mailbox patent: In US patent practice, many Japanese inventors simply want their JPO applications translated into English and then filed with the USPTO without change. The resulting US patent is probably not as high-quality as it would be if an American patent attorney or agent were free to adapt the Japanese application to US practice.

Market segment: A cluster of customers having similar purchasing behaviour.

Misappropriation: The unauthorized, improper or unlawful use of property for a purpose other than that for which it was intended; stealing.

Moral rights: The rights of the creator of a work of intellectual property regardless of who owns the work. Not all legal systems recognize these rights. Moral rights applicable to authors of copyrighted works include the right to claim authorship, the right to prevent use of one's name for works which one did not author, the right to prevent the use of one's name on works which have been distorted or mutilated, the right to prevent intentional distortion or mutilation, and the right to prevent change or destruction of a work of recognized stature.

Multitechnology corporation: A corporation operating in several technologies (as a result of technology diversification).

Non-obviousness requirement: An invention is not patentable if, at the time it was made, a person with ordinary skill in the relevant art and knowledge of all relevant prior technical information would have been able to make the invention, for instance by combining the information contained in the prior art documents.

Pacing technology: A technology in an early development stage with a verified potential for influencing product performance, quality and/or production cost.

Patent: The term is short for 'letters patent' (see, for example, David 1993 for the origin of the term). A patent is a limited-term exclusive right provided to inventors/applicants who file an adequate patent application. All patents will be published so that the general public will know of the invention and be informed of how it works.

Patent family: A set of patents granted in different countries for the same original invention.

Patent flooding: See 'file early, file often'. Patent flooding is a slightly more extreme version, used, for example, in Japan to force cross-licensing arrangements between holders of basic patents and holders of many patents with minor variations of the basic patent.

PCT: Patent Cooperation Treaty. This treaty permits a single patent application to be filed in multiple countries. The patent's filing date is the date on which it was filed in the first signatory country. PCT applications receive their patent search in the first country in which they are filed. The subsequent search report is provided to all the national patent offices which subsequently review the application. This treaty is the closest agreement presently in force which amounts to an international patent.

Pending: The term 'patent pending' means a patent has been applied for but not yet granted.

Piracy: See 'counterfeit'.

Plaintiff: A person who seeks remedial action for an injury to rights in a court of law.

Preliminary injunction: An injunction which may be granted to a plaintiff upon an inter-party showing that the defendant is likely to continue with, or refrain from doing, an act, the right to which is in dispute. While injunction practice is complex, the granting of a preliminary injunction should occur when: $P \cdot H_p > (1 - P) \cdot H_d$, where P is the plaintiff's probability of winning the trial, H_p is the harm to the plaintiff from not granting the injunction, and H_d is the harm to the defendant from granting the injunction.

Priority: Two different inventors may submit patent applications on the same invention. The priority date is the date of the earliest invention. In first-to-file systems, the priority date is the same as the filing date. In first-to-invent systems, the priority date is effectively the earliest date upon which the invention was conceived.

Priority application: The original patent application filed at some patent office in the world for a particular invention. This application then gives the applicant priority to the invention for a certain amount of time for filing patent applications at other patent offices for the same invention.

Product diversification: The expansion of the range of product areas of a company, in other words, the process by which new product areas are entered by a company.

Prophylactic disclosure: Disclosure of technical information with the intention to hinder patenting.

Reverse engineering: An engineering process by which a product or a production process is disassembled and analysed with the purpose of learning its design and function.

Revocation: A process by which a patent is declared invalid. This can occur either in a court of law or by action of the patent office.

Settlement: Since litigation is expensive and time-consuming, the parties generally benefit by concluding their dispute prior to a full courtroom battle. Settlements can be reached in a variety of ways, including arbitration, negotiation, and mediation. Settlements do not generally require the approval of the court.

Strategic patent: A patent that efficiently keeps others out of an area, that is, a patent with insurmountable R&D costs necessary to invent around.

Strategic patenting: Strategic patenting is loosely defined as working towards maximizing the asset value of an invention. This relates not only to when the patent is allowed to be issued, but also to which part of the technology is protected. It also entails monitoring competitors' products and proactively reviewing the scope of patent claims to ensure that, on issue, the patent is likely to cover those competing products. If correctly managed, strategic patenting can result in a patent portfolio of significant commercial value.

Submarine patent: In the USA, patent applications were previously kept in secret until a patent was granted, that is, there was no pre-grant publication system. Because patent applications may take years, in some cases many years, before being patents, an invention might mature into a patent long after others have started using the invention. This time lag allowed a company to create a so-called submarine patent, which essentially forced those using the underlying technology to purchase a licence on the patent or face a lawsuit for patent infringement when the patent was finally granted and published. In those patent systems which routinely publish all patent applications within a specified time after filing (18 months) this is a minor problem.

Sub-technology: A specialized knowledge part of a technology. In a classification of technologies, a certain technology at some level of classification is disaggregated into sub-technologies at lower levels.

Sui generis: A unique legal solution which does not fit into any pre-existing legal category. Latin: of its own kind or class; that is, of no other kind.

Surrounding patents: Patents related to one particularly important patent (for example, an essential, strategic or basic patent) in such a way that commercial use of the latter in products or processes requires the former. Typically, surrounding patents relate to different applications or complementary modifications of the surrounded patent.

Technical performance variable: Physically measurable attribute of a product, process or system pertaining to its technical functioning.

Technology: A body of knowledge about techniques and technical relationships, typically regarding ways to transform material matter to achieve more desirable physical effects. The body of knowledge referred to may be more or less specialized.

Technology base: Essentially the same as a technology system, but any interdependencies that may or may not be present are not explicitly referred to. Usually a technology base is considered in connection with a product (or service) or an actor who is in possession or some sort of control of the technologies in question.

Technology diversification: The process by which a company (or more generally an economic entity, such as a nation, region, organization, individual) extends its activities into technologies new to the company, thereby extending its range of technologies.

Technology system: A set of interrelated technologies. The technologies may be interrelated conceptually or causally, and in the latter case they are inter-dependent. A technology system is moreover to be distinguished from a technical system, which essentially is a set of physical parts or products or artefacts, that is, a 'hard' system.

Technology trade: Trade with patents, technology licences and technical know-how.

Technology transition (or technology base shift): A change in a technology base that involves an addition and/or deletion (substitution) of one or more technologies, rather than just an advancement of knowledge within given technologies.

Tort: A private or civil wrong or injury.

Trade secret: A pattern, formula, device or compilation of information which is valuable to a given business and not publicly known. The owners of trade secrets are protected against the theft of their secrets by others. The owner of a trade secret must usually make efforts to keep it secret in order to obtain any legal protection through trade secret rights.

Trademark: A distinctive mark (word or figure) through which products of particular manufacturers may be distinguished from those of others. Most of the world's major trading nations maintain offices in which trademarks may be registered.

Wilful infringement: Infringement by intent. For instance, counterfeiting, whereby the infringer knowingly or wilfully copies a protected work.

Writ: A written judicial order to perform a specified act. Failure to respond to the writ may be punishable as a crime.

References

Aaker, D.A. (1991), *Managing Brand Equity: Capitalizing on the Value of a Brand Name*, New York: Free Press.

Aaker, D.A. (1996), *Building Strong Brands*, New York: Free Press.

Abramovitz, M. (1956), 'Resource and output trends in the United States since 1870', *American Economic Review, Papers and Proceedings*, **46**, May, 5–23.

Abramovitz, M. (1986), 'Catching up, forging ahead and falling behind', *Journal of Economic History*, **46** (2), 385–406.

Abramovitz, M. (1990), 'The catch-up factor in postwar economic growth', *Economic Inquiry*, **28**, January, 1–18.

Abramovitz, M. (1991), *Thinking about Growth and Other Essays on Economic Growth and Welfare*, Cambridge: Cambridge University Press.

Acs, Z. and D. Audretsch (eds) (1991), *Innovation and Technological Change*, London: Harvester Wheatsheaf.

Adelstein, R.P. and S.I. Peretz (1985), 'The competition of technologies in markets for ideas: copyright and fair use in evolutionary perspective', *International Review of Law and Economics*, **5**, 209–38.

Adler, P.S., D.W. McDonald and F. MacDonald (1992), 'Strategic management of technical functions', *Sloan Management Review*, **33** (2), 19–37.

Aghion, P. and P. Howitt (1998), *Endogenous Growth Theory*, Cambridge, MA: The MIT Press.

Albach, H. and S. Rosenkranz (eds) (1995), *Intellectual Property Rights and Global Competition: Towards a New Synthesis*, Berlin: Sigma.

Alimpiev, V. and A. Sokolov (1997), 'The Institutional Structure of Applied R&D', in Gokhberg et al. (1997), pp. 34–56.

Ames, E. and N. Rosenberg (1963), 'Changing technological leadership and industrial growth', *Economic Journal*, **73**, March, 13–29.

Anawalt, H.C. and E. Enayati (1996), *IP Strategy: Complete Intellectual Property Planning Access and Protection*, New York: CBC (Clark, Boardman, Callaghan).

Andewelt, R. (1986), 'Recent revolutionary changes in intellectual property protection and the future prospects', *Albany Law Review*, **50**, 509–21.

Anton, J.J. and D.A. Yao (1994), 'Expropriation and inventions: appropriable rents in the absence of property rights', *American Economic Review*, **84** (1), 190–205.

Aoki, M. (1988), *Information, Incentives, and Bargaining in the Japanese Economy*, Cambridge: Cambridge University Press.

Aoki, M. and R. Dore (eds) (1994), *The Japanese Firm: Sources of Competitive Strength*, Oxford: Oxford University Press.

Aoki, M. and T.J. Prusa (1995), 'Product development and the timing of information disclosure under U.S. and Japanese patent systems', Cambridge, MA: NBER, Working Paper No. 5063.

Aoki, M. and N. Rosenberg (1987), 'The Japanese Firm as an Innovating Institution', in Shiraishi and Tsuru (1987), pp. 137–54.

Arai, H. (1997), 'IPR Protection in the 21st Century', International Intellectual Property Training Institute 10th Anniversary Memorial Ceremony Speech by Commissioner, Japanese Patent Office, Tokyo.

Archibugi, D. (1992), 'Patenting as an indicator of technological innovation: a review', *Science and Public Policy*, **19** (6), 357–68.

Archibugi, D. and P. Pianta (1992), *The Technological Specialization of Advanced Countries*, Dordrecht: Kluwer Academic Publishers.

Arora, A. (1995), 'Licensing tacit knowledge: intellectual property rights and the market for know-how', *Economics of Innovation and New Technology*, **4**, 41–59.

Arora, A. (1996), 'Contracting for tacit knowledge: the provision of technical services in technology licensing contracts', *Journal of Development Economics*, **50**, 233–56.

Arrow, K.J. (1962), 'Economic Welfare and the Allocation of Resources for Invention', in NBER (1962), pp. 609–25.

Arrow, K.J. (1974), *The Limits of Organization*, New York: W.W. Norton & Co.

Arthur, W.B. (1988), 'Competing Technologies: An Overview', in Dosi et al. (eds), pp. 590–607.

Arundel, A. and I. Kabla (1998), 'What percentage of innovations are patented? Empirical estimates for European firms', *Research Policy*, **27** (2), 127–41.

Athreye, S.S. (1998), 'On markets in knowledge', *Journal of Management and Governance*, **1**, 231–53.

Austin, M.M. and P. Vidal-Nauget (1980), *Economic and Social History of Ancient Greece: An Introduction*, Berkeley, CA: University of California Press.

Azmi, I.M. (1996), 'Basis for the recognition of intellectual property in light of the Shari'ah', *IIC, International Review of Industrial Property and Copyright Law*, **27** (5), 649–74.

Babbage, C. (1832), *On the Economy of Machinery and Manufactures*, London: Charles Knight.

Banner, D.W. (1986), 'The creation of the Federal Circuit Court of Appeals and the resulting revitalization of the patent system', *Albany Law Review*, **50**, 585–91.

Barnett, H.G. (1953), *Innovation: The Basis of Cultural Change*, New York: McGraw-Hill.

Barton, J.H. (1991), 'Patenting life', *Scientific American*, **264** (3), 40–46.

Barton, J.H. (1993), 'Adapting the Intellectual Property System to New Technologies', in NRC (1993), pp. 256–83.

Barton, J.H. (1995), 'Patent scope in biotechnology', *IIC, International Review of Industrial Property and Copyright Law*, **26** (5), 605–18.

Barzel, Y. (1968), *Economic Analysis of Property Rights*, Cambridge, MA: Cambridge University Press.

Basberg, B.L. (1987), 'Patents and the measurement of technological change: a survey of the literature', *Research Policy*, **16** (2-4), 131–41.

Battelle (1985), *Patent Trend Analysis. Tracking Technology Change for Business Planning. Battelle Technical Inputs to Planning*, Report No. 44, Columbus, OH: Battelle Memorial Institute.

Baxter, W.F. (1966), 'Legal restrictions on exploitation of the patent monopoly: an economic analysis', *Yale Law Journal*, **76** (2), 267–370.

Beck, R.L. (1983), 'The prospect theory of the patent system and unproductive competition', *Research in Law and Economics*, **5**, 193–209.

Becker, G.S. (1964), *Human Capital*, Chicago, IL: University of Chicago Press.

Becker, G.S. (1993), *Human Capital: A Theoretical and Empirical Analysis, with Special Reference to Education*, 3rd edn, Chicago and London: University of Chicago Press.

Bertha, S.L. (1996), 'Intellectual property activities in U.S. research universities', *Journal of Law and Technology*, **36** (4), 513–41.

Bertin G.Y. and S. Wyatt (1988), *Multinational Industrial Property – the Control of the World's Technology*, Hertfordshire: Harvester-Wheatsheaf.

Besen, S.M. and L.J. Raskind (1991), 'An introduction to the law and economics of intellectual property', *Journal of Economic Perspectives*, **5** (1), 3–27.

Bidault, F., B. Page and P. Sherwood (1989), *Technology Pricing: From Principles to Strategy*, New York: St. Martin's Press.

BIE (1995), *The Economics of Intellectual Property Rights for Designs*, Bureau of Industry Economics, Occasional Paper 27, Canberra: Australian Government Publishing Service.

Bohlin, E. (1995), *Economics and Management of Investments: An International Investigation of New Technology Decision-Making in Telecommunications*, PhD Dissertation, Department of Industrial Management and Economics, Chalmers University of Technology, Göteborg, Sweden.

Boitani, A. and E. Cicotti (1990), 'Patents as Indicators of Innovative Performance at the Regional Level', in Cappellin and Nijkamp (eds) (1990), pp. 139–63.

Borrus, M. (1990), 'Macroeconomic Perspectives on the Use of Intellectual Property Rights in Japan's Economic Performance', in Rushing and Brown (1990), pp. 261–76.

Bouchaert, B. (1990), 'What is property?' *Harvard Journal of Law & Public Policy*, **13** (3), 775–816.

Bowonder, B. and T. Miyake (1993), 'Japanese technological innovation strategy: recent trends', *Engineering Management Review*, Summer, 38–48.

Brandi-Dohrn, M. (1994), 'The unduly broad claim', *International Review of Industrial Property and Copyright Law*, **25** (5), 648–57.

Branscomb, A.W. (1994), *Who Owns Information? From Privacy to Public Access*, New York: Basic Books.

Branscomb, L.M. and F. Kodama (1993), *Japanese Innovation Strategy, Technical Support for Business Visions*, Center for Science and International Affairs, Occasional Paper No. 10, Harvard: Harvard University.

Bresnahan, T. and M. Trajtenberg (1995), 'General purpose technology: engines of growth?', *Journal of Econometrics*, Special Issue, January, **65** (1), 83–108.

Bright, J.R. (1964), *Research, Development and Technological Innovation: An Introduction*, Homewood, Illinois: Richard D. Irwin Inc.

Brockhoff, K.K. (1992), 'Instruments for patent data analyses in business firms', *Technovation*, **12** (1), 41–58.

Brooking, A. (1996), *Intellectual Capital: Core Asset for the Third Millennium Enterprise*, London: Thomson International Business Press.

Bureau of Economic Analysis (1994), *Survey of Current Business*, **72** (9), 111–14.

Bush, V. (1945), *Science – The Endless Frontier: A Report to the President*, Washington, DC: US Government Printing Office.

Calder, K.E. (1993), *Strategic Capitalism: Private Business and Public Purpose in Japanese Industrial Finance*, Princeton, NJ: Princeton University Press.

Cantwell, J. (1989), *Technological Innovation and Multinational Corporations*, Oxford: Basil Blackwell.

Cantwell, J. (ed.) (1994), 'Transnational Corporations and Innovatory Activities', in UN Library on Transnational Corporations, introductory chapter.

Cantwell, J. (1995), 'The globalisation of technology: what remains of the product cycle model?', *Cambridge Journal of Economics*, **19**, 155–74.

Cantwell, J. and L. Piscitello (1996), *The Diversification and Internationalization of Corporate Technology: From a Strategic Choice Historically to a Complementary Combination Today*, mimeo, University of Reading.

Cappellin, R. and P. Nijkamp (eds), *The Spatial Context of Technological Development*, Aldershot: Gower.

Carpenter, M.P., M. Cooper and F. Narin (1980), 'Linkage between basic research literature and patents', *Research Management*, **23** (2), 30–35.

Carpenter, M.P. and F. Narin (1993), 'Citation rates to technologically important patents', *World Patent Information*, **5** (3), 180–85.

Carpenter, M.P., F. Narin and P. Woolf (1981), 'Citation rates to technologically important patents', *World Patent Information*, **3** (4), 160–63.

Castells, M. (1998), *The Information Age: Economy, Society and Culture, Volume III: End of Millennium*, Oxford: Blackwell.

Caves, R., H. Crookell and P. Killing (1983), 'The imperfect market for technology licenses', *Oxford Bulletin of Economics and Statistics*, **45** (3), 249–67.

Chakrabarti, A.K. (1989), 'Technology indicators: conceptual issues and measurement problems', *Journal of Engineering and Technology Management*, **6**, 99–116.

Chakrabarti, A.K. and M.R. Halperin (1990), 'Technical performance and firm size: analysis of patents and publications of U.S. firms', *Small Business Economics*, **2**, 183–90.

Chandler, Jr, A.D. (1990), *Scale and Scope – The Dynamics of Industrial Capitalism*, Cambridge, MA and London: Belknap Press of Harvard University Press.

Cheung, S.N.S. (1982), 'Property rights in trade secrets', *Economic Inquiry*, **20** (1), 40–52.

Cheung, S.N.S. (1986), 'Property Rights and Invention', in J. Palmer, pp. 5–18.

Chisum, D.S. (1986), 'The patentability of algorithms', *University of Pittsburgh Law Review*, **47**, 959–1022.

Clark, K.B., R.H. Hayes and C. Lorenz (1985), *The Uneasy Alliance. Managing the Productivity–Technology Dilemma*, Boston, MA: Harvard Business School Press.

Clarke, T.E. and J. Reavley (1993), *Science and Technology Management Bibliography 1993*, 4th edn, Ottawa: Stargate Consultants Ltd.

Cockburn, I. and R. Henderson (1994), 'Racing to invest? The dynamics of competition in ethical drug discovery', *Journal of Economics & Management Strategy*, **3** (3), 481–519.

Coleman, A. (1992), *The Legal Protection of Trade Secrets*, London: Sweet & Maxwell.

Columbia Law Review (1994), Symposium: Toward a Third Intellectual Property Paradigm, **94** (8).

Collins, S.M. and B.P. Bosworth (1994), *The New GATT: Implications for the United States*, Brookings Occasional Papers, Washington, DC: Brookings Institution.

Comanor, W. and F.M. Scherer (1969), 'Patent statistics as a measure of technical change', *Journal of Political Economy*, **77** (3), 329–98.

Conrad, C.A. (1984), 'The advantage of being first and competition between firms', *International Journal of Industrial Organization*, **1**, 353–64.

Cooper, C.C. (1991), *Shaping Invention: Thomas Blanchard's Machinery and Patent Management in Nineteenth-Century America*, New York: Columbia University Press.

Cordero, R. (1991), 'Managing for speed to avoid product obsolescence: a survey of techniques', *Journal of Product Innovation Management*, **8**, 283–94.

Cordray, M.L. (1994), 'Gatt v. Wipo', *Journal of the Patent and Trademark Office Society*, **76** (2), 67–144.

Cornelli, F. and M. Schankerman (1995), *Optimal Patent Renewals*, mimeo, London Business School.

Cox, G.B. (1986), 'Law and technology', *Albany Law Review*, **50**, 495–500.

Dahmén, E. (1970), *Svensk industriell företagsverksamhet. Kausalanalys av den industriella utvecklingen 1919–1939*, IUI, Stockholm 1950. Translated and published in 1970 under the heading 'Entrepreneurial Activity and the Development of Swedish Industry 1919–1939' by the American Economic Association, Translation Series, Homewood: Richard D. Irwin Inc.

Dasgupta, P. (1988), 'Patents, priority and imitation or, the economics of races and waiting games', *Economic Journal*, **98**, 66–80.

Dasgupta, P. and P.A. David (1987), 'Information Disclosure and the Economics of Science and Technology', in Feiwel (1987), pp. 519–42.

Dasgupta, P. and J. Stiglitz (1980), 'Uncertainty, industrial structure and the speed of R&D', *Bell Journal of Economics*, **11**, 1–28.

David Hume Institute (1997), 'Innovation, incentive and reward: intellectual property law and policy', *Hume Papers on Public Policy*, **5** (3), Edinburgh: Edinburgh University Press.

David, P.A. (1985), 'Clio and the economics of QWERTY', *American Economic Review*, **75** (2), 332–7.

David, P.A. (1993), 'Intellectual Property Institutions and the Panda's Thumb: Patents, Copyrights, and Trade Secrets in Economic Theory and History', in NRC (1993), pp. 19–61.

Davis, M. (1989), 'Patents, Natural Rights and Natural Property', in Weil and Snapper (1989), pp. 241–9.

DeBrock, L.M. (1985), 'Market structure, innovation, and optimal patent life', *Journal of Law and Economics*, **2** (1), 223–44.

Deiaco, E. (1993), *Halkar Sverige efter? Sveriges position i det globala patentlandskapet*, Stockholm: IVA (Ingenjörsvetenskapsakademin IVA-R: 402) (Royal Swedish Academy of Engineering Sciences, IVA. In Swedish.)

Demsetz, H. (1967), 'Toward a theory of property rights', *American Economic Review, Papers and Proceedings*, **57**, 347–59

Denison, E. F. (1985), *Trends in American Economic Growth*, Washington, DC: Brookings Institution.

de Solla Price, D. (1973), 'The Relations Between Science and Technology and Their Implications for Policy Formation', in Simons and Strasser (1973).

De Waal, F. (1982), *Chimpanzee Politics*, London: Jonathan Cape.

Diamond, S.A. (1983), 'The historical development of trademarks', *Trademark Reporter*, **73** (3), 222–47.

Doi, T. (1980), *The Intellectual Property Law of Japan*, Alphen aan den Rijn, The Netherlands: Sijthoff & Noordhoff.

Dosi, G., C. Freeman, R. Nelson, G. Silverberg and L. Soete (eds) (1988), *Technical Change and Economic Theory*, London and New York: Pinter.

Dosi, G., R. Gianetti and P.A. Toninelli (eds) (1992), *Technology and Enterprise in a Historical Perspective*, Oxford: Oxford University Press.

Dreyfuss, R.C. (1989a), 'General Overview of the Intellectual Property System', in Weil and Snapper (1989), pp. 17–40.

Dreyfuss, R.C. (1989b), 'The federal circuit: a case study in specialized courts', *New York University Law Review*, **64** (1), 1–77.

Drucker, P.F. (1993), *Post-Capitalist Society*, New York: HarperCollins.

Dunning, J.H. (1988), *Multinationals, Technology and Competitiveness*, London: Unwin Hyman.

Dutton, H.I. (1984), *The Patent System and Inventive Activity during the Industrial Revolution 1750–1852*, Manchester: Manchester University Press.

Eaton, J. and S. Kortum (1996), 'Measuring technology diffusion and the international sources of growth', *Eastern Economic Journal*, **22** (4), 401–10.

Edvinsson, L. and M.S. Malone (1997), *Intellectual Capital*, New York: HarperCollins.

Ehrnberg, E. (1996), *Technological Discontinuities and Industrial Dynamics*, PhD Dissertation, Department of Industrial Management and Economics, Chalmers University of Technology, Göteborg, Sweden.

Eisenberg, R.S. (1987), 'Proprietary rights and the norms of science in biotechnology research', *Yale Law Journal*, **97** (2), 177–231.

Eisenberg, R.S. (1989), 'Patents and the process of science: exclusive rights and experimental use', *University of Chicago Law Review*, **56** (3), 1017–86.

Ellul, J. (1990), *The Technological Bluff*, Grand Rapids, Michigan: William B. Eerdman.

EPO (various years), *Annual Reports*, Munich: European Patent Office.

EPO, JPO and USPTO (1995), *Trilateral Statistical Report*, 1995 edition, Munich: European Patent Office.

Ernst, H. (1995), 'Patenting strategies in the German mechanical engineering industry and their relationship to company performance', *Technovation*, **15** (4), 225–40.

Etemad, H. and L.S. Dulude (1987), 'Patenting patterns in 25 large multinational enterprises', *Technovation*, **7**, 1–15.

Eto, H. (ed.) (1993), *R&D Strategies in Japan: The National, Regional and Corporate Approach*, Amsterdam: Elsevier.

European Commission (1997), *Building the European Information Society for Us All*, Luxembourg: Office for Official Publications of the EC.

European Commission (1998), 'Impact on competition and scale effects – intangible investments', *The Single Market Review*, Subseries V, 2.

Evenson, R.E. (1984), 'International Invention: Implications for Technology Market Analysis', in Z. Griliches (ed.), *R&D, Patents, and Productivity*, Chicago, IL: University of Chicago Press.

Farrell, J. (1989), 'Standardization and intellectual property', *Jurimetrics*, **30** (1), 35–50.

Farrington, B. (1965), *Greek Science*, Baltimore: Penguin Books.

Faust, K. (1990), 'Early identification of technological advances on the basis of patent data', *Scientometrics*, **19** (5/6), 473–80.

Feiwel, G. (ed.) (1987), *Arrow and the Ascent of Modern Economic Theory*, London: Macmillan.

Finley, M.I. (1965), 'Technical innovation and economic progress in the ancient world', *Economic History Review*, 2nd series, **XVIII** (1), 29–45.

Florida, R. and M. Kenney (1992), *Beyond Mass Production: The Japanese System and its Transfer to the U.S.*, Oxford: Oxford University Press.

Folk, G.E. (1942), *Patents and Industrial Progress: A Summary, Analysis and Evaluation of the Record on Patents of the Temporary National Economic Committee*, New York: Harper & Brothers.

Foray, D. (1994), *Production and Distribution of Knowledge in the New Systems of Innovation: The Role of Intellectual Property Rights*, Paper prepared for the conference: 'Intellectual Property Rights and Global Competition', Berlin Science Center for Social Research, 21–22 April 1994.

Forbes (1997), The World's Richest People 1997 Database, http://www.forbes.com/tool/toolbox/billnew/index.asp

Foster, F.H. and R.L. Shook (1993), *Patents, Copyrights and Trademarks*, 2nd edition, New York: John Wiley & Sons, Inc.

Frame, J.D. and F. Narin (1990), 'The United States, Japan and the changing technological balance', *Research Policy*, **19** (5), 447–55.

Francks, P. (1992), *Japanese Economic Development. Theory and Practice*, London: Routledge.

Frank, R.H. and Cook, P.J. (1995), *The Winner-Take-All Society*, New York: Free Press.

Fransman, M. (1994), 'Knowledge Segmentation – Integration in Theory and in Japanese Companies', in Granstrand (1994), pp. 165–87.

Fransman, M. (1995), *Japan's Computer and Communications Industry: The Evolution of Industrial Giants and Global Competitiveness*, Oxford: Oxford University Press.

Freeman, C. (1987), *Technology Policy and Economic Performance. Lessons from Japan*, London: Pinter.

Freeman, C., J. Clark and L. Soete (1982), *Unemployment and Technical Innovation*, London: Pinter.

Freeman, C. and C. Perez (1988), 'Structural Crises of Adjustment: Business Cycles and Investment Behavior', in Dosi et al. (1988), pp. 38–66.

Freeman, C. and L. Soete (1997), *The Economics of Industrial Innovation*, London: Pinter.

Friedman, D.D., W.M. Landes and R.A. Posner (1991), 'Some economics of trade secret law', *Journal of Economic Perspectives*, **5** (1), 61–72.

Fruin, W.M. (1992), *The Japanese Enterprise System, Competitive Strategies and Cooperative Structures*, Oxford: Clarendon Press.

Fudenberg, D., R. Gilbert, J. Stiglitz and J. Tirole (1983), 'Preemption, leapfrogging and competition in patent races', *European Economic Review*, **22**, 3–31.

Fujita,Y. (1991), *An Analysis of the Development and Nature of Accounting Principles in Japan*, New York: Garland.

Funk, J.L. (1993), 'Japanese product-development strategies: a summary and propositions about their implementation', *IEEE Transactions on Engineering Management*, **40** (3), 224–36.

Gallini, N.T. (1992), 'Patent policy and costly imitation', *RAND Journal of Economics*, **23** (1), 52–63.

Gallini, N.T. and R.W. Winter (1985), 'Licensing in the theory of innovation', *RAND Journal of Economics*, **16** (2), 237–52.

Gardner, H.S. (1988), *Comparative Economic Systems*, Chicago, IL: Dryden.

Gerlach, M.L. (1992), *Alliance Capitalism: The Social Organization of Japanese Business,* Berkeley, CA: University of California Press.

Geroski P. (1995), 'Markets for Technology: Knowledge, Innovation and Appropriability', in Stoneman (1995), pp. 90–131.

Gerschenkron, A. (1962), *Economic Backwardness in Historical Perspective*, Cambridge, MA: Belknap.

Gilbert, R. and C. Shapiro (1990), 'Optimal patent length and breadth', *RAND Journal of Economics*, **21** (1), 106–12.

Gilfillan, S.C. (1964a), *Invention and the Patent System*, US Congress, Joint Economic Committee, Washington DC: Government Printing Office.

Gilfillan, S.C. (1964b), 'The Social Principles of Innovation', in Bright (1964), p. 11.

Gire, J. (1992), 'Current literature in intellectual property', *IDEA: Journal of Law and Technology*, **33** (1), 109–16.

Glazier, S.C. (1995), *Patent Strategies for Business*, 2nd edition, London: Euromoney Books.

Glismann, H.H. and E.-J. Horn (1988), 'Comparative invention performance of major industrial countries: patterns and explanations', *Management Science*, **34** (10), 1169–87.

Gokhberg, L., M.J. Peck and J. Gacs (eds), *Russian Applied Research and Development: Its Problems and its Promise*, Laxenburg, Austria: IIASA.

Goldstein, P. (1994), *Copyright's Highway: From Gutenberg to the Celestial Jukebox*, New York: Hill & Wang.

Goldstein, P. (1997), *Copyright, Patent, Trademark and Related State Doctrines*, 4th edn, Westbury, NY: Foundation Press.

Grabowski, H. and J. Vernon (1986), 'Longer patents for lower imitation barriers: the 1984 Drug Act', *American Economic Review*, **76** (2), 195–8.

Graham, G.S. (1956), 'The ascendancy of the sailing ship 1850–85', *Economic History Review*, **IX** (1), 74–88.

Granstrand, O. (1982), *Technology, Management and Markets: An Investigation of R&D and Innovation in Industrial Organizations*, London: Pinter.

Granstrand, O. (1984), *The Evolution of the Video Cassette Recorder Industry and the Main Frame Computer Industry in Japan*, CIM Working paper 1984:07, Chalmers University of Technology, Department of Industrial Management and Economics, Göteborg, Sweden.

Granstrand, O. (1988), *Patents and Innovation: A Study of Patenting Practices and Trends in Sweden With a Brief Outlook on the US*, CIM Working paper No. 4, March, Chalmers University of Technology, Department of Industrial Management and Economics, Göteborg, Sweden.

Granstrand, O. (1993), *Patenting Profiles in Japanese and Swedish Large Corporations*, mimeo, Chalmers University of Technology, Department of Industrial Management and Economics, Göteborg, Sweden.

Granstrand, O. (ed.) (1994), *Economics of Technology: Seeking Strategies for Research and Teaching in a Developing Field*, Amsterdam: North-Holland.

Granstrand, O. (1998), 'Towards a theory of the technology-based firm', *Research Policy*, **27** (6), 465–89.

Granstrand, O. (1999), 'Internationalization of Corporate R&D: a study of Japanese and Swedish corporations', *Research Policy*, **28** (2-3), 275–302.

Granstrand, O., E. Bohlin, C. Oskarsson and N. Sjöberg (1992a), 'External technology acquisition in large multi-technology corporations', *R&D Management*, **22** (2), 1–35.

Granstrand, O., L. Håkanson and S. Sjölander (eds) (1992b), *Technology Management and International Business: Internationalization of R&D and Technology*, Chichester: John Wiley & Sons.

Granstrand, O. and C. Oskarsson (1994), 'Technology diversification in "MUL-TECH" corporations', *IEEE Transactions on Engineering Management*, **41** (4), 355–64.

Granstrand, O., P. Patel and K. Pavitt (1997), 'Multi-technology corporations: why they have "distributed" rather than "distinctive core" competencies', *California Management Review*, **39** (4), 8–25.

Granstrand, O. and J. Sigurdson (1981), *Technological and Industrial Policy in China and Europe*, Proceedings from the First Joint TIPCE Conference 1981, Technology & Culture, Occasional Report Series No. 3, Research Policy Institute, Lund, Sweden.

Granstrand, O. and J. Sigurdson (1992), *Sweden's Position in the Global Technological Development*, (Summary Report), Chalmers University of Technology, Department of Industrial Management and Economics, Göteborg, Sweden.

Granstrand, O. and J. Sigurdson (1993a), *A Questionnaire Study of IPR and Patent Management in Japanese and Swedish Corporations*, mimeo, Chalmers University of Technology, Department of Industrial Management and Economics and University of Lund, Research Policy Institute, Göteborg and Lund, Sweden.

Granstrand, O. and J. Sigurdson (1993b), *The Role of Patenting in Technology Commercialization: A Study of Patent Management Practices in Some Large Japanese Corporations and a Comparison with Sweden*, mimeo, Chalmers University of Technology, Department of Industrial Management and Economics and University of Lund, Research Policy Institute, Göteborg and Lund, Sweden.

Granstrand, O. and S. Sjölander (1990a), 'Managing innovation in multi-technology corporations', *Research Policy*, **19** (1), 35–60.

Granstrand, O. and S. Sjölander (1990b), 'The acquisition of technology and small firms by large firms', *Journal of Economic Behavior and Organization*, **13**, 367–86.

Granstrand, O., S. Sjölander and S. Alänge (1989), 'Strategic technology management issues in Japanese manufacturing industry', *Technology Analysis and Strategic Management*, **1** (3), 259–72.

Green, J. and S. Scotchmer (1995), 'On the division of profit in sequential innovation', *Rand Journal of Economics*, **26**, 20–33.

Griliches, Z. (1964), 'Research expenditures, education, and the aggregate agricultural production function', *American Economic Review*, **54**, 961–74.

Griliches, Z. (1984), *R&D, Patents, and Productivity*, Chicago, IL: University of Chicago Press.

Griliches, Z. (1989), 'Patents: recent trends and puzzles', *Brookings Papers on Economic Activity: Microeconomics*, **1**, 291–330.

Griliches, Z. (1990), 'Patent statistics as economic indicators: a survey', *Journal of Economic Literature*, **28** (4), 1661–707.

Griliches, Z. (1996), 'The discovery of the residual: a historical note', *Journal of Economic Literature*, **34**, 1324–30.

Griliches, Z., B. Hall and A. Pakes (1988), *R&D, Patents and Market Value Revisited*, Cambridge, MA: NBER, Working Paper No. 2624.

Grindley, P.C. (1995), *Standards, Strategy, and Policy: Cases and Stories*, Oxford: Oxford University Press.

Grindley, P.C. and D.J. Teece (1997), 'Managing intellectual capital: licensing and cross-licensing in semiconductors and electronics', *California Management Review*, **39** (2), 8–41.

Grupp, H. (1991), 'Innovation Dynamics in OECD Countries: Towards a Correlated Network of R&D Intensity, Trade, Patent and Technometric Indicators', in OECD (1991).

Grupp, H. (1994), 'The Dynamics of Science-Based Innovation Reconsidered: Cognitive Models and Statistical Findings', in Granstrand (1994), pp. 223–51.

Hall, B.H. (1993), *The Value of Intangible Corporate Assets: An Empirical Study of the Components of Tobin's q*, University of California at Berkeley, Department of Economics, Working Paper No. 93-207

Hall, B.H. (1994), *Industrial Research during the 1980s: Did the Rate of Return Fall?* Cambridge, MA: NBER.

Hall, B.H. (1998), *Innovation and Market Value*, Paper prepared for the NIESR Conference on Productivity and Competitiveness, London, 5–6 February 1998.

Hall, B.H., A.B. Jaffe and M. Trajtenberg (1998), *Market Value and Patent Citations: A First Look*, mimeo, Cambridge, MA: NBER.

Harhoff, D., F.M. Scherer and K. Vopel (1997), *Exploring the Trail of Patented Invention Value Distributions*, Mannheim: ZEW, Zentrum für Europäische Wirtschaftsforschung GmbH, Discussion Paper No. 97-30.

Harvey, C. and G. Jones (eds) (1992), *Organizational Capability and Competitive Advantage*, London: Frank Cass & Co. Ltd.

Hayes, R.H. and W.J. Abernathy (1980), 'Managing our way to economic decline', *Harvard Business Review*, **58** (4), 66-7.

Helfgott, S. (1990), 'Cultural differences between the U.S. and Japanese patent systems', *Journal of the Patent and Trademark Office Society*, **72** (3), 231–8.

Henderson, R., A.B. Jaffe and M. Trajtenberg (1995), *The Bayh-Dole Act and Trends in University Patenting 1965-1988*, Center for Economic Policy Research No. 433, Stanford, CA: Stanford University.

Hodkinson, K. (1987), *Protecting and Exploiting New Technology and Designs*, London: E & F.N. Spon.

Hofer, R.E. (1986), 'The real world of juries, damages, and injunctions in patent cases', *Albany Law Review*, **50**, 593–9.

Holmes, O.W. (1878), 'Possession', *American Law Review*, **12**, 688–701. Published in Novick (1995), Vol. 3, pp. 37–60 and modified as a lecture on pp. 220–41.

Horgan, J. (1996), *The End of Science: Facing the Limits of Knowledge in the Twilight of the Scientific Age*, Reading: Addison-Wesley.

Hughes, T.P. (1971), *Elmer Sperry: Inventor and Engineer*, Baltimore, MD: Johns Hopkins Press.

ICC (1997), *'Countering Counterfeiting: A Guide to Protecting and Enforcing Intellectual Property Rights'*, Paris: ICC (International Chamber of Commerce) Publishing.

IIP (1994), *Report on the Basic Issues Concerning Economic Effects of Intellectual Property* (Summary), Tokyo: Institute of Intellectual Property (IIP).

IIP (1995), *Study in Issues between Intellectual Property Rights and Technical Standards*, Tokyo: Institute of Intellectual Property (IIP).

Imai, K.-I. (1992), 'The Japanese Pattern of Innovation and its Evolution', in Rosenberg et al. (1992), pp. 225–46.

Imai, K.-I., I. Nonaka and H. Takeuchi (1985), 'Managing the New Product Development Process: How Japanese Companies Learn and Unlearn', in Clark et al. (1985), pp. 337–75.

Imai, M. (1986), *Kaizen: The Key to Japan's Competitive Success*, New York: Random House.

IVA (1993), *Profit from Innovation*, Stockholm: Royal Swedish Academy of Engineering Sciences (IVA).

Jacobsson, S. and C. Oskarsson (1995), 'Educational statistics as an indication of technological activity', *Research Policy*, **24** (1), 127–36.

Jacobsson, S., C. Oskarsson and J. Philipson (1996), 'Indicators of technological activities – comparing educational, patent and R&D statistics in the case of Sweden', *Research Policy*, **25** (4), 573–85.

Jaffe, A.B. (1989), 'Characterizing the "technological position" of firms, with application to quantifying technological opportunity and research spillovers', *Research Policy*, **18** (2), 87–97.

Jaffe, A.B., M. Trajtenberg and R. Henderson (1993), 'Geographic localization of knowledge spillovers as evidenced by patent citations', *Quarterly Journal of Economics*, **108** (3), 577–98.

Jantsch, E. (1967), *Technological Forecasting in Perspective*, Paris: OECD.

Johnson, C. (1982), *MITI and the Japanese Miracle: The Growth of Industrial Policy, 1925–1975*, Stanford, CA: Stanford University Press.

Johnson, C. (1993), 'Comparative capitalism: the Japanese difference', *California Management Review*, **35** (4), 51–67.

Johnson, C., L. Tyson and J. Zysman (eds) (1989), *Politics and Productivity: How Japan's Development Strategy Works*, New York: Harper Business.

JPO (1994), *Guide to Industrial Property in Japan*, Tokyo: JPO (Japanese Patent Office).

JPO, USPTO, EPO (1996), *Trilateral Statistics Report 1996*, http://www.jpo-miti.go.jp/

Julian-Arnold, G. (1992), 'International compulsory licensing: the rationales and the reality', *IDEA: Journal of Law and Technology*, **33** (4), 349–71.

Kahn, A.E. (1940), 'Fundamental deficiencies of the American patent law', *American Economic Review*, **30** (3), 475–91.

Kamien, M.I., S.S. Oren and Y. Tauman (1992), 'Optimal licensing of cost reducing innovation', *Journal of Mathematical Economics*, **21**, 483–508.

Kaplan, R.S. and D.P. Norton (1996), *The Balanced Scorecard: Translating Strategy into Action*, Cambridge, MA: Harvard Business School Press.

Katz, M. and C. Shapiro (1985), 'On the licensing of innovations', *Rand Journal of Economics*, **16**, 504–20.

Kaufer, E. (1989), *The Economics of the Patent System*, New York: Harwood Academic Publishers.

Kerin, R.A., P.R. Varadarajan and R.A. Peterson (1993), 'First mover advantage – a synthesis, conceptual framework and research propositions', *Engineering Management Review*, Winter, 19–33.

Kingston, W. (ed.) (1987), *Direct Protection of Innovation*, Dordrecht: Kluwer Academic Publishers.

Kingston, W. (1990), *Innovation, Creativity and Law*, Dordrecht: Kluwer Academic Publishers.

Kingston, W. (1992), 'Is the United States right about "first to invent"?', *European Intellectual Property Review*, **7** (223), 375–9.

Kingston, W. (1994), 'Compulsory licensing with capital payments as an alternative to grants of monopoly in intellectual property', *Research Policy*, **23**, 661–72.

Kingston, W. (1995), 'Reducing the cost of resolving intellectual property disputes', *European Journal of Law and Economics*, **2**, 85–92.

Kingston, W. (1997), 'Patent protection for modern technologies', *Intellectual Property Quarterly*, **3**, 350–69.

Kitch, E. (1977), 'The nature and function of the patent system', *Journal of Law and Economics*, **30** (1), 265–90.

Klemperer, P. (1990), 'How broad should the scope of patent protection be?', *RAND Journal of Economics*, **21** (1), 113–30.

Klevorick, A.K., R.C. Levin, R.R. Nelson and S.G. Winter (1995), 'On the source and significance of interindustry differences in technological opportunities', *Research Policy*, **24** (2), 185–205.

Kline, S.J. and N. Rosenberg (1986), 'An Overview of Innovation', in Landau and Rosenberg (1986), pp. 275–305.

Kodama, F. (1986), 'Technological diversification of Japanese industry', *Science*, **233**, 291–6.

Kodama, F. (1995), *Emerging Patterns of Innovation: Sources of Japan's Technological Edge*, Boston, MA: Harvard Business School Press.

Kogut, B. (ed.) (1993), *Country Competitiveness*, Oxford: Oxford University Press.

Kortum, S. and J. Lerner (1997), *Stronger Protection or Technological Revolution: What is behind the Recent Surge in Patenting?*, mimeo, Cambridge, MA: NBER.

Kotabe, M. (1992), 'A comparative study of U.S. and Japanese patent systems', *Journal of International Business Studies*, **23** (1), 147–68.

Krech, D., R.S. Crutchfield and E.L. Ballachey (1962), *Individual in Society: A Textbook of Social Psychology*, New York: McGraw-Hill.

Kretschmer, M. (forthcoming), 'Intellectual property in music: a historical analysis of rhetoric and institutional practices', *Studies in Cultures, Organisations and Societies*, special issue *Arts Management and Culture Industry* (edited by Paul Jeffcutt, John Pick and Robert Protherough).

Kuflick, A. (1989), 'Moral Foundations of Intellectual Property Rights', in Weil and Snapper (1989), pp. 219–40.

Kuhn, T.S. (1970), *The Structure of Scientific Revolutions*, 2nd edn, International Encyclopedia of Unified Science, 2 (2), Chicago, IL: University of Chicago Press.

Lakatos, I. and A. Musgrave (eds) (1970), *Criticism and the Growth of Knowledge*, Cambridge, MA: Cambridge University Press.

Landau, R. and N. Rosenberg (eds) (1986), *The Positive Sum Strategy: Harnessing Technology for Economic Growth*, Washington, DC: National Academy Press.

Landes, M. (1969), *The Unbound Prometheus: Technological and Industrial Development in Western Europe from 1750 to the Present*, Cambridge, MA: Cambridge University Press.

Lanjouw, J.O. and J. Lerner (1997), *The Enforcement of Intellectual Property Rights: A Survey of the Empirical Literature*, Cambridge, MA: NBER, Working Paper No. 6296.

Lee, J.-Y. and E. Mansfield (1996), 'Intellectual property protection and U.S. foreign direct investment', *Review of Economics and Statistics*, **78** (2), 181–6.

Leonard-Barton, D. (1995), *Wellsprings of Knowledge: Building and Sustaining the Sources of Innovation*, Boston, MA: Harvard Business School Press.

Lerner, J. (1994), 'The importance of patent scope: an empirical analysis', *RAND Journal of Economics*, **25** (2), 319–33.

Levin, R.C. (1986), 'A new look at the patent system', *American Economic Review*, **76** (2), 199–202.

Levin, R.C., A.K. Klevorick, R.R. Nelson and S.G. Winter (1987), 'Appropriating the returns from industrial research and development', *Brookings Papers on Economic Activity*, **3**, 783–831.

Lewellen W.G. and S.G. Badrinath (1997), 'On the measurement of Tobin's *q*', *Journal of Financial Economics*, **44**, 77–122.

Lieberman, M.B. and D.B. Montgomery (1988), 'First mover advantages', *Strategic Management Journal*, **9**, 41–58.

Liebowitz, S.J. and S.E. Margolis (1990), 'The fable of the keys', *Journal of Law & Economics*, **XXXIII** (1) 1–25.

Lindholm, Å. (1994), *The Economics of Technology-Related Ownership Changes: A Study of Innovativeness and Growth through Acquisitions and Spin-offs*, PhD Dissertation, Department of Industrial Management and Economics, Chalmers University of Technology, Göteborg, Sweden.

List, F. (1841), *The National System of Political Economy*, English edition, London: Longman (1904).

Long, P. (1991), 'The openness of knowledge: an ideal and its context in 16th century writings on mining and metallurgy', *Technology and Culture*, **32**, 318–55.

Machlup, F. (1958), *An Economic Review of the Patent System*, Study No. 15 of the Subcommittee on Patents, Trademarks, and Copyrights of the Committee on the Judiciary, US Senate, Washington, DC: US Government Printing Office.

Machlup, F. (1962), *The Production and Distribution of Knowledge in the United States*, Princeton, NJ: Princeton University Press.

Machlup, F. (1980), *Knowledge, Its Creation, Distribution, and Economic Significance, Vol. 1, Knowledge and Knowledge Production*, Princeton, NJ: Princeton University Press, p. 80.

Machlup, F. (1984), *The Economics of Information and Human Capital*, Princeton, NJ: Princeton University Press.

Machlup, F. and E. Penrose (1950), 'The patent controversy in the nineteenth century', *Journal of Economic History*, **10** (1), 1–29.

MacKay, E. (1990), 'Economic incentives in markets for information and innovation', *Harvard Journal of Law & Public Policy*, **13** (3), 867–909.

MacLeod, C. (1988), *Inventing the Industrial Revolution: The English Patent System, 1660–1800*, Cambridge: Cambridge University Press.

MacLeod, C. (1991), 'The paradoxes of patenting, invention and its diffusion in 18th and 19th century Britain, France and North America', *Technology and Culture*, **30/32**, 885–910.

MacPherson, C.B. (ed.) (1978), *Property: Mainstream and Critical Positions*, Toronto: University of Toronto Press.

Mainers, R.E. and R.J. Staaf (1990), 'Patents, copyrights and trademarks: property or monopoly?', *Harvard Journal of Law & Public Policy*, **13** (3), 911–47.

Malerba, F. and L. Orsenigo (1995), *On New Innovators and Ex-Innovators*, mimeo, Department of Economics, Bocconi University, Milan.

Malerba, F. and L. Orsenigo (1996), 'Schumpeterian patterns of innovation are technology-specific', *Research Policy*, **25** (3), 451–78.

Mansfield, E. (1985), 'Public Policy toward Industrial Innovation: An International Study of Direct Tax Incentives for Research and Development', in Clark et al. (1985), pp. 383–407.

Mansfield, E. (1986), 'Patents and innovation: an empirical study', *Management Science*, **32** (2), 173–81.

Mansfield, E. (1988a), 'Industrial innovation in Japan and the United States', *Science*, **241**, 1769–74.

Mansfield, E. (1988b), 'The speed and cost of industrial innovation in Japan and the United States: external vs. internal technology', *Management Science*, **34** (10), 1157–68.

Mansfield, E. (1994), *Intellectual Property Protection, Foreign Direct Investment, and Technology Transfer*, Discussion Paper 19, Washington, DC: International Finance Corporation (IFC).

Mansfield, E. (1995), *Intellectual Property Protection, Direct Investment, and Technology Transfer: Germany, Japan, and the United States*, Discussion Paper 27, Washington DC: International Finance Corporation (IFC).

Mansfield, E., M. Schwartz and S. Wagner (1981), 'Imitation costs and patents: an empirical study', *Economic Journal*, **91** (December), 907–18.

Mansfield, E., J. Rapoport, A. Romeo, E. Villani, S. Wagner and F. Husic (1977a), *The Production and Application of New Industrial Technology*, New York: W.W. Norton.

Mansfield, E., J. Rapoport, A. Romeo, S. Wagner and G. Beardsley (1977b), 'Social and private rate return from industrial innovations', *Quarterly Journal of Economics*, **71** (May), 221–40.

Marshall, A. ([1890] 1994), *Principles of Economics*, London: Macmillan Press.

Mazzoleni, R. and R.R. Nelson (1998), 'The benefits and costs of strong patent protection: a contribution to the current debate', *Research Policy*, **27** (3), 273–84.

McKinnon, R.I. (1996), *The Rules of the Game: International Money and Exchange Rates*, Cambridge, MA: MIT Press.

McKinnon, R.I. (1997), *Dollar and Yen: Resolving Economic Conflict between the United States and Japan*, Cambridge, MA: MIT Press.

Merges, R.P. (1988), 'Commercial success and patent standards: economic perspectives on innovation', *California Law Review*, **76** (3), 803–76.

438   *The economics and management of intellectual property*

Merges, R.P. (1992), *Patent Law and Policy: Cases and Materials*, Charlottesville, VA: The Michie Co. Law Publishers.

Merges, R.P. (1994), 'Intellectual property rights and bargaining breakdown: the case of blocking patents', *Tennessee Law Review*, **62** (1), 75–106.

Merges, R.P. (1995a), 'Intellectual property and the costs of commercial exchange: a review essay', *Michigan Law Review*, **93** (6), 1570–615.

Merges, R.P. (1995b), *Contemporary Pressure Points in Patent Law and Litigation: Economic Perspectives*, Paper presented at the American Economic Association meeting, January 1996, San Francisco.

Merges, R.P. (1996), 'Contracting into liability rules: intellectual property rights and collective rights organizations', *California Law Review*, **84** (5), 1293–393.

Merges, R.P. and R.R. Nelson (1990), 'On the complex economics of patent scope', *Columbia Law Review*, **90** (4), 839–916.

Merton, R.K. (1935), 'Fluctuations in the rate of industrial invention', *Quarterly Journal of Economics*, **49** (3) 454–74.

Merton, R.K. (1973), *The Sociology of Science: Theoretical and Empirical Investigations*, Chicago, IL: University of Chicago Press.

Merton, R.K. (1988), 'The Matthew effect in science, II – cumulative advantage and the symbolism of intellectual property', *ISIS*, **79**, 606–23.

Meurer, M.J. (1989), 'The settlement of patent litigation', *RAND Journal of Economics*, **20** (1), 77–91.

Miyazaki, K. (1995), *Building Competencies in the Firm: Lessons from Japanese and European Optoelectronics*, New York: St. Martin's Press.

Mody, A. (1990), 'New International Environment for Intellectual Property Rights', in Rushing and Brown (1990), pp. 203–39.

Mogee, M.E. (1991), 'Using patent data for technology analysis and planning', *Engineering Management Review*, Winter 1991, 46–51.

Mokyr, J. (1990), *The Lever of Riches: Technological Creativity and Economic Progress*, New York and Oxford: Oxford University Press.

Momberg, D. and A. Ashton (1986), *Strategy in the Use of Intellectual Property: A Guide to Managing Business' Most Valuable Asset*, Hong Kong: Gerundive Press.

Montgomery, C.A. (1994), 'Corporate diversification', *Journal of Economic Perspectives*, **8** (3), 163–78.

Morita, A. (1986), *Made in Japan*, New York: E.P. Dutton.

Mowery, D. (1992), 'The US national innovation system: origins and prospects for change', *Research Policy*, **21** (2), 125–44.

Mowery, D. and N. Rosenberg (1979), 'The influence of market demand upon innovation: a critical review of some recent empirical studies' *Research Policy*, **8** (2), 102–53.

Mowery, D. and N. Rosenberg (1989), *Technology and the Pursuit of Economic Growth*, Cambridge, MA: Cambridge University Press.

Nance, D.A. (1990), 'Owning ideas', *Harvard Journal of Law & Public Policy*, **13** (3), 757–73.

Narin, F. (1993), 'Patent citation analysis: the strategic application of technology indicators', *Patent World*, April, 25–30.

Narin, F., M.B. Albert and V.M. Smith (1992), 'Technology indicators in strategic planning', *Science and Public Policy*, **19** (6), 369–81.

Narin, F., M.P. Carpenter and P. Woolf (1984), 'Technological performance assessments based on patents and patent citations', *IEEE Transactions on Engineering Management*, **EM-31** (4), 172–83.

Narin, F. and E. Noma (1985), 'Is technology becoming science?' *Scientometrics*, **7** (3-6), 369–81.

Narin, F., E. Noma, and R. Perry (1987), 'Patents as indicators of corporate technological strength', *Research Policy*, **16** (2-4), 143–55.

NAS (1994), *Corporate Approaches to Protecting Intellectual Property: Implications for US–Japan High-Technology Competition*, Report of a workshop, National Academy of Sciences (NAS), Washington, DC: National Academy Press.

NBER (1962), *The Rate and Direction of Inventive Activity*, National Bureau of Economic Research, Princeton, NJ: Princeton University Press.

Nelkin, D. (1984), *Science as Intellectual Property: Who Controls Research?*, New York: Macmillan.

Nelson, R.R. (1992), 'The Roles of Firms in Technical Advance: A Perspective from Evolutionary Theory', in Dosi et al. (1992).

Nelson, R.R. (ed.) (1993), *National Innovation Systems: A Comparative Analysis*, New York and Oxford: Oxford University Press.

Nelson, R.R. and N. Rosenberg (1993), 'Technical Innovation and National Systems', in Nelson (1993), pp. 3–21.

Nelson R.R. and S.G. Winter (1977), 'In search of useful theory of innovation', *Research Policy*, **6** (1), 36–76.

Nelson R.R. and S.G. Winter (1982), *An Evolutionary Theory of Economic Change*, Cambridge, MA: The Belknap Press.

Niosi, J. (ed.) (1994), *New Technology Policy and Social Innovations in the Firm*, London: Pinter.

Nonaka, I. (1990), 'Redundant, overlapping organization: a Japanese approach to managing the innovation process', *California Management Review*, **32** (3), 27–38.

Nonaka, I. and M. Kenney (1991), 'Towards a new theory of innovation management: a case study comparing Canon Inc. and Apple Computer Inc.', *Journal of Engineering and Technology Management*, **8**, 67–83.

Nordhaus, W.D. (1969), *Invention, Growth and Welfare*, Cambridge, MA: MIT Press.

North, D.C. (1981), *Structure and Change in Economic History*, New York: W.W. Norton & Company.

Novick, S.M. (ed.) (1995), *The Collected Works of Justice Holmes*, Vols 1–5, Chicago, IL: University of Chicago Press.

NRC (1993), *Global Dimensions of Intellectual Property Rights in Science and Technology*, National Resource Council, M.B. Wallerstein, M.E. Mogee and R.A. Schoen (eds), Washington, DC: National Academy Press.

OECD (1991), *Technology and Productivity – The Challenge for Economic Policy*, Paris: OECD.

OECD (1996), *Innovations, Patents and Technological Strategies*, Paris: OECD.

OECD (1997), *Patents and Innovation in the International Context*, OCDE/GD(97)210, Paris: OECD.

O'Brien, T.I. (1986), 'Establishing a company policy and program for intellectual property rights', *Albany Law Review*, **50**, 539–56.

Odagiri, H. and A. Goto (1993), 'The Japanese System of Innovation: Past, Present and Future', in Nelson (1993), pp. 76–114.

Ogburn, W.F. and D.S. Thomas (1922), 'Are inventions inevitable?', *Political Science Quarterly*, **37**, 83–98.

Okimoto, D.I. (1983), *Pioneer and Pursuer: The Role of the State in the Evolution of the Japanese and American Semiconductor Industries*, Occasional paper of the Northeast Asia–United States Forum on International Policy, Stanford, CA: Stanford University.

Okimoto, D.I. (1989), *Between MITI and the Market: Japanese Industrial Policy for High Technology*, Stanford, CA: Stanford University Press.

Okimoto, D.I. and Y. Nishi (1994), 'R&D Organization in Japanese and American Semiconductor Firms', in Aoki and Dore (1994), pp. 178–208.

Oman, R. (1986), 'Technology and intellectual property: the view from Capitol Hill', *Albany Law Review*, **50** (1), 523–32.

Ordover, J.A. (1991), 'A patent system for both diffusion and exclusion', *Journal of Economic Perspectives*, **5**, 43–60.

Oskarsson, C. (1993), *Technology Diversification: The Phenomenon, its Causes and Effects*, PhD Dissertation, Department of Industrial Management and Economics, Chalmers University of Technology, Göteborg, Sweden.

Ostry, S. and R.R. Nelson (1995), *Techno-Nationalism and Techno-Globalism: Conflict and Cooperation*, Washington, DC: Brookings Institution.

OTA (1992), US Congress, Office of Technology Assessment, *Finding a Balance: Computer Software, Intellectual Property, and the Challenge of Technological Change*, OTA-TCT-527, Washington, DC: US Government Printing Office.

Pakes, A. (1986), 'Patents as options: some estimates of the value of holding European patent stocks', *Econometrica*, **54** (4), 755–84.

Pakes, A. and M. Simpson (1989), 'Patent Renewal Data', *Brookings Papers on Economic Activity, Microeconomics*, Washington, DC: Brookings Institution, 331–410.

Palmer, J. (ed.) (1986), *The Economics of Patents and Copyrights*, Research in Law and Economics, Vol. 8, Greenwich, CT: JAI Press Inc.

Palmer, T.G. (1990), 'Are patents and copyrights morally justified? The philosophy of property rights and ideal objects', *Harvard Journal of Law & Public Policy*, **13** (3), 817–65.

Parr, R.L. and P.H. Sullivan (1996), *Technology Licensing: Corporate Strategies for Maximising Value*, Chichester: John Wiley & Sons.

Patel, P. and K. Pavitt (1995), *Technological Competencies in the World's Largest Firms: Characteristics, Constraints and Scope for Managerial Choice*, Laxenburg, Austria: International Institute for Applied Systems Analysis, Working Paper 95-66.

Pavitt, K. (1985), 'Patent statistics as indicators of innovative activities: possibilities and problems', *Scientometrics*, **7** (1-2), 77–99.

Pavitt, K. (1991), 'Key characteristics of the large innovating firm', *British Journal of Management*, **2**, 41–50.

Pearce, R. (1994), 'The internationalisation of research and development by multinational enterprises and the transfer sciences', *Empirica*, **21**, 297–311.

Penrose, E.T. (1951), *The Economics of the International Patent System*, Baltimore, MD: Johns Hopkins University Press.

Penrose, E.T. ([1959] 1972), *The Theory of the Growth of the Firm*, 5th impression, Oxford: Basil Blackwell and Mott Ltd.

Phillips, A. (1971), *Technology and Market Structure: A Study of the Aircraft Industry*, Lexington, MA: Heath Lexington Books.

Plant, A. (1974), *Selected Economic Essays and Addresses*, London and Boston: Routledge & Kegan Paul.

Polanyi, M. (1962), *Personal Knowledge: Towards a Post-Critical Philosophy*, New York: Harper & Row.

Popper, K.R. ([1962] 1968), *Conjectures and Refutations: The Growth of Scientific Knowledge*, New York: Harper & Row.

Porter, M.E. (1980), *Competitive Strategy: Techniques for Analyzing Industries and Competitors*, New York: Free Press.

Porter, M.E. (1990), *The Competitive Advantage of Nations*, London and Basingstoke: The Macmillan Press, Ltd.

Posner, R.A. (1983), *The Economics of Justice*, Cambridge, MA: Harvard University Press.

Prior, W.J. (1991), *Virtue and Knowledge: An Introduction to Ancient Greek Ethics*, London and New York: Routledge.

Quigg, D.J. (1986), 'The patent system: its historic and modern roles', *Albany Law Review*, **50**, 533–8.

Rahn, G. (1983), 'The role of industrial property in economic development: the Japanese experience', *International Review of Industrial Property and Copyright Law*, **14** (4), 449–92.

Rahn, G. (1994), 'Patentstrategien japanischer Unternehmen', *Gewerblischer Rechtsschutz und Urheberecht, Internationaler Teil*, **5**, 377–82.

Ravenscraft, D.J. and F.M. Scherer (1987), *Mergers, Sell-offs, and Economic Efficiency*, Washington, DC: Brookings Institution.

Reichman, J.H. (1994), 'Legal hybrids between the patent and copyright paradigms', *Columbia Law Review*, **94** (8), 2432–558.

Reichman, J.H. and P. Samuelson (1997), 'Intellectual property rights in data?', *Vanderbilt Law Review*, **50** (1), 52–166.

Reinganum, J. (1982), 'A dynamic game of R&D: patent protection and competitive behavior', *Econometrica*, **50**, 671–88.

Rogers, E.M. (1995), *Diffusion of Innovations*, 4th edition, New York: Free Press.

Rose, M. (1993), *Authors and Owners. The Invention of Copyright*, Cambridge, MA: Harvard University Press.

Rosenberg, N. (1963), 'Technological change in the machine tool industry 1840–1910', *Journal of Economic History*, **23** (4), 414–43.

Rosenberg, N. (1982), *Inside the Black Box: Technology and Economics*, Cambridge, MA: Cambridge University Press.

Rosenberg, N. (1989), 'Why do firms do basic research? (with their own money?)', *Research Policy*, **19** (2), 165–74.

Rosenberg, N. (1992), 'Economic experiments', *Industrial and Corporate Change*, **1**, 181–203.

Rosenberg, N. (1994), *Exploring the Black Box*, Cambridge: Cambridge University Press.

Rosenberg, N. and L.E. Birdzell Jr (1986), *How the West Grew Rich: The Economic Transformation of the Industrial World*, New York: Basic Books.

Rosenberg, N. and C.R. Frischtak (1984), 'Technological innovation and long waves', *Cambridge Journal of Economics*, **8**, 7–24.

Rosenberg, N., R. Landau and D. Mowery (eds) (1992), *Technology and the Wealth of Nations*, Stanford, CA: Stanford University Press.

Rosenberg, N. and R.R. Nelson (1994), 'American universities and technical advance in industry', *Research Policy*, **23**, 323–48.

Rosenberg, N. and W.E. Steinmueller (1988), 'Why are Americans such poor imitators?', *American Economic Review*, **78** (2), 229–34.

Rosenbloom, R.S. (1985), 'Managing Technology for the Longer Term: A Managerial Perspective', in Clark et al. (1995), pp. 297–335.

Rosenbloom, R.S. and M.A. Cusumano (1987), 'Technological pioneering and competitive advantage: the birth of the VCR industry', *California Management Review*, **29** (4), 51–76.

Rushing, F.W. and C.G. Brown (eds) (1990), *Intellectual Property Rights in Science, Technology, and Economic Performance: International Comparisons*, San Francisco, London and Boulder, CO: Westview Press.

Samuels, R.J. (1994), *Rich Nation, Strong Army, National Security and the Technological Transformation of Japan*, Ithaca, NY: Cornell University Press.

Samuelson, P. (1993), 'A Case Study on Computer Programs', in NRC (1993), pp. 284–318.

Samuelson, P., R. Davis, M.D. Kapor and J.H. Reichman (1994), 'A manifesto concerning the legal protection of computer programs', *Columbia Law Review*, **94** (8), 2308–431.

Schankerman, M. (1989), 'Measuring the value of patent rights: uses and limitations', *OECD: Science and Technology Indicators*.

Scheinfeld, R.C. and G.M. Butler (1991), 'Using trade secret law to protect computer software', *Rutgers Computer and Technology Law Journal*, **17** (2), 381–419.

Scherer, F.M. (1972), 'Nordhaus' Theory of optimal patent life: a geometric reinterpretation', *American Economic Review*, **62**, 422–7.

Scherer, F.M. (1977), *Economic Effects of Compulsory Patent Licensing*, Monograph Series in Finance and Economics, No. 2, New York University, New York.

Scherer, F.M. (1980), *Industrial Market Structure and Economic Performance*, Chicago, IL: Rand McNally.

Scherer, F.M. (1982), 'The office of technology assessment and forecast industry concordance as a means of identifying industry technology origins', *World Patent Information*, **4** (1), 12–17.

Scherer, F.M. (1983), 'The propensity to patent', *International Journal of Industrial Organization*, **1** (1), 107–28.

Scherer, F.M. (1991), 'Changing Perspectives on the Firm Size Problem', in Acs and Audretsch (1991), pp. 24–38.

Scherer, F.M. (1993), 'Research on patents and the economy: the state of the art', in European Patent Office and IFO Institute for Economic Research, *Results and Methods of Economic Patent Research*, Munich: IFO, pp. 41–56.

Scherer, F.M. (1998), 'The size distribution of profits from innovation', *Annales d'Economie et de Statistique*, No. 49/50.

Scherer, F.M., A. Beckenstein, E. Kaufer and R.D. Murphy (1975), *The Economics of Multi-Plant Operation: An International Comparisons Study*, Cambridge, MA: Harvard University Press.

Scherer, F.M., S.E. Herzstein Jr, A.W. Dreyfoos et al. (1959), *Patents and the Corporation: A Report on Industrial Technology under Changing Public Policy*, 2nd edn, Boston, MA: privately published.

Scherer, F.M. and D. Ross (1990), *Industrial Market Structure and Economic Performance*, 3rd edn, Boston, MA: Houghton Mifflin.

Scherer, F.M. and S. Weisburst (1995), 'Economic effects of strengthening pharmaceutical patent protection in Italy', *International Review of Industrial Property and Copyright Law*, **26** (6), 1009–24.

Schiff, E. (1971), *Industrialization without Patents*, Princeton, NJ: Princeton University Press.

Schlicher, J.W. (1996), *Licensing Intellectual Property: Legal, Business and Market Dynamics*, Chichester: John Wiley & Sons.

Schmookler, J. (1950), 'The interpretation of patent statistics', *Journal of the Patent Office Society*, **32** (2), 123–46.

Schmookler, J. (1966), *Invention and Economic Growth*, Cambridge, MA: Harvard University Press.

Schnaars, S.P. (1994), *Managing Imitation Strategies: How Later Entrants Seize Markets from Pioneers*, New York: Free Press.

Schon, D.A. (1967), *Technology and Change*, New York: New Heraclitus, Delacorte Press.

Schumpeter, J.A. (1912), *Theorie der Wirtschaftlichen Entwicklung*, Leipzig: Duncker & Humblot. Revised English translation (1934), *The Theory of Economic Development: An Inquiry into Profits, Capital, Credit, Interest, and the Business Cycle*, Boston, MA: Harvard University Press.

Schumpeter, J.A. ([1943] 1976), *Capitalism, Socialism and Democracy*, London: George Allen & Unwin.

Scotchmer, S. (1991), 'Standing on the shoulders of giants: cumulative research and the patent law', *Journal of Economic Perspectives*, **5** (1), 29–41.

Scotchmer, S. and J. Green (1990), 'Novelty and disclosure in patent law', *RAND Journal of Economics*, **21** (1), 131–46.

Shapiro, A.R. (1990), 'Responding to the changing patent system', *Research Technology Management*, **33** (5), 38–43.

Shariq, S.Z. (1997), 'Knowledge management: an emerging discipline', *Journal of Knowledge Management*, **1** (1), 75–82.

Shepard, A. (1987), 'Licensing to enhance demand for new technologies', *RAND Journal of Economics*, **18** (3), 360–68.

Shiraishi, T. and S. Tsuru (1987), *Economic Institutions in a Dynamic Society: Search for a New Frontier*, London: Macmillan.

Sigurdson, J. (ed.) (1990), *Measuring the Dynamics of Technological Change*, London: Pinter.

Sigurdson, J. (1995), *Science and Technology in Japan*, London: Cartermill.

Sigurdson, J. (1996), *Future Advantage Japan? Technology Strategies for Pharmaceutical and Chemical Corporations*, London: Cartermill.

Simon, E. (1986), 'US trade policy and intellectual property rights', *Albany Law Review*, **50**, 501–7.

Simons, E.M. and G. Strasser (eds) (1973), *Science and Technology Policies*, Cambridge, MA: Ballinger.

Sirilla G.M., G.P. Edgell and A.R. Hess (1992), 'The advice of counsel defense to increased patent damages', *Journal of the Patent and Trademark Office Society*, **74** (10), 705–28.

Soete, L. and S. Wyatt (1983), 'The use of foreign patenting as an internationally comparable science and technology indicator', *Scientometrics*, **5**, 31–54.

Sokoloff, K.L. (1988), 'Inventive activity in early industrial America: evidence from patent records, 1790–1846', *Journal of Economic History*, **48**, December, 813–50.

Solow, R.M. (1957), 'Technical change and the aggregate production function', *Review of Economics and Statistics*, **39**, August, 312–20.

Spanner, R.A. (1984), *Who Owns Innovation? The Rights and Obligations of Employers and Employees*, Homewood, IL: Dow Jones-Irwin.

Spero, D.M. (1990), 'Patent protection or piracy – a CEO views Japan', *Harvard Business Review*, **68** (5), 58–67.

Stalk, G. Jr and T.M. Hout (1990), *Competing Against Time: How Time-based Competition is Reshaping Global Markets*, New York: Free Press.

Stephan, P.E. (1996), 'The economics of science', *Journal of Economic Literature*, **34**, September, 1199–235.

Stewart, T.A. (1994), 'Your company's most valuable asset: intellectual capital', *Fortune*, **130** (7), 68–73.

Stewart, T.A. (1997), *Intellectual Capital*, New York: Doubleday.

Stigler, G.J. (1991), 'Charles Babbage (1791 + 200 = 1991)', *Journal of Economic Literature*, **29**, September, 1149–52.

Stoneman, P. (ed.) (1995), *Handbook of the Economics of Innovation and Technical Change*, Oxford: Basil Blackwell.

Sveiby, K.E. (1989), *The Invisible Balance Sheet*, Stockholm: Affärsvärlden, Ledarskap.

Sveiby, K.E. (1997), *The New Organizational Wealth: Managing and Measuring Knowledge-based Assets*, San Fransisco, CA: P. Berrett/Koehler.

Swais, N. (1996), *Protecting Trade Secrets*, Vancouver: International Self-Counsel Press.

Takahashi, T. (1994), *Intellectual Property Rights and Corporate Strategies: One Aspect of Competition in the U.S. and Japanese Electronics Industry*, Tokyo: Nomura Research Institute.

Tandon, P. (1982), 'Optimal patents with compulsory licensing', *Journal of Political Economy*, **90** (3), 470–86.

Taylor, C.T. and Z.A. Silberston (1973), *The Economic Impact of the Patent System: A Study of the British Experience*, Cambridge: Cambridge University Press.

Teece, D.J. (1982), 'Towards an economic theory of the multiproduct firm', *Journal of Economic Behavior and Organization*, **3** (1), 39–63.

Teece, D.J. (1987), 'Profiting from Technological Innovation: Implications for Integration, Collaboration, Licensing and Public Policy', in Teece (1987b), pp. 185–219.

Teece, D.J. (ed.) (1987b), *The Competitive Challenge*, Cambridge, MA: Ballinger.

Thurow, L.C. (1996), *The Future of Capitalism: How Today's Economic Forces Shape Tomorrow's World*, New York: William Morrow & Company Inc.

Thurow, L.C. (1997), 'Needed: a new system of intellectual property rights', *Harvard Business Review*, Sept–Oct, 95–103.

Tirole, J. (1988), *The Theory of Industrial Organization*, Cambridge, MA: The MIT Press.

Tisell, H.G. (1907), *Internationell patentstatistik för åren 1885-1904*, Lund: Håkan Ohlssons boktryckeri. (In Swedish)

Tisell, H.G. (1910), *Undersökning öfver uppfinnareverksamhetens variationer inom olika industriklasser i Sverige, Tyskland, Frankrike, England, Österrike och Ungern*, Lund: Statsvetenskaplig Tidskrift. (In Swedish)

TNEC (1941), *Investigation of Concentration of Economic Power: Technology in our Economy*, TNEC Monograph No. 22, Washington, DC: US Government Printing Office.

TNO (1995), *Immaterial Investments as an Innovative Factor*, Appledorn: TNO Centre for Technology and Policy Studies, Report No. STB/95/029.

Tobin, J. (1969), 'A general equilibrium approach to monetary theory', *Journal of Money, Credit and Banking*, **1**, 15–29.

Tobin, J. and W. Brainard (1968), 'Pitfalls in financial model building', *American Economic Review*, **59**, 99–102.

Towse, R. (1997), 'Copyright as an economic incentive', *Hume Papers on Public Policy*, **5** (3), 32–45.

Trajtenberg, M. (1990), 'A penny for your quotes: patent citations and the value of innovations', *RAND Journal of Economics*, **21** (1), 172–87.

Tushman, M. and P. Anderson (1986), 'Technological discontinuities and organizational environments', *Administrative Science Quarterly*, **31**, 439–65.

Tyson, L.D. (1992), *Who's Bashing Whom? Trade Conflict in High-Technology Industries*, Washington, DC: Institute for International Economics.

Ueda, A. (ed.) (1994), *The Electric Geisha*, Tokyo: Kodanska International.

UN Library on Transnational Corporations (1994), Vol. 17, London: Routledge.

Urabe, K., J. Child and T. Kagono (eds) (1988), *Innovation and Management: International Comparisons*, Berlin: de Gruyter.

US Congress, Office of Technology Assessment (1992), *Finding a Balance: Computer Software, Intellectual Property, and the Challenge of Technological Change*, OTA-TCT-527 Washington, DC: US Government Printing Office. (Same as OTA, 1992)

Utterback, J.M. (1994), *Mastering the Dynamics of Innovation*, Boston, MA: Harvard Business School Press.

van Raan, A.F.J. (ed.) (1988), *Handbook of Quantitative Studies of Science and Technology*, Amsterdam: Elsevier, North Holland.

Vaughan, F.L. (1925), *Economics of our Patent System*, New York: Macmillan.

Veblen, T. ([1958] 1965), *The Theory of Business Enterprise*, New York: New American Library.

Vernon, R. (1966), 'International investment and international trade in the product cycle', *Quarterly Journal of Economics*, May, 190–207.

Vlastos, G. (1991), *Socrates, Ironist and Moral Philosopher*, Ithaca, NY: Cornell University Press.

von Bertalanffy, L. (1968), *General System Theory: Foundations, Development, Applications*, New York: George Braziller.

von Hippel, E. (1976), 'The dominant role of users in the scientific instrument innovation process', *Research Policy*, **5** (3), 212–39.

von Hippel, E. (1982), 'Appropriability of innovation benefit as predictor of source of innovation', *Research Policy*, **11** (2), 95–115.

von Hippel, E. (1988a), *The Sources of Innovation*, New York: Oxford University Press.

von Hippel, E. (1988b), 'Trading trade secrets', *Technology Review*, **91** (2), 58–63.

Wallerstein, M.B., M.E. Mogee and R.A. Schoen (eds) (1993), *Global Dimensions of Intellectual Property Rights in Science and Technology*, Washington, DC: National Academy Press. (Same as NRC 1993.)

Warshofsky, F. (1994), *Patent Wars*, Chichester: John Wiley.

Weil, V. and J.W. Snapper (eds) (1989), *Owning Scientific and Technical Information: Value and Ethical Issues*, New Brunswick and London: Rutgers University Press.

Wernerfelt, B. (1984), 'A resource-based view of the firm', *Strategic Management Journal*, **5**, 171–80.

Westney, E. (1993), 'Country Patterns in R&D Organization: The United States and Japan', in Kogut (1993), pp. 36–53.

Westney, E. (1994), 'The Evolution of Japan's Industrial Research and Development', in Aoki and Dore (1994), pp. 154–77.

Wilkins, M. (1992), 'The Neglected Intangible Asset: The Influence of the Trade Mark on the Rise of the Modern Corporation', in Harvey and Jones (1992), pp. 66–95.

Williamson, O.E. (1985), *The Economic Institutions of Capitalism: Firms, Markets, Relational Contracting*, New York: Free Press, London: Collier Macmillan Publishers.

Wilson, E.O. (1975), *Sociobiology: The New Synthesis*, Harvard: Belknap Press.

Winter, S.G. (1987), 'Knowledge and Competence as Strategic Assets', in Teece (1987b), pp. 159–84.

Winter, S.G. (1989), 'Patents in Complex Contexts: Incentives and Effectiveness', in Weil and Snapper (1989), pp. 41–60.

Woronoff, J. (1992) *The Japanese Management Mystique: The Reality Behind the Myth*, Chicago, IL: Probus Publishing Company.

Wright, B.D. (1983), 'The economics of invention incentives: patents, prizes, and research contracts', *American Economic Review*, **73** (4), 691–707.

Wright, G. (1990), 'The origins of American industrial success, 1879–1940', *American Economic Review*, **80** (4), 651–68.

Yamaji, K. (1994), *Market Economy and Intellectual Property Oriented Management*, Speech at LES International Conference in Beijing, May 7, 1994.

Yamaji, K. (1997), *One Proposes, God Disposes. My Curriculum Vitae*, Tokyo: Nihon Keizai Shimbun, Inc.

Index of names

Index of subjects

trademarks 52, 86, 95, 419
  history 28, 43
  trademark management, Sony 244,
    245–7
  trademark strategies 242–7
  value of 8, 9
training *see* education and training

uncertainty 354
underinvestment 90, 91, 93
United Kingdom
  patents 92, 158–9
    anti-patent movement 35
    history 28, 29, 34, 42, 44
    international comparisons 149
United States of America 2, 14–15
  anti-trust policies 8, 38–9, 49
  history of intellectual property in 29,
    34, 36–7, 38–41, 42, 43, 44, 141
  as intellectual capitalist state 331
  mergers and acquisitions 192
  organization of intellectual property in
    279
  patents 4, 8, 53, 73, 76, 145, 172,
    173
    exploitation of technology and
      186

international comparison 144–54,
    163
  research and literature on 87, 92
  Structural Impediments Initiative and
    30, 37
  technology in 176–7
  trademark protection in 246
  wage differentials in 328
Universal Copyright Convention 30
universities 200
users *see* customers/users
USSR/Commonwealth of Independent
    States (CIS) 31, 51, 54, 145, 172
utilitarianism 24, 26–7

value
  of knowledge 326
  markets 15, 16
  of patents 73–6, 80–2, 101
  rising value of intellectual property
    8–10
  of trademarks 8, 9
Venice 24, 28, 32, 42, 93
video recording standards 203, 231

wage differentials 328
welfare distribution 101